A Surgeon
with Stilwell

A Surgeon with Stilwell

Dr. John H. Grindlay and Combat Medicine in the China-Burma-India Theater of World War II

Alan K. Lathrop

McFarland & Company, Inc., Publishers
Jefferson, North Carolina

Frontispiece: Dr. John H. Grindlay (used with permission of the Mayo Foundation for Medical Education and Research; all rights reserved)

LIBRARY OF CONGRESS CATALOGUING-IN-PUBLICATION DATA

Names: Lathrop, Alan K., 1940– author.
Title: A Surgeon with Stilwell : Dr. John H. Grindlay and Combat Medicine in the China-Burma-India theater of World War II / Alan K. Lathrop.
Description: Jefferson, North Carolina : McFarland & Company, Inc., Publishers, 2018 | Includes bibliographical references and index.
Identifiers: LCCN 2018035672 | ISBN 9781476673509 (softcover : acid free paper) ∞
Subjects: LCSH: Grindlay, John H. | World War, 1939–1945— Medical care—United States. | United States. Army— Surgeons—Biography. | Surgeons—United States—Biography.
Classification: LCC D807.U6 G75 2018 | DDC 940.54/7573092 [B]—dc23
LC record available at https://lccn.loc.gov/2018035672

BRITISH LIBRARY CATALOGUING DATA ARE AVAILABLE

ISBN (print) 978-1-4766-7350-9
ISBN (ebook) 978-1-4766-3306-0

© 2018 Alan K. Lathrop. All rights reserved

No part of this book may be reproduced or transmitted in any form or by any means, electronic or mechanical, including photocopying or recording, or by any information storage and retrieval system, without permission in writing from the publisher.

Front cover image: Captain John H. Grindlay (date is unknown but likely after his return to the U.S. in 1944; photograph courtesy of Grindlay family); background map Library of Congress

Printed in the United States of America

McFarland & Company, Inc., Publishers
 Box 611, Jefferson, North Carolina 28640
 www.mcfarlandpub.com

To the men and women who served
in the war in Asia, 1941–1945

Table of Contents

Preface and Acknowledgments   1

Introduction   5

1. Aid for China   13
2. AMMISCA Goes to China   19
3. Grindlay Goes to China   23
4. AMMISCA Settles In   30
5. War Begins for AMMISCA   38
6. Enter Stilwell and Goodbye to China   54
7. Joining Seagrave in Burma   65
8. Stilwell's Escape from Burma: Preparing for the Walkout   84
9. The Walkout   93
10. Hambleton's Story (Continued)   109
11. The British, Chinese and Civilian Exodus   122
12. Ramgarh: The Beginnings   133
13. Days and Nights at Ramgarh, 1942–1943   143

14. Winding Down at Ramgarh	156
15. Back to Burma and Home	159
Epilogue	199
Chapter Notes	209
Bibliography	236
Index	243

Preface and Acknowledgments

This book is a modest attempt to fill a gap in a much larger gap. The larger gap is the war that the United States fought in East and Southeast Asia from 1941 to 1945. Although this conflict has been covered in previous books, the output does not begin to compare with the thousands of volumes devoted to the European and Pacific conflicts. The smaller gap, rather than being concerned with combat operations, focuses on the practice of medicine in an area of the war that was every bit as vicious as the other theaters. This volume offers a very personal look at the medical war in the China-Burma-India (CBI) theater as seen and experienced by combat surgeon John H. Grindlay. Unlike other aspects of World War II, the medical history of the war is not extensive, especially as written by people who experienced it.

Needless to say, a book that looks at warfare from a personal, subjective viewpoint—foxhole observation, if you will—will be narrow in its coverage. The reader of this book will find little about the bigger picture in the theater because it has been well covered by others and because Grindlay was not privy to a great deal of the larger events, although he was generally aware of what was going on outside his small sphere of concern. He was well acquainted with General Joseph W. Stilwell, the theater commander, but Stilwell did not discuss plans (except on a need-to-know basis) with someone of Grindlay's status.

I was extremely fortunate to unearth many new sources and have incorporated excerpts from some of them in this book. Historians and readers interested in the China-Burma-India theater will find this account a valuable addition to the existing literature on the subject.

During a span of more than 40 years, I have been collecting information for a book on the CBI theater. The central figure in this book, Grindlay, passed away in 1968, before I had an opportunity to meet him or, for that matter, had even heard of him and of his adventures in China, Burma, and

India. He was brought to my attention by my father-in-law, who had been well acquainted with Grindlay at the Mayo Clinic and who arranged for me to meet Betty Grindlay about two years after her husband's death. She told me of Dr. Grindlay's diary, which he had kept during his service in the CBI theater.

At the time of this meeting, I was collecting source material for a projected article on the Chinese Nationalist troops in the first Burma campaign of 1942. Much to my delight, Mrs. Grindlay kindly made copies of relevant pages from the diary that concerned Grindlay's experiences with the American Military Mission to China (AMMISCA) in China and Dr. Gordon Seagrave's hospital in Burma and the subsequent retreat, led by Lieutenant General Stilwell, from Burma to India in May of that year. I incorporated entries from these pages in my article "The Employment of Chinese Nationalist Troops in the First Burma Campaign," which was published in the summer 1981 issue of the *Journal of Southeast Asian Studies*.

Almost fifteen years later, I contacted Mrs. Grindlay about obtaining a copy of the full diary. Her declining health at the time forced her to pass on my request to her daughter, Lorna, who kindly made a photocopy of the diary for me. Once I received it, I set about producing a transcription of the diary on my home computer and printing the transcribed version for easier use. Dr. Grindlay's handwriting was unclear in a number of instances, especially given the hastiness with which many of the entries were written. There were also many unfamiliar names of men with whom he served and place names in Burma that at first defied transcription; it took me many months to identify and correct their misspellings. Often, Grindlay heard names without seeing them in writing and used phonetic equivalents in his diary.

The diary is a gold mine of information about well-known personalities (particularly Stilwell and Gordon Seagrave) and chronicles, as no other document does, day-to-day details about the first Burma Campaign in 1942; medical facilities and activities in the Chinese training center at Ramgarh, India; and the Allied return to Burma in 1943 to begin construction of the Ledo (later renamed the Stilwell) Road and to push the Japanese out of northern Burma. The availability of Dr. Grindlay's diary turned my research in the direction of writing a history of the medical aspects of the war in the CBI.

As time went on and the structure of the book began to take shape, I discovered many blanks in the story that required further research to fill. The search for source material led me to such amazing documents as the diary of Colonel Edward MacMorland, at Widener University Archives, Chester, Pennsylvania, as well as the rich resources of the U.S. Army Heritage and Education Center (AHEC), Carlisle, Pennsylvania, where I found the diary of Robert P. Williams, the papers of Anna Mae Hayes, and other materials that shed new and valuable light on the medical war in China and Burma;

the National Archives and Records Administration, College Park, Maryland, which holds many of the official records of the U.S. Army in the CBI; the American Field Service Archives, New York City, an extremely rich source of information about medical and ambulance units that accompanied the British 14th Army in Burma; and the University of Pennsylvania Archives, Philadelphia, where the records of the 20th General Hospital are preserved and where the archivist asked whether I would like to see the newly received papers of Father Louis Meyer, a Roman Catholic chaplain based at the 20th General Hospital who had also ministered to men building the Ledo Road. I was the first researcher to use the Meyer papers, and they turned out to be a gold mine of new information about life at the 20th General and, wonder of wonders, contained a copy of the diary of Captain Roscoe Hambleton, a daily chronicle of his final tragic weeks in Burma in 1942. A number of these sources had been either only sketchily used by other researchers or not consulted at all, as evidenced by the numerous documents that had never been declassified since 1945 at AHEC and the National Archives.

Many years ago, I was fortunate enough to become acquainted with Mrs. Henrietta Thompson. About 1970, she became interested in Stilwell's walkout from Burma. She and her family would take walks at the army marching pace of 110 steps per minute, the rate that Stilwell had maintained during the trek. She searched out the survivors of the walkout, military and civilian, and flew around the world to meet personally with each of them and record their reminiscences of the event. Henrietta heard that I, too, was interested in the Stilwell walkout and contacted me by phone to learn what I had done so far and what I hoped to do. She was kind enough to make her extensive notes available to me and invited me to her home in Maine to review them and make copies. She then self-published the interviews in a compendium called *Walk a Little Faster*; I have referred to that book and her unpublished notes many times in this volume. As I remarked in a chapter note, her interviews with survivors of the trek are absolutely invaluable. Almost all of the people she spoke to are now dead, and Henrietta's work stands as the only collection of their memories extant, clearly and concisely. Her book is available in a few libraries across the nation; I am fortunate enough to have two copies that she gave me long ago.

The staffs of several other archival institutions also provided an enormous amount of expertise and guidance. These include the Mayo Clinic Archives in Rochester, Minnesota; the Tulsa (Oklahoma) Historical Society; the Hoover Institution for War, Revolution, and Peace at Stanford University, Palo Alto, California; the American Baptist Historical Society in Atlanta, Georgia; California State University, Fullerton; the Center for Military History, Department of the Army, in Washington, D.C.; the National Archives in Kew, Richmond, England; and the India Office and Library in London.

In order to get this book researched and written, the cooperation of many people over the years was vital and greatly appreciated. First and foremost, my patient and loving wife, Peggy, provided support, assistance, encouragement, and a great deal of love that kept me going. Second, thanks go to members of the Grindlay family, especially Mrs. Betty Grindlay, Dr. Lorna Grindlay Moore, and Professor Josh Grindlay, who made available the remarkable diary of Dr. John Grindlay and his collection of photographs dating from the years he spent in the CBI theater. Third, a much-loved and sorely missed friend, Keith Stevens, lent invaluable information and advice from the British perspective. Fourth, I must acknowledge my father-in-law, William Dunnette, who always took a deep interest in any project I was working on and who introduced me to Mrs. Grindlay many years ago.

Many individuals gave invaluable assistance to my research on the CBI theater: Mr. Nicholas Dennys, Brigadier General (Retired) Frank "Pinky" Dorn, Ray Kaupilla, Ronald Bleecker, Dr. Ann Thompson, Peter Lutken, Robert Maynard, Lester Gilbertson, Vicky Bryant, Ophelia Fortune, Robert Bullock, Sterling Seagrave, Jack Flynn, Les Opheim, Mr. and Mrs. Floyd Homstad, Linda Willis, Ruth Case, Henrietta Thompson, Constance Putnam, Linda Willis, Bill Brough, and Glyn Owen. I deeply apologize to anyone whose name has been inadvertently omitted and to those whose rich and unique stories were not included in the book due to space limitations. A special note of thanks goes to the University of Minnesota's Office of the Graduate School and the University of Minnesota Retirees Association for a research grant in 2010 that enabled me to travel to New York, Pennsylvania, and Washington, D.C.

To all of these people and institutions, I owe a deep, heartfelt expression of gratitude for their assistance and cooperation in the research conducted for this book.

The author takes full responsibility for all errors of fact, omission, and misinterpretation that may appear in this book.

Introduction

On a stiflingly hot afternoon in the fall of 1942 in eastern India, a day when only "mad dogs and Englishmen" went out in the midday sun, Captain John H. Grindlay, a U.S. Army surgeon, spent several weary hours operating on a badly injured Chinese soldier in the U.S. military hospital at Ramgarh, two-hundred-odd miles northwest of Calcutta. The hospital was staffed by a unique assemblage of U.S. Army surgeons and medical technicians, a few civilian surgeons, and a contingent of native Burmese nurses who made up the Seagrave Hospital Unit under the direction of the prominent medical missionary Dr. Gordon Seagrave, now a major in the U.S. Army.

The Chinese soldier had suffered horrible wounds on his buttocks from a beating at the hands of one of his own officers as punishment for a minor infraction (losing a blanket), and Grindlay fought to repair the damage to exposed muscles and ligaments. As he worked, the fatigue, the unrelenting heat, and the terrible, merciless and seemingly unjustified injuries to the innocent soldier provoked in the surgeon a smoldering rage. After the surgery was completed, Grindlay stormed over to the office of his commanding officer, where his anger and frustration exploded in a fiery outburst. Brigadier General Haydon Boatner, the Chief of Staff of Chinese forces in the China-Burma-India theater, sat with uncharacteristic patience as Grindlay shouted, "General, I'm fed up with your × × × [sic] Chinese and I quit. No matter what you say, nor what you do, I quit. I'll never treat another of your × × × [sic] Chinese."

Boatner listened calmly to the tirade and at the end admitted that there was little he could or should do to interfere with Chinese army discipline. His commander, Lieutenant General Joseph W. Stilwell, had so ordered, and Boatner's hands were tied. The general invited Grindlay to cool off with him and several of his closest subordinates over dinner and drinks. "We killed [a bottle of whiskey]," Boatner later wrote to Grindlay's children, "and ate our dinner amidst everyone cussing about our own personal problems with those x x x [*sic*] Chinese … [Grindlay] went back to the hospital that night feeling no pain and we never again discussed the incident … [He] was superbly qualified for his job, and … so he kept on blowing off steam at me but stuck to his job—like the extremely high-class surgeon, soldier and man he was."[1]

In a war that made strange bedfellows—none more so than one that saw Americans and Chinese fighting shoulder to shoulder—incidents of this kind were sure to happen. Neither nation fully understood the other's culture, and the resulting lack of comprehension and appreciation was a constant challenge for both sides.

How did the United States come to be waging a war in far-flung India? How did a man like John Grindlay, a typical American Midwesterner with little more than a romantic notion of what the Far East was like, end up in the remoteness of the Indian subcontinent performing surgery on Chinese soldiers? What was the chain of events that led to this unimaginable episode in his life and that of thousands of other men, both American and Asian? The full story is as improbable as any to come out of World War II or any other war.

The United States' entry into World War II was quite sudden and unexpected, although it should not have been a surprise, given the fact that American military intelligence had been intercepting and decrypting Japanese coded diplomatic and military traffic for a decade prior to the war's outbreak.[2] The Japanese attack on Pearl Harbor on 7 December 1941 caught the nation in a state of embarrassingly inadequate military preparedness: the army was woefully undermanned and underequipped, the navy consisted mostly of First World War vintage vessels, and there was no air force worthy of the name. A few voices were raised in the 1930s to strongly advocate for an immediate and vigorous program to correct these inadequacies, but most Americans in and out of the government preferred to watch the war already under way in Europe from a distance and shuddered at the thought of being dragged into another global conflict. If U.S. participation in the war could be avoided, as the non-interventionists argued, so much the better.

Americans generally were aware that a war was raging in East Asia between an increasingly militant and belligerent Japan and a weak and vulnerable China. They also vaguely knew that Japan was fortifying its islands in the Pacific, some of them former German possessions that had been granted to Japan by the League of Nations after World War I. Newspapers and magazines reported the growing threat to the countries and colonies of Southeast Asia, as the Japanese were declaring their desire to create an "Asia for Asians." All of that sounded like nationalistic machismo to the Americans, and, anyway, it was happening thousands of miles away, far over the horizon, and seemingly of little direct concern to the United States. But the army and navy kept a wary eye on Japan's expansion and formulated plans for eventual conflict with the Japanese as early as the 1920s, and American diplomats maneuvered quietly behind the scenes to reach an accommodation with Japan, a goal that increasingly seemed more and more distant and unattainable.

Japan began its war in East Asia in remote Manchuria in September 1931. A small, harmless explosive device was detonated by Japanese troops alongside the tracks of the Chinese Eastern Railway near Harbin while a trainload of Japanese soldiers was passing by. Although no one was injured, Japan charged that it was a provocation by the local Chinese warlord, Chang Tso-lin, aimed at disrupting traffic on the line; the Japanese used this act as an excuse to grab military and political control of Manchuria. Their aggression extended to Shanghai the following year, again after citing anti-Japanese incidents of belligerence among the Chinese armies in the area. The Chinese military forces fought creditably, thanks to the training they had received from German advisors dispatched to assist the government of Chiang Kai-shek, the Nationalist leader of pre-war and wartime China, in building a modern army.[3]

The "Shanghai Incident" resulted in more than 3,000 Japanese casualties and more than 14,000 Chinese casualties, many of the latter civilians who were killed and wounded by bombing and shelling. The incident was concluded by a shaky truce signed on 5 May 1932, and an international commission (headed by Lord Bulwer-Lytton, former governor of Bengal, and consisting of representatives from China, Japan, Italy, the United States, Great Britain and France) was appointed by the League of Nations to police the truce.[4] The League condemned Japan's actions; in response, the Japanese delegation walked out and went home.

Full-scale war erupted between China and Japan in July 1937, following a minor incident at the Marco Polo Bridge southwest of Peiping. A company of Japanese troops marched to the Yungting River near the bridge to conduct night maneuvers. As they stopped on the river bank to eat a meal, live shells fell into their midst, presumably fired from nearby Chinese fortifications. A soldier was discovered to be missing, though he reappeared at dawn; however, the episode was deemed sufficiently serious to flare into skirmishing, and eventually open warfare, despite efforts at negotiation on both sides.

China's desperate plight won the sympathy of the Franklin D. Roosevelt administration in the United States. The question of whether to supply military aid to China, however, was another matter; it stalled for several years while the U.S. government debated what its policy should be. Passage of the Neutrality Acts in the late 1930s prevented any kind of direct assistance, but President Roosevelt sought, behind the scenes, some way to circumvent the law and send aid to China. The problem was further complicated by the growing menace of Nazism in Europe. After Germany's annexation of Czechoslovakia in March 1939, the Roosevelt administration was primarily concerned with the containment of further Nazi aspirations but also kept a watchful eye on East Asia. The president wished to avoid provocation, and the State Department and military leaders saw no vital American interests at stake in China.[5] American involvement thus remained constrained, even in the face of growing Japanese aggression that took the form of a widening war in China and occupation of Hainan Island in early 1939 (the latter act effectively controlling access to Indochina and the Red River supply route to China). These moves, along with Japan's annexation of the Spratly Islands between Indochina and the Philippines, were viewed as a threat to U.S. interests in East and Southeast Asia (as well as those of the British, French, Dutch, and Australians) and precipitated markedly important policy changes: the first was a secret understanding between Britain and the United States whereby the latter would send its Pacific fleet to Singapore in case of a Japanese threat against Malaya or the Dutch East Indies; second was an announcement to Japan on 26 July 1939 that the United States intended to terminate its 1911 commercial treaty in six months' time. After 26 January 1940, the United States was free to restrict its trade with the Japanese however it saw fit, a clear warning to Japan that American shipments of oil, machinery and metals vital to war making could be curtailed.[6]

The declaration of war between Germany, France and Britain following the Nazi attack on Poland on 1 September 1939 gave Roosevelt the loophole he had been seeking. The following year, he signed the destroyers-for-bases agreement with the British that made a number of aging vessels available to Britain, and in March 1941, he signed the Lend-Lease Act, according to which military supplies could be legally "loaned" to nations facing aggressors. China was included in this interpretation.

In response to Japanese pressure on Southeast Asia, especially following the signing of the neutrality pact between the Soviet Union and Japan on 13 April 1941, which freed the Japanese from having to worry about a Russian threat in the Far East, Roosevelt demonstrated to the world that his policy of Japanese containment was not faltering by authorizing the release of American army and navy pilots to join the American Volunteer Group (AVG; better known as the "Flying Tigers") in China as civilian combatants. Simultaneously, the War Department began poring over shopping lists of military supplies submitted by the Chinese in order to determine which requests could be filled, how, and when. Out of this effort came the American Military Mission to China (AMMISCA).

On the home front, support for China was being vigorously promoted by Henry R. Luce, publisher of *Time* magazine, one of America's most influential news sources. Luce had privately proposed to President Roosevelt in 1940 that the United States should dispatch aging destroyers to Britain in exchange for leases to British air bases, which Roosevelt followed up on two months later. Luce's news magazines, *Time* and *Life*, published stories and

Asia in 1988 (John R. Borchert Map Library at the University of Minnesota; revisions by Patrick Lathrop).

editorials that depicted the Chinese as "virtuous victims" and the Japanese as "predatory cockroaches." Most striking to readers were maps that showed Japan's expansionism and its growing competition for shrinking world industrial markets.[7]

China ultimately became one part of a much wider struggle as the Japanese sought to secure their lines of sea communication and supply by dramatically enlarging their territorial aspirations to Southeast Asia and the Pacific. This decision to up the ante only came after a great deal of debate, persuasion, and, ultimately, coercion of Japan's politicians by its military leaders. Beginning in the late 1930s, the Japanese army began developing a strategy to oust the Soviet Union from East Asia. The Soviets, as Communists, were viewed by the Japanese army leaders as extremely dangerous to the region's political and military stability. The Japanese strategy of "driving north" was put forth in very persuasive terms in 1938 in the form of a small-scale skirmish around a promontory called Changkufeng along the Tumen River, which forms an ill-defined border near its lower end, where Korea, Manchuria, and Russia meet.[8] This half-month-long indecisive battle was followed the next year by a large-scale attack against the Russian forces guarding their side of the Manchurian-Mongolian border. This incident was an example of the Kwantung Army (the occupier of Manchuria) stepping up its belligerency in the region. The fighting continued over a period of three months in the vicinity of Nomonhan, ultimately costing the Japanese one entire division. The Russians were damaged but not seriously; their tanks and artillery saved them, as was to be the case in their war against Germany two years later.[9]

The Japanese retreated, licking their wounds, and the army's influence with the politicians, especially the emperor, waned. This development provided a golden opportunity for the navy to push forward with its own strategic plan, a "drive south" scheme aimed at gaining economic and military control of French Indochina and the Netherlands East Indies to ensure that the vital sea lanes leading from the oil- and rubber-rich region back to the home islands would be protected against enemy attack. The success of the "drive south" plan was evident in the Japanese occupation of Indochina in the summer of 1941, an opportunity suddenly created by the fall of France a year earlier and its inability to defend its colonial territories in Southeast Asia.

By the end of 1940, the Japanese had formed an ambitious plan for dominating an arc of territory stretching from Manchuria (renamed Manchukuo) and Northeast China south and westward through Indochina, the East Indies, and Malaya to Burma and the very doorstep of India. The area that was the object of this conquest would be included in Japan's so-called "Greater East Asia Co-Prosperity Sphere." Plans to conquer India were only beginning but would take more definite shape later, after the vital territory was firmly in Japanese grasp, offering a springboard from which to launch an attack on the subcontinent. Ambitious, yes, but the region seemed ripe for the picking. No colonial military force capable of fighting off tough, resilient, well-trained, and (in some cases) blooded Japanese divisions and the accompanying naval and air forces was in sight anywhere in the territory.

A further refinement of the Japanese plan for Asian conquest eventually called for the inclusion of the Philippines. This plan was risky because it included the possibility of a confrontation with the United States, an unknown but dangerous foe with enormous resources, the only country with the potential strength to effectively oppose Japan in its drive to secure the raw materials necessary to sustain its military and industrial base. Still, the naval leaders argued, in order to fully secure the vital sea lanes, there was no alternative to attacking the Philippines and other American bases in the Pacific so as to create the outermost of two or three concentric rings of defense for the Asian possessions and the home islands.[10]

The stage was set, then, militarily and politically, for the opening of full-scale war in East Asia and the Pacific Ocean by the end of 1941.

1

Aid for China

By mid–1941, the conflict between China and Japan had been raging for four years. Photographs in American magazines and newspapers portrayed the savage nature of the combat, and the fortitude and stoic endurance of the Chinese people and the steadfast Nationalist government of Generalissimo Chiang Kai-shek made them heroic symbols in the United States of the struggle against Japanese aggression. The grim war and the toll it was taking on China motivated the U.S. government to consider sending a military mission to China with the intention of establishing an effective means of coordinating and administering Lend-Lease aid to the hard-pressed Chinese Nationalist armies and providing modern military training to make them more effective.[1]

During his campaign for a third term, President Franklin D. Roosevelt gave notice in a speech on 2 November 1940 of his intention to find a way to help friendly nations that were at war, declaring, "Our policy is to give all possible material aid to the nations which still resist aggression across the Atlantic and Pacific Oceans." This statement implied that some means would be found to assist both Britain and China in waging war as a way to keep the United States out of the conflict, thus appeasing the isolationists. Non-involvement, as the isolationists pointed out, was in accord with the spirit of the Neutrality Acts passed in 1935, 1937, and 1939, but Roosevelt sought a way of circumventing the acts without illegally rendering direct military aid. He therefore quietly resorted to backdoor economic measures by initiating a series of ever-tightening embargoes against Japan during 1940 and 1941, starting with high-octane aviation gasoline. Added to the list were scrap steel and iron, copper, zinc, nickel, bronze, brass, carbon black, titanium, petroleum coke, and, finally (and most disastrously for the Japanese), by mid–1941, oil. At the same time, Japanese assets in the United States were frozen and a trade embargo was declared as a consequence of the Japanese occupation of Indochina. The British and the Dutch soon followed suit.

Roosevelt was utterly convinced of the necessity for the United States to enter the European conflict, believing that the defeat of Nazi Germany and everything it stood for was vital to America's long-term interests. Until Germany was defeated, he was anxious to avoid a war with Japan, which would drain scarce resources and supplies from the European theater and embroil America in a perilous two-front conflict. The Lend-Lease Act, which Roosevelt signed into law on 11 March 1941, was the first important step toward ending the isolationist stance of the United States and actively entering the war. Lend-Lease opened the door for direct military aid to Great Britain and other nations whose defense was deemed by the president to be "vital to the defense of the United States."[2] It also made possible the extension of such aid without violating the letter or the spirit of the Neutrality Acts, which prohibited Americans from selling or transporting arms and granting loans to any nations declared by the president to be in a state of war. A "cash and carry" provision was added to the Neutrality Acts in 1939 that enabled Britain to keep trading with the United States as long as the goods were paid for in advance, but this gesture was not extended to other nations, including China.

From the outset, the Chinese were excluded from any direct U.S. military aid under Lend-Lease. The defense of China was not considered vital to U.S. interests, and, in spite of intense Chinese lobbying in Washington for military supplies and equipment, assistance was restricted to credits from the American Export-Import Bank solely for civilian materials.[3] The War Department was willing to make some aid available but found that China's requests (submitted through its representative in Washington, T.V. Soong, the head of China Defense Supplies, Inc., a front organization for the Nationalists' lobbying efforts in the United States) contained a "general air of vagueness and unreality." This left a bad impression in the minds of military planners and made it very difficult to determine China's actual requirements.

Roosevelt did not declare that China was eligible for military assistance until 6 May 1941. T.V. Soong, meanwhile, had submitted a request for $50 million in aid at the end of March, including 1,000 planes and a host of other materials.[4] Lauchlin Currie, one of Roosevelt's confidential advisors, was charged by Harry Hopkins, the president's influential aide and informal administrator of Lend-Lease, with expediting arms shipments to China. Currie sent Soong's shopping list to the War Department for review. Secretary of War Henry Stimson responded with his own list of available supplies and equipment that could be allotted to China without affecting the program of aid to Britain or putting too great a strain on American weapons reserves and manufacturing.[5] Stimson's final list was some $30 million less than Soong's request. The first shipment of three hundred trucks was under way less than two weeks after Roosevelt's 6 May announcement.

By the summer of 1941, the United States was preparing to ship thousands of tons of weapons, vehicles, and aircraft to China. The looming question in the minds of top War Department officials was how such aid would be effectively distributed and used once it arrived in China. Behind their concern was a fundamental distrust of Chinese intentions for Lend-Lease, based on reports of corruption in high government circles as well as the obvious lack of reality in the Chinese requests and their unfamiliarity with modern weapons and equipment. It became clear that a military mission had to be sent to China to coordinate the disbursement of Lend-Lease aid as well as provide assistance and training to the Chinese in assessing their actual needs and using the material once it arrived.

The impetus for an advisory American military mission originated with a recommendation by Lieutenant Colonel William Mayer, U.S. military attaché in Chungking, at the suggestion of Major General Lancelot Dennys, head of the British Military Mission. By mid-1941 the British had already authorized and put into place a mission that would aid the Chinese by providing training in the use of weapons and conduct of special operations. On 15 June 1941, Mayer suggested to the office of the adjutant general of the War Department that an officer of general rank be appointed to succeed him as military attaché and act as an advisor to Chiang Kai-shek in addition to administering Lend-Lease aid. Mayer reported that the British had already established a mission under a high-ranking officer, which implied that they could control the use and distribution of Lend-Lease unless an American officer of similar rank was dispatched to China. Mayer recommended Major General Joseph W. Stilwell and Brigadier General John Magruder as possibilities for the post, since both men were of general rank, had previously served as military attachés in China, and knew the language and culture.[6]

On 16 June, Colonel Haydon L. Boatner of the Supply Division of the War Department General Staff (G-4) drafted a paper for Brigadier General Eugene Reybold, the acting assistant chief of staff (G-4), urging that aid to China be carefully restricted and supervised. Boatner was an "old China Hand" who had seen service in China and knew whereof he spoke. "Our Government must supervise the shipment, receipt, storage, distribution and use of all equipment sent to China," he wrote. Boatner also suggested that a military mission be sent to China to coordinate the Nationalists' requests for the disbursement of materiel.[7] Army Chief of Staff General George C. Marshall approved the document on 3 July and passed it on to the Joint Planning Committee (JPC) of the Joint Chiefs of Staff (JCS) for final approval.

The JPC issued its response on 12 July in a report titled "Aircraft Requirements of Chinese Government," in which the members recommended that the United States and Great Britain provide China with aircraft, armament, and parts "sufficient for effective action" and instructor pilots to "render advisory assistance in the maintenance and employment of all training and combat aircraft, and equipment pertaining thereto." The same report acted on the suggestions of Lieutenant Colonel Mayer and Colonel Boatner to formally recommend that a military group be sent to China to "act in an advisory capacity" to assist the Chinese in determining and procuring their Lend-Lease requirements, to oversee their distribution (scheduled to begin in the fall of 1941), and to watch out for the interests of U.S. military personnel.[8] The report was approved by the Joint Board of the JCS on 12 July and subsequently by the secretaries of war and the navy and somewhat reluctantly by President Roosevelt on 23 July, who scribbled on it, "OK—but restudy Military Mission versus the Attaché method." Representatives of the army and the State Department considered the matter and ultimately decided to send a mission rather than rely on the military attaché to administer Lend-Lease material in China. In fact, by 14 July, General Magruder had already been officially chosen to lead such a mission, over Generals Stilwell and A.J. Bowley, although both were considered officers who could ably perform the job.[9]

John Magruder had a career stretching back to World War I. He was judged to be one of the army's top experts on China and was described as intelligent, scholarly, suave, charming, and tactful. He served in France with the American Expeditionary Force and then was assigned as assistant military attaché in Peking from 1920 to 1924 before being transferred to the Artillery School and subsequently to the Command and Staff School, where he distinguished himself as a student. From there, he served successively as military attaché in China from 1926 to 1930; as an instructor at the Virginia Military Institute; as military attaché in Berne, Switzerland; as chief of the Intelligence Branch, Military Intelligence Division; and finally as commander of Fort Devens, Massachusetts, by December 1940.

By mid–July, wheels were beginning to turn in earnest. On 11 July, Brigadier General Sherman Miles,

Brigadier General John Magruder (U.S. Army).

assistant army chief of staff, wrote to Magruder outlining the duties of leading a military mission and asking for the latter's comments. Subsequently, Magruder was ordered to Washington and began wading through reports and other documents to review the background of the situation in China. He received orders from the secretary of war a month later to organize a military mission and was given five tasks, which had been approved by the Joint Board and which were forwarded to him by the undersecretary of war:

1. To advise and assist the Chinese Government in all phases of procurement, transportation and utilization of military materials, equipment and munitions requisite to the prosecution of its military effort;

2. To advise and assist the Chinese Government in the training of Chinese personnel in the use and maintenance of materials, equipment and munitions;

3. To assist the Chinese Government in obtaining prompt and coordinated administrative action by U.S. authorities necessary to insure the orderly flow of materials and munitions from the Lend-Lease agencies to the Chinese military forces;

4. To explore vital port, road and railroad facilities with a view to the establishment and maintenance of an adequate line of military communications; and

5. To assist the personnel of the U.S. government departments in carrying out their respective duties in furtherance of the objectives of the Lend-Lease Act as pertains to China.[10]

Magruder's primary responsibility was to advise and assist with Lend-Lease and to investigate the means of expediting shipment of supplies and equipment to China. He had no authorization to take any other action and was not told what to do in case war broke out between the United States and Japan because no decisions on that score had yet been made by authorities in Washington.[11] The army high command was adamant that the aid mission be responsive only to the *orders* of the American government and—so far as was possible—to *requests* from the Chinese government for supplies and training of personnel. The mission was also charged with securing transportation to China for the men and equipment included in the aid mission. Magruder was informed that an initial sum of $800,000 was to be requested from Lend-Lease funds for financing the mission's operations until 30 June 1942.[12]

Magruder set up two locations for his mission: one was an office in Washington that would correct flaws or mistakes in the Chinese program and work with China Defense Supplies, Inc. (T.V. Soong's organization) to prepare and expedite formal requests for military supplies and equipment and help arrange for their transportation to China; the other was an operating group based in China to screen Chinese requests and prioritize them for the Washington office as well as to improve the supply lines through Burma. The China group would also observe Chinese ordnance production and make recommendations for ways to increase production and enhance utilization of Lend-Lease weapons and provide instruction in their use as necessary.[13]

Magruder began assembling a staff with a variety of skills and experience to conduct and support the multiple functions of the mission. Personnel were drawn from the financial, transportation, chemical warfare, artillery, signal corps, infantry, and medical branches of the army and brought to Washington for interviews prior to being selected for participation in one of three staff groups: permanent staff (part of which was to be stationed in Washington); task specialists (to be sent to China and remain there until their assigned duties were completed); and administrative staff (in both the United States and China). Officers who were selected were to be those "with highest qualifications," for the mission's success depended heavily on the "prestige of the personnel in Chinese eyes." To get the right men for the demanding jobs ahead, the army foresaw the need to detach some personnel from their current stations rather than rely entirely on volunteers. The importance of each duty justified the "arbitrary assignment … of certain competent key officers—a type which will not voluntarily be released by their present chiefs."[14]

2

AMMISCA Goes to China

The selection of the personnel complement for the American Military Mission to China was well under way by August 1941. Magruder preferred that his top officers have some knowledge or experience with China, but such men were few and far between. Magruder himself had been a military attaché in China in the late 1920s and probably was acquainted with many, if not all, of the men in the army who were China specialists. He managed to recruit several of whom he knew and was fortunate enough to attract others with a strong interest in the country. Yet, only about a third of AMMISCA's complement knew anything at all about China.

For his chief of staff, Magruder selected Colonel Edward MacMorland (1892–1978) of the Ordnance Corps. MacMorland was acquainted with Chinese officials, including T.V. Soong, through his service as secretary of the Army-Navy Munitions Board. MacMorland had a long record of foreign service in the army starting in World War I, including his participation in the American Expeditionary Force, a stint as a commander of the Transportation Corps of the American North Russia Expeditionary Force (1918–1919), and service with the Interallied Baltic Military Mission in 1919 (which monitored the withdrawal of German troops from Courland and Latvia).

Lieutenant Colonel George W. Sliney (1889–1966) accompanied the mission as the chief artillery advisor to the Chinese. He went on to serve as the highly competent commander of artillery under Stilwell's Northern Area Combat Command in Burma and India until 1944.

Lieutenant Colonel Edwin M. Sutherland's (1897–1967) specialty was supply; after his AMMISCA service, he became the commander of Services of Supply Base Section 3 in northeast India, and then, when it was disbanded and merged with Base Section 2, he commanded that unit with headquarters in Calcutta. In late 1942 he left the China-Burma-India theater and became chief of the Pennsylvania Military District training camp in Indiantown Gap, and, in 1944, he was assigned as commander of 119th Infantry Regiment of the 30th Division in Europe after D–Day.

Lieutenant Colonel Arcadi Paul Gluckman (1896–1983) was selected to be in charge of supplies as AMMISCA's G-4. He, too, was an expert in supply problems, in addition to being fluent in Chinese. Gluckman was commissioned a second lieutenant in the Army Reserve in 1917 and served as assistant military attaché in China in the early 1930s.

Major Joseph Aaron Mendelson (1891–1986), who headed the medical team, also spoke Chinese, the result of living in China for a total of ten years on three different occasions before the war.[1]

Major Harry Aldrich had served in China under Magruder and was fluent in Chinese. He later compiled a two-volume study of the Chinese language that became a standard in the field.

Lieutenant Marcus Ogden (1895–1964) had risen through the ranks from private, serving for a time as a sergeant on the staff of the military attaché in Peking in 1934. He was a member of the army's Finance Corps.

On 18 September, MacMorland departed from Washington, D.C., with Magruder and Sliney. The group flew to San Francisco via Tucson and Los Angeles, arriving mid-morning of 19 September. They were met by Major Aldrich, Lieutenant Colonel Sutherland, and Lieutenant Ogden and immediately went into a staff meeting with Magruder. Aldrich was assigned as leader of the men who would be traveling by sea to Burma and driving over the Burma Road to China with the twenty vehicles and supplies for the mission. The ship carrying this group would leave from San Francisco within a few weeks.[2]

On 21 September, Magruder and his accompanying officers left late in the afternoon for the seventeen-hour flight to Hawaii on a Pan-American clipper that also carried Lord Louis Mountbatten, who, MacMorland wrote in his diary, "told us many thrilling tales of his experiences in this war, particularly in Crete." Mountbatten had been on a goodwill tour of the United States to help strengthen contacts between the Royal Navy and the U.S. Navy, and he was en route to Pearl Harbor to meet top naval officers and inspect the port's facilities. Besides Mountbatten and the American army officers, there were three women on board who were staying in Hawaii, and, as Colonel MacMorland remarked in his diary, a "miscellaneous hodge podge of other adventurers, like ourselves en route to the Far East."[3]

After tours of the army and naval facilities, they flew to Midway Island on 28 September, MacMorland noting that the island was a "hive of National Defense activities in charge of the Navy" and "a good deal like a Concentration Camp [sic]" because of the tight security. Wake Island, their next destination, was in the process of being transformed from a sleepy overnight stop for Pan-American Airways' trans-Pacific clippers into a U.S. Marine base with an airstrip, barracks, warehouses, and sheds to house men and their supplies, plus storage tanks for aviation and vehicle fuel, roads, and gun emplacements. When MacMorland and his group arrived, Wake Island was taking on the appearance of a fortified military base.[4] The group was shown around the island by the marine commander, Major Lewis A. Hohn, who told them that the contractor had a thousand men at work at "fancy wages, and yet they stay an average of only 4 months."[5]

The next stop was Guam, which they reached at 4:00 in the afternoon of 1 October. There they found three other members of the AMMISCA party who had been stranded for a week by engine trouble on their clipper. Two large parties of passengers were packed into the two dozen hotel rooms near the airport, ten miles from the main town, Agana. Magruder arranged to get his party out the following day, ordering two members of the stranded group to remain behind and catch the next clipper to the Philippines.

On 2 October the group had a smooth, uneventful flight to Manila, covering fifteen hundred miles in ten hours, landing at Cavite at 2:00 in the afternoon and driving to the Manila Hotel. The next day was hectic: a meeting with MacArthur took place in the morning, where they heard his views on the situation in China; in the afternoon they met with Brigadier General Henry B. Clagett,[6] air commander in the Philippines; and that night they dined with General and Mrs. MacArthur, as well as Sir Robert Brooke-Popham (British commander-in-chief at Singapore) and two of his staff officers, plus

Colonel Edward MacMorland (courtesy Widener University Archives).

Admiral Thomas C. Hart, U.S. Asiatic Fleet commander. That same evening the Pacific clipper arrived with the two AMMISCA members who had been left behind at Guam.

The day of 4 October was spent in more conferences and lunch with the Chinese Chamber of Commerce of Manila. There was no dinner engagement in the evening, so all hands could get to bed at a reasonable hour for the 7:00 takeoff for Hong Kong next morning. The flight to Hong Kong was about six hours in duration, made on three naval PBYs. "Apparently we caused quite a stir when we came over HongKong [sic]," MacMorland wrote in his diary. "The Chinese were impressed when the symbol of U.S. assistance landed in China in Navy planes." The next several days were spent in meetings and dinners with Chinese and British officials, along with tours of the defenses, hosted by Major General Christopher Maltby, the British commander.[7] The group purchased a refrigerator to be shipped to Rangoon, where it would be held by the Standard Oil Company until the group that was driving along the Burma Road could pick it up.

The men of AMMISCA were off to Chungking on the evening of 9 October. Their departure was made in secrecy on a China National Airways Corporation (CNAC) DC-3, which flew first north, then northwest, to avoid the Canton area, which was occupied by the Japanese. The American pilot was an expert flier and safely delivered his passengers to a military airfield forty miles north of Chungking. A large delegation of Chinese officials met the members of the AMMISCA party and drove them to their quarters in Chungking, a comfortable house complete with a bath, electric lights, and running water, where a sumptuous supper had been prepared for them.

Despite his hectic schedule, MacMorland found time to stroll through the streets and noted the cheerfulness of the people, who had already endured four years of warfare. "It is hard to understand how the swarms of people connected with each little shop can find a living from traffic in the very small stocks in each," he wrote on 19 October. "I cannot conceive of Americans standing what the Chinese have experienced."[8]

3

Grindlay Goes to China

The main contingent of the AMMISCA staff made up of many of the lower-ranking officers, plus noncommissioned officers and enlisted men, who formed the working core of the mission. These men included medical, transportation, and supply personnel, filling support positions under Magruder's top officers, and were dispatched to China by ship along with bulk of the unit's equipment and supplies.

The medical staff was under the command of Major Joseph Mendelson and consisted of a surgeon and two technicians, who would provide medical support for the mission, help set up equipment, and conduct laboratory work. The surgeon was First Lieutenant John Happer Grindlay, known as "Grumpy" among his friends, a thirty-one-year-old physician from Ohio and a member of the Army Reserve who was on the staff of Walter Reed General Hospital when he learned about AMMISCA from a fellow medical officer. In his diary (which he started keeping in September 1941 after hearing of the formation of AMMISCA and methodically kept until the end of his war service overseas), Grindlay related the chain of events that led him to volunteer to join the group:

> [September] 4. *Heard of Mil.Mis. to China ... while in* [Walter Reed General Hospital's] *library for afternoon. Surgeon wanted.*
>
> [September] 6. *Can't shake idea of China Mission.... Mission to go to Chungking & study Chinese needs, also observe. I would* [be] *surgeon with opportunity to help Chinese in hospitals there. I would go by boat to Rangoon & up Burma Road. The thrill of it surpasses any thrills ... I've ever had.*
>
> [September] 8. *Gave my answer ("yes")*[1]

Born in Philadelphia on 13 November 1909, Grindlay received his AB degree at Oberlin College in 1931 and his MD from Harvard Medical School in 1935. He entered Dartmouth Medical College as a fellow in pathology (1935–1936) and served an internship on the house staff at Mary Hitchcock Memorial Hospital at Dartmouth for another year (1936–1937). From 1937 to

1939 Grindlay attended the Mayo Clinic Graduate School of Medicine in Rochester, Minnesota, as a fellow in surgery, and he received his MS in surgery from the University of Minnesota in 1940. He joined the U.S. Army Reserve as a medical officer the following year and was assigned to Walter Reed. He married Elizabeth (Betty) Ellis in 1939, and the couple had a child, Sara, a year later.

Grindlay's term of service, like that of others in the mission, was of indefinite tenure, and he was warned that he should plan to stay in China a year or more due to the nature of "the international situation." His surgical expertise was sought not only to provide medical support for AMMISCA's personnel but also to investigate the general medical situation in China. The latter charge included looking into requirements for medical supplies, what uses were being made of those already available, and the possibilities of training Chinese medical personnel. Grindlay's duties also included advising on the medical needs of Chinese workers who were constructing a rail line from Kunming to Lashio, which the Americans were contemplating finishing.[2]

On 8 September, Grindlay was relieved from his duties at Walter Reed and started the paperwork in preparation for transfer to AMMISCA. He notified his wife, Betty, who promptly began packing his bags. Three days later, mission members dined with Lauchlin Currie and Tommy Corcoran, President Roosevelt's special envoys and advisors, at which time they learned more about the situation in China and the expectations the administration had for them once they arrived. Corcoran had secretly formed a shadowy government agency, called China Defense Supplies, that was charged with sending Lend-Lease materials to China and had worked closely with Claire Chennault in setting up the American Volunteer Group, popularly known as the "Flying Tigers" (a name suggested by Corcoran's son David). Currie was a long-time member of Roosevelt's "Brain Trust" and the president's leading eco-

Captain John H. Grindlay. Date of photograph is unknown but likely taken after his return to the United States in 1944 (courtesy Grindlay family).

nomic advisor. He had traveled to China at Roosevelt's request to discuss the country's war needs with Generalissimo Chiang Kai-shek and Communist leader Chou En-lai and returned to urge Roosevelt to add China to the Lend-Lease program. T.V. Soong (1891–1971), Chiang Kai-shek's brother-in-law, former finance minister and soon-to-be minister of foreign affairs, who was in Washington to filter requests for Lend-Lease supplies from Chungking to the War Department and to exert influence in their acquisition, also joined the dinner meeting. Eight days later Grindlay boarded a train for San Francisco to meet the ship that would carry twelve of the AMMISCA crew, their vehicles, and equipment to Rangoon.[3]

The ship, Grindlay noted curiously, bore no name on its bow. (It was in fact the *Hoegh Silverdawn*, a freighter owned by a large Norwegian shipping company, and had entered service the year before.[4]) He discovered that there would be a long delay in sailing due to a slowdown caused by the unionized longshoremen, who lacked work and wanted to stretch out the little they had. Grindlay found himself at loose ends and spent much of his time sightseeing: as he wrote to his parents on 2 October, he had been walking "a good 10 miles a day, much of it up steep hills. My shoes are getting thin rapidly."[5] He discovered, however, that "even enchanting [San Francisco] grows dull." His baggage finally went aboard that morning, and he joined it at midnight. The next day, at 6:30 a.m., the ship left the pier, steamed a short distance up the bay, and "loaded 2 barges of dynamite." At 3:00 in the afternoon of 4 October, they set sail for Rangoon.

Just outside the Golden Gate, the ship stopped to put off the pilot, and the captain opened his sealed orders. Grindlay learned that they would sail to Rangoon by way of Manila, Borneo, Soeribaija, Batavia, and Penang. A strong wind was blowing, and the ship pitched and rolled sickeningly.

> [October] 4. The gale lasted all night but abated during day slowly. Four men got very sick and two others kept to their bunks.... One man was thrown from his bunk. Nearly all the deck cargo shifted & some of the crates of the trucks were smashed. (Our hatches & main deck are completely covered by deck cargo, mainly crates of trucks for China & two piles of onions).

He paused in his diary to list the members of the mission who were aboard, including four officers and eight enlisted men:

> Major George Vaughn, Q.M.C. (commander of the contingent)
> Captain Roscoe Hambleton, Spec. [Engineer]
> First Lieutenant Marcus Ogden, Inf.
> First Lieutenant John Grindlay, M.C.
> Warrant Officer Albert Norem
> Technical Sergeant W.O. Gardner, D.E.M.L. [Detached Enlisted Men's List[6]]
> Technical Sergeant Frank Marek, D.E.M.L.

Staff Sergeant Jacob Moul, D.E.M.L.
Staff Sergeant Hubbard White, D.E.M.L.
Staff Sergeant J.R. Lytle, D.E.M.L.
Staff Sergeant Francis Astolfi, D.E.M.L.
Staff Sergeant Melvin E. Tingly, M.C.

Of this group, Grindlay and Tingly were from the Medical Corps. They would join Major Mendelson and Technical Sergeant Ray Chesley (a first-rate laboratory technician) in Chungking as the mission's medical team. Major Vaughan had replaced Major Aldrich as commander of the group traveling along the Burma Road from Rangoon to Chungking. Vaughan was described by Grindlay as "short, slim, small mustache, agreeable [and] at first glance not imposing. However he turns out to be intelligent, decent [and] capable." Hambleton was a "short, slender, intelligent chap. A Cornell graduate [mechanical engineer, class of 1917] who has spent 15 yrs in China with his own [engineering] company.... A true world traveler." Marcus Ogden (introduced in the previous chapter) was, as Grindlay noted in his diary, a "character & old China hand, formerly an N.C.O. attached to [the] legation in Peking. A walrus mustache, ruddy face, great good nature, knows all the ins & outs of the army & has learned how to take it as it comes. Married a month I hear."

Grindlay also described the enlisted men in his diary, but in briefer terms. Some of them would be assigned as advisors to the Chinese in various capacities; others would be given responsibility for troubleshooting and correcting obvious problems concerning the routing of Lend-Lease supplies to the Chinese. For example, several were mechanics and transportation specialists who would be stationed along the Burma Road to assist in improving its efficiency. Warrant Officer Norem was the only one who was not a technician, being a chief clerk and a "lean, nervous rather neurotic but dependable man" who spoke Norwegian (and thus could converse with the crew of the ship). Tingly was "tall, blond & quiet"; Gardner was "6'4" & way over 200 [pounds]"; Marek was "handsome and huge"; White was "stocky & handsome"; Moul was "roly-poly, good natured"; Astolfi appeared "tall, good-looking, rather naïve & sweet"[7]; and Lytle was "short & intelligent."

During the nightly cocktail hour, Grindlay learned that the ship and its crew had barely escaped from Denmark before the German invasion. The captain, Dag Jorgen Arnesen, was a "short chap of average build with a bright kindly eye & ruddy face. A Norwegian nose & English is fair. Very quiet talking really only when questioned." Both Arnesen and his executive officer, Captain Alf Slaatten, had not seen their families for two and a half years, and both had children they had never laid eyes on. Slaatten, Grindlay discovered, had worked on a whaling ship for three years. The vessel had been crushed by an iceberg near Antarctica; half of the crew was lost, and Slaatten and other survivors had clung to the iceberg for two days before rescue came. He had suffered frozen feet and spent three months recuperating in a hospital.[8]

The trip across the Pacific was uneventful. Grindlay wrote to his parents from Manila on 23 October that he had little to do on board except read, walk around the deck where there was space to sunbathe, and swim in the saltwater tank. "The meals ... are very good," he happily reported. Breakfast consisted of fruit, cereal, eggs, meat, toast and coffee. Lunch and dinner were five-course affairs, "one of which is fish and another course is always meat. Then there is always tea in the afternoon." He had to admit, however, that he longed for his family and while "I ... think the opportunity is good ... it's the last sacrifice I make for a career." They made 13.5 knots at full speed and sailed non-stop to Manila, where the ship was reprovisioned and refueled, and additional supplies were taken on for the mission. Here, Slaatten left the ship to take a clipper to Singapore to assume command of another Hoegh-owned freighter.

After two days in port, the *Hoegh Silverdawn* sailed on to Soerabaija on Java, where part of its cargo of dynamite was unloaded. Grindlay and the others spent three days sightseeing before journeying to Semerang, and then on to Batavia. "They are fine cities," he wrote his parents from Rangoon on 16 November. "They are beautifully laid out with wide streets & lawns & gardens. The buildings are most modern [and] like all else are clean & spotless."

On 7 November, the ship sailed to Singapore, arriving two days later and delivering more cargo. The city impressed Grindlay with its blend of Chinese, Malays, and Indians. Most of the taxis were driven by Sikhs, "huge turbaned ... full bearded fellows." He went to dinner at the Raffles Hotel with Captain Arnesen and the ship's chief engineer. The famous hotel struck Grindlay as "a beautiful place but almost [everyone] there [was] in uniform (only a few women). I saw many colorful uniforms of the various regiments." The ship then steamed on to Rangoon, where the long sea voyage ended on 15 November, about five days later than expected.

Hoegh Silverdawn anchored five miles downriver from the city because of its dangerous cargo of dynamite and was met by Major Aldrich, who had arrived in the Far East with the Magruder party a month earlier.[9] After checking into their hotel, Grindlay and his comrades were briefed about what to expect in the days ahead. All of the vehicles that came with them were to be driven up the Burma Road to China by the AMMISCA members and hired Chinese and Burmese drivers. Through negotiation with the government of Burma, the men were issued driver's licenses that would expire upon the convoy's arrival at Wanting, China.

The men spent most of their time overseeing the unloading of supplies from the ship, which kept Grindlay so busy that he was unable to find time to write in his diary. Finally, in a spare moment, he recorded the week's events:

> [November] 23 ... *This has been a busy week. Beginning at 6 AM Monday* [17 November] *we have worked daily until 5 PM* [with] *an hour for lunch, at the Godowns* [warehouses] *of Brooking St. Wharf. For 2 days we checked the tons of crates boxes, etc., of equipment, from med. supplies to canned goods and auto parts. Everything arrived, at least all the medical. Then we sorted out some things & sent it off to go to Lashio by rail.... The motor transport men (Vaughan* [sic]*, Marek, Gardner & White) have labored hard at conditioning & repairing the cars, carryalls, pickups & trucks.... We have uncrated & sorted & packed all the rest of the equip—making kits for each of us & those here & at Lashio & Kunming. Kits of personal equip, also stationery & other supplies. We have worked like hell, sweating gallons; we are the first whites I am sure the coolies ever saw working. We have had a dozen of the coolies daily—hard-working, thin but strong Kuoringis—carrying & lifting boxes from one of our spots to the other.* [It is not known who the "Kuoringis" were, though Grindlay may have meant the Kalingas from the Philippines.] *Finally, we are in partly good shape. All the equipment now is over* [in] *our godown, the one we are to have permanently; I have finally heard that we will be able to take the hospital* [truck] *as far as Lashio at least—there is the question of whether its 8' width can navigate a few bridges in Burma further on.*

The hospital truck was Grindlay's pride and joy. It had been custom built in the shops at the Presidio and was fully equipped with medical supplies, and Grindlay was fiercely determined to get the truck safely through to China.

Rangoon, Grindlay noted, was a city like Singapore—a hodgepodge of races. It seemed to him as though

> *in the town itself the Burmese & Chinese, though numerous, are out-numbered by Indians. There is every type of the latter, in all degrees of filth & all types of costumes ...* [with] *all ways of wearing the cloth they drape in many ragged* [filthy]*, deformed beggars. There is no room at the town's best hotel* [the Strand] *so our party is staying at the next best, none too good, with only a few light bulbs & rudimentary plumbing, etc. I had lunch with the officers here and Gen. Magruder and a Chinese Gen. (Kuo).*

The trees in a park across the street from the hotel were teeming with squawking ravens while huge kites the size of eagles circled overhead. According to Grindlay, "There are all kinds of bugs and mosquitos at night and we sleep under nets.... Betel nut juice is spattered all over the streets, looking like blood." He found that natives slept on the streets and in doorways at night, and there were "countless rickashas pulled by Indians." On the next day (17 November), he planned to squeeze in a visit to the Burma General Hospital "and have a look around and meet some of the men there." Grindlay heard, to his relief, that the Burma Road was said to be in good shape, with "no military activity and no threats of any," he wrote to his parents. "We will be safe, albeit suffering a few hardships in lack of conveniences, etc.... Don't worry about my health or safety for there is no danger—only inconveniences."

At 7:15 a.m. on 27 November, the twenty-vehicle convoy rolled out of Rangoon and began the long trek up the Burma Road and on to Kunming and, eventually, Chungking, which was reached on 21 December. The journey was largely uneventful, except for mechanical breakdowns, wrangles with the Chinese drivers, and minor illnesses brought on by the frequent rains and chilly, damp air in the mountains. En route, the group traveled through some of the world's wildest and most rugged country on roads that were still being constructed by coolie labor, cut by hand from steep mountainsides. The convoy struggled laboriously up treacherous inclines and inched its way around hairpin turns and down precarious slopes into deep valleys and over rickety bridges spanning roaring streams. Grindlay provided a graphic description of the scenery in a letter to his parents from Chungking, dated 2 January 1942:

> The Burma Road was a real experience. I can't begin to describe it. Thru jungles and the wild primitive tribes of the Shan States in [northern] Burma, then the equally wild southern Yunnan province. We have nothing like it. The mountains are rugged, the highest sheer cliffs I've seen ... you'd never believe it. The lower slopes are almost as steep, but are laced with rice terraces—for as far into the horizon as you can see. The wretched people—all women with bound feet, some areas the people having huge goiters, gangs of women, men, and children breaking rock or digging the road out of the cliff. The villages are of mud brick, the larger ones, walled. The smaller hills and entrances to the gorges all have fortresses thousands of years old. We paralleled the ancient "Silk Road" of Marco Polo—tiny arched bridges, stone paving, steps cut into the cliffs, caravans of hides, furs, silk, etc.—some from Tibet. The motor road is appallingly thrilling, up and down, over one range after another. Hairpin loops (72 down one cliff), over sheer cliffs dropping 1000-5000 ft. Narrow—you'd have to see to believe. We slept in our tents each night and cooked almost all our meals from canned rations. We had 3 days rest each at Lashio and Kunming—each delightful spots.[10]

As feared, the bridges on the Burma Road were very narrow, but the travelers managed to squeeze the vehicles, including the ambulance truck, through all but the "69th Mile Bridge," a British-built suspension affair on the road between Lashio and the border town of Wanting.[11] The convoy leaders drove ahead to arrange for the bridge's stone and concrete abutments to be chiseled out sufficiently to permit the hospital truck to scrape through. The group paused in Lashio until they received word that the bridge was ready for them.[12]

They arrived in the murky winter climate of Chungking four days before Christmas and were warmly welcomed by the other members of AMMISCA. Grindlay described the city to his parents in his letter of 2 January:

> Chungking is quite a place. It is deadly dull now. Rain, mist, and fog continually. Never sun. The town has been bombed to ruins in the past 4 years. However, a few houses have been rebuilt, such as ours. And a lot of shacks have been put up by the natives. It is a big place, on a Gibralter-like rock at the junction of the Yangtze and Chialing rivers, both large and terribly swift. On the opposite banks are steep cliffs, and behind ragged but not high mts. It is the usual Chinese city—crowds of poor coolies, pushing and dragging heavy carts, and carrying heavy loads with shoulder yokes. All barefoot and clothes ... in rags. Many sick, crippled, and all showing some evidence of disease.[13]

4

AMMISCA Settles In

When the AMMISCA members arrived in China, they found a country that had been at war for more than four years. The Japanese had driven the Nationalist armies of Generalissimo Chiang Kai-shek out of eastern China, including the coastal ports, into the protective mountain fastnesses of the southwest. The Nationalist government and its minions shouldered their way into Chungking (a city of about a million people that clung precariously to steep cliffs along the Yangtze and Chialing rivers) in late 1937, after they were pushed out of the former capitals at, first, Nanjing (about 1,400 miles to the east along the Yangtze) and then Wuchang (one of three cities that comprised the urban confluence of Wuhan, some 450 miles from Chungking and one of a few inland concessions granted to Western powers by the last empress of China). Both the city and the government were exhausted from almost half a decade of warfare, having suffered enormous losses to the armed forces and equally enormous expenditures that had brought Chiang's government to the brink of financial collapse, in addition to an urban fabric that was blasted to ruins by Japanese aerial attacks. Chungking's population grew astonishingly when thousands of refugees and many factories and universities and cultural organizations were relocated from eastern China following the government's exodus. To escape the constant bombing, huge shelters were dug into the cliffs to provide a safe refuge for civilians during the attacks. Despite the attempts of the Japanese to kill it, the city remained a center for education, publishing, news media, and museums and libraries. Besides hosting hordes of Chinese newcomers, Chungking was also a temporary home to hundreds of foreigners.[1]

Among the foreigners were the men of AMMISCA. After Magruder and six members of his staff arrived in Chungking on 9 October, they began to hold regular meetings with Chiang Kai-shek, who, immediately prior to their arrival, had begun stepping up his requests for military equipment. T.V. Soong, acting as the Generalissimo's representative in Washington, had requested 1,000 antiaircraft guns by the end of October and a large quantity of pack howitzers by the end of the year. The War Department was startled by the unrealistic size of the request and explained that only a small portion could be delivered by the dates requested due to a shortage in the weapons stockpiles. An angry Lauchlin Currie memoed his boss, Harry Hopkins, the coordinator of Lend-Lease, early in October that, aside from 500 Bren guns obtained from Canada, "we haven't shipped one gun yet to China on lend-lease [sic]." Under pressure from the White House, the War Department released from its stockpiles 48 75mm howitzers, 11,000 Thompson submachine guns, 500 Bren guns, 100 50-caliber machine guns, 35 scout cars, and a huge quantity of ammunition.[2]

The Tenth of October in China was hailed as "Double Ten," the anniversary of the founding of the republic on 10 October 1911, and Colonel Mac-Morland noted that there were celebrations and decorations everywhere in Chungking. He and several other members of Magruder's staff began a whirlwind round of visits and meetings in the midst of the Double Ten festivities that were to consume most of the days that followed. They called on U.S. Ambassador Clarence Gauss on 11 October, using a launch loaned by General Ho Ying-chin, China's war minister, to cross to the south bank of the Yangtze River, where the American embassy was located. The embassy was "a rather poor building," in Mac-Morland's view.

Gauss was a man of somewhat sour disposition, a career diplomat who had served in China almost continuously since 1907 and was recognized as perhaps the most able foreign service officer in the Far East and one who had seen everything. He had fearlessly defended U.S. interests against Japanese encroachment and, in doing so, came to the attention of his superiors in Washington. Gauss was named ambassador to China by President Roosevelt

Clarence Gauss, U.S. ambassador to China (National Archives and Records Administration, College Park, Maryland).

in February 1941 and arrived in Chungking from his previous post in Australia in May. He received a cool reception from the Chinese, who suspected that his reputation for toughness might interfere with their requests for Lend-Lease aid. Gauss was not sympathetic to such requests and was willing to approve anything that was reasonable and could be handled over the Burma Road. However, by late 1941 he had come to the conclusion that China's military weakness would only permit the country to maintain a defensive posture and any American supplies should go toward keeping Chinese armies in the war to pin down large numbers of Japanese. This was exactly the same conclusion that the Joint Chiefs of Staff had already reached.[3]

The next day Magruder and his staff were shown a dugout to be used in case of bombing, which was dug into a hill situated about one hundred yards from their house and furnished with wooden floors and electric lights. The air raid warning system was a series of visual relay signals manned by volunteer spotters consisting of lanterns and paper balls of different shapes and colors raised on poles denoting that Japanese planes had left their airfield at Hankow to the east and their position vis-à-vis Chungking. Crude as it was, the system gave the city forty minutes' advance notification of a bombing attack, time enough for most of the citizenry to reach one of the enormous shelters carved into the hills. The same system was adopted by Claire Chennault to provide a warning of approaching Japanese bombers in Kunming, where his Flying Tigers (the American Volunteer Group) were based. In the late afternoon, the Americans crossed the river again in the company of Hollington Tong (1887–1971), a journalist, newspaper editor, and the Chinese government's liaison to the press, to call on H.H. Kung (1881–1967), Chiang Kai-shek's wealthy banker brother-in-law and China's finance minister. "In reaching Kung's house," MacMorland later wrote in his diary, "we passed through some [11 miles of] attractive mountain scenery to a small village from which we ascended endless stairs up the mountain to the house. We were in a sweat when we got there, but were pleasantly surprised by Madame and Mr. Kung and had tea."

More visits occurred on 12 October, and then a small party of the officers traveled to the airport on an island in the Yangtze River at 1:00 in the morning to meet a group who had flown up from Hong Kong to join AMMISCA, including Major Joseph Mendelson (the chief medical officer), Captain William M. Clarkson (adjutant general), and Colonel Otto George (Army Air Corps). Later that same morning, MacMorland and Magruder called on Major General Lancelot Dennys, head of the British mission (called 204 Military Mission), and the British ambassador, Sir Archibald Clark Kerr. A discussion of the tasks of both missions and "some things with which they will have to help with the Burmese Govt." was followed by dinner that night, MacMorland recorded in his diary.

4. AMMISCA Settles In

General Archibald Wavell (commander-in-chief of the American-British-Dutch-Australian Command [ABDACOM]), General Mao Pang-tsu (Chinese Nationalist Air Force), and Major General Lancelot Dennys (commander of 204 [British] Military Mission). Photograph taken in late 1941 or early 1942 in China (courtesy Nicholas Dennys).

Clark Kerr (1882–1951) was born in Australia and had been in China since 1938. He was known to have leftist sympathies but was by no means a Socialist or a Communist. He was tall, distinguished, skillful, courageous, and well spoken. He and his diminutive wife, Tita (a blonde Chilean twenty-nine years his junior), made a glamorous couple in diplomatic circles, although it was whispered that Sir Archie had homosexual proclivities and his wife had dalliances of her own. Whether or not there was any truth in these rumors, Tita's sudden departure in February 1941 caused excited gossip in diplomatic and journalistic circles that she had run off with an American military attaché, a fact hotly denied by Clark Kerr's biographer many years later.[4] Clark Kerr was described by MacMorland as "a very likeable human type, who immediately remembered me. I had seen him for only a few minutes at the Gov. General's luncheon in HongKong [sic]. Gen. Dennys is an active, imaginative officer, who has only himself at present for a large job. I believe we can cooperate fully with these British representatives."

On 15 October MacMorland spent time working out plans for the motor column that was to drive up the Burma Road from Rangoon, which would include John Grindlay and the other members of AMMISCA who were still on the high seas. The rest of the staff began outlining the relationships that each team member would have with their opposite numbers in the Chinese government. Major Mendelson would be working with the Chinese surgeon general and Red Cross head, Dr. Robert Lim; Lieutenant Colonel Walter Soderholm would assist Major General Yu Ta-wei, the chief of the Chinese ordnance department, with weapons and ammunition requirements. The Chinese government assigned General Tseng Hsi-kuei from the Office of Foreign Affairs to Magruder's office as a kind of secretary and liaison. Soon afterward, small groups of men were dispatched to inspect the Chinese system of military communications, assess the state of their weapons arsenals, and determine the types and condition of equipment currently being used by the Chinese army and air force. This information would enable AMMISCA to knowledgably advise the Chinese about what types of equipment would be most needed and how to effectively deploy such devices after they arrived. The Americans, however, soon discovered that the Chinese resented any activity related to training the Chinese armies in the use and maintenance of Lend-Lease goods, pointing out that they had been at war for four years and had much more experience in warfare than did the U.S. military. AMMISCA's good intentions were met by polite but stubborn resistance. The British mission had already encountered the same attitude, and General Dennys was becoming increasingly frustrated.

It will be recalled that AMMISCA's primary assignment was to expedite the shipment and transfer of Lend-Lease aid to China. In accordance with this directive, Magruder set up a team charged with studying the capacity of the Burma Road, the most important supply route into China, with an eye to increasing the tonnage carried over the road. This study encompassed a review of the road's condition and the use and maintenance of the equipment operating on it. It was somewhat of a duplication of effort, as another group had surveyed the road the previous summer. At President Roosevelt's urging, Harry Hopkins had dispatched Daniel Arnstein, president of the New York Terminal Cab Company, along with Harold Davis and Marco Hellman (veterans of the American trucking industry), to Burma to find out why, as Hopkins said with some exaggeration and no trace of eloquence, "not a god-damn thing was moving over the Burma Road." Their report was sent to Hopkins, Roosevelt, and Chiang Kai-shek—who may have passed on a copy to Magruder, although there is no evidence of such. Another survey made by the assistant American military attaché to China, Major David Barrett (1892–1977), had identified many worsening problems, including increasing congestion and insufficient equipment, repair facilities, drivers, fuel, or personnel to coordinate the flow of material over the road, not to mention the deteriorated condition of the road itself. The more the situation was examined, the more difficult the problem seemed to become. In any event, Magruder rolled up his sleeves and plunged into the transportation morass once again, putting staff members to work not only on how to increase the efficiency of the Burma Road but also studying the feasibility of building a pipeline for the transportation of petroleum (one of his pet projects) and of planning and directing the construction of the Yunnan–Burma railroad, for which Grindlay was detailed to provide medical support.[5]

Meetings about the Burma Road situation were held on 17 and 18 October with Major James Wilson, an army transportation specialist who flew in from Lashio.[6] Supplies were piling up at the Rangoon docks because of inadequacies and glitches in the transportation and distribution systems. Smuggling and sabotage only added to the problems, complicated by a shortage of mechanics to repair broken-down trucks. Japanese bombing caused minimal damage to equipment along the road, but their notorious inaccuracy often resulted in landslides that blocked the road for days on end. To MacMorland's relief, word reached Chungking that thirty-five mechanics were sailing from San Francisco on 7 November, which would help alleviate the repair situation, but the men were not due to arrive for another two months.

On 25 October, Magruder issued a directive to his staff reminding them that no member could engage in negotiations with the Chinese that would commit the U.S. government to any policy decision. Yet he found himself drawn into just such a discussion two days later at a meeting he called at his residence. Chiang Kai-shek informed Magruder that his intelligence had discovered Japanese preparations to launch an attack from Indochina northwestward to Kunming with the intention of severing the Burma Road. While Chiang felt that his ground forces could hold back the Japanese, his weak air defenses could not prevent them from subjecting Kunming to serious bombing attacks and possibly capturing the city. "The loss of Kunming," the Generalissimo warned, "means that China [could] no longer offer any effective resistance" because vital supplies that would otherwise come in over the Burma Road would be cut off. The Chinese had expected the British to lend assistance with their air forces from Singapore, but the British refused to cooperate. Madame Chiang entered the discussion at this point, bitterly pointing out that the Chinese had offered to launch a ground attack against Japanese forces in Indochina as a diversion in case the Japanese attacked Singapore. And yet, she continued, "the British did not seem inclined to help China now with the Singapore air force unless British territory is invaded."[7]

Chiang asked Magruder to send a telegram to Washington urging that pressure be applied to the British to come to China's aid. He argued that the potential Japanese attack from Indochina was an extension of Japan's southward advance, a test of the announced policy of the United States to stand firm against further southward enemy expansion. Madame Chiang asked whether the air forces of the Dutch East Indies could lend assistance, and Magruder said he felt that they could not. In the face of pressure from the

Generalissimo and his wife, Magruder buckled and agreed to immediately send a message to Washington on the subject, outlining Chiang's concerns and his request for British aid. Magruder plucked up the courage to emphasize that the supply route of the Burma Road must remain intact and that AMMISCA stood ready to give technical advice on improvements in its operation, but the Chinese must deal with any political aspects relating to operation of the road.[8]

MacMorland and Magruder wrote a report of the meeting and transmitted it to Secretary of War Henry Stimson. A separate note from the Generalissimo went directly to President Roosevelt, who passed it on to Secretary of State Cordell Hull for action. Hull, in turn, referred it to the War Department, where a series of conferences were held to discuss the situation. The army chiefs concluded that air support could only come from the RAF at Singapore or from the U.S. garrison in the Philippines, but taking aircraft away from the latter would weaken the forces needed in case of Japanese attack, the threat of which was increasing every day.[9]

In the meantime, Major Harry Aldrich, the ranking AMMISCA officer in Rangoon, was called to a meeting on 31 October with Burma's governor-general, Sir Reginald Dorman-Smith, to discuss American-British relations. Dorman-Smith was especially anxious to obtain the Americans' six-month plans for aid and support of the Chinese. Aldrich said he did not know of any such plans and therefore could not provide them. The governor-general then informed him—much like a cat pouncing on a canary, in Aldrich's words—that he could confiscate American Lend-Lease supplies in Burma if the need arose but hoped that there would only be good relations maintained between the British and American military missions. He also asked if Magruder was planning a trip to Rangoon and was told that one was in the offing.

Magruder left for Rangoon on 5 November and, when he returned on the afternoon of 17 November, MacMorland found him "a bit discouraged with the way [the] British and Chinese want to hand over their problems to us, including of course paying for everything." Late the next afternoon, the two officers paid a visit to Chiang Kai-shek and conferred for almost two hours, discussing Chinese communications and aviation problems. These matters had been presented to the Generalissimo by Colonel Ross Hoyt of the U.S. Army Air Corps three days earlier.[10] Hoyt found the Chinese air force to be sadly deficient in combat training and proficiency, in addition to suffering from low morale. The Generalissimo agreed and asked that the United States take over total control of the bomber command.

On 20 November Magruder was in the air again, this time traveling to Singapore for a conference with the British on possible air support for any Japanese attacks on Kunming. Colonel Claire Chennault accompanied him, joining the small party (which also included Chinese general Kuo Chan [1894–1950]) in Burma. The same CNAC plane that carried Magruder, Chennault, and Kuo to Singapore brought in Major (later Colonel) Frank Merrill (1903–1955) from the Philippines, where he was on General MacArthur's staff. Before that, Merrill had served as military attaché in Tokyo and studied the Japanese language. Later in the war, he would be placed in command of the only American ground combat troops in the China-Burma-India theater, a force nicknamed "Merrill's Marauders." After his arrival in Chungking, Merrill was asked by MacMorland to give an account of the conditions in Japan to the assembled officers, based on his lengthy service there both as military attaché and as an observer of the Japanese army. Merrill's remarks are not recorded.

* * *

Thanksgiving for AMMISCA in Chungking was celebrated early. Three dressed turkeys were flown in from Hong Kong and, on finding that they would not last until Thanksgiving, it was decided to have the feast a couple of days early. The military attachés were invited, plus correspondent Leland Stowe. A bottle of vermouth and some whiskey was located, and Manhattan cocktails were produced before dinner. In the meantime, MacMorland noted glumly that news reports "seem to indicate that war with Japan is a grave possibility. Talks in Washington are getting nowhere."

The inactivity of the mission was starting to wear on everyone's nerves, affecting morale. It was difficult to get the Chinese to take action regarding their war materiel requirements. Officers poised to visit various facilities often were unable to obtain transportation or were "stood up" by escorts, including translators. Lieutenant Colonel Soderholm returned from touring Chinese armaments works with a very bitter opinion of their progress. "He is such a good friend of mine that I hate to see him take a sour attitude," MacMorland wrote. Mendelson blamed the morale problem on grumbling and disaffection with the mission: "There is such an interesting problem here that I fail to see why the 'can't take it' fellows do not find something constructive to do." But finding something constructive to do was difficult in circumstances where the Chinese obstructed and blocked action. A significant part of the morale problem, at least for some of the men, lay in not understanding what the mission was expected to achieve. Magruder finally held a staff meeting on 1 December to clarify matters. "Some do not seem to understand what it's all about even after all this time," MacMorland wrote later with an air of surprise.

5

War Begins for AMMISCA

When war with Japan erupted in December 1941, the United States had no plans for coordinating military operations with China. Planners in Washington viewed China solely as a base from which operations could be mounted against Japan, a strategy that never changed throughout the war.[1] President Roosevelt especially saw Lend-Lease aid as a means of enabling Chinese armies to continue fighting, thus tying down large numbers of Japanese troops who might otherwise be deployed elsewhere in Asia and the Pacific.

The presence of the military aid group in Chungking had been very much a sore point in the negotiations between the United States and Japan in Washington leading up to the Pearl Harbor attack. The Japanese made withdrawal of AMMISCA and curtailment of military aid to China a critical bargaining chip in the talks that had been dragging on since March 1941. The United States, in turn, demanded that the Japanese respect the territorial integrity of China and withdraw from the areas they occupied. These two stumbling blocks ultimately proved insurmountable.[2]

On 8 December, the day of the Japanese attack on Pearl Harbor (this was the date in the Far East, west of the International Date Line, though it was 7 December in the United States), Colonel MacMorland was awakened at 6:30 a.m. by General Magruder and told that the Japanese had attacked Manila. "Our marines at Peking are captured," he wrote glumly in his diary. The North China marine contingent numbered 203 men (140 in Peking, 48 in Tientsin, and 15 in Chinwangtao), along with 14 navy medical officers and enlisted men. The marines in Peking and Tientsin were legation guards; the Chinwangtao detachment was stationed at Fort Holcomb, 140 miles northeast of Tientsin.

Magruder continued:

> The gunboat "Wake" has surrendered.[3] Report of ships sunk east of Hawaii [the reports were in error]. One report that battleship "Oklahoma" is sunk. Japs are also landing at

5. War Begins for AMMISCA   39

Kraz [Kra Isthmus] *Peninsula north of Singapore. Report that island of Wake is captured and Guam under attack. Bombing here and there in the Philippines. Apparently many of C.N.A.C. planes destroyed in bombing of Kai Tai* [Kai Tak] *airport, Hong Kong. They will try to fly out the rest of them tonight.... Besieged by reporters.... Air of tenseness among our officers.*

By evening, AMMISCA had also received messages reporting that the Japanese were engaged in combat with British forces in Malaya.

Chiang Kai-shek called a conference at his residence at 9:00 that night. In attendance were the Chinese war and foreign ministers, Sir Archibald Clark Kerr, General Dennys, General Magruder, Colonel MacMorland, and Colonel Hoyt.[4] The Generalissimo expressed sympathy for the American losses and surprised Magruder by asking whether he had seen a Chinese intelligence report from a week earlier outlining Japanese plans for simultaneous assaults against Hong Kong, the Philippines, the Netherlands East Indies, Thailand and Malaya. As far as is known, Magruder never saw it, and whether the report existed at all is questionable. Chiang asked if Magruder had thought of a possible plan of cooperation or conclusion of a military alliance among the various powers now engaged in the Pacific and Asia—China, Britain, the Netherlands, and the United States. Magruder, always sensitive to the political implications of any remarks along these lines, delicately side-stepped the question and responded that the Western nations would have to adopt a defensive posture until their army and naval strength increased. The Generalissimo offered Chinese troops to the British in Burma, and General Dennys answered that providing food for one regiment was all he could promise. Chiang replied that he could supply a division and try to feed two of its three regiments. He then tried again to draw Magruder into a political thicket by asking him to convey a request to the American government that Washington and London raise the question of declaring war on Japan simultaneously with the Soviet Union. Magruder once again avoided a trap and remarked that the matter was not appropriate for AMMISCA but should be transmitted through the American embassy. He told the Generalissimo that he believed the enemy would encounter "great difficulties" attacking on the ground from Thailand and thought an air attack on supplies at Rangoon and Lashio presented more of a threat.[5]

Two days later, Magruder and Dennys were told by General Ho Ying-chin, China's war minister, that Chiang Kai-shek had decided to put all of China's resources into the war. The question was, how could China help? Ho noted there were four outstanding issues that needed to be resolved: reinforcement of Hong Kong; Allied assistance to Malaya and Burma; exchange of information between the Allies; and conclusion of an American-British-Chinese-Russian pact. The first issue would be settled by deployment of three Chinese armies to the Canton area and the second by British and Chinese cooperation in the defense of Burma. Magruder said that the United States could offer no immediate support, but he would recommend to Washington that naval and air deployment be considered as available. Dennys cautiously asked that the Chinese send a diversionary attack against French Indochina and that Chinese forces be available for deployment through Yunnan. Magruder clung stubbornly to his erroneous belief that a land attack on Burma was unlikely.[6]

Later that same day, Magruder and MacMorland met at Chiang's residence, where the Generalissimo expressed his concern that the Allies had no war plan for the Far East. He further declared that, unless they developed a plan within one week, they would not be prepared for a major war. He asked that Magruder and Dennys send recommendations to their respective governments to formulate a plan. Magruder replied that such a decision was the responsibility of the commanders-in-chief in the Far East, but he would send a recommendation to Washington and would also speak to General Dennys, who was not present at the meeting.

On 15 December, Chiang's prayers of an Allied alliance were partly answered when a message arrived from President Roosevelt requesting that a high-level military conference be convened in Chungking to discuss military cooperation among the Allies and plans for the defense of China and Burma. Major General George Brett (1886–1963), U.S. Army Air Forces chief of staff, was being sent to act as Roosevelt's representative and to investigate the possibility of basing heavy bombers in China. The president asked that the conference convene on 17 December, but it had to await Brett's arrival and his whereabouts were unknown.[7]

* * *

In the meantime, Grindlay and the rest of AMMISCA had arrived in Chungking via the Burma Road and were settling into their quarters. Twelve officers, including Grindlay, were assigned to House Number 98, located on the edge of Chungking, three miles from the houses that the rest of the AMMISCA team occupied and away from the heavily bombed areas in the city.

Grindlay found himself sharing the house with Major Frank Merrill and several other officers. He wrote to his wife that his quarters were "splendid for this part of the world ... but really barren for an American house." It was, he noted, "typical of the few European houses [in the city], large, walled, nice formal gardens and European plumbing conveniences," including a bathtub and a toilet, "but typically the water, which we [in the United States] turn a tap to get, is carried by coolies each morning up steps cut in the cliff from the Chialing river about 1000 ft. just below us." Major Mendelson had jerry-rigged a makeshift system that required the coolies to pour the water into a leaky wooden tank, and then pump it into another leaky wooden tank next to the house. When a spigot was turned in the bathrooms, the occupants enjoyed running water until evening, when it was used up. The water was heated by running it through a pipe that passed through a coal-fired oven. Distilled drinking water was carried by coolies from seven miles away. Electricity was sporadic and unpredictable in its timing and intensity. The electric-powered light was brightest during the day, but from dusk until about 10:00 at night "you have to look hard to see the light," Grindlay wrote, because it was so dim. "We use candles," he went on, "for everything and are having as much trouble getting them as soap." Food was prepared by Chinese cooks who had been on American river gunboats and thus knew something about cooking food to American tastes and specifications. Grindlay and the rest of the medical personnel took turns keeping a close eye on food preparations and the general sanitary conditions of the kitchen to prevent contamination and the spread of disease.

One of Grindlay's duties was to unpack the medical supplies and equipment that the convoy had brought up from Rangoon, including a motor generator "liberated" from an unattended supply dump along the Burma Road. The new materials were installed in a dispensary that Grindlay helped set up, along with a portable X-ray machine that was flown from Karachi, the dental records of the American Volunteer Group (Flying Tigers), medical X-rays from the U.S. riverboat *Tutuilla*, and vaccines provided by the Chinese Institute of Health. The medical staff also worked constantly to improve sanitary conditions for the Americans and to arrange medical care for U.S. mechanics and motor technicians stationed along the Burma Road in cooperation with the Chinese National Health Administration, which would staff and administer aid at eleven points on the road. AMMISCA reimbursed the Chinese for all such aid, except that resulting from venereal disease and alcoholism. The Royal Army Medical Corps was likewise compensated for treating American military personnel in Rangoon, and civilian hospitals in Mandalay and Lashio were assigned responsibility for Americans as well.[8]

On Christmas Eve, Grindlay and his fellow officers were invited to a party at the home of General Cheng Chen, Chinese army chief of staff, given for the staffs of the U.S. Embassy, Navy, and AMMISCA. "Upper class Chinese girls" who could not dance with any degree of competence or speak much English were provided as dancing partners, and the music was from "an old, worn phonograph augmented by a few Chinese soldiers with instruments, who had no idea of occidental music," Grindlay noted. The Chinese, he wrote to his wife, "tried to give us an American Christmas and we loved it, but it was as funny as if we had tried to give them a Chinese holiday celebration." Each man received a gift from Magruder. The next day, the men stayed home and had roast goose and liquor contributed by everyone. Later, a group of

Americans, including Grindlay, went to the Press Club and partied with the correspondents. Grindlay reported, "I shot the bull with Harrison Forman, the NBC commentator here.... He is a man with a lot of experiences as a Tibetan explorer and I had much to ask him."[9] In the evening he and Colonel Adrian St. John drove to "Daisy's Cafe," operated by a flaming red-haired "Amazon," as Grindlay described her. He found it "filled with Chinks & their girls—a dismal dark cheap place [with] some phonograph records. Had coffee, sweet cherry brandy (which made St. John sick next day) & vodka—poor stuff. Left & home again at 10....Today supposed to have raid but too foggy for Japs. No news or music from home."[10]

Grindlay reported in a letter to his wife on 29 December that no one knew how long the mission would stay in Chungking or what its ultimate fate would be. "Perhaps they will be sending reinforcements here and a different headquarters will be found," he wrote of some of the rampant speculation. "As a matter of fact there is talk of our forming a [army] division here now, using foreigners & Chinese, at least until Americans can get here." Then, to relieve the anxieties of the folks at home, he added, "Don't get worried about me for this is the least active of all the War areas now and even if it gets active it will be a safe place. [The city] is riddled with caves and the wide open spaces are wide." Possibilities and facilities for conducting surgery were almost nonexistent, and he expressed his frustration with the inactivity: "[There] are no materials in this country to work with and none seems to be coming in. If nothing can be done before I leave here, I'm going to forge in and do my cutting [surgery] on the street, on anything I can catch."

The Tulsa Incident

In the midst of the Christmas celebrations, AMMISCA was facing its first serious crisis. On 18 December, 12,950 pieces of American Lend-Lease signals communication equipment and munitions arrived in Rangoon aboard the freighter SS *Tulsa*.[11] The War Department fully appreciated that Burma was critical to the defense of China and radioed Magruder that he should try to persuade the Chinese to transfer part of the cargo to the British. Chinese authorization was required, since, under the terms of the Lend-Lease agreement, they held title to all China-bound shipments as soon as they left the United States.

Lieutenant Colonel Joseph Twitty, the American officer in charge of liaising with the British government of Burma and of expediting Lend-Lease through Rangoon, feared that the valuable cargo would be lost if the Japanese bombed the port. The stevedores were deserting, and the British were threatening to confiscate the entire cargo. Twitty asked Magruder for advice and,

5. War Begins for AMMISCA

SS *Tulsa* (date of photograph unknown) (Tulsa Historical Society).

while waiting for a reply via the inadequate communications system with Chungking, he asked the British to transport all Lend-Lease stocks, including those on the *Tulsa*, to a "safe place" ashore to protect them from loss or damage by Japanese aerial attacks and fifth column activity. When Twitty told General Yu Fei-peng, the senior Chinese representative in Rangoon, of his actions, Yu did not seem upset. He suggested that a committee be formed to divide the stocks, and Twitty agreed. However, when word of the impounding of the stocks and the establishment of the committee reached Magruder, he told Twitty that the Lend-Lease material could not be impounded or transferred without the Chinese government's agreement. Major General Brett, who was en route to Chungking for the joint military conference, happened to be in Rangoon and told Magruder that he was taking responsibility for the incident and would discuss it further when he arrived in the Chinese wartime capital.[12]

A conference was held between the allies late on the morning of 23 December to prepare for a larger meeting in the afternoon that included Australian minister Sir Frederick Eggleston and Chiang Kai-shek. Among the items discussed was the *Tulsa*'s arrival and delivery of almost 13,000 pieces of signal equipment, which, British General Archibald Wavell pointed out, was "badly needed in Burma." Magruder repeated that this equipment was Lend-Lease material designated for the Chinese and that their permission was required for any transfer. If the British would supply a list of their specific needs, Magruder continued, the transfer could probably be made quickly. Wavell grumbled that he had only taken command in Burma a short time before and did not know what their needs were.

The meeting was broken off, and the men moved from the AMMISCA headquarters to the (Chinese) National Military Council. General Ho Ying-chin joined the meeting and offered Chinese troops for the defense of Burma; Wavell's response was controversial then and remains so to this day among World War II historians. He said that while he appreciated the offer of Chinese troops to defend Burma, he thought that British troops alone could defend the country; a few minutes later he may have recognized the apparent rudeness of his remarks and modified his statement to add that he was not prepared to accept the Chinese armies because he was not able to provide adequate lines of communication and supply for them and the British forces at the same time. Ho took Wavell's refusal as an insult and a loss of face, and the misunderstanding only served to deepen the Chinese mistrust of the British that already existed.[13]

The larger and lengthier afternoon meeting, which included the Australian minister and the Generalissimo, convened at 4:00 p.m. and lasted until 12:30 the next morning. Wavell presented a summary of the morning discussion, which centered on four points: (1) how to use the available air forces, including the American Volunteer Group (Flying Tigers); (2) possible sharing by the Chinese of Lend-Lease supplies with the British; (3) what assistance the Chinese could give to the war in Burma; and (4) the importance of keeping the Japanese under attack everywhere in China. On the last point, Wavell cautioned that the Chinese should not make "hasty, ill-planned offensives in every direction" and advised that the enemy lines of communication should be systematically attacked to prevent the movement of reinforcements from China to other theaters, thus keeping the Japanese forces distracted. Wavell stressed that the defense of Burma was of primary importance, not only from the British viewpoint but also for the protection of China.

Chiang Kai-shek urged implementation of the first three points and added his assent to President Roosevelt's suggestion that a combined military body be established in Washington to direct political and military action against the Axis Powers and to formulate a grand strategy for the defeat of Japan. Chiang and the other Allied leaders also agreed that a secretariat should be set up in Chungking to plan and coordinate the war in Asia. Wavell appointed General Dennys, General Brett appointed General Magruder, and the Generalissimo appointed General Ho to make up the secretariat.

The *Tulsa* incident continued to be a major sticking point between the Chinese and their allies: whether and how to pool Lend-Lease supplies remained a thorny issue. Chiang combined his concern over losing these precious materials to the British with a threat that much more would have to be given to China to prevent the country from collapsing or making peace with Japan and to enable the Chinese to keep the Japanese pinned down. He argued again that there needed to be a plan for the defense of Burma and China cou-

5. War Begins for AMMISCA

pled with the assurance that supplies would continue to flow into China to maintain the war effort. The Generalissimo insisted that any message to Roosevelt on the outcome of the meeting must convey the message that "maintenance of the China front" be included, and he "desired to make it plain that Chinese forces will go anywhere but that they want to know the plan of operations in advance."[14]

Magruder and General Wavell met on the morning of 23 December to discuss the ramifications of the *Tulsa* incident. Magruder told Wavell that all Lend-Lease allocations were part of his authority and that transfer of material could only take place with the formal agreement of the Chinese. Once their agreement was obtained, Magruder could release supplies and equipment to the British. Wavell argued that the switchboards, wire, and other equipment that had arrived on *Tulsa* were badly needed in Burma, but Magruder firmly stated that those materials were designated for two battalions of Chinese field artillery for fire control and communications. He went on to emphasize once again that the British could not arbitrarily take Lend-Lease material consigned to China and that they had only to submit a list of requirements to him and he would forward it to the Generalissimo for approval. Magruder also told Wavell that Roosevelt was committed to continuing Lend-Lease supply to China for "bucking up Chinese resistance," despite the heavy demands of the war, and implied that the Chinese would probably agree to transfer whatever material was required for the defense of Burma. He reiterated that his instructions did not authorize transferring material to the British without Chinese approval. Wavell argued that Chungking and Washington should designate Burma a priority theater in order to "obviate political difficulties" in the United States regarding the taking of equipment from the Chinese. Magruder could do nothing more than repeat his instructions but pointed out that the British already were in disfavor in the War Department stemming from their refusal to supply ammunition to the American Volunteer Group (AVG) stationed in Burma. Instead, ammunition had to be drawn from critically low stocks in the Philippines. Wavell grumbled that "if it were decided that all Lend-Lease was to go to the Chinese, he himself would have to get along without it." The somewhat rancorous meeting closed indecisively, stalemated on the matter of seeking and obtaining Chinese approval to share the Lend-Lease aid.[15]

On the day after Christmas, Magruder, MacMorland, Owen Lattimore, Hollington Tong (a Chinese press secretary who acted as interpreter), and Mr. Li (a secretary of Chiang Kai-shek) met with the Generalissimo and Madame Chiang at their private residence to discuss the *Tulsa* incident and its ramifications further. Chiang presented two telegrams he had received from General Yu Fei-peng, his consul-general in Rangoon, and the report of an interview he had held with a messenger from General Yu concerning the

British impounding of the *Tulsa* shipment and General Brett's decision that the material should be held pending approval of the Generalissimo and General Wavell as to its disposition. Brett had gone on to state that this seizure was in accordance with U.S. policy. Chiang threatened to end all cooperation between China and Britain, calling the seizure "unprecedented" and "unfriendly to say the least." Magruder found himself siding with the Generalissimo and said that General Brett had no authority to approve the impounding of Lend-Lease supplies and recalled Twitty to Chungking for a full report of his actions.[16]

Two weeks later, another high-level conference was held with the Generalissimo at which the entire simmering issue was thrashed out all over again. Ultimately Chiang tamped down his anger by allowing some supplies and equipment to be shared with the British for the defense of Burma. But only, he added, if it would not seriously harm his own armies' needs in defending China.

AMMISCA Medicine

While the *Tulsa* incident was occupying the high command, there remained little for Grindlay to do in the first weeks of his assignment in Chungking. The medical group of which Grindlay was a member had as its charge the assessment of medical conditions in China and in the Chinese army as well as reviewing requisitions for American Lend-Lease medical materials. The group was also directed to establish a liaison with the British to prepare for establishing medical facilities for the Chinese expeditionary force if and when it moved into Burma.

A great part of the medical group's time was absorbed in setting up aid for the mission members, the staff of the American embassy, war correspondents, Burma Road personnel, missionaries, and Chinese officials and their staffs. While doing so, Grindlay learned much about living and medical conditions in China. "I learned that China is a medieval country, that the Burma Road was a pitifully fragile line of communication. I learned that the Chinese Medical Corps was only about 5 percent effective and for all practical purposes, non-existent," the surgeon wrote home.

Before Grindlay arrived in Chungking, Major Mendelson had started to review the Chinese medical situation, and on 28 November he had compiled a report for Magruder that contained a list of recommendations covering personnel, training, supply, and transportation. He suggested that the Chinese Red Cross be placed under the office of China's surgeon general, that competing organizations be reduced in size, and that Red Cross personnel be used to supplement the Chinese Army Medical Services (CAMS). To increase the number of trained doctors and technicians in the CAMS, Mendelson recommended that civilian physicians be recruited (and be paid salaries to attract candidates) and that medical schools be upgraded to improve training. His strongest recommendation was to reorganize the entire Chinese army medical services into a unit independent of other branches of the armed forces and other political entities.

Mendelson's report noted the inefficiency of having competing agencies and decentralization of purchasing, distribution, and accounting of supplies. He suggested that the entire system be placed under the supervision of a foreigner. As to transportation, Mendelson again pointed out the lack of central organization and coordination, and he advised that all motor transport, fuel and lubrication should be purchased, distributed, dispatched, and pooled centrally. He also recommended that drivers be better trained and an increased effort made to train mechanics and to supply spare vehicle parts. Mendelson concluded his report with a stern warning: "If the above advice cannot be followed, it is recommended that all Medical Lend-Lease and Red Cross funds be withheld and the medical members of the Mission be returned to the United States as superfluous."[17]

The medical situation only improved marginally in the months and years to come, despite the efforts of AMMISCA and subsequent American struggles to make it more efficient and effective. While the Chinese Communists were much better at reorganizing and upgrading their medical facilities, thanks in part to an influx of Western volunteers and supplies before and during the war, the Nationalists remained stuck in the nineteenth century in spite of having a trained Western physician in charge of their medical organization; the only modern facilities were a few American-, French-, or British-run hospitals and clinics, such as the Red Cross and the Seagrave Hospital in Burma, of which more will be said later.

In the closing days of December, Grindlay and several others visited the French Catholic hospital in Chungking, which had had its surgical wing destroyed by Japanese bombs. The nursing sisters had done an amazing job of keeping what was left of the hospital clean, but "it would be a darn hard job to do one operation a day" in it, Grindlay wrote to his wife on New Year's Day 1942. Built around 1900, the hospital had no electricity and was "like a dark damp old feudal castle, no heat etc. ... NO way of sterilizing except to boil on a tiny stove in the operating room." Most of the equipment salvaged from the surgical wing was stored out in the country, away from the threat of further bomb damage or loss. Grindlay was pleased to note, however, that there was a

> well-stocked pharmacy [with] old fashioned crude drugs. Ward beds like Chinese beds, [where the patients are] wrapped in cotton quilts to keep warm.... Private rooms [are] large—whole family of [the patient] often occupy the [patient's] room & eat [with]

him, cooking on stove, etc. Large Chinese kitchen—cat [lying] on rice pot lid. Chin[ese] doc. drawing blood while bundled in overcoat.... Many foundlings.[18]

The hospital had one admirable advantage over AMMISCA's medical and living quarters: it possessed filtered and chlorinated running water that came from the city water works on a cliff above the hospital. The Japanese had been trying for years to knock out the water works, Grindlay noted, but thanks to their notoriously inaccurate bombing, it was one of the few undamaged structures. The hospital might adequately house whatever surgical cases he would have to face in the future, "but a lot of work would have to be done to improve their improvised operating facilities."

Grindlay, Lieutenant Colonel Arcadi Gluckman (AMMISCA's G-4), and Lieutenant Marcus Ogden (an infantry officer with the mission) also visited the battered and aging American naval gunboat *Tutuila*, anchored in the Yangtze River and due to be towed eight miles downstream and decommissioned. Two months later it was transferred to the Chinese under the American Lend-Lease program. The vessel was built in Shanghai in 1926–1928 by the Kiangnan Dock and Engineering Works along with its sister ship *Panay*, which had been bombed by the Japanese in 1937, causing substantial loss of American lives and provoking an international incident. The *Tutuila* was armed with three-inch guns fore and aft and, when Grindlay saw it, had armor plates propped up above the rail on the main deck as further protection. The ship was painted "mud yellow," Grindlay reported in his diary. (Just how much of this appearance was discoloration from the murky Yangtze River is open to question, as gunboats were usually painted white.) Grindlay picked up six bandoliers of rifle or machine gun ammunition from *Tutuila*'s personnel, plus a Springfield rifle, and arranged for twelve Lewis guns to be transferred to AMMISCA. On the way home, he took a detour through the Thieves Market and bought more curios to send home to his wife and parents.[19]

But outings like this one were relatively rare. Inactivity was the general rule, and the idleness was taking a toll on the men, who were becoming increasingly restless and irritable. Tempers flared over minor concerns, and petty feuds erupted. Many were disgruntled with Magruder for not getting Washington to assign them more responsibilities. Mendelson, the senior medical officer, accused Major Aldrich of sneaking gin over the Burma Road and submitted a letter to the inspector general through Magruder asking for an investigation and to be relieved of his duties. Aldrich was disliked by a number of the men, and especially by Mendelson after he discovered that Aldrich had been prescribing himself mineral oil for constipation without a doctor's authorization; as a result, Grindlay had to treat him for hemorrhoids. After receiving Mendelson's letter, Magruder summoned Mendelson to a meeting, who attended cheerfully armed with two bottles of vodka, hoping to celebrate both his relief and Aldrich's reprimand. A rancorous argument ensued,

5. War Begins for AMMISCA

Mendelson later told Grindlay, after which the medical officer promised to support Magruder "to the hilt" and Magruder promised in turn to keep Aldrich away from the medical stocks. Mendelson asked his officers to support "the Old Man," arguing that Magruder was feeling as discontented and frustrated at the inactivity as the men were and, besides, was under a great deal of strain from having to keep the Chinese happy. Magruder told Mendelson that he would "do his best by each & all" of them.[20] Mendelson's complaint resulted in action two days later when Magruder sent a message to Washington analyzing AMMISCA's situation and its mission, possibly hoping to spur the War Department into assigning a more important role to the unit.[21]

Over the course of several weeks Grindlay had become acquainted with Dr. Robert ("Bobby") Lim (1897–1969), the dynamic and well-respected founder of the Chinese Red Cross, who was the inspector general of medical services for the Nationalist government. He had arrived in Chungking on 6 January from his headquarters in Kweiyang, more than 300 miles south of Chungking, accompanied by Dryhurst Evans from the American Red Cross, a big, ruddy-faced, jovial Welshman, and Cheng Pao-nan, director of the American Bureau for Medical Relief to China.[22] The energetic Lim impressed Grindlay, who normally did not think highly of the Chinese, as a small man who spoke "faultless Oxford English [with] some Scotch tang [Lim was educated at Edinburgh University], very quiet, wastes few words, very keen, damned good man." Lim was a widower with two children and the "most famous medico in China," who had fallen out with the Nationalist government for a time in the late 1930s after arranging for medical aid to be sent to the Communists. He and Grindlay discussed research and plans for modernizing the Chinese army medical organization. Lim was in charge of the only training school for medical officers in the Chinese army.

The next night at dinner, Grindlay met another distinguished visitor, the scholar and traveler Owen Lattimore, who had arrived in Chungking on 19 July to begin serving as an advisor to Chiang Kai-shek. Grindlay thought Lattimore a fascinating and "brilliant scholarly young real gentleman" who held forth at dinner on his knowledge of Chinese and Mongol history and his travels, including his search for the grave of Genghis Khan in Mongolia. Lattimore was living in "Kungshaven," T.V. Soong's modern concrete villa featuring a bathroom (with a bidet) for every bedroom. It was called the "most modern house & best in Chungking," Grindlay reported.[23]

On 8 January the AMMISCA's staff learned that Majors Vaughn and Aldrich had been promoted to the rank of lieutenant colonel. A small drinking celebration was held for Major Vaughn, but Grindlay failed to mention whether one was held for the unpopular Aldrich.[24] Orders had also been received for Lieutenant Colonel Walter Soderholm of the Ordnance Department to return to the United States. "[He] is overjoyed," Grindlay wrote.

> He is a brilliant fellow who fought in last war & has been running arsenal shops for years. His work surveying Chinese arsenals [was] over long ago & he has been bitching & going really crazy at inactivity ever since. A very nice chap, rather sarcastic but not bitter, amazingly keen wit, good vocabulary & well-chosen words. He promises to tell general staff at home of [the] way this thing [AMMISCA] is. General [Magruder] knows about & has sent in reports of true Chinese situation, not, however, suggesting we be sent home. Apparently, [Soderholm] says at least, arsenals here can do fair work, & a lot more than they are now doing.[25]

Four days later, Lim, Evans, Mendelson, and Grindlay met to discuss plans for American and Chinese medical cooperation, and Lim described the state of Chinese medical services. He invited Grindlay to visit his training facility at Kweiyang; shortly thereafter, permission was given for Grindlay to make the trip.

He left Chungking on the morning of 16 January for the two-day drive to Kweiyang in an ambulance truck over terrible roads. The "most impressive part" of the trip, as Grindlay recorded in his diary, was "the continuous pounding up & down jolting, bruising my back & chafing the shin until I was in misery. This & the raw penetrating cold."[26] The day after his arrival, Grindlay was given a tour of the various parts of the compound, including a truck repair shop, power plant, and medical supply center, where he watched girls packing kits for drugs, making dressings from gauze rolls, and tailoring clothing. Sterile surgical packs were also made up for distribution in the field, as were laboratory test kits. Lim took Grindlay through the hospital, which the latter found to be a series of wards, each in a separate building with plastered-bamboo walls and grass roofs. The beds were board platforms on wooden sawhorses, covered with thin straw ticking and a cotton quilt. The floor was dirt, and windows were filled with paper. The operating room, recently built, had thick stone walls and a wooden floor. The scrub room had "overhead tanks & chin-controlled valves" and "pressure cooker autoclaves." There was an observation gallery for the students. Although crude by American standards, the facilities were clean and unstained.

Grindlay wrote to his parents on 31 January, after his return to Chungking:

> You would be amazed at the splendid work being done there—making equipment, rehabilitating soldiers, etc. They make shoes, stockings, artificial limbs, soap, clothing, dressings; they have crude, small scale foundry, machine & carpenter shops. Everything is crude from our point of view, but really remarkable considering what they have to work with. Heat is unknown & it was very wet, foggy, & cold. I was quite uncomfortable after each morning operating, although I was warmly dressed.

During the tour, Grindlay was told something that very few Americans knew until well after the end of the war—that the Japanese were engaging in bacteriological warfare in China. Evidence of this attack had been collected

5. War Begins for AMMISCA   51

in Changteh, a large transportation hub in Hunan Province, and brought to Lim's facility for analysis. It was shown to Grindlay, who recorded the event in his diary:

> In late November [1941] there was an air raid. Everyone left town & when they returned the town was covered by these strange seeds & some cotton wads. The Chinese suspected plague because there was a similar experience linked to a plague outbreak previously. These seeds & wadding [were] collected. In 7–10 days plague broke out & quite a few died. It was proved plague; episodes recurred steadily for several weeks & then the plague died out. It is reasoned that Japs released bags of grain in which there was wadding containing infected rat fleas. The grain attracted native rats & some fleas got on these rats, others bit human victims.[27]

Grindlay spent five days at Lim's training center, observing the activities and conducting surgeries daily for the benefit of the students. All the surgical procedures were on abdominal cases, mainly colons and small intestines.[28] The operations were conducted in "icy cold," with the lights going off and on. Despite the primitive conditions and discomfort, Grindlay greatly enjoyed doing surgery again after months of inactivity.[29]

He began the return trip from Kweiyang on the afternoon of 24 January, bouncing over the same roads in the same uncomfortable ambulance. Accompanying him were Dr. Lanto Kaneti,[30] a Bulgarian who had served in the International Brigade during the Spanish Civil War; Mr. Ma, a Chinese transport man; and an unidentified Chinese woman with her three children, who rode in the back of the vehicle. After an overnight stay in Tsunyi, they arrived at Chungking late in the afternoon of 25 January. On his return, Grindlay was immediately plunged into highly welcome activity.

While Grindlay was away, the mission compound in Chungking experienced a sudden change of pace when, on 23 January, a group of twenty-four British ordinary seamen and sixteen officers who had escaped from Hong Kong on Christmas Day arrived. These men were from the 2nd Motor Torpedo Boat Squadron under Lieutenant C.J. Collingwood, and they had made a hazardous and adventurous trip overland, assisted part of the time by the Chinese underground. En route, one of the trucks in their convoy skidded on a muddy road and overturned, injuring several of the men. Among them, too, was a suspected case of typhoid. Grindlay happily treated the injured after he returned, and he helped, with several Chinese doctors, to get the newcomers cleaned up and settled in heated barracks.

After dinner, the group talked about their experiences. As Grindlay recorded in his diary:

> [The sailors] had been sent on a mission to occupy a point in the harbor between artillery & machine gun fire & to silence these. They did for a while but saw it was hopeless & on night of Dec. 25 slipped out in fast torpedo boats going north & landing at end of a bay just above [Hong Kong]. Went ashore & climbed 2 mt. ranges here—a

> stiff exercise for sailors, one 68 yrs. old. Then by rail back & forth a long ways to Kweilin, thence to Kweiyang by truck. Stated battle of Hongkong [sic] a huge Brit. disaster. Jap troops each had detailed up to date map of city & had organized objectives. No Brit. troops there until recently [when] fresh Canadian troops sent over. These manned defenses; however they stayed in pillboxes at night (instead of getting out as Sikhs & Gurkhas did) & were then easily taken by Japs. Defenses easily broken thru. Indians took as prisoners & didn't expect to be taken prisoners. Japs cruel toward whites—bayoneting those that surrendered etc. Rumored that surviving whites taken to labor camps in Formosa.[31]

Grindlay also found, upon his return to House Number 98, another new arrival: Paul Hawkins, a U.S. Army Reserve officer and employee of the National City Bank of New York, who had escaped from Shanghai in December 1941 disguised in Chinese clothes and was helped across the country by Chinese guerrillas. Hawkins was exhausted from his adventure and had numerous cuts, scrapes, and insect bites. He struck Grindlay as "a queer duck who is considerable of an exhibitionist" with "psychopathic tendencies"; Grindlay also applied powdered sulfa to an ulcer on Hawkins' leg. Hawkins was hired as a civilian employee by the mission in the capacity of a general clerk until he could be checked through the War Department and ordered to active duty. He ultimately failed a physical for the regular army and was denied permission to join the Chinese partisans. He left China to rejoin his bank's Bombay branch, traveling via Burma and Calcutta, and worked there for a few months before returning to the United States in August 1942.[32]

The monotony of daily life in Chungking was relieved on 30 January when Grindlay and the other officers were invited to a dinner at General Magruder's house, attended by Generalissimo and Madame Chiang Kai-shek ("the big shot & his wife," he wrote to his parents next day). This was an opportunity to meet the wartime leaders of China, and, with his antenna quivering, the surgeon took in details of the couple's appearance and those of other distinguished guests. He wrote a description of Chiang and his wife in his diary that night with a physician's eye:

> Sat about a bit waiting for [the Chiang Kai-sheks] & finally Madame C. entered. I was by [the] door so mine was first hand she shook. Looks like her pictures; about 40, nice Chink features, clean hair done up well, & combination Western-Shanghai dress. Next was [the Generalissimo] in short black Chin. coat, black shirt—both silk. No insignia. He is shorter than I, well-built & wiry appearing [with] lean face & form, but rather small bones & delicate frame & face. Good Chin. features. Hair coon gray & cut to about ¼ inch. No scars on scalp. Grinning the usual Chin. howdoyoudo.

Other guests included British ambassador Archibald Clark Kerr, American ambassador Clarence Gauss ("plump, pudgy, thick glasses, sour looking chap"), and Major General Lancelot Dennys. Clark Kerr ("lean, hawk-nosed, reddish faced, charming & capable chap") asked Grindlay to accompany him

5. War Begins for AMMISCA   53

to his new post in Moscow. Grindlay was flattered by the invitation and accepted gladly but doubted that General Magruder would release him. "Wish it could have been arranged," Grindlay wrote wistfully to his wife later that night. He tried to strike up a conversation with Madame Chiang

> but soon saw she had only cool, polite interest in pleasantries; somehow she summoned in turn Sir A [Clark Kerr] & [Captain E.R.] Manning [an Australian pilot who commanded RAF No. 221 Group in Burma], asked them questions & all the time slouched in her chair on one hand [with] other holding a cigarette, peering intently [with] her cold eyes thru her smoke, listening, & turning to side only to give instructions I gathered. Never saw her smile during this.... Finally the Madame saw fit to go, so the Gissimo followed.... Wish I could write of the intrigue & machinations which that woman delves in.

6

Enter Stilwell and Goodbye to China

On 7 February 1942, AMMISCA's tedium was broken when important news arrived that would greatly alter all the members' lives. As Grindlay reported in his diary, there was an

> *assembly of officers & men at [House] #2 this [morning] to tell them a Gen. Stillwell [sic] (close friend of Gen. Marshalls [sic]) is coming over & will be in charge. Don't know what this means.... Perhaps there are some plans for activity here & perhaps I'll get something to do. Stillwell [sic] will have a staff of about 15 [with] him & we'll be absorbed.*

Lieutenant General Joseph Warren Stilwell (1883–1946) had served as U.S. military attaché in China in the late 1930s, spoke fluent Chinese, and knew the people and politics of China intimately from two extended tours of duty. He was appointed by General George Marshall, army chief of staff, at the direction of President Roosevelt, to head all U.S. forces in the newly created China-Burma-India (CBI) theater, administer Lend-Lease aid in the theater, serve as chief of staff to Chiang Kai-shek, and take charge of all forces then operating in Burma, including the British and Chinese. Secretary of War Stimson interviewed Stilwell before he left for China and was very favorably impressed with the officer's knowledge of China. "In half an hour," Stimson recalled later, "he gave me a better first-hand picture of the valor of the Chinese armies than I had every received before." Stilwell told Stimson that the success of any American mission depended on whether Generalissimo Chiang Kai-shek would hand over command of his armies to an American, something he had never done before. If that happened, Stimson wrote, "Stilwell said that the possibilities of the [mission] were unbounded and he was very enthusiastic about it.... So I went to bed with a rather relieved feeling that I had discovered a man who will be very useful."[1]

Stilwell's orders explicitly directed him to increase the effectiveness of U.S. aid, best accomplished by pushing for reform of the Chinese armies and

6. Enter Stilwell and Goodbye to China 55

improving their combat efficiency through more rigorous training. Stilwell's mission, therefore, was extremely complicated: "As U.S. Army representative he was under the Secretary of War. As supervisor and controller of lend-lease he was under the President. As Chief of Staff of the Generalissimo's Joint Staff he was under the Generalissimo and at the same time the representative of the U.S. Government."[2]

One of several important decisions to come out of the First Washington Conference (ARCADIA), a series of meetings held in Washington between the British and the Americans from 22 December 1941 to 14 January 1942, was that the primary objective of the war was to defeat Nazi Germany first and then turn full attention to the Japanese in the Pacific and Asia. China was not initially discussed; however, it loomed large in American strategic thinking, but not in that of the British, whose priority was the survival of India and Burma. Roosevelt's overriding fear was that China might collapse militarily and thereby release large numbers of Japanese for service in Southeast Asia and the Pacific. To prevent that outcome, he insisted that Chiang Kai-shek's armies be kept supplied with arms and equipment and that China be made a great world power.

At ARCADIA, Roosevelt and Churchill agreed that a Supreme Command should be created for American, British, Dutch, and Australian (ABDA) forces in the southwest Pacific and Southeast Asia, including Burma, and that there should be a similar command for China. To that end, on 31 December, Roosevelt sent a message to Chiang Kai-shek proposing that the Generalissimo become supreme commander of the China theater. This message was not routed through Magruder's office, as were other official communications between Washington and Chiang's government; instead, it inexplicably went to the naval attaché, Captain James McHugh, who was junior in rank to Magruder. McHugh informed Magruder of the message and magnanimously invited him to go along when it was delivered to Chiang. Magruder seethed over this breach of military etiquette and complained to Washington about it. Regardless, Chiang agreed to the proposal and assumed command of China on 5 January; he then requested that an American of at least lieutenant general rank be appointed to act as his chief of staff. The process of identifying this individual had already started in Washington.

On 4 January, the War Department informed Magruder that, pending Chiang Kai-shek's agreement, an officer of "very high rank and prestige" would be posted to Chungking. Magruder was initially told that he would retain command of all American troops in China and Burma, but early in February, in reply to Magruder's persistent messages asking for clarification of his mission, General Marshall radioed that Stilwell would be in command. The matter was settled once and for all when Stimson radioed Magruder on 15 March that Stilwell would have "complete freedom of action to make use of [AMMISCA] personnel ... as he may deem appropriate.... Without reference to the War Department, personnel of Mission may accordingly be transferred." A follow-up message from General Marshall to Stilwell on 9 April ordered the latter to reassign AMMISCA personnel to other areas of the CBI theater.[3]

The War Department hoped that the presence of a senior American military officer in Chungking—especially one with command responsibilities—would solve the problem of AMMISCA's ineffectiveness. It had already become obvious to Magruder and others in the mission that the Chinese did not view AMMISCA with any sort of respect. A clear example occurred on 10 February, when Grindlay got wind of an angry message that Magruder sent to Washington detailing an incident representative of the treatment he and his staff were receiving in China:

> In [the wire Magruder] *reported an incident yesterday when he called on the Gissimos* [sic] *secretary (the G. is in Burma) & gave him verbally some secret dope. A boy bringing tea at the time happened to bump a screen & revealed 4 crouching eves-dropping* [sic] *servants.*

Magruder's message went on to inform the War Department that the situation in China was hopeless and

> *to stop handing out radio reports of Chinese victories. They sound foolish to folks here (who know the Chinks are sitting on their asses) & they delude the people at home (& give them false impression). He said that,* [with] *the divisions Japs have on Siberian front there can't be more than 20 poorly equipped Jap divisions in all China—& the Chin. are doing nothing about it as usual. Yet the Chin. ask (& get) loads of equipment which simply disappears; they aren't using it but ask for huge stores.... This is a political, not a military mission & should be called off.*

Stilwell was initially due to arrive on 15 February, but Grindlay learned ten days later that the general had not departed from the United States until 14 February, noting caustically in his diary that "where the hell he has been is now accounted for." Magruder departed from Chungking on a trip to Burma on 19 February; a week later, a message came through British radio sources that Stilwell wanted to meet Magruder in Calcutta. AMMISCA headquarters tried frantically to locate Magruder to tell him of Stilwell's message, finally delivering it the next day. After their meeting, the two men flew to Kunming on separate aircraft; then they traveled together on Stilwell's plane to Chungking, where they arrived on 4 March at 2:30 p.m. During the flight, Magruder irked the old China hand, who was admiring the terrain below, by gloomily commenting, "Isn't that a hell of a looking country?" Stilwell, Lieutenant Colonel Frank Roberts (G-2), and aides Lieutenant Colonel Frank Dorn and First Lieutenant Dick Young were billeted in House #2, "Kungshaven" (T.V. Soong's former residence, occupied by Owen Lattimore earlier in the year).[4]

6. Enter Stilwell and Goodbye to China   57

Grindlay could not report to his parents or his wife on these developments because of the rigid censorship, but he recorded in his diary the first meeting that the AMMISCA crew had with Stilwell the day after the general arrived. He developed an almost immediate admiration for the new CBI commander that would never to fade.

> The General told us he was going to sit tight a bit, until he had seen & heard things & talked [with] the Gissimo. He reminded us (he is an old China hand, formerly a mil. attaché & is wise on China) we were allied [with] the Chinese & must remember it. I liked his bluff, homely manner.[5]

Soon after Stilwell arrived, he assumed control of all Lend-Lease allocation and distribution and assigned Magruder to command the Division of General Affairs, a staff position with no effective authority and responsible only for obtaining and coordinating information regarding the shipment of Lend-Lease supplies from Rangoon to Kunming. Stilwell assembled a staff of thirty-one men, among them Colonel Robert P. Williams, who became the theater surgeon of U.S. forces in the CBI. Williams was born in Greencastle, Indiana, on 29 August 1891, a graduate of the University of Cincinnati Medical School (1913), and a career army officer since 1915. When he arrived in Chungking, he took charge of all medical operations in the theater and relegated Major Mendelson to the post of station surgeon. Besides supervising the reorganization of medical services in the theater, American and Chinese, Williams also established and maintained a liaison with the Chinese surgeon general, the director-general of the National Health Administration, and the director-general of the National Red Cross Society of China. He was soon to be assigned to Stilwell's rear echelon headquarters in New Delhi, leaving Mendelson alone at forward echelon headquarters in Chungking.

Meantime, tension was building in Rangoon as the Japanese advanced closer to the city, and evacuation of the civilian populace and the military was beginning. The Japanese had invaded Burma from Siam (Thailand) on 20 January 1942 and marched against weak British resistance to the Sittang River, east of Rangoon. The British dug in to defend the important railroad bridge on the line that ran to Rangoon, but the overwhelming enemy attack forced the bridge to be blown on 23 February after less than half of the British forces had crossed it. With the British defenses in shambles, the Japanese drove on toward the key port of Burma.

AMMISCA established a headquarters in a small white house on the edge of Rangoon, from which point the arrival and distribution of Lend-Lease supplies were coordinated. The group stationed there was commanded by Colonel Adrian St. John and included Major Frank Merrill, Major John Russell (a specialist on Burmese transportation routes), Captain Roscoe Hambleton (also an engineer and transportation specialist), Major Ted Haywood (an army administrator), and Staff Sergeant Francis Astolfi. There were also a number of servants and orderlies employed from the local labor base. St. John had orders from Chungking to destroy all the Lend-Lease supplies left in the port whenever it was "necessary and advisable."

Captain Nevin Wetzel arrived on 17 February to lend assistance in the destruction of the Lend-Lease material. As a member of the Corps of Engineers, Wetzel had traveled from Lashio, where he had assisted Major John E. Ausland, the chief advisor to the Chinese government on the construction of the Yunnan–Burma railroad. Wetzel and St. John, along with a Mr. Shu of China Defense Supplies, toured the warehouses (*godowns*) in the port area where the goods were stored and also began a search for dynamite. Failing that, they arranged for several barrels of gasoline to be strategically placed around the warehouses and then sat down to wait for the right time to ignite them.[6]

There were upward of ten warehouses filled with tires, blankets, industrial machinery, electrical equipment, and construction materials. The *godowns* also held 1,200 trucks still in their crates, waiting to be moved to the General Motors assembly plant on the edge of the city, which had been virtually closed down due to a shortage of labor. The factory was reopened by the Americans, using whatever local laborers could be scrounged, plus 200 Chinese army mechanics, and, in the weeks before its eventual demolition, most of the trucks were assembled and loaded with Lend-Lease supplies and driven north to Mandalay. Nine thousand tons of supplies and equipment were shipped out of Rangoon in one month and put on trains at Mandalay to be forwarded to Lashio and on to China. Another 516 jeeps were assembled in a field near the GM plant at night to avoid Japanese air attacks.[7]

The headquarters staff began burning their files and loading two sedans with food and readying their trucks for evacuation. On the morning of 24 February, word was received that the Japanese had encircled the 17th Indian Division east of the Sittang River and two of its brigades were trapped there when the bridge mentioned previously was prematurely blown on 19 February. Many of the soldiers managed to escape by swimming to the west bank, but a large number did not. Rumor had it that the Japanese were racing to occupy Prome, thus cutting off escape from Rangoon. Colonel St. John decided that the time had come to begin destroying the vast stores of Lend-Lease materials.[8]

Between the hours of 2 a.m. and 5 p.m. on 24 February, the General Motors assembly plant and the warehouses containing trucks, tires, and other supplies were burned. St. John, Wetzel, Merrill, and Astolfi drove across town to torch a warehouse holding 50,000 blankets. They spread gasoline throughout the building and laid a sawdust trail as a fuse; however, the gasoline fumes exploded when the sawdust was lit, blowing St. John out of the doorway and

6. Enter Stilwell and Goodbye to China   59

thirty feet into the adjacent yard. Merrill was blown off a pile of rails that he had been standing on, and Wetzel was trapped under the door when it came off its track (fortunately, he managed to get out before being burned). All four men were "black as spades" and suffered numerous cuts and bruises; St. John had a wrenched shoulder and knee. They frantically drove a hundred miles out of the city that night before stopping for a few hours of sleep. The next day they raced through Prome and spent the night at Magwe. On the third day they passed through the oil complex at Yenangyaung (destined to be the scene of a fierce battle in mid–April and already being prepared for demolition by the British almost two months before the Japanese threatened it) and arrived in Maymyo on 26 February. Two days later, Wetzel returned to his assignment on the Burma Road at Lashio.[9]

Rangoon was also the scene of the quiet arrival of the American Volunteer Group (AVG), famously known as the "Flying Tigers." It consisted of 240 volunteers, including pilots drawn from the army, navy, and marines (plus mechanics, medics, armorers, and radio operators), who were recruited through the efforts of Claire Chennault with funds from China and the United States. Chennault (1890–1958) had originally gone to China in 1937, after leaving the U.S. Army Air Corps, to survey the Chinese air force and report on its condition. Two years later, he returned home and began drumming up the idea of assembling a group to fight the Japanese as well as train Chinese pilots. He eventually won approval from the War Department to take over a shipment of P-40C Tomahawks that the British had rejected and begin his project.

The AVG pilots signed lucrative contracts for one year with the Central Aircraft Manufacturing Company (CAMCO), a Shanghai airplane assembly company owned by American businessman William D. Pawley, to conceal the War Department's involvement in furnishing aircraft and spare parts to China, a clear violation of the Neutrality Acts. The pilots and ground crewmen were dispatched to Rangoon in mid–1941; the planes started arriving in crates and were transported to an RAF facility at Mingaladon airfield, outside Rangoon, for assembly. From there, they were flown to another RAF airfield near Toungoo, where the pilots began training in the new planes as the monsoon season was in progress with its storms, rain, and steamy heat.[10]

Upon the outbreak of the war in December, the AVG based one squadron at Mingaladon and flew combat missions against Japanese bombers. The other two squadrons were ordered to Kunming by Chiang Kai-shek. As the Japanese steadily captured air bases in Burma, the AVG eventually moved to Loiwing, China, from which point they continued to fly missions in defense of the Burma Road as well as against Japanese forces in eastern China. By the early spring of 1942, men and planes were worn out, including Chennault himself. He met with the pilots at Loiwing on 18 and 19 April and told them that he was now a brigadier general in the U.S. Army Air Forces and they had to obey his orders. The men told him that their planes were in poor condition, their numbers were dwindling, and the enemy had them outnumbered. Chennault refused to let them resign and warned them that if they refused to fly, they could be charged with desertion. On 19 April Chennault sent a radio message to Colonel Clayton Bissell's headquarters in Chungking urging that the group be reinforced at the earliest possible date and returned to its original assigned mission.

> Group literally worn out nerves morale shot Stop Pilots quitting because of present employment of low altitude reconnaissance and lack of support from any other air unit Stop Can hold group together only if employed properly as interceptor pursuit Stop Please consult Madame Chiang and advise as immediate decision necessary Stop Copy to Gen. Stillwell [sic] End.[11]

The Flying Tigers were designated the 23rd Fighter Group in July 1942 after being absorbed into the U.S. Army Air Forces. On 11 March 1943, the Fourteenth Air Force was activated, under Chennault's command, and the 23rd became part of its structure.

* * *

On 14 March, AMMISCA was shaken by news of the loss of several group members in an airplane crash less than four miles from the airfield at Kunming. An aging CNAC DC-2 (the last such aircraft still left in the fleet) crashed and burned after taking off for Chungking at 9:45 the previous night. It came down on the edge of woods not far from the airstrip. Among the thirteen passengers who died were Major General Dennys; Lieutenant Colonel Otto ("Gus") George (a close friend and housemate of Grindlay's); Second Lieutenant Frederick Kohler; Mrs. Joyce Lowe and her 5-year-old son David (both Canadians); Dr. Fenimore Lynch (an advisor to the Central Bank of China); pilot Emil Scott; and co-pilot William Schuler.[12] Colonel George had been with AMMISCA since October, and Lieutenant Kohler was en route to join Stilwell's staff. Lieutenant Colonel Harvey Edward, also part of Stilwell's staff, escaped injury. General Claire Chennault, commander of the American Volunteer Group in Kunming, and his chief flight surgeon, Colonel Thomas C. Gentry, took charge of burying the American dead. Grindlay reported with great sadness and in sometimes insensitive (if not gruesome) detail the circumstances and consequences of the crash and the enormous impact it had on the men of AMMISCA.

> After lunch we heard the news—Gus was on the plane & instantly killed. The whole house might have fallen in on us. Gus gone! Good old dry-humored, common-sense, generous, noble Gus. Not an unclean thing in his character. And the hell of it is he was there on a futile mission & he knew it & said so. He went to Kunming to get the dope on fields, fuel & bombs for a mission that Gen. Brady wanted to run against the Japs.

6. Enter Stilwell and Goodbye to China

> *Waiting for all the consents from the Chinese (who opposed it in fear the Japs would retaliate!) took so long that it could no longer be done—but Gus was sent anyway. A few days before, on a trip to Kweilin he had to turn back* [with] *engine trouble in Chenaults* [sic] *Beechcraft & 6 Chinks who accompanied him in another plane crashed & were all killed. Then Gus was ordered back here to report to Magruder—& Magruder left yesterday* [for Rangoon without] *waiting for Gus! The boys who talked* [with] *Gus at* [Kunming] *last night said he joked about this. The port engine, which had been acting up for several days caught fire & the pilot had to make a forced landing. The tail broke off & Edwards* [sic] *& 3 Chinese in it were thrown clear, Edwards* [sic] *uninjured. Gus & the others were "instantly killed" & burned to a crisp. We all feel lousy & took solace in drink—but no real relief in that either. After dinner Coudray & I went to Press Hostel to try to get it off our minds. There we heard the rumor confirmed that Gen. Dennis* [sic] *... was also killed & fried. All the correspondents busy* [with] *writing & sending off the story. Yet all were grief-stricken for they too knew Gus. Sorry about Kohler too, though I never saw him. And losing Dennis* [sic] *is a blow—of course it is a great loss to the British—I knew him, have talked* [with] *him at many functions & liked him tremendously. He was the finest type of Britisher. His wife was like him. Together they were a magnificent pair. She'll take it like a hero but it will be a hell of a blow to her.*[13]

An inventory was taken of Lieutenant Colonel George's personal effects—"hell of a trial for us who lived [with] him." "We sold a few things & the rest was packed to send to his wife," Grindlay wrote in his diary afterward.[14] General Dennys was succeeded as head of the British 204 Military Mission by Major General John G. Bruce, another veteran of the Indian Army (he had also been a member of the expeditions of 1922 and 1924 that attempted to climb Mount Everest).

Grindlay was recovering from a two-week bout with flu, made worse by a severe reaction to plague vaccine administered on the same day that Lieutenant Colonel George's effects were dispatched to the United States, and the fever and general bodily ache associated with it forced him to focus on his condition, thus mercifully helping to wipe the horrible incident from his mind. He wrote to his wife, "I was terribly sick for a couple days last week—just a reaction from some plague vaccine. I never had a reaction before but this one was a dozen rolled into one."[15]

Adding to Grindlay's doldrums was the ongoing monotony that infected him and most of the other members of AMMISCA: "all [of us] chafe under this inactivity." Treating minor medical problems among the men while he was recovering from the plague vaccine reaction and making occasional excursions to visit hospital facilities in Chungking, or to the Thieves' Market or the Press Hostel for drinks, were the only breaks in his boring life. But all of that was about to dramatically change as the pace of events accelerated rapidly for Grindlay and several others.

On 28 March, a wire was received ordering Grindlay to Maymyo, Burma, "by first available plane," there to join Stilwell's forward command post as a surgeon. "I was overjoyed, albeit a little worried about it," he admitted in his diary that day. He went up to House #2 and obtained a plane ticket; then he went into the city to pick up some film he had had developed. "Came home & had cocktails (the usual gin & syrup) [with] Evans [the American Red Cross official] & Col. Joseph Heinrich as guests.[16] We had a songfest afterwards." The next day, Grindlay spent the morning packing but was unsure of when he would actually be leaving, since the plane departing that day was full. He also received word of his promotion to captain.

In the meantime, Major John Russell, part of AMMISCA's group in Rangoon, visited Grindlay's house and reported on his recent trip to Calcutta, where he had found things in a high state of disorder. As Grindlay wrote in his diary:

> *Calcutta was a disgrace. No preparation. "Business as usual." One million tons of shipping tied up in harbor of this city, the 2nd largest in Brit. empire. The Brit. still take their tea & hang around the hotels & clubs & quit work at 5 PM.*[17]

Major Russell was due to be reassigned to Kunming, where Magruder was now stationed, heading the "general affairs" division of AMMISCA after its absorption by Stilwell's command. Magruder and his staff, including MacMorland, were devoting their time to maintenance and traffic on the Burma Road—a truly boring assignment, in Grindlay's view. "Thank God I'm not with them," he wrote with relief on 29 March.

That afternoon Grindlay attended a memorial service at the Methodist Mission compound for the victims of the airplane crash at Kunming.

> *The British & Am. military & embassy groups sat in front* [with] *the Chinese Army & Gov't officials.* [Finance Minister H.H.] *Kung was in front of me (fat* [with] *Chinese silk cap, short coat & shirt—like the rest of the officials) & Madame Chiang in back of me. Mrs. Dennis* [sic] *sat across aisle & whenever I dared glance at her she was listening or singing* [without] *sign of her undoubted great grief. The "church" was merely a room in one of the bldgs. The Bishop of Eastern (a Britisher) Szechwan preached a hell of a disorganized sermon & the Bishop of West. Szechwan gave a long dull prayer punctuated by lots of amens. The Brit. ambassador read the 90th Psalm poorly* [Sir Horace Seymour] *is a tall red-faced decent-looking chap.... Lots of hymn singing. A truly pagan senseless ritual. On the way home we all said poor Gus would have turned in his grave at it. Had a few drinks when we got back & after dinner sang a lot of songs, one a good Negro spiritual led by Gluckman. Before dinner listened to a good German choral concert. All our music that is any good is from the Berlin* [radio] *station.*

On 29 March, Grindlay watched another plane take off in the morning without him: "I was told I could have gone on it if I had been at [the] airport, though it was also said that 'several pieces of baggage had to be removed because of overloading.'" He took a second plague shot, despite his severe reaction to the first one, and repacked his gear in the afternoon, getting it all into two bags, a footlocker and a small steamer trunk. He paid his outstanding

6. Enter Stilwell and Goodbye to China

bills and had some final cocktails with various members of the mission. Grindlay also wrote in an optimistic vein to his parents that same day:

> I should tell you in this letter that I am going to a country south of here, for how long I don't know. I am told that there is a lot of surgery to be done there. I will be very glad to do all I can. A lot of our group are down there—you probably know all about it from the papers. The group I came out here with has been absorbed & placed on the staff with our new general [Stilwell]—who brought a number of new men with him. I like the new set up.

It was to be the last letter he would write to his parents for two months.

The next day, Grindlay awoke feeling "slightly achy from the plague [shot] yesterday," but he apparently did not have the same severe reaction that he did with the first one. He received word that he would leave the following day for Burma and spent his last day in China walking through some of the neighborhoods above House #2. He visited an old Christian burial ground on top of the hill, which afforded a view of the Chialing River valley and the cliffs, as well as Chiang Kai-shek's "Chin[ese] style rather decrepit house next door."

AMMISCA was winding down, and its staff was being scattered. A few, including Major Merrill and Grindlay, were assigned to Stilwell's command in Burma. Magruder had mentioned to Ambassador Gauss on 8 May that there was a possibility that the mission would be withdrawn. Gauss cautioned against taking any action that would make the Chinese suspect that the United States lacked confidence in them as allies. The State Department urged General Marshall to retain the mission, and he cabled AMMISCA to continue giving aid to the Chinese. An office was maintained in Chungking for this purpose as a subordinate agency under Stilwell's command. A few days later, Magruder requested a transfer to the United States for medical treatment. His request was approved, and he finally departed on 18 May, sending a message to Stilwell in Burma that he was leaving. Stilwell did not respond personally, only forwarding a note of thanks from General Ho Ying-chin and asking Marshall for details of Magruder's departure. After his treatment at Walter Reed Hospital, Magruder served in the Army Service Forces in Washington until October 1943, when he was assigned to the OSS as deputy director. He remained there until his retirement in 1945 at the rank of brigadier general.

AMMISCA thus effectively ended with a whimper, silently absorbed into Stilwell's command as a subordinate office and gradually disappearing from history. It had been largely ineffective in its capacity of supervising the lending of military aid to China, though it had much more success as an advisory group. Although the mission had been dispatched with high hopes, it suffered from the prevailing confusion in the War Department over its objectives as well as from Chinese interference. AMMISCA was a harbinger of the later frustrations, failures, and personality clashes that would plague Stilwell's mission. To most of the men who served in AMMISCA, it seemed to be a waste of time and energy, an exercise in idleness and futility. To the Chinese, it was an instrument to manipulate and through which to funnel requests, complaints, and propaganda to the United States. To Washington, it seems to have been a token gesture, a means of dealing with large problems with the Chinese with the least expenditure of effort.

The American planners were uncertain of what role AMMISCA should play because they could not define a China policy, and the mission naturally suffered. Only with Stilwell's entry upon the stage and the creation of the CBI theater did the United States finally make plain its intention to support Chiang Kai-shek and to placate the Chinese without becoming too deeply entrenched in mainland Asian politics or warfare. U.S. war plans never envisioned mainland Asia—especially China—as vital to the defeat of Japan. Therefore, AMMISCA and its successor, the CBI, would of necessity be little more than advisory groups. To say that frustration and boredom ranked at the top of mental attitudes afflicting most American servicemen in the mission and the theater would not be an understatement.

7

Joining Seagrave in Burma

The United States was forced to assume a major role in the conflict in the Far East when Japan attacked Pearl Harbor, and afterward the U.S. military quickly found its advisory role in China expanding into a full-fledged support mission in Burma and India. To demonstrate its solid and ongoing military and political commitment to its allies as well as to expeditiously administer its burgeoning military presence in the region, the United States created the China-Burma-India theater in March 1942.

Abbreviated thereafter as the CBI, the theater was a geographical microcosm of world climate extremes. Terrain varied from dismal, treacherous swamps to the world's tallest mountains, from bone-dry deserts where annual rainfall could be measured in a teacup to jungles assaulted by monsoons whose rains were gauged in feet. In the dry season between monsoons, the ground in some areas turned powder dry and stone hard; when the rains came, from May to October annually, humans and animals sometimes waded through mud that was waist-deep on men and stomach-deep on mules and horses. Small, lazy streams were transformed into raging torrents that became extremely dangerous, if not impossible, to cross. Transportation was difficult on primitive roads and trails that were often no more than footpaths through the jungles. Dust was an enemy of men and machines in the dry season, clogging radiators and air filters and infiltrating engines and fuel lines. In the rainy season humidity was extreme: the fetid heat and dampness promoted the growth of luxuriant vegetation, and lush mold and fungus proliferated along with many exotic varieties of animals, insects and plants that harbored dangerous (and often fatal) diseases. Daytime temperatures ranged from well below 0 degrees F in the highest elevations to well above 100 degrees F in the lowland deserts and jungles.

The combination of an enervating climate that caused a high percentage of illness and death among men and animals, great difficulty in waging warfare in inhospitable terrain, and frequent shortages of equipment and supplies due to being at the farthest end of the shipping lanes from the United States, coupled with the low military priority given to the theater, contributed to its infamous reputation. The CBI's relative remoteness from the rest of the world led the men and women who served in this theater—British, Americans, Indians, Chinese, Australians, West Africans, Nepalese (Gurkhas), and many others—to deservedly call it "The Forgotten War."[1]

A newly promoted Captain John H. Grindlay finally left Chungking for Lashio, Burma, at 10:45 in the morning of 31 March on a CNAC transport plane, which departed in a rush after hearing that Japanese bombers were on the way. There was a stopover in Kunming to refuel, and then the overloaded plane took off with a virtual "who's who" of CBI personalities: General Hsung, chief of staff of the Chinese army group at Kunming; Colonel Edward Mac-Morland, deputy commander of AMMISCA; Colonel Thomas Gentry, chief surgeon of the Flying Tigers; Sir Horace Seymour, British ambassador to China; and Lieutenant Colonel George Vaughn, Major James Wilson, and Major T.M. Haywood of the AMMISCA group. Grindlay had a few minutes to dash off a brief letter to his wife to reassure her about his future in Burma: "[Don't] worry about my safety. I shall be doing a lot of cutting, I hear, when I arrive—there are lots of wounds down there. But I shan't be in the front lines by any means. I'll be in a protected base. Still it will be interesting." Little did he realize just how interesting it would turn out to be, and not nearly as "protected" as he assumed. "Lord, but it's hot waiting here," he wrote, craving an American cigarette after months of smoking cheaper-quality British brands. "How do Am[erican] cigarettes taste, by the way?" he asked plaintively.

The flight to Lashio was rough, and almost everyone except Grindlay became airsick. They landed just as darkness fell. That night Grindlay learned that he was to join the Seagrave Hospital Unit at Pyinmana. He departed from Lashio by car the next morning with "a hell of a driver" named Boas and arrived in Maymyo, the former British hill station east of Mandalay in central Burma, at 5:00 in the afternoon after a horribly dusty ride. He reported to Colonel Robert Williams, theater surgeon, who had been alerted to Grindlay's arrival by Major Mendelson, and dined with Williams and Robert Lim. The next day, Grindlay departed for Seagrave's facility with an Anglo-Indian driver named Edward Henderson, who was much better—and safer—than Boas.[2]

Williams had arrived in Burma by way of Calcutta on 19 March. He had been stationed at Fort Lewis, Washington, when he received orders to go to the Philippines, but by the time he arrived at his first stop at Fort Ord, California, his orders had been changed and he was instructed to go to India as part of Stilwell's group. Williams then flew to Washington and met his new boss, who briefed him on his assignment as theater surgeon. On 26 February Williams joined other members of Stilwell's staff in Miami, including

7. Joining Seagrave in Burma

Brigadier General William Gruber, Colonel Benjamin Ferris, Captain Paul Jones, Technical Sergeant Dean Chambers (the group's radio man), State Department Foreign Service Officer John Paton Davies, and several others. (Ferris, Jones, and Chambers would accompany Williams on Stilwell's epic retreat from Burma less than two months later.) They all boarded a Pan-American clipper and flew to Liberia, where they changed planes for the flight across the Sahara to Khartoum, up the Nile River to Cairo, then on via Karachi to Calcutta and, finally, Lashio on the Burma Road.[3]

From Lashio, Williams set off for Stilwell's headquarters at Maymyo with a truckload of medical supplies; he was accompanied by Olaf Skau, a Seventh-day Adventist missionary. He and Skau took turns driving the 136 miles to the old British hill station. Williams found Stilwell's headquarters in a two-story American Baptist mission rest house and was assigned a room with Frank Merrill. He also met the British commander, General Harold Alexander, and Brigadier Treffry Thompson, the chief surgeon and deputy director of medical services (DDMS) under Alexander. Skau and Williams picked up more medical supplies from the British and drove to the front near Pyawbwe, 156 miles away. There, at the Americans' forward command post southeast of Meiktila, close to the headquarters of the Chinese Fifth Army, Williams encountered Stilwell; Lieutenant Colonel Frank Dorn, Stilwell's longtime aide; Major General Franklin Sibert, liaison to the Chinese Fifth Army; Lieutenant Colonel William Wyman, Sibert's assistant at the forward command post; and others, including Dr. Wesley May, an army surgeon. After the supplies were unloaded, Williams returned to Maymyo and met Grindlay on 2 April.[4]

* * *

Japanese forces had invaded southern Burma from Thailand in December 1941, and they had been steadily pushing back the woefully outnumbered, outmaneuvered, and ill-equipped British and Indian defenders of the British colony ever since. The enemy attack aimed first at capturing Rangoon and then advancing northward in two prongs: one roughly followed the Sittang River in the east, and the other followed the Irrawaddy River through Burma's heartland.

The Japanese began bombing Rangoon almost immediately, and, after more than a month of bombardment, a mad scramble to evacuate the city began in earnest in mid–January. Civil disorder erupted after Rangoon was emptied of the civilian and police authorities who had been in control of political and law enforcement institutions. The increasing chaos was witnessed by, among others, an attractive Philadelphia socialite and journalist working for *Collier's* magazine, Alice-Leone Moats, who arrived in the city on 13 January. She found scores of foreigners, including Americans, making preparations to leave. The lobby of the prestigious Strand Hotel was packed with salesmen, oil company workers, and business and government types who were trying to get out of Burma while soaking up what night life was still available at the hotel's famous Silver Grill.

Moats wanted to travel to Kunming over the Burma Road but had trouble finding transportation. She finally arranged with a member of the International Red Cross to ride in his convoy, which was supposed to leave in two days, but the convoy's departure was ultimately delayed for two weeks due to difficulties in obtaining trucks, whose bodies had to be built on chassis sent from the United States. Then followed seemingly endless wrangles with customs officials. According to Moats, "A one-per-cent transit duty had to be paid on all goods. (For some things like liquor there was a 99-per-cent duty.) There were three forms—A, D, and E—to be filled out for export permits. D and E could be handed in at any time; A only after the trucks were loaded, which meant a delay of at least two days after a convoy was ready to go."[5] The process could be speeded up, Moats pointed out, if palms were greased with silver rupees.

To fill her time while the convoy was being assembled and battles with the bureaucracy were being fought, Moats found recreation in limited touring ("There wasn't anything in the way of sight-seeing to do, as Rangoon didn't offer much in that line, aside from a pagoda which looked like a giant gilt corkscrew") and spending nights at the popular Silver Grill to watch an exotic dancer bump and grind to music provided by a "tone-deaf" orchestra. The young sophisticate concluded that "the customers' principal amusement was drinking." She went dancing a few times, both at the Silver Grill and at the Gymkhana Club, "a barn of a place with a ballroom that could have comfortably accommodated one hundred couples," she sniffed, although far fewer were in attendance most nights. Many people either had already left the city or were in no mood for gaiety.[6]

Moats' Red Cross convoy finally departed Rangoon on 30 January, loaded with gasoline, tires, and spare parts, but no medical supplies. They made their way up the Burma Road via Mandalay, Maymyo, and Lashio. The latter, she commented, "looked like a mining town during a boom. It had increased to three times its size since the opening of the Burma Road, and new buildings were springing up all over." The group again experienced delays due to vehicle breakdowns and the "innumerable formalities that had to be gone through to obtain still more permits for crossing the border [into China]." Moats encountered the same obstacles that Daniel Arnstein and Magruder's commission had discovered the previous year:

> Supplies were going over the road in a trickle. This was due to British red tape, inefficiency, and some graft; to Chinese inefficiency and graft, the lack of good mechanics, and to Chinese overseas drivers, a tough, irresponsible, not too honest crew who were never in a hurry.... Besides, there was mutual distrust between the two nations.

7. Joining Seagrave in Burma

The British couldn't forget that Burma had once belonged to China, who they feared might want to take her old territory back. The Chinese hadn't forgiven the closing of the road [the previous year] and sometimes suspected that the British wanted to give them just enough supplies to keep the Japs busy but not enough to win a complete victory, which might leave them too powerful. That was why, at that time, it was cheaper for the Chinese to pay squeeze money to pass supplies through the Japanese lines from Hong Kong than to get them from Burma.[7]

The Chinese government was indeed alarmed at the prospect of losing the vital Burma Road, inefficient and corrupt as it was, because it was the only overland supply route into China. In December 1941, Chiang Kai-shek offered the British two armies, the Fifth and Sixth, to help fight the Japanese in order to keep the road open; these troops, as previously noted, were at first refused by General Wavell (who wanted to defend the British possession with Commonwealth forces), creating a diplomatic furor. The Chinese were later accepted after American pressure was applied, and the first troops began arriving in Burma in February, though it was not until mid-March that they were deployed in force along the eastern sector of the front, too late to save Rangoon (which fell on 8 March) or to effectively prevent the loss of the Burma Road.

Thus, when Stilwell arrived in Burma on 19 March, he found a chaotic and nearly hopeless situation. As the defenses were crumbling, the British were retreating and, worse, being outflanked by the experienced and better-trained and -equipped Japanese divisions. One enemy division was driving northward along the Irrawaddy River, with its water, rail, and road links to Mandalay, Myitkyina, and ultimately China, while two others were thrusting rapidly along the Salween and Sittang river valleys in the east to cut off the retreating Chinese. There was no chance of organizing an effective defense, in spite of the arrival of General Harold Alexander to take overall command of the British and Chinese armies on 3 March. Alexander had commanded at Dunkirk and had already seen enough retreating to last a lifetime. He was unwilling to become saddled with another failure, but he unfortunately lacked the manpower and equipment to effectively stop the Japanese. In addition, the fighting took place during the hottest, driest part of the year in Burma, with dust and debilitating heat taking a terrible toll on men, machines, and pack animals.

Adding to these problems was the reluctance of most Chinese commanders to follow the orders of anyone except Chiang Kai-shek, though the Generalissimo's orders were often contradictory or capricious. Stilwell, who reported to Alexander, told the latter of the Chinese unwillingness to obey his orders and received a sympathetic ear from the British general, but that was about all he could offer: Alexander had his own troubles with trying to rally the British army and, at the same time, plan a defensive line in the higher ground in northern Burma. Despite Stilwell's spirited and tireless attempts to browbeat the Generalissimo and the Chinese generals into establishing defensive positions to try to halt the Japanese (if only temporarily), it was inevitable that repeated failure and meddling by the Generalissimo would lead to discouragement, as reflected in Stilwell's diary entry for 1 April, written after less than two weeks in the field:

> *Wed. APR. 1 ... CKS himself was ordering retirement to Pyinmana line. (IS THIS TO BE APRIL FOOL'S DAY FOR ME?)—At 12 went down* [to Chiang Kai-shek's headquarters] *& threw the raw meat on the floor. It was quite a shock. Pulled no punches & said I'd have to be relieved.*[8]

Toungoo, a key town and defensive position on the main road and railway into the eastern Shan States, fell to the Japanese on 30 March after a stubborn battle with the Chinese 200th Division, one of three reliable units that Stilwell had. Fearing the worst, and with one eye on the approaching monsoon season, the British decided to withdraw to the Mandalay area and develop three possible routes of retreat from Burma: one, via the Chindwin River to Kalewa and overland by a hastily prepared road to Tamu and Imphal in India; two, by rail to Myitkyina, and then by road and jeep track through the Hukawng Valley and into northern Assam, a northeastern province of India (a treacherous course in the rainy season); and three, to China by way of Maymyo and the Burma Road through Lashio to Kunming.[9]

The medical services available to Stilwell were woefully inadequate and not nearly sufficiently equipped to deal with the flood of casualties—Chinese and British—streaming from the combat areas. The few British field hospitals in operation in Moulmein, Rangoon, and Mingaladon at the beginning of the campaign were withdrawn to Mandalay by rail and river steamer, from which point it was planned to evacuate casualties by train and road to Shwebo or Myitkyina (and then hopefully on to India by plane). Brigadier Treffry Thompson, the British DDMS in Burma, reported to Brigadier H.C.D. Rankin (DDMS India) that all but four or five truckloads of medical supplies and equipment were evacuated from Rangoon's civil hospitals, druggists' shops, and docks. This material was sent to the Agricultural College in Mandalay, where a medical depot was established in which to sort the supplies prior to dispatching them to the various military units and supply dumps. Thompson also acknowledged that the British had succeeded in evacuating 150 patients from part of the lunatic asylum in Rangoon (many had been released into the streets, along with inmates of the Rangoon jail, where they added significantly to the danger and chaos in the city). A total of two hundred tons of medical stores were transported to Lashio, Shwebo, and Monywa, as well as Myitkyina, but it was not nearly enough to keep up with the increasing patient loads.[10]

Some British casualties were evacuated to India by hospital ship before the port of Rangoon was closed. Riverboats ferried wounded British and Chinese soldiers as far as Mandalay, but after Rangoon fell and the Japanese moved farther up the Irrawaddy and the river's water level had fallen perilously low in the dry season, boat crews refused to endanger their crafts or their own lives in trying to navigate the shoals and other underwater hazards by returning southward to pick up more patients. Hospital trains that were organized to carry casualties and medical staffs to Myitkyina or Shwebo for evacuation to India were marked with Red Crosses; Brigadier Thompson reported that there were no cases in which the Japanese had attacked any of them in spite of rumors to the contrary. Air evacuation to India started on a small scale in March and expanded in April through the use of U.S. and RAF transport planes. Still, the numbers of casualties evacuated by air amounted to only a few thousand, as aircraft were in critically short supply and were also detailed to pick up civilian refugees. The congestion was by no means improved by the appearance of aircraft without advance notice, which meant that only the medical cases already waiting at the airfield could be loaded on board.[11]

On 3 April, Mandalay was bombed by the Japanese, who, along with fifth columnists, set fires that burned out much of the southern part of the city, including the residential district, the railroad station, and the bazaar. (Grindlay saw the distant smoke from these fires while en route to Pyinmana.) The British military and government center in Fort Dufferin and all buildings within the walls marked with a Red Cross escaped bombing, but a large hospital caught fire when sparks ignited the roof, and another facility on the western side of the city was threatened by the spreading blaze. All the patients were safely moved to other locations. Two Chinese military and civilian hospitals were also bombed, forcing their evacuation to the north with the aid of a British Casualty Clearing Station unit newly arrived in Mandalay.[12]

Colonel Williams arrived in Mandalay with Frank Merrill during the morning of 4 April. "[Smoldering] ruins through center of city, south and west of Fort Dufferin," he wrote in his diary. "Bombing extensive [but] fire did the damage." He promised the British a hospital train, and then he drove to the railroad yards and conferred with British officers about getting a train together. "[They] couldn't say how much damage had been done to rails, nor when amb[ulance] train in yards could be moved, nor whether any trains were on Lashio lines—this was 29 hours after the bombing. [I] left in disgust." In the meantime, Williams phoned Lashio and arranged for a surgical team, dressings, and forty trucks to be in Maymyo by the next morning.[13]

There were no U.S. Army field hospitals or medical evacuation units in Burma, and Stilwell and his staff had to rely on either the British or the Seagrave Hospital Unit for medical assistance for the Americans and Chinese.

Chinese medical staffs were overwhelmed, poorly supplied, and mostly inadequately trained. The Harper Memorial Hospital was the best available, operated by Dr. Gordon S. Seagrave, the famed "Burma Surgeon," the son of Baptist missionaries who was born and raised in Burma. After graduating from Johns Hopkins University's medical school and undergoing an internship at Union Memorial Hospital in Baltimore, Seagrave and his wife took over operation of a hospital at Namkham in northeastern Burma in 1922 from another medical missionary, Dr. Robert Harper. Harper had been at Namkham since his arrival in 1903 to replace the ailing Dr. M.B. Kirkpatrick, who had established the clinic and hospital almost a decade earlier. Seagrave enlarged the facility and started a training program for native nurses and physicians. By 1942, the Harper Memorial Hospital (as Seagrave named it in honor of Dr. Harper) had a capacity of 100 beds and a staff of two doctors and eleven native nurses (later increased to nineteen). After war in Burma broke out, the British assigned the Seagrave unit to provide mobile medical support for the Chinese Sixth Army, which was operating in the Shan States in eastern Burma. (It was thereafter commonly referred to as the Seagrave Hospital Unit.) The unit's first base of operations was Toungoo.

When Stilwell arrived, Seagrave requested that he and his staff be placed under American command; Stilwell agreed and subsequently issued orders that the medical group should move to just behind the front lines in the vicinity of Pyinmana, about two hundred miles north of Rangoon near the Sittang River. When the Chinese retreated shortly afterward, Seagrave and his stalwart nurses relocated their mobile surgical hospital to a former government agricultural station north of Pyinmana. Seagrave's unit relied primarily on the British for medical supplies and had to constantly journey back and forth between their hospital and the nearest British supply depot to fetch what they needed.

At the same time that Stilwell added the Seagrave Hospital Unit to his command, he informed Seagrave that a group from the Friends Ambulance Unit (FAU) was to join him. The FAU members had been recruited in England in 1940 from among Quakers and other conscientious objectors to serve in China as ambulance drivers and to work in various non-combat activities. Peter Tennant, whose father had been British under-secretary of state for war during the First World War, was the leader of the group, and he interviewed about 150 men, of whom ultimately about forty were chosen. Tennant and three others were in an advance party that had landed in Rangoon in July 1941. The rest arrived in September, assembled their ambulances, and drove them to China over the Burma Road. When war came to Burma, some of the group members volunteered to serve the British Red Cross, and others were assigned as ambulance drivers for the Chinese. The latter group included Bill Brough, Bill Duncumb, Martin Davies, Eric Inchboard, Tom Owen, George

7. Joining Seagrave in Burma 73

Parsons, Brian Jones, Kenneth Grant, Tony Reynolds, and (later) Tennant. They were joined by Paul Geren, an American and former staff member of Judson College in Rangoon who fled the city in January 1942 and joined the Chinese armies in the southern Shan States as an ambulance driver. By March Geren was part of the FAU and remained with them for the duration of the campaign and through the unit's retreat with Stilwell to India in May.[14]

For the first three months of 1942, the men of FAU spent their time ferrying medical supplies and salvaging spare vehicle parts from the docks in Rangoon and from cars and trucks abandoned along the roads.[15] During the month of February, they rescued £120,000 worth of supplies from Rangoon as well as oil from the fields at Yenangyaung. Much of this material was first dropped at Lashio and subsequently moved into China in March as the Japanese pushed farther north.

In early April, a section of the FAU under Bill Brough was sent to work with the Seagrave field hospital, evacuating wounded members of the Chinese Fifth and Sixth Armies from the front to the hospital. When Brough and the others arrived at Seagrave's base, they found two men—an American and a Burmese—trying to get a patient on a stretcher through a doorway. Brough pitched in to help, only to be told by the American, Paul Geren, that they were trying to get the stretcher *out*, not in.

When not out on the road, the FAU members sometimes assisted in surgery by

> pouring chloroform from a dropper bottle to induce anaesthesia, then maintaining it with ether.... Chloroform gave an easier induction [than ether] but was more dangerous. Initially on occasions the surgeon would tell us that the patient was too deeply anaesthetized and the blood had turned darker. As our experience increased this observation was heard less often, and later hardly ever heard it at all.[16]

At the start of the war, Seagrave added another medical missionary, Dr. Theodore Gurney, to his team. The British-born Gurney and his wife Agnes had worked in Ethiopia from 1937 to 1939 under the auspices of the Bible Churchman's Missionary Society, based in England. The couple transferred to Burma in 1939 and set up a medical mission at Panglong, and then at Langhko in the Shan States, until the Japanese invasion in late 1941 forced Gurney to evacuate his wife and their children to England while he remained behind and joined Seagrave's hospital. It is not known where Gurney obtained his medical education and training, but Grindlay came to greatly respect Gurney's abilities as a surgeon.[17]

Another medical officer arrived at Seagrave's hospital just ahead of Grindlay: Captain Donald O'Hara, a dentist and oral surgeon, who had come to Asia to join Stilwell's staff. He was flying to China when his plane made a stop at Bhamo in Burma. While sitting around waiting to continue, O'Hara discovered that his name was on a list to get off in Burma. He stayed behind when the plane took off; it crashed soon after, killing everyone on board. "It did kind of shake me up when we learned we were going to Burma instead of China," he said later,

> particularly when I was told to join Seagrave and the Baptist Mission. I thought, "Hell, the way I like to drink and smoke and swear, I'll just get on with the missionaries like that!" ... I asked if there was some way I could get out of it and they said there wasn't and I went down there as unhappy as the devil.... Then I saw the outfit and met Seagrave and he opened his desk drawer and offered me a drink! Then I met the nurses and all of a sudden I took a liking to the whole bunch.... Some of the nurses were smarter than the MD's [sic]. They could talk to the patients ... they knew all the fevers and they had a better idea of what was going on than the American doctors.[18]

O'Hara's training as an oral surgeon had made him familiar with the structure of the skull and face; this knowledge was put to good use in repairing head wounds. He also arranged with Lieutenant Colonel Frank Dorn, Stilwell's aide, to get ambulances for the Friends Ambulance Unit (which O'Hara referred to as "that Quaker outfit," despite the fact that not all of the men were Quakers, though all were pacifists). The ambulances that the FAU originally had were too wide to fit through most of the narrow gates in Chinese town walls, so they were traded with the Americans for smaller Chevrolet chassis with bodies built in Rangoon.

And then "another [American army] captain turned up today [3 April] while I was matching the nurses for blood transfusion," Seagrave wrote in his diary. "Captain Grindlay trained in the Mayo Clinic.... Looks just like a Mayo Clinic man, too! I will have to keep a stiff upper lip and do the best surgery I can."[19]

Grindlay had no sooner reached Seagrave's hospital than the FAU brought in two truckloads of Chinese bomb casualties. "I did my first amputation 5 minutes after I joined the group in Pyinmana," he wrote to his wife on 26 May. His diary captures the breathless pace and the horrible injuries that occupied him that morning and for the next month.

> One had 2 legs off at thigh & horrible burns. Sick at stomach. Scrub. Just started amputating the legs of this case when he died. Then I took one [with] shrapnel [wound in the] buttock. Found it passed in front of sacrum. Opened belly—full of blood. 10 holes in p.i. & probably pelvic vein torn. Died. Seagrave working on another belly case—it died. Both worked on a brain case—2 large trephine holes parietal region—torn & bloody brain. [I used a] Vaseline wick.[20]

The FAU came in from the front lines and said that the Chinese forces were retreating to positions behind their own, leaving the hospital exposed and undefended. "Worked like hell—nurses harder than I—until 1 PM," Grindlay wrote in his diary that night. "Sent 30 [patients] to Meiktila [a city about 90 miles north of Pyinmana].... Took brain cases & 2 plaster cases

7. Joining Seagrave in Burma

[with] us on[the] end [of]one truck. Everything else packed up. Left 1:15 PM.... Wound over side [road] to ... Shwemyo Cliff. About 30 mi. north [of Pyinmana]." The doctors and nurses unpacked at a former Public Works Department bungalow atop a bluff overlooking the Sittang River—which, as it turned out, was an excellent potential target for Japanese pilots. Grindlay fell into bed at 4:00 a.m. at the end of a long, exhausting first day in combat surgery, one of many more to come.

The men of the FAU who had driven the thirty Chinese patients to Meiktila returned at noon the next day. Their trucks, Grindlay reported, were

> strafed along the road. 4 tires & radiator connector tube hit on one truck & it had to be towed in. Hot & windy—dry. Forest fires & haze.... Scorpions & cobras about here. Numerous air alarms—about every ½ hr. a flight of Jap bombers passes down valley. Tried to nap. Got tired of running to gulch behind us [with] girls.

A report came in of soldiers wounded by the strafing. One of FAU men raced off in a truck to check. He returned at the end of dinner—"the inevitable rice, soup & spiced beef stew slop," Grindlay grumbled, eaten with one's fingers—with one case aboard, though the driver said two more truckloads were following. Grindlay pitched in immediately, working by lamplight.

> I hop[p]ed on the case & got going—had thru & thru bullet [wound] rt. wrist—shattering ulna & thru & thru [wound] rt hip to left scrotum hitting greater trochanter [and] crest [of the] ilium & destroying left testes. Took out left testes, debrided scrotum & drained both sides. Debrided hip & wrist & did a Trueta cast of rt. arm.... Lamp light & bugs.... High wind.[21]

After supper the next day (5 April), a "hot windy day," Grindlay helped pack up and move the unit to Tatkon, a town eight miles north of their previous location on the road to Meiktila. The nurses worked hard, as usual, and lent an air of civility to the proceedings by singing. "Girls singing native Kachin, Burmese & English & American songs," Grindlay wrote with admiration. "Affectionate pretty hard-working little creatures," he told his wife in a letter written at the end of May. They are "wonderful little girls. Very, very shy, very polite and generous and terribly hard workers.... No white woman could have done what they did." Besides their nursing duties, the women also performed most of the laundry tasks in addition to bathing the men at wells and rivers.

They arrived at their new quarters (a school) at midnight, unloaded and went to bed. Grindlay was suffering from "renal colic & tough backache." He "[took] a slug of Drambuie & got enough relief to put out bedding. Got little sleep during night [with] my back, the colic did subside though."

The unit moved yet again the next day to a former agricultural station a quarter of a mile away. It was less sheltered than their previous quarters but somewhat more comfortable. The day was quiet, and Seagrave was able to organize a hymn sing by the nurses that evening. During the morning of 7 April, the Japanese strafed the Chinese troops on the road south of them; the FAU went out to pick up casualties while Grindlay, Seagrave and O'Hara scrubbed.

> About 1 [p.m.] *the trucks returned, 34 wounded, only one* [with] *minor* [wounds]. *Two brain cases died on table. Rest all horribly shattering compound fractures etc.—requiring lots of work—several needing amputations. Soldiers filthy & lousy* [with] *lice & scabies malaria & probably syph*[ilis] *&* [tuberculosis]. *Worked alone from 6 PM on while Seagrave went up for supplies. One "storm-king" lantern. Usual bugs & poor asepsis. Back (rt. kidney) aching. Finally finished 11 PM & ate usual slop.*

Twenty-five more casualties were brought in after breakfast the next day. Four of them had malaria, and the rest were wounded. Grindlay wrote, "Two belly cases 2 days old. I did one & resected 2 ft. bowel—a tough job. All our cases have at least one serious shattering [wound], most have 2 or three. One I did yesterday had 4 bad compound fractures." Most fractures were the result of bullets or shell fire, the impact of which broke bones.

Casualties continued to pour in. Grindlay arose at 10 a.m. on the morning of 10 April "more dead than alive feeling." Everyone pitched in to clean and disinfect the dining room, hospital and dispensary. After lunch, thirty-five wounded arrived. According to Grindlay, "On one I took out a spleen (bleeding from bullet [wound])—[with] an untrained nurse & bugs falling into [the surgical] field."

Colonel Williams, accompanied by Bobby Lim and Colonel "Limey" Wang (a Chinese liaison officer), dropped in on 12 April to visit Seagrave's hospital. "Seagrave, with Captains Grindlay and O'Hara, doing all surgery for [Chinese] Fifth Army," Williams recorded in his diary. His group had driven through Meiktila half an hour after it was bombed, where the British 1 Casualty Clearing Station was receiving wounded from the attack. Williams, Lim, and Wang went on to Kyaukse and noticed that one surgical team was handling 400 seriously injured cases. Up until 18 April, Williams personally delivered medical supplies to Seagrave.[22]

The frantic pace was beginning to exhaust Grindlay. By 14 April, he reported "no pep left in me." Indian soldiers were being brought in with dressings made from a paste of chopped leaves. "[Wounds] badly infected," he wrote. Thirty-five cases came in at 10:30 p.m., and he worked on them until 2 a.m.: "I had 2 belly cases to start [with]. One with hole in liver which I packed & one [with] hole thru splenic flexure—for which I did a transverse colostomy (no feces in belly) & I put a drain thru to the splenic flexure region. Other horrible dirty shattering wounds—one with buttocks & anus ripped off for whom I did ... some of Harrison-Crips [sic] op."[23]

The intense heat made it extremely difficult to relax or sleep. "No sleep today. Too blasted hot," Grindlay grumbled on 16 April. News arrived of the

7. Joining Seagrave in Burma

Major General Robert Lim, left (inspector general of medical services, Chinese Army) and Colonel Robert Williams (chief surgeon in the CBI theater). Photograph taken in April 1942 at Headquarters of Chinese Fifth Army, Pyawbwe, Burma (Gerard J. Casius Collection, United States Army Heritage and Education Center, Carlisle, Pennsylvania).

two-pronged Japanese advance up the Irrawaddy River through central Burma and the eastern Shan States, flanking the Seagrave unit. "Seagrave knows the geography well & thinks we are in danger of being cut off. Just as I got to bed another truck of severely wounded [arrived]. Only 15 [patients] so I did them alone & got to bed 4:30 Am, very tired & feeling lousy." On 18 April Stilwell ordered Seagrave to evacuate north of Meiktila because the fast-retreating British were uncovering the right flank of the Chinese defenders at Pyinmana. "Off before the [Chinese] had the road blocked [with truck traffic]." They drove through Meiktila, and Grindlay and Seagrave scouted for a new location, which they finally found just outside the town of Kume, an hour and a half by road northeast of Meiktila. It was a former government bungalow that had "a fine wall & lots of water in the canal by door." The house was surrounded by palm trees with ruins of pagodas across the canal. The local natives built a thatch-roofed hut next to the house to provide an operating room.

By this time Grindlay's skill as a surgeon was coming to the attention of Stilwell's staff and winning their admiration. Lieutenant Carl Arnold, an aide in Stilwell's headquarters in Maymyo, later said:

> Grindlay in his field was just great. He'd call me over to watch an operation ... and he never backed away from anything because he didn't have the facilities to do it. I've seen him open up a little Chinese [soldier] and get the excess blood that was in the abdominal cavity into a bottle and put it back in him, for crying out loud, and two days later the guy's walking around. He was excellent in his field.[24]

On 20 April, while Seagrave went off to Stilwell's headquarters to protest Grindlay's rumored reassignment to another mobile surgical hospital, wounded soldiers continued to flood in by the truck load

> all the burning hot day & right thru the night. O'Hara had several jaw cases & did a few other small cases. Otherwise I was alone, living on coffee & cigarettes, bloody, plaster coated, sweaty, wearing only Shan pants & shoes. Many plaster cases—[compound fractures of] femurs etc.

By 2:00 p.m. the next day, they had worked on 120 patients—"all bad," Grindlay wrote. "Absolutely exhausted—twitching & temper short." He also continued to suffer from renal colic, which further debilitated him.

He was asleep "in heat & flies after lunch" when Williams came in to wake him. The news was grim: the Chinese Sixth Army, which was defending the area around them, had fallen apart under Japanese attacks. They might stay in Kume for another week, but then they would have to evacuate. Stilwell and most of his staff were going to Shwebo, between forty and fifty miles northwest of Mandalay, on a potential evacuation route to India; a few others were sent to Lashio to be flown out to China. With the Japanese threatening to cut off the Burma Road, retreat to India was rapidly becoming the only option. That night Grindlay fell into bed tense with exhaustion, taking sleeping pills to relax.

On 23 April, Seagrave returned from Stilwell's headquarters with a commission as a major in the U.S. Army and reported that Grindlay would be allowed to stay on with him. However, the unit only spent two more days at Kume, operating steadily on a stream of casualties with little rest. They were also ordered to move north to Shwebo on 25 April to join Stilwell's headquarters and that of Lieutenant General Thomas Hutton, the British Burma army commander and chief of staff to General Archibald Wavell. Grindlay had recovered from his renal colic by then and felt more energetic. "Started packing 5 PM. Usual mess & confusion but off about 9 PM." Unfortunately, the Seagrave unit got separated in the darkness amid a mass of British tanks and trucks on the road. Grindlay assembled part of the group and led them through Mandalay and "over Ava bridge over Irrawaddy [River near Mandalay]. Held them in Sagaing village on other side until Seagrave came up. Then found a camp along river in an [American Baptist Missionary] compound. Some slept on pews in church.... I slept [with] the Sikhs on the lawn. Very tired."

On 27 April, Grindlay saw Stilwell and his staff at Shwebo and was asked to stop and share a whiskey with them. They were

> idle & awaiting decision from [Washington] & Gissimo [Chiang Kai-shek] what to do. Battle [of] Burma over.... Stilwell [sic] talked [with] me for long time about type of med. equip. to take [on the retreat from Burma] before going to bed. Doesn't regard [Colonel] Williams opinions. Next move is rumored to India, unless we have to go to China.

Grindlay hoped their destination would be India, which, as events proved, was the only viable retreat route.

Shwebo was heavily bombed on 28 April, the same day that the Seagrave unit was told that India would be their destination. "Present plan is by rail to Myitkina [sic] & then walk or plane to India," Grindlay wrote happily, a plan that Stilwell proposed to Chiang Kai-shek and was subsequently approved. Seagrave and Grindlay drove into Shwebo the next morning looking for whatever supplies that they could scrounge. Soon after they arrived, Japanese bombers "flew over & dropped about 150 bombs. I just laid on ground & passed cigarettes. Seagrave & I drove thru town looking for casualties but [saw] no one but soldiers in town. Bomb holes, fallen trees & huge fires blocked most of streets & there were [occasional] explosives." They returned to Shwebo late in the afternoon but still found no casualties. Instead, they discovered a bottle of gin and drank it on the way back to the hospital: they "arrived tight," Grindlay wrote later.

Williams and Bobby Lim went to Kyaukmyaung on the Irrawaddy River, 46 miles north of Mandalay, on 29 April to arrange for a hospital boat to evacuate some of the wounded. Stilwell split his headquarters that afternoon, sending most of the men upriver by boat and leaving a small number behind to remain with the Chinese army. These men included Williams, Jack Belden, and Captain Roscoe Hambleton, a transportation specialist who was given a "special mission" by Stilwell to coordinate the ferrying of the Chinese 22nd Division across the Irrawaddy at Kyaukmyaung, the first leg of their trek to safety in India.[25]

On 1 May Grindlay volunteered to stay behind for a day at Kyaukmyaung to perform emergency surgery on any Chinese wounded he could find. He took with him two FAU drivers (Eric Inchboard and Ken Grant) and two Chinese orderlies (Ling Sing and La Wong) to the ferry landing on the Irrawaddy. He conducted surgery alone through the day with the town burning around him and the Japanese closing in. O'Hara said later that he never expected to see Grindlay and the others again after he left them to rejoin the Stilwell group at Zigon, where the Chinese Sixth Army was temporarily headquartered.

Grindlay found the chaos at Kyaukmyaung almost unimaginable: "Burning & half sunk ships. Flies. Indian refugees.... Brit. troops." His group brewed coffee after finding a pile of cans abandoned by the British on the bank of the Irrawaddy. An argument was raging at that point between Brigadier John Crawford Martin (a British liaison officer with the Chinese), General Tu Li-ming (the commander of the Chinese Fifth Army), and General Eric Goddard (the chief British administrative officer who was in charge of transportation) over the one remaining riverboat of the Irrawaddy Flotilla Company. Brigadier Martin and General Tu both wanted to use the boat to evacuate the Chinese 22nd Division across the river, while Goddard wanted it to carry gasoline to Bhamo. Martin and Tu eventually won the day. Grindlay, Grant, Williams, Hambleton, and Belden were invited by Brigadier Martin to come aboard the boat for dinner at 12:30 that night, with Colonel Drysdale (the boat's commander) and his wife. The boat's crew reconnoitered wrecks in the river to see if they could make a bridge for the Chinese troops, but "no luck." Martin commandeered the riverboat for 48 hours to ferry the Chinese, but the vessel's commander protested and went off to find General Alexander to have the orders countermanded. Hambleton told Grindlay that he was staying behind, per Stilwell's orders, to get the 22nd Division across the river after the bulk of its troops arrived from Mandalay.[26]

There were no more casualties to be treated, and Grindlay's group joined Colonel Williams, Belden, and several other men who were setting off in search of Stilwell, leaving Hambleton behind. It was the last they saw of him.

Grindlay drove all night on a narrow track atop a paddy dike, a task made more exhausting and stressful by Chinese trucks parked in the road, blocking traffic. He lost Grant and Inchboard, both of whom had diarrhea and had to stop several times, and went on ahead in a jeep with the two Chinese orderlies in the cold and darkness while separated from Williams and Belden and worried about being left behind. At dawn, much to his relief, Grindlay suddenly encountered Stilwell, his staff, and the Seagrave group just as they were coming out of a dried-out rice field in the vicinity of Khin-U, from the direction of Shwebo to the south, on another dike road that led north to Zigon. Williams, Belden, Inchboard and Grant also caught up with Stilwell at about this time.

The track petered out after a while, and the column followed a trail next to a railroad line. Just after noon, they left the trail when they heard Japanese planes bombing behind them. "[Scared the] hell out of me," Grindlay later wrote. He stopped and directed traffic, dispatching the vehicles one by one across a vulnerable open stretch of ground to a more sheltered trail. When all were across, he brought up the rear. "Hot, dusty. [The road was] only ruts winding thru paddies & teak forest—little foliage. Hands & legs sunburned. Ruts too wide for jeep.... No wind screen—dust choking." That night they camped at Pintha, just southwest of Zigon. Grindlay stripped and had a welcome bath at a well, with one of the Seagrave nurses, Little Bawk, washing him, much to Stilwell's amusement. The villagers gave the travelers small, delicious bananas, and they ate the last of their K-ration canned fruit. Grindlay slept that night next to the trucks with the nurses, his sunburned arms and knees raw and sore.

The next day, 3 May, the group left Pintha at sunrise and journeyed about 35–40 miles. Their progress was slowed when they discovered that heavy Chinese trucks had broken through weak and rotted wooden bridges at Meza, which necessitated laborious detours hacked through the jungle. One of their ammunition-carrying trucks overheated and caught fire, and the driver fled when bullets started popping. The truck also had on board the luggage of many of the officers, including Stilwell's, but most of it was salvaged. Grindlay supervised the rerouting of the rest of the convoy around the burning vehicle and the cutting of a trail through bamboo thickets along the road. A wind and rain storm brought blessed relief from the heat and dust, and they arrived in Kawlin, a town near Wuntho that Grindlay noted was filled with pagodas.

The group was working its way north-northwest, gradually heading toward India. Stilwell had received instructions from Chiang Kai-shek to head to Myitkyina with the Fifth Army, which was following the Irrawaddy, but it was apparent to the American commander that "we can no longer be of much use." The situation was beyond hope, the defenses had crumbled and everyone was fleeing the doomed country. Stilwell was losing control of the Chinese: "Tu [Fifth Army commander] is doing just as [he] pleases. Lo has no control over him.... Why keep Americans in hot water?" he wrote in his diary. General Lo Cho-ying (1896–1961), the Chinese army commander-in-chief and Stilwell's chief of staff, was begging for an airplane to pick him up in Myitkyina after causing a train wreck that closed the line to Myitkyina, leaving Stilwell no choice but to go by road as far as possible. His objective now was to stay "ahead of the deluge" (meaning the masses of disorganized Chinese army troops, hordes of panicky Indian civilians, and the Japanese).[27]

Roscoe Hambleton's Fate

Captain Roscoe Hambleton experienced the kind of nightmare trek that Grindlay was spared when he fortunately stumbled on Stilwell's group at dawn north of Shwebo. Hambleton managed to get the 22nd Division across the Irrawaddy in two days to link up with the rest of Fifth Army on the east bank and begin the trek to Myitkyina. "Dirt, disease, danger, despair," he wrote in his diary on 2 May. The next day he "finished [his] job at Kyaukmaung [sic], packed up and boarded the S.S. *Heron* for a trip up river to Katha. The boat laid up for the night after traveling three miles. No food, sleep, etc. What a mess." Hambleton was accompanied by Lieutenant Denis Guy Lean, a liaison officer of the Indian army assigned to the Fifth Chinese Army, and a Colonel Tsen of the 38th Division.[28]

The trip resumed on the morning of 4 May; two days later they arrived at Katha. The town had been bombed by the Japanese, and the crew and passengers decided to leave the boat and start walking. They soon discovered that they were cut off from all escape routes other than those that led to India. Hambleton, Lean and Tsen rode in an oxcart for two hours on their way to a camping spot. "Never so tired before, but what a relief to leave Katha," Hambleton wrote. He had gone about ten miles since leaving the boat in mid-afternoon. He had also left "a lot of stuff" on the boat, including money, a camp bed, blankets, sheets, and other items. On 8 May, as the travelers were riding in the cart, a small convoy consisting of a number of Chinese in a jeep, a scout car, and a truck drove up and told the men that they had heard that Stilwell and his party were just ahead at Mansi, a village on the Chaunggyi River that led to the Uyu, a tributary of the Chindwin, which formed part of the border with India.

Hambleton's party, now joined by the Chinese, raced off and arrived in the town at 2:00 a.m. on 9 May but found no trace of the Stilwell group. Unknown to Hambleton, the Americans had moved on two days earlier and were about three days from Homalin, to the north and west on the Chindwin River, near the border with India. Hambleton and his companions turned back and met General Tu and the headquarters troops of the Chinese Fifth Army near Indaw. They had dinner and felt better, except for being grimy with dust and dirt from the road. Tu told them that his plan (based on orders from Chiang Kai-shek) was to break through the Japanese positions at Myitkyina and escape to Tengchung, China. "Cross your fingers, darling," Hambleton worriedly wrote to his wife in his diary.

On Sunday, 10 May, Hambleton had access to a radio and sent a message, which he copied in his diary, to Claire Chennault's base in Kunming: "Relay information that Stilwell left Mansi 8th attempt cross Chindwin and walk India STOP I was delayed and forced return Indaw join 5th Army which leaving tonight by trucks to fight through Myitkyina to Tengchung End Hambleton."[29] It is not known whether this message reached Chennault or whether it was relayed to India.

That night a regiment of the 38th Division tried to drive the Japanese out of Katha, but this effort failed because a supporting regiment from the 22nd Division did not arrive in time. The regiment of the 38th was badly mauled, so, the next day, General Tu decided on a new plan: rather than lose more men in a hopeless cause, he would take an alternate route via the Burma Road to China, bypassing Myitkyina and crossing the Irrawaddy, and then marching south and east to Hsipaw and over the mountains to Paoshan in

Yunnan. This was a dangerous gambit because it would take the Fifth Army through Japanese-occupied areas. The following day, Hambleton and Lean rode in the scout car to gain some badly needed rest. They made seventeen miles in fourteen hours—a long day. Everyone kept "an eye out for a place to run if [enemy] planes appear."

During the morning of 14 May, the vehicles were abandoned twenty miles from Mansi. From then on, the Chinese advanced at a snail's pace, averaging ten miles a day. Hambleton found the confusion and disorganization in the Chinese army frustrating. A bugle roused the soldiers early in the morning, and then they would sometimes wait for hours before the column started out. The Fifth Army reached the Uyu River, north of the Chaunggyi, a few days behind Stilwell, and they began walking downstream. Hambleton's clothes and shaving kit were soaked from wading in the water. After a time, the riverbed turned from rocks to sand and became easier to walk on, but the monsoon season was starting, and thereafter everyone's clothes and blankets were seldom dry. Lean developed foot trouble and had to ride on a pony, and, after an exhausting day of steep climbs, Hambleton was forced to mount a pony, too.[30]

By this time General Tu had evidently changed his mind about retreating to China, as, near Hpakan, at the headwaters of the Uyu River, he discovered that there was a considerable force of Japanese in the way and the route to Sumprabum, north of Myitkyina, was cut off by the enemy. Also at this time Hambleton noticed that he was steadily losing weight from the walking and inadequate food. His strength was ebbing, and he tired more quickly. Hambleton, after all, was not a young man; he would turn forty-seven years old on 8 June 1942. "Am entirely and completely exhausted," he wrote in his diary on 21 May. One of the Chinese doctors gave him an injection and pills for dysentery, as he was "passing only water and no control as just bursts out any time." The next day he noted that it had been eight months since he had left Washington with the AMMISCA group. He rode a mule all day and felt more rested. The army arrived at a village named Haungpa near Hpakan, where they stopped for a day of rest and to consider their next step after learning that the Japanese were in Sumprabum. It now appeared that the most feasible route of retreat was through the dreaded Hukawng Valley, a malarial jungle trek that would become a death trap for thousands of refugees and soldiers alike in the weeks ahead. Hambleton and Lean decided for some reason that when they got to Maingkwan, which was partway up the Hukawng, they could pick up a jeep road to Myitkyina. What they planned to do there is not known, though they must have surmised that if the Japanese were already in Sumprabum, they must also be in Myitkyina to the south. It seemed like a way of escaping Burma and avoiding the Hukawng. But "Qien sabe [who knows?]," Hambleton wrote philosophically.[31]

8

Stilwell's Escape from Burma
Preparing for the Walkout

While Hambleton was still desperately trying to find an escape route from Burma, Stilwell had already reached India, leading a column of 110 soldiers and civilians guided by natives and a missionary. He had split his staff at Shwebo on 1 May and dispatched most of them to India by air to form a rear echelon headquarters in New Delhi and establish liaisons both with the U.S. Tenth Air Force, commanded by Major General Lewis Brereton (General Douglas MacArthur's air force commander in the Philippines from 1941 into early 1942), and with the RAF to facilitate supply drops to the column. Among the thirty-seven staff members who were put aboard the plane at Shwebo were Colonel Richard Sandusky, Lieutenant Colonel Frank Roberts, Lieutenant Kenneth Haymaker, Lieutenant Carl Arnold, and Colonel John McLaughlin (acting adjutant general of U.S. Army Headquarters, Burma). Arnold later noted that they left in a "terrific hurry. The Japs were strafing and dive-bombing and Haines [*sic*], the pilot, was quite anxious to get off and when we took off we flew close to the ground for about forty minutes so that they couldn't spot us and I've never been so scared in my life!"[1]

Twelve officers remained with Stilwell, who refused to be flown out to "save face," arguing that the Americans needed to somehow salvage part of their shattered prestige after the loss of the Philippines by showing the Chinese that they would not run away and leave them to their fate. "If I run out now that will be one more defeat, one more surrender. I could not command the Chinese again," he told his staff. At the same time, Stilwell clung to the slim hope that he could somehow direct the Chinese as his duty dictated and maintain contact with their fragmented army to try to either form a defensive line in northern Burma before the monsoon season began or get them safely evacuated from Burma. But it finally became all too apparent to Stilwell that the "jig was up," in his words, and there was no choice but to let the Chinese forces see to their own safety and to get his people out before the Japanese caught up with them.

Colonel Caleb Vance Haynes (1895–1966) was commander of the Assam-Burma-China Ferrying Command. He and Colonel Robert Lee Scott (1908–2006), Haynes' executive officer, were ordered to fly to Shwebo to pick up Stilwell and his staff. Flying in "black storms" (which signaled the onset of the monsoon season) to Myitkyina, they refueled, learned from a British pilot where the airfield at Shwebo was located, and found it by following the Mandalay–Shwebo rail line at tree-top level. They arrived just after a Japanese bombing raid. On landing, Haynes went off in search of Stilwell while Scott guarded the aircraft. Haynes was told that Stilwell was going to walk out and that about forty people would be on the return flight to Calcutta. Scott and Haynes flew them safely to India and were determined to return to pick up Stilwell—by force, if necessary. But when Scott and Haynes arrived again at Shwebo, they found no one except some British and American wounded. One of the officers on Stilwell's staff gave Scott the itinerary of the walkout to pass along to General Brereton and the RAF, and Scott helped plan, organize, and fly drops of food, medicines, blankets, and other supplies along the route. But, in the absence of recognition codes, Scott later wrote that they were unable to locate the Stilwell group even though they dropped supplies to every group they saw.[2]

Before Stilwell left Burma, Major James Vivian Davidson-Houston (a member of the Royal Engineers Corps and commander of the British commando contingents in Burma, part of 204 Military Mission), and his aide, Major O.C.T. "Sailor" Dykes (a former Royal Marine who had transferred to the Gurkhas), appeared at Stilwell's Maymyo headquarters on 20 April. The men had been sent from Chungking four days earlier by General John Bruce, General Dennys' successor, to organize the deployment of the British 204 MM commandos returning from China as well as Chinese commandos from "Surprise Battalions" operating in Hunan.[3] Davidson-Houston had served as assistant military attaché in Hong Kong before the war. At the same time, he and Dykes also reported to General the Honorable Harold Alexander (1891–1969), commander-in-chief of British forces in Burma, who impressed Davidson-Houston with his quiet confidence.

About a week later, while with Stilwell, the British soldiers encountered Brigadier Christopher Ronald Spear (1897–1942) at Kyaukse. Spear was a colorful character who had served in China as a British military attaché and was detained by the Japanese (along with a language officer named Lieutenant Cooper) in Mongolia in 1939 on suspicion of espionage. The men were released after a couple of weeks in confinement, and Spear left China for Britain in the autumn of 1939 due to a mental breakdown. In early 1942, Spear was appointed chief British liaison officer with the Chinese Fifth Army, the position he was holding when Davidson-Houston met him in late April. One evening, while drinking whiskey and water on the veranda of Spear's quarters, they noticed a flickering glow in the mountains to the east. "Just another fire," Spear said calmly. "A lot of Burmese are going about lighting fires. It's partly the love of doing damage and partly pre-arranged signals to the enemy."[4]

Davidson-Houston and Dykes had been told by Major General Sibert on 21 April that the military situation in Burma had deteriorated so much that they were not needed and should return to China. However, by then the Japanese were attacking Lashio and they were stuck in Burma. Davidson-Houston and Dykes were ordered to take a train to Myitkyina. They got as far as just north of Shwebo, traveling with Major George Eliot "Beaver" Barton, a former member of the (British) Bush Warfare School at Maymyo, when they discovered that the rail line was blocked by a train collision. The tracks were cleared within a day or so, and the train continued on, bearing General Lo Cho-ying and the British officers, among many others.

When they arrived at Indaw, they discovered that there was another serious train wreck beyond and that they could not move farther. The next morning, the train yards were filled with cold, lifeless locomotives and parties of people setting off on foot northward and westward in hopes of finding trails over the hills to India. General Lo had also departed and, in the absence of orders, confusion reigned. In the midst of this mayhem, Davidson-Houston, Dykes, and Barton met a forest officer, Major Herbert E. Castens, and then they encountered Stilwell (along with his convoy of jeeps and trucks) and rejoined his party. The Americans, Davidson-Houston later wrote, were not at all happy to have the "Limeys" attach themselves to the group. None of them had any rations of their own, and none had ever been west of the Chindwin and so knew nothing about the country between there and India. Davidson-Houston took command of the British party, which by this time also included Major W.D. Haigh, a sapper with the Royal Engineers; a Sikh subaltern named Lieutenant G.B. Singh; a former unnamed member of the Burmese navy; three officers from British army headquarters; and five other ranks.[5] The British members remained with Stilwell through the rest of the walkout. Dykes said later that they felt "somewhat guilty at not being with the British troops who were having a pretty rough time. However, they didn't seem to need our services, so I suppose it was a case of 'sauve qui peut.'"[6]

Around 1 May, an American agricultural missionary was added to the Stilwell unit. He was the Reverend Brayton C. Case, who had long experience in Burma and was conversant in several native languages, and who conferred with Stilwell about various escape routes to India. He accompanied the Stilwell group on the walkout, and, after arriving in India, the general asked Case to join his headquarters staff because the missionary knew Burma and could provide a great deal of knowledge about the country. Stilwell assured him that there would be plenty of work to do. Case was willing to lend whatever help and expertise he could and would prove to be a valuable guide for the Stilwell party in the days to come.[7]

The days that followed were a mad rush for the Seagrave unit, including the FAU, as its members prepared to trek out with Stilwell to India. Bill Brough and Brian Jones had been separated from the rest of the FAU after being sent north on a British hospital train to Myitkyina, one of the last to get through before the rail line was blocked. Brough was in dire straits, with severe dysentery and cerebral malaria, and Jones had a broken collar bone from a jeep accident and went along to look after his comrade. At Myitkyina they were placed on one of the last planes to fly out to India. Brough fully recovered in a Calcutta hospital and returned to service, eventually abandoning his conscientious objector status and transferring to Detachment 101 of the OSS in Burma.[8]

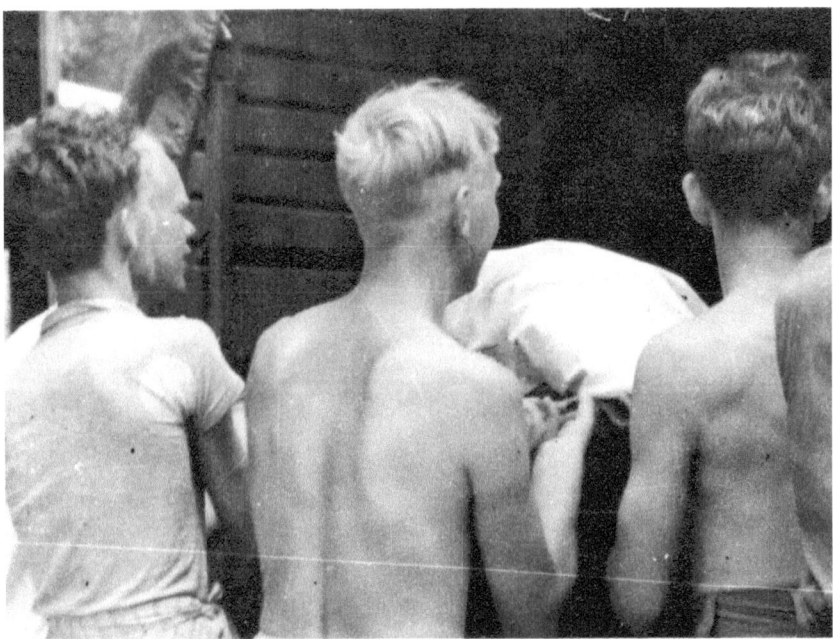

A stretcher-bearing Bill Brough (Friends Ambulance Unit member) being loaded onto a train for evacuation to Myitkyina, about 1 May 1942. Location unknown, but probably Shwebo, north of Mandalay. Brough was seriously ill with dysentery and was flown to India, accompanied by Brian Jones, another FAU member. By the time he reached Calcutta, Brough had almost shaken the dysentery, but then he developed a case of the far more serious cerebral malaria. He recovered after a week's stay in a hospital. Grindlay is visible at far left. Blond man in center may be Brian Jones, Brough's companion on the flight (U.S. Army photo, courtesy Grindlay family).

Prior to the start of the walkout, the Stilwell group was organized into four echelons, with Stilwell commanding the first, Colonel Adrian St. John the second, Grindlay the third, and Seagrave the fourth. They found a forest bungalow in which to spend the night and where they had three hours' sleep and a meal of rice and sardines. "Off again on the dot of three on the morning of May 6," Seagrave noted in his diary.[9] They arrived in Mansi (which Hambleton and the Chinese reached a week later), and all the vehicles except the jeeps were abandoned where the road ended at a small bamboo bridge that a large Chinese truck had broken through. In a clearing, Stilwell assembled the group and told them what was ahead: they would walk or ride in the jeeps as far as the vehicles could go, switch to rafts on the Uyu River to Homalin, and from there walk over the mountains to India.[10] He ordered that all nonessential articles of clothing and equipment be discarded and that packs weigh no more than ten pounds. All food was to be turned in to a common pool. Grindlay was devastated by the theft of his camera with the photographs he had taken in the previous weeks.

Two other British soldiers suddenly appeared in the clearing: Jack Croft and Hughie Campbell, officer cadets from the Bush Warfare School. Croft had lived in China for several years as a youth, and Campbell was a former employee of the Burmah Oil Company. They had met at school, and during the campaign they were assigned to go south and salvage whatever they could from abandoned vehicles. By the end of April, they found themselves members of a party of officers and cadets who managed to reach Shwebo and took a train to Indaw, where, like Stilwell's staff and others, they learned the line was blocked to the north and so decided to head west to India. They walked for a couple of days before encountering Stilwell's party on 6 May. Croft recalled years later:

> There were huge piles of equipment and stores to one side and some of these were being burned. A pall of dust and smoke hung over the whole place. We were standing there observing all this when we were abruptly confronted by a testy American officer who rudely remarked, "My God, not more Limeys!" I took exception to this and answered tartly that though he might not like our company, neither were we too keen on his. But since we all seemed to be engaged in the same effort of escaping, wouldn't it be sensible for us to stick together?

The unidentified officer cooled off and conferred with Stilwell, and the newcomers were allowed to stay. They joined Davidson-Houston's group, some of whom "were on crutches and were wearing filthy bandages and their attitude seemed to be, 'If the Japs want Burma, they can have it!'" Croft said later.[11]

"I looked around me and what impressed me was the *color* of the *scene*," journalist Jack Belden remembered. "All these people from different countries, how they were reacting and making their preparations. The girls, the little Burmese nurses, were throwing away all their belongings, their colorful skirts and silks, tossing all their garments up into the trees, laughing and having a good time."[12] Belden, a stringer for Henry Luce's Time-Life news organization, had known Stilwell four years earlier in China and had been covering the war in Burma since the Americans had arrived. He willingly chose to stay with the American general instead of being evacuated by air, for the sake of the companionship and in hopes of obtaining an exclusive story. He later wrote a book about his experiences, *Retreat with Stilwell*, one of the best published narratives of the walkout.

Paul Geren, the former faculty member at Judson College in Rangoon who had joined Seagrave's unit as an ambulance driver, wrote to friends that

> every man among us had to tear himself away from all his possessions, except the clothing he wore, a blanket for sleep, and whatever small treasures he could carry in his pockets, saving his carrying capacity for food and weapons which assumed a value above all other things.... I discarded what I had not already lost in Rangoon and Namkham (I supposed the retreat would be by way of Namkham where I had deposited my valuables, but before I knew it the Japanese were between Namkham and me), leaving me with practically nothing of what I brought from America or had bought since.... As we left the scene of great abandonment, a friendly Burman marched his wife out and loaded her with our shaving kits, clothing, bed rolls, etc., and marched her off, not bothering to strain himself with a load.[13]

Nurses and others are seen discarding nonessential items in a jungle clearing at the start of the "walkout" on 6 May 1942. "There were huge piles of equipment and stores to one side and some were being burned," said a British soldier who accompanied the march (U.S. Army photo, courtesy Grindlay family).

Lieutenant Fred Eldridge, an army public relations officer, was discovered the next day to be carrying a bedroll and extra clothing on one of the pack mules, in clear violation of Stilwell's orders. The general called the entire group together to point out the selfishness of one person and ordered Eldridge to carry no more than a small pack, his camera, and a rifle. Eldridge later said, "When the General heard about it, I got chewed out all right! It was an incident I wasn't very proud of and when he chewed me out, he was right, dead right."[14]

A final radio message was transmitted on 6 May before the trek began. Stilwell warned headquarters in New Delhi of the looming crisis:

> The Indian Government should be warned rice comma police and doctors urgently needed by refugees on all routes to India from Burma stop Large numbers on way stop All control gone stop Catastrophe is quite possible stop Am heading for Homalin and Imphal with party of one hundred period Hope to make Homalin May tenth period If possible comma send 500 pounds of food from Imphal by carriers to meet us at Homalin period Stilwell.

He also gave the group's itinerary to be followed in the weeks ahead:

General Stilwell in the jungle clearing on 6 May 1942, surrounded by his Chinese bodyguard and others who would follow him on the walkout. He was briefing everyone on the rules of the retreat, explaining that vehicles were being abandoned and that they would be walking to India in the days ahead (U.S. Army photo, courtesy of the Grindlay family).

Lieutenant Fred Eldridge, left, and General Stilwell, 1944 (location unknown) (U.S. Army photo, courtesy Grindlay family).

We abandon all transportation here. Our route will be Maingkaing—by raft down the Uyu River to Homalin—across Chindwin [River]—on foot over mountains to Ukhrul and Imphal.... This is our last radio message repeat our last message. Stilwell.

Then they took turns smashing the radio beyond repair to prevent it from being used by the Japanese and burned their codes and all file copies of messages.

Grindlay heard that a meeting had taken place among some of the American officers where a proposal was made by Colonel Benjamin Ferris, Stilwell's chief of staff, that the British and Seagrave units should be left behind. To drown his sorrows, Grindlay guzzled part of a bottle of Scotch that Colonel St. John was carrying with him, and then he went to Stilwell to lodge a vigorous protest, saying that he would rather be court-martialed than let the group be abandoned. Afterward, the surgeon took another stiff drink and passed out, later revived by St. John, who tossed him in the river. "When the general heard of the plan," Grindlay later wrote to his wife, "he got us together and in his famous speech ... told us he would never allow anyone to be left." The group lay down on the grass next to a stream to rest for the night and prepare for the strenuous day ahead.[15]

So far, the Stilwell group was staying ahead of the hordes of Chinese soldiers and civilian refugees that were pouring over jungle trails toward India. The Japanese were also closely pursuing the Americans and the British, but not fast enough. Second Lieutenant Hirano Mibu of the 214th Infantry Regiment of the 33rd Division recalled that his unit was slowed for five days by an outbreak of cholera. Lacking sufficient quantities of Ringer's saline solution (used to combat the dehydrating effects of cholera), the Japanese medics ingeniously resorted to injecting the men with juice from young palm fruit buds, laced with salt. The treatment worked, and the troops resumed their pursuit of the British. Hirano wrote later, "When we arrived at Shwegyi, a river crossing point to Kalewa, we found a large number of trucks and tanks left on the roadside but all British [and] Indian troops had already retreated towards India. To me, it was strangely impressive to see white mosquito nets left by the enemy swinging in the jungle."[16]

9

The Walkout

On the morning of 7 May, Stilwell's "walkout," as it came to be called, began. Grindlay's diary, which he scrupulously kept during the ordeal, clearly (and sometimes brutally) illuminates the pain, discomfort, exhaustion, and dangers the party experienced in the days that followed. "The first half of the 14 day march was hell, as was the second," he wrote to his wife after arriving in India. Colonel Robert Williams also continued his diary during the walkout, and while its entries are briefer than Grindlay's, it remains an excellent day-by-day chronicle of the escape. Both diaries present an accurate day-by-day picture of events and new viewpoints for observing the walkout throughout its grueling two weeks from Burma to India.

The walkers now included native guides, plus the Reverend Brayton Case; Stilwell's staff and his Chinese bodyguards under General Tseng; the contingent of British officers and enlisted ranks, as well as a couple former British forestry officials (including Major Castens), led by Colonel Davidson-Houston; the Seagrave unit with the FAU drivers; and some Indian civilian refugees—all told, about 110 people.

According to Grindlay,

> *Off after daybreak* [with] *Gen. S*[tilwell] *leading & carrying Tommy gun. Crossed river wading.... Then down the primeval jungle river the long undulating single file column led by yo-yo pole toting high stepping Burman, then Stillwell* [sic]. *Girls kept me in line (exhausted) & sang—causing those ahead to turn about (they were all exhausted & thought mornings hike equal to a 30 mi. march). Tea on bank along river then down river for a mile in pitch black—meeting luminous water rushes—feet now blistered & blisters worn off.*

The only sounds were the nurses singing and the usual noises of birds and the barking and hooting of monkeys, gibbons and deer. The walkers followed an elephant trail and stopped that evening next to an elephant camp, where the jangling of the animals' wooden bells kept them awake all night.

By sheer chance, a string of twenty empty pack mules turned up on the evening of the first day with three disreputable-looking handlers from Yunnan who said they were on their way to India. Williams wrote to his wife that these men were the "wildest looking ruffians you ever saw, with tiny mules."[1] Stilwell suspected they were opium smugglers but hired them immediately to carry mess equipment and bedrolls (which otherwise would have had to be discarded) and, later, men who collapsed from the heat, sunstroke and overexertion. At the same time, sixty local bearers were hired to help tote food and other necessities. "Oh, boy, what a break!" Stilwell exulted in his diary. The mules and drivers were placed in the charge of Lieutenant Eugene Laybourne and sent overland to rendezvous with the Stilwell column at Homalin. The rest of the group started hiking to Maingkaing, part of the time walking on shore, part of the time wading in the Chaunggyi River to the point where it joined the Uyu. Major Frank Merrill passed out from sunstroke (later identified as a heart attack, the first of three that he suffered during his CBI service), as did Lieutenant Tommy Lee, one of Stilwell's aides. Grindlay and others loaded Lee, Merrill, Colonel Henry Holcombe, and Major Felix Nowakowski onto air mattresses, which the FAU men towed through the river. General Sibert had "a hard time with sun," Grindlay noted,

Major Herbert "Beaver" Barton, left (British army), General Stilwell, center, and Jack Belden (*Time-Life* correspondent) somewhere in Burma (U.S. Army photo, courtesy Grindlay family).

9. The Walkout

Paul Geren, center, and Peter Tenant (head of China contingent of the Friends Ambulance Unit) pulling an inflatable mattress with an unidentified member of the Stilwell party aboard. Man at left unidentified (U.S. Army photo, courtesy Grindlay family).

which meant that he probably was suffering from either heat exhaustion or sunstroke as well.

They arrived at Maingkaing on the Uyu River in the late afternoon of 9 May, where they built rafts of bamboo to carry them west to Homalin. The men spent much of their time trying to keep the rafts afloat, "for [they] were grounded or breaking up all the time.... One night we were 2 ½ hours in a whirl pool and the other [night] we exhausted ourselves keeping the raft together after it hit bars or snags," Grindlay reported in a letter to his wife.

At the start, Stilwell had laid down strict rules to be followed on the walkout regarding daily food distribution and consumption, washing, shaving, and other matters, to maintain discipline, keep morale as high as possible, and ensure that people were kept fit enough to stay with the column. Stilwell promised that no one would be left behind, and so, if the group was to keep ahead of the Japanese, they had to keep moving, one way or another. The following routine was developed: have breakfast of coffee and oatmeal before daylight; march until 10:00 a.m.; rest for tea and sleep until 3:30 p.m.; eat a dinner of rice and chicken stew (when chickens were available for purchase from local villagers); resume walking until dark; camp and drink more tea; and go to bed. Most of the heat of the day was thus avoided, as was dehydration.

Building rafts on the Uyu River (U.S. Army photo, courtesy Grindlay family).

Quinine was dispensed liberally by Williams to stave off malaria (after the first airdrop, which included a bag of pills, was received), and all water was boiled before drinking. Despite the regimen of quinine, however, there still were several cases of malaria in the group, and, after they reached India, Grindlay had to continue treatment for at least four lingering cases among the officers.

The FAU men and other members of the Seagrave group were looked after by the nurses. According to George Parsons, "[They] walked with us in their little flip-flop sandals. They helped to keep us alive for we had almost no food ... and they knew how to collect roots and berries from the jungle which they would cook for us to eat."[2] The sweltering hot weather made riding rafts on the river much more preferable to marching, Williams and others had to admit. Badly blistered feet were beginning to heal under treatment administered by Williams, Grindlay and Ray Chesley, who spent evenings bandaging and wrapping blisters, scrapes, and cuts. On 11 May an RAF Wellington bomber dropped bully beef, crackers, cigarettes, British medical dressings, and adhesive tape. Grindlay had earlier lost Williams' medical officer's kit and Williams had lost the emergency tropical box he packed before the trek, so the fresh dressings and tape were most welcome. Grindlay and the nurses wove thatched roofs for the rafts to provide shade from the torrid sun. "Won admiration [from] Stillwell [sic]—our group did—& his appreciation later for [without] mat roofs it would have been unbearable," he wrote proudly in his diary.³

The group arrived at Homalin on the Chindwin River on the afternoon of 12 May, having chased off a rogue elephant along the way and abandoned the rafts, which were starting to fall apart anyway after three days of use. Two members of the FAU accompanied Tun Shein, the native "gofer" of the Seagrave unit, on a trip into town to buy shoes; they persuaded a shopkeeper to open his closed store and sell them twelve pairs. The group felt rested and relieved to be almost out of danger, but the forbidding mountains across the Chindwin looked "horribly high." Journalist Jack Belden begged Stilwell for a "sound bite" quote, and the latter said, not without rancor and sarcasm, "Here we are, damn it!" They stayed in a Buddhist monastery that night, the Seagrave group being assigned to the nunnery. Kukis and Nagas, staunch allies of the British, were substituted for the bearers who came from Maingkaing; these were hardy men who were acclimated to steep trails and high altitudes, which the walkout members would soon have to face.⁴

The next day, as they were about to leave, Laybourne's mule train, which had left them on 6 May, was spotted coming toward the town. The column,

Stilwell party in rafts on the Uyu River (U.S. Army photo, courtesy Grindlay family).

now united, crossed the river in dugouts and started trekking into the mountains on a trail that had recently been remade by the British to better accommodate horses and soldiers. By day's end, they had climbed from 500 feet to 4,000 feet and slept in nipa shacks on the mountain top. On 14 May, they were met by Thomas Arthur "Tim" Sharpe, president of the Manipur State Darbar (legislative body), who had been dispatched from Imphal with pack ponies and porters, his presence offering clear evidence that either the radio message of 6 May had been received in India or the Americans who were evacuated by air had reported Stilwell's walkout to his headquarters in New Delhi. Sharpe told the travelers, to their great relief, that from this point on the column would have three meals a day and "plenty of coolies [and] horses." He also brought news that Captain O'Hara had been promoted to major.[5]

Heavy rain, a sign of the fast-approaching monsoon season, fell on the mountain trail, causing men, mules and horses to slip, slide, and stick in the gluey mire as they trudged up and down the heights of the Chin Hills. Grindlay wrote, "Uphill over very steep trail, [with] alternate dense jungle & open dense, tall jungle grass patches.... For last hour of stiff climb [we] had drenching tropical thunder shower." Leeches were making their presence felt: O'Hara picked one off of his ankle, and Williams doused the wound with iodine and placed a bandage over it to prevent infection. He also "knocked [a leech] off

Major General Franklin Sibert (left) and Paul Geren (right) playing cards on a raft (U.S. Army photo, courtesy Grindlay family).

9. The Walkout

Officers resting at Homalin after the trip down the Uyu and Chindwin rivers. From left: Colonel Frederick McCabe, Colonel Robert Williams, and Lieutenant Eugene Laybourne (U.S. Army photo, courtesy Grindlay family).

St. John, stepped on it, [and] blood spurted to his knees." The group, now accompanied by about thirty ponies and 200 native bearers, was strung out for hundreds of yards along the trail. Fortunately, there were food dumps, which the tea planters and natives under Sharpe's direction had placed at each halt, and there was much rejoicing at the news that only about a week's marching remained to reach safety in India. That night two pigs were provided by the local villagers, killed and roasted while everyone dried out their clothes over fires, and Williams tried out a ration of British rum, which he pronounced, "Not bad." The Seagrave group ate heartily and then collapsed into welcome sleep in two huts.

The next day (15 May) was just as challenging:

> Up early [Grindlay wrote].... Up very stiff trail, largely thru jungle grass [with] marvelous view [of] Chindwin & Uyu [Rivers] valley—we can see easily our entire course of past [week].... Hot, sunny, shadeless, humid.... Again passing rain for last 2 hours, cold as we crossed a knife edge cornice, wetting the trail, causing our 28 horses to slip, drenching & chilling us. Just before dusk, on down slope of ridge [with] fleecy clouds below & last view of Chindwin behind for good, arrived at a Kuki village.... Another full meal, drying of clothes & to bed.

The Stilwell group needed their rest that night, for the following day they laboriously struggled "over a [mountain] shoulder & down to the deepest chasm of a rocky ravine I [Grindlay] ever saw. Then up the longest, steepest, hottest grinding trail, passing over the ridge & just beyond to our noon halt. Terrible strain—the men all nearly collapsed, several of the girls very weary & I had to have them await the ponies." At the lunch halt in a Naga village, they were served frothing rice beer in a gourd and another unidentified alcoholic beverage sipped through a bamboo straw. "Got a bit of a jag [with] Jack Belden on these 2," Grindlay wrote.[6]

It was at this stop that Williams received news of his promotion to full colonel and, in a brief ceremony, was sworn in by Frank Merrill, to the delight of the villagers who gathered around to watch. Williams also handed out quinine, as he had been doing all along, but cases of malaria still broke out, either because some people avoided the medicine or because, like Colonel St. John, it upset their stomachs and they could not hold it down.[7]

The travelers were off again at 2:00 p.m., descending a steep gorge and reaching the bottom at 4:00 p.m. "Bathed in rushing river & ate," Grindlay wrote that night. The group camped in four long thatched sheds of bamboo, where they ate that night around the cooking fires. He had contracted conjunctivitis a day or so previously, and the smoke made his eyes "miserable

A rest break at Homalin: from left, Lieutenant Colonel George Sliney, Major Frank Merrill, Major Felix Nowakowski (U.S. Army photo, courtesy Grindlay family).

[with] pus, [causing] sticking lids." The group slept on platforms made of bamboo, and "[the] knots & bends of the branches were hell—& turning over an experience."

By this time the group was more than twenty miles into India, passing through an area that would be the scene of savage fighting two years later when the Japanese army launched a massive attack on British defenses in Assam. At noon they halted at another Naga village, where trees were "hung [with] tiger and miffin skulls," as Grindlay observed, and the houses had elaborate carvings on them. They had walked fourteen miles in half a day over rugged terrain, and, after a lunch of tea and biscuits, they "went on up, up & up thru pine forest to village of Omphin," on a hilltop. Here, in an "alpine setting [with] huge sheer [mountain] back drops," it was "cold, clear & dry." This camp was

Even high-ranking officers get hot. General Sibert and Lieutenant Colonel Sliney cool off in their underwear on a rest break (U.S. Army photo, courtesy Grindlay family).

called the "flea stop" after the Seagrave group spent the night scratching the pests' bites.

On 18 May they arose in the dark, breakfasted, and were on the trail by 5:15. They zigzagged up a ridge that Grindlay estimated to be several thousand feet in height. They had seen the trail the day before from the opposite side of the valley and dreaded its ascent. Once over the mountain, a treacherously steep decent was followed by another stiff climb until the group reached Ukhrul, Sharpe's home and the largest village yet encountered, situated at an altitude of 6,500 feet. While talking with the British soldiers in the group about the "hot spots & highlights" of Calcutta, Grindlay passed a Naga school and a camp of Ghariwallis, soldiers reputed to be as tough as the Gurkhas; they marched a mile farther on to Sharpe's house, "a red sheet iron roofed white stucco place," Grindlay noted. The American and British officers were quartered in the main house, while the Seagrave group stayed in the guest house. Their baggage finally arrived: "Naga bearers straggling more than usual for they stopped for beer in their home village." The Seagrave party took baths "in icy air in [a] well & girls washed clothes. Had clinic for feet & drying clothes by roaring fire in our house. Picked fleas.... Did 21 miles today."

The next morning, soon after starting out at 5:30 a.m., a torrential rain started. "Kept along ridge for 11 miles in clouds & rain & bitter cold," Grindlay reported. The travelers descended a steep, slippery trail, and then they went up a steeper one that Grindlay estimated at 3,000 feet. The noon halt took place in rain and clouds, where they ate sausage and biscuits. It was so muddy that no one could sit down. The rain finally stopped after lunch, and the group dried out.

The days of grueling climbs and descents were taking a toll on Grindlay. "I was getting absolutely exhausted for some reason," he wrote on 19 May. Late that afternoon they reached a narrow steel suspension bridge "on other side of which was end of motor [road coming from India]." A party of American officers arrived, some of them the men from Stilwell's staff who had been

Major Nowakowsi drinking Naga beer through a bamboo straw during the march out of Burma, May 1942 (U.S. Army photo, courtesy Grindlay family).

9. The Walkout

From left, General Stilwell, Lieutenant Colonel Frank Dorn, and Jack Belden take a rest break somewhere on the walkout (U.S. Army photo, courtesy Grindlay family).

evacuated from Burma by air before the walkout began and who had prepared for Stilwell's arrival in India. Stilwell lined the group up and told them that trucks were coming, but there was better ground across the bridge and they would camp on the other side. Everyone listened raptly to the report of how these officers had tried to find the walkers. The last radio message sent from Burma before the radio was smashed was received by Major General Lewis Brereton, commander of Tenth Air Force, in India, "& this was all that they had in evidence we were heading for Imphal." Then, three nights before, a runner was dispatched with messages from Stilwell and Jack Belden that disclosed which trail they were taking so food stocks could be sent to them. Grindlay was elated that "[they] brought in a couple bottles whiskey (I had a nip) a few cigarettes & some chocolate (how delicious). Told us of outside news, most sensational was bombing of Tokyo by our medium bombers under Doolittle." Williams was pleased that toothbrushes and toothpaste had also been brought to them, besides the candy and cigarettes. In his diary he told a slightly different story from Grindlay's, reporting that after the radio message was received, the Americans began patrolling all the trails exiting the Chin Hills and aircraft were sent up to search for them.[8]

Then Stilwell took Grindlay aside "& asked [me] about health of the ill ones—Seagrave taking too much sulfanilanide accounts for his symptom of heart [disease] etc. I thought." St. John and Chesley were suffering from malaria, as Williams had noted three days earlier. The Seagrave unit set up camp in an auto shed after crossing the bridge, rudely kicking out the Indian refugees who had already occupied it.

On 20 May, they boarded seven British trucks and two ambulances for the trip to Imphal. After a slippery, slithering ride of twenty-three miles over mountainous muddy roads, they reached the town, where Stilwell held a press conference. Glaring at news cameras and reporters, he made no secret of his frustration and anger with the events of the past three months in Burma: "I claim we got a hell of a beating. We got run out of Burma and it is humiliating as hell. I think we ought to find out what caused it, go back and retake it."

Stilwell and his staff later prepared a post-campaign report for the War Department, which was so critical of the Chinese and British efforts that it was ordered suppressed. Among his conclusions, Stilwell noted that the loss of Burma could not be blamed on any single person or government. It was impossible to "create a picture of the [campaign] with all its tragedy, its absurdities, its broken promises, and its stupidities" in a single report. "But," Stilwell continued, "the system of political appointments, official ineptitude,

A group of Chin porters who were hired to carry supplies for the walkout members (U.S. Army photo, courtesy Grindlay family).

Colonel Robert Williams showing off the beard he grew during the trek out of Burma, May 1942 (U.S. Army photo, courtesy of the Grindlay family).

the hope that someone else would do the job, the indifference—all reflected in individuals the attitude of the higher agencies of the governments they represented." The British civil authorities seemed to resent what they viewed as "undue interference with their prerogatives by the British military establishment, and failed to co-operate until forced to do so by events." As a result, stocks of rice were woefully inadequate, both for civilian refugees and for the Chinese armies in Burma. In addition, hundreds of tons of salt stored in warehouses in Mandalay were lost to the Japanese through the bungling of the civil government, Stilwell alleged. Chinese delays in providing transportation for their men, combined with "reticence on the part of the Chinese high command to push vigorously the defense of Burma," were among the causes for the "final disaster."[9]

On 24 May, in a meeting with Major General Lewis Brereton, commander of the Tenth Air Force, in Calcutta, Stilwell unloaded more anger and frustration. "He is fuming mad about things he saw on his retreat," Brereton wrote in his diary. "Among the things that rankled in his soul are ... 800 trucks standing idle at Lashio when he, asking for 150 to move troops into action, got 34 ... trucks moving north into China carrying loot while soldiers go hungry ... a Chinese Lieutenant General of the Quartermaster Corps heading north along the Burma Road with a Buick sedan on a 2 ½ ton truck that should have been carrying guns and ammunition ... British soldiers throwing away ammunition and weapons on their way out of Burma."[10]

Paul Geren wrote a circular letter for friends a week later that described how twenty Indian refugees in the party that had followed the Stilwell group died en route to the railhead, while six others died on the station platform. Grindlay borrowed a razor and shaved off his "heavy red & white beard. Left mustache." The Seagrave unit treated the malaria cases among the American officers (including St. John, Chesley, and Holcombe) and turned them over to Williams for further medication. Williams found time on the night of 22 May to send a radio message to his wife, Barbara ("Bobbie"), via correspondent Alfred Wagg's radio link: "Out of Burma tired but OK, love, Bob."[11]

On 23 May, Stilwell's staff (including Grindlay and the sick men) was put on a special train at Dimapur and taken via Gauhati on the Brahmaputra River to Calcutta. The train was delayed at one point for twenty-two hours due to a collision with another locomotive. Paul Geren reported that the train was "reeking as an Indian train only can reek with scores of cases of dysentery."

The Seagrave unit remained behind at a fifty-two-bed American Baptist Missionary Women's Hospital at Gauhati. The unit was "not needed" at Imphal, in the estimation of the deputy director of medical services of the British army, mainly because of a shortage of rations.[12] Before leaving for Calcutta with the American army contingent, Grindlay walked down to visit the quarters of the hospital group to say goodbye, the nurses yelling "Uncle Grindlay, Uncle Grindlay" and sobbing. Even the tough army surgeon was teary-eyed.[13]

"On 24th May, a group of weary, filthy, bearded men dumped their bags down in the lobby of the Great Eastern Hotel in Calcutta and demanded rooms." They were Stilwell's staff—"Uncle Joe's Mob," as they had been dubbed. Wilfred G. Burchett (1911–1985), an Australian journalist who had worked in Burma, was there when the men trudged into the hotel. He noted that Colonel Adrian St. John's appearance had gone from being red-faced, hearty, and weighing more than two hundred pounds to that of a man with "a tremendous greying beard[;] his clothes hung as if all their supports had been withdrawn, his face was pallid and hollow." St. John was still suffering from the effects of malaria, but he had regained some of his feisty spirit, enough to explode to Burchett, "If anybody brings rice near me again, I'm gonna disembowel 'em with a chopstick." Burchett asked Fred Eldridge how Stilwell had held up on the walkout: "Hell, that was one picnic excursion for him. He's just made of steel wire, rubber and concrete for guts."[14] The weary travelers spent a day and a half in luxury at the Great Eastern, although Grindlay reported that he was feeling miserable with renal colic in the same kidney that had given him a "perfect hell of a day" back in Burma.

Grindlay took St. John to their room, put him to bed, washed his pajamas, and then had a hot bath with beer on the side. Afterward, he went to the bar and enjoyed cocktails with "a bunch of young Am[erican] lieut[enants], the pilots etc. who had bombed Tokyo [i.e., Doolittle's raiders]. Told how they hedge-hopped & dropped bombs on unprepared targets. Also that they had bailed out just over Chinese lines & lost every plane (med[ium] bombers) but not a man—but hush hush! Huge dinner of many courses. Then to a movie in a real theater [with] Eldridge & O'Hara." The next day Grindlay's renal colic returned, with dull nausea, cramps, and backache. He ate only a little ice cream all day, which did not help to alleviate his symptoms, although he summoned enough energy to draw pay from the Services of Supply office near the hotel and to accompany St. John and Chesley to Whiteway, Laidlaw & Company (one of Calcutta's largest department stores) to purchase a change of clothing.[15]

From Calcutta the military personnel were flown to Stilwell's rear echelon headquarters in New Delhi. The ailing personnel from the walkout—Americans, British and Chinese—were treated for several weeks by Grindlay and other doctors in a new, air-conditioned hospital. Grindlay also had four officers with malaria living with him in his hotel suite, including Colonel St. John, and he took treatment for it himself, even though he did not have a clinical case of it. The surgeon was down to 135 pounds but starting to feel much better after having regular baths, clean clothes, and good meals.[16]

Meanwhile, Seagrave's unit, along with two of his doctors (Bill Cummings and Ted Gurney), plus the FAU drivers and the nurses, began receiving Chinese wounded coming in from Burma at the hospital in Gauhati on the banks of the Brahmaputra River.[17] By the end of June, the facility was filling up with civilian refugees who were in deplorable condition from their trek out of Burma. "They are starved and emaciated and suffering so much from lack of vitamins that they can't swallow," Seagrave wrote. "With this starvation background they have picked up the most virulent forms of malaria, amoebic and bacillary dysentery." Fortunately, there were no cases of cholera among the refugees: those victims had already died along the trails. Drugs were virtually nonexistent. The dysentery cases were housed in one of the former dormitories, where flies proliferated. Many of the patients were also plagued with Naga sores (infected leech bites), which only added to their misery. Seagrave minced no words in blaming much of their condition on the enemy:

> I can't help but feel that the Japanese were very clever when they decided to let the Indian refugees leave the country. They took pains to see that the refugees would starve by robbing them of their money and food supplies as they went through their lines.... Making starvation enroute certain, the Japs thereby also made inevitable the acquisition of the worst forms of contagious disease, and the arrival, in a poorly prepared province of India, of thousands of sick who would each one be a source of contagion to the whole country. It seems like a new variety of bacterial warfare![18]

The Seagrave party stayed at Gauhati until July and then moved to Ramgarh, a road junction about two hundred air miles northwest of Calcutta and the site of a British POW base that once housed more than 5,000 German and Italian prisoners of war (mostly captured in North Africa). The medical personnel were assigned buildings in the former Italian section of the camp and set up a hospital to treat the thousands of Chinese soldiers struggling out of Burma well into the summer and fall of 1942. These men would form the nucleus of a new, rearmed and reinvigorated army that would return to Burma in 1943 to begin the reconquest of the country they had tried so hard to defend.

10

Hambleton's Story (Continued)

While all of the members of the group led by General Stilwell had successfully escaped to India, Captain Roscoe Hambleton was still struggling to flee Burma with the Chinese Fifth Army headquarters staff and bodyguard of troops and the 22nd Division, which remained intact despite having lost many of its men in engagements with the Japanese. On 23 May, the same day that Grindlay and the Stilwell staff left Gauhati by train for Calcutta, Hambleton and Lieutenant Lean of the British army decided to try to follow a jeep track from Maingkwan via Myitkyina to Ledo and safety. This plan seems to have been greatly misguided, because reports were being received that Myitkyina had fallen to the Japanese, which would effectively block any attempts to reach Ledo by road. Once the news had time to sink in, Hambleton and Lean realized that their only option was to remain with the Chinese.

The Fifth Army contingent, consisting of perhaps 2,500 men, had made slow but steady progress after crossing the Uyu River and was heading northwest toward India. They followed a path along a creek but found few natives and many deserted villages. The army was undisciplined and untrained, in Hambleton's estimation, which angered and frustrated him by turns and caused him a great deal of stress and hardship in the days to come. The food supply varied from day to day, between ample and almost nothing, causing him additional emotional and physical upset. One day (26 May) Hambleton wrote in his diary, "Food pretty limited—only rice and sardines. No lunch." The next day, however, he had a lunch of fresh fish and some kind of juice and a good dinner of beef, liver and fish.

Hambleton probably did not know that an exchange of conflicting radio messages had occurred between Fifth Army headquarters and Chungking. Over the span of a few days, Chiang Kai-shek sent orders to General Tu Li-ming, the Fifth Army commander, first directing Tu to set up a defensive line at Myitkyina, then changing his mind when it became apparent that the

Japanese were going to beat them there and ordering the army to evacuate to China. But all of the escape routes were effectively cut off by the Japanese, and the army would have to fight its way through about two hundred miles of enemy-occupied territory, so further orders were received to head for Maingkwan, ninety miles northwest of Myitkyina, and on to India via Shingbwiyang in the Hukawng Valley. It is doubtful whether Hambleton or General Tu, or anyone else in the army, had any inkling of how difficult such a trek would become.[1]

By this time, General Tu was sick with a relapsing fever he had caught from bed bugs and lice and was being carried on a litter. The army crossed the Chindwin River and took a "fairly easy road" that paralleled the watercourse to a tributary, where the Chinese paused until a means of fording was found. It was finally decided to use native dugouts, and, once across, Hambleton had a good dinner and good rest, even taking a relaxing swim in the river. He wrote hopefully that perhaps the hardest part of the trek was over. On 1 June, after a dusty day, he wrote that he was "tired and very dirty." Word was received that Stilwell had reached India and the 200th Division was in China. The news that others had escaped depressed him. Two days later the conditions had gone from dust to rain. "Worse and worse—cold and soaked," Hambleton noted. He made a shelter for the night of leaves and his raincoat, where he was able to dry out a little, and he ate some rice for dinner. All night he and Lieutenant Lean sat up "through long hours on my bedroll and [tried] to dodge leaks in [the] roof. Baggage sodden and rain steady and heavy," Hambleton wrote gloomily. It was the onset of the monsoon season in Burma.[2]

The rains continued almost nonstop for the next two days. Hambleton and Lean shared some of the last tinned rations that Hambleton was saving. They were soaked and spent one night with five Chinese soldiers in a leaf hut with no food and no water, choking on a smoky fire. As on previous nights, they sat up "with rain dripping on shoulders, back and face. What a mess." Hambleton's left leg was left bloody after a big leech had worked its way under his pant leg. The group caught up to the headquarters unit after three days of trying and walked all day on 5 June with the army surgeon, Dr. Cheng Jen-yu, as they followed General Tu's litter. That night they camped in a roomier shelter with the doctor and four others, plus Tu's dog. Hambleton ate some dry rice and drank coffee. "No sugar," he complained. He then stretched out on the damp ground, even though the quarters were cramped, and smoked before falling asleep to the sound of pouring rain and leeches crawling into the shelter and feasting on the men.[3]

The following day the rain slackened and the sun came out for a time, but the steep trail was deep in mud. Hambleton stayed near General Tu to be sure of getting some food. A heavy thunderstorm broke out early in the evening, and the column halted, as the darkness and rain made it hard to see

10. Hambleton's Story (Continued)

the trail. It was impossible to light a fire because of a lack of matches and dry wood, so the men sat on the wet ground all night. Once again Hambleton's frustration bubbled to the surface. "Most irritable," he grumbled to his diary, "example of inefficiency, stupidity, and indifference to other men. Damn mess this whole business as we wander all over muddy hills instead of being on direct route."

By the next morning the rain had stopped, but after five hours they reached a river swollen with runoff and impossible to cross. Everyone sat down and did nothing. "No more rice or food supplies," Hambleton wrote. "All colossal stupidity. Am covered with dirt, insect bites, and scratches." He conferred with General Tu, who had recovered from his fever, and learned that there were five tributaries ahead of them that had to be crossed, which meant they would have to build rafts. "Maybe reach Shingbwiyang in [a] week," Tu estimated. In the meantime, Doctor Cheng (along with four mules carrying food and medical supplies) was lost somewhere behind them. They dined that night on "dead mule meat, banana roots, pumpkin, and muddy water. Slept on damp ground on slope."[4]

Conditions did not improve in the following days. On the bank of the Chindwin, men were cutting bamboo for rafts. Hambleton passed a miserable birthday on 8 June (his forty-seventh), suffering as he was from swollen feet, with a ten-day growth of beard, his shirt caked stiff with mud, "hands and feet in bad shape," and lacking tobacco. All the men and the animals were suffering from hunger and fatigue. The army was camped on a hillside, with General Tu on the top, who asked questions about the United States and hoped to visit there after the war. The food supply remained undependable: one day there was only oatmeal for breakfast, while the next day the general distributed some chicken in broth. That night there was beef from a bullock that the 65th Regiment had brought to the general, supplemented with rice and washed down with coffee. The next morning a little more of the bullock appeared in a weak broth.

The outlook for Fifth Army was worsening by the day. General Liao Yao-hsiang commander of the 22nd Division (which was following the Fifth Army headquarters), arrived in camp on 9 June and said that his men were suffering severely from lack of food. "What a farce this trip is," Hambleton grumbled, "unnecessary suffering and death from bad decisions and lack of foresight. A pitiful group now. River rising—spirits falling. No food. News that 38th Div arrived in India week ago—left Mansi few days after us.... Waited in rain and got some of Gen Tu's pumpkin. Back to miserable shelter. Rain all night.... Path [to a bridge] is small river of mud. No fire for coffee tonight. Two toenails have rotted off. [Road to] Shing[bwiyang] OK hereon. This is most appalling, wretched experience man could have without proper equipment ... large numbers of men have died—drowned and starved."[5]

The rain and hardships continued. Hambleton and Lean crossed the river on a small bridge built by Chinese engineers. Hambleton tried to get his baggage mule across, but it balked. He ate a brief dinner of rice, horse meat gravy, and a piece of dried beef, and he borrowed some tobacco and smoked in the dark while "battling biting insects." He fantasized that night of "better times ahead, also as every day we will eat, back in civilization and that Sunny [his wife] is going to fix for us." The next morning, 11 June, the mule was finally urged to swim across the river, but it drowned midstream, leaving Hambleton with only two small shoulder bags and a blanket roll. With his heavy raincoat, the load made his shoulders sore. On 12 June he reported that the road was deep "slimy, slippery sticky mud," and, having no food or water, he had to use all of his strength to keep going. Two days later he discovered that it was hard to sleep because his bones stuck out too much and he needed padding on which to lie comfortably.

Then, on 17 June, things began looking up. Near Taro, American and RAF transport planes flew over and made three supply drops, totaling 27,200 pounds, which General Tu had requested two days earlier. Most of the goods were in the form of free drops—that is, dropped without using parachutes so that more would hit the drop zone and not float off into the jungle. "Troops rejoiced as planes were dropping supplies. We are also very grateful," Tu radioed to India after the air drop. "In the forenoon, supplies were mostly dropped on wrong locations, across the [Chindwin] river. They were mostly picked up by Indian & British troops.... Please drop 30 percent on top of estimated quantity. Also drugs for digestive disorder." In addition, Tu asked for food, medicine and salt sufficient for 7,000 men for five days.[6]

Colonel Haydon Boatner and his staff in Dibrugarh, from which most of the air drops originated, understood the dire situation faced by Fifth Army but also learned that General Tu and his men were grabbing most of the supplies and letting the soldiers of the Chinese 22nd Division starve. A radio message from General Liao on 25 June told of the Fifth Army headquarters troops taking 80,000 pounds of supplies and leaving the 22nd Division to feed on grass and roots. Also, some 30,000 pounds of goods promised by the Chinese government had not arrived. "We earnestly request [that supply drops be concentrated] on 26 and 27 June without regard to weather. This will enable us to resume march to Shingbwiyang," Liao radioed. In the meantime, General Tu continued to send what the Americans considered greatly exaggerated requests for food and supplies, and they accused Tu of inflating the number of troops in his headquarters force. However, Hambleton presented a different picture in his diary, noting that even Tu and his headquarters unit were living off horse meat, handfuls of rice, and anything else that could be either foraged from natives or made up from jungle ingredients, an indication that the air drops were insufficient.

10. Hambleton's Story (Continued)

Unquestionably, despite being inadequate, the three drops on 17 June were a great relief to the Chinese army, including as they did rice, salt, dried fish, canned vegetables, and medicines. The weather cleared, and Hambleton happily reported that he had obtained an empty can in which to boil water for washing his shirt, underwear, and handkerchief. He was able to relax and smoke, wash his hair, and watch the sun set. But he was afflicted with an infected and badly swollen left foot, and he could not get his shoe on. The swelling subsided somewhat a couple of days later, and he was able to wear his shoe again, but the foot remained sore and swollen. He was happy that he was having good bowel movements—apparently his tension was easing. And, of course, a better diet was helping the situation.

The rains started again after a brief dry spell, but the going was slightly easier because the road along the Chindwin had leveled. The food shortage was relieved by more air drops; canned bully beef arrived, as did turnips, rice, and cheese and milk. On 23 June Hambleton wrote that they had passed "many bodies and skeletons (45–50) last couple days," which he thought might have been men from the 96th Division, which was also heading for Shingbwiyang and then on to Fort Hertz via Putao. This division was brutally looting and victimizing the natives as it progressed up the Hukawng Valley ahead of the Fifth Army headquarters and the 22nd Division. Only after General Tu arrived in Shingbwiyang and took command of the division did something approaching control appear. As word spread of the Chinese approach, the natives abandoned their villages and fled into the jungle to hide. Thus, when Hambleton and the rest of the Fifth Army headquarters came through the area, they found only deserted villages and dilapidated buildings in which to seek shelter.[7]

On 27 June, the army made a tortuous climb up steep trails on slippery rock ledges and passed through two villages filled with skeletons. Hambleton did not note whether they were Chinese soldiers or civilian refugees, who were also pouring through the area by the thousands as they tried to reach safety in India. Tu and his headquarters force were within three miles of Shingbwiyang and set up camp in a valley on level ground. It rained hard, and in the morning Hambleton and Lean "discovered we were in a small lake." Lean set off to find higher ground and dropped his pipe in the water, which was almost hip deep. "Everyone scrambled up to higher ground." The rain continued all night. "No food, no rest, no nothing—tempers getting short. Some of the Chinese had food but refused to share it." Planes could be heard overhead, but the inclement weather prevented them from locating the column. The 22nd Division at Taro experienced the same conditions, reporting to Boatner's headquarters in Assam, "Food and medical supplies ... in this division totally lacking and our present position ... hindered by flood, is particularly desperate." Supplies were requested for 5,000 men for ten days.[8]

Adding to the problems was the almost constant confusion resulting from poor guides and their inability to find trails. Soldiers were put to work cutting a new road because they had lost the main trail to Shingbwiyang; instead of reaching the town on 30 June, they were forced to pitch camp again after encountering swamps and swollen rivers. "What a disorganized mess," Hambleton fumed. "[Don't] even know where they are." The next day the army set out to march to Shingbwiyang but was blocked by the Taron River in flood. Hambleton's growing frustration is painfully evident in his diary entry for 1 July:

> Word passed we would go back to starting place and not Shingbwiyang.... This aimless wandering is inhuman under these conditions. Worse part was to see Army planes overhead dropping supplies at Shingbwiyang only a few miles away. We pulled ourselves together and started back—slow going—nearly to last nights camp and then off on new path just cut.... Came to river crossing on logs again ... got over safely. Word that Hq is only three hours away, but on and on again. Dark settled down and then hard rain. Darling [he wrote to his wife]—I needed all the courage right there, but strength almost gone. Pitch dark and stumbled along through bamboo tunnels and slimy path. Couldn't see a thing. At last some shouting and saw fires ahead. Came to shelters.... Had smoke ... with rain dripping all over me. Entirely soaked. Put our coat on roof but little help. Sat crouched all night, shivering. Mind only on things ahead as I'd go nuts worrying about present. How many more days of this wandering desperately. 22nd Div also coming in [to the] same place.... No food of course.

Rumors spread that General Tu had gone ahead and reached Shingbwiyang, and Hambleton, Lean, and a few others were ordered to join him in a boat that would cross the river to the town. The baggage was piled in the boat, but when another person jumped on board, the boat sank. "Got now entirely and completely soaked." They finally got the boat righted and crossed over to the road to Shingbwiyang. The general sent them some broken cookies, which Hambleton, Lean, and their Chinese servant boy stuffed into their mouths as fast as possible. A messenger from Shingbwiyang arrived with cans of bully beef and cauliflower and some dried apricots, which tasted like nectar to the half-starved men. They staggered into the town and were "shocked" to see that there were only a few houses instead of a big settlement, as they had thought it would be. Still, they were all hopeful that the worst was over and were temporarily assigned to one of the "houses" (which were in reality only crude sheds) by Clive North, the local British administrator.

> [Shingbwiyang is] run by North, Asst. District Commissioner—in house next door. Headquarters was his servants' place.... Peculiar chap—half sick after looking after this Indian refugee camp. Gave us each cigarettes, milk, and we shared tin of PEACHES. Almost too much luxury and change for stomach. Got lowdown on whole situation. English planes bringing in Indian supplies—large amounts looted by Chinese (Advance 65th Regiment) and helluva mixed up situation.[9]

10. Hambleton's Story (Continued)

Hambleton and Lean were assigned to a shed on the edge of the dropping field with other English refugees, almost all of them British soldiers. He listed their names in his diary:

> Captain Young, [Sergeant] Shaw, Corporal Cornec, Russell (Contractor in Burma), Carroll (weak sister RMC), Sergeant Florence (Anglo-Indian), Pop (Indian campaigner of last war), Baxter (Anglo-Indian).

Captain Young and Sergeant Shaw had walked through the Hukawng Valley from Myitkyina. They had volunteered to accompany a group of orphaned children and staff from the Bishop Strachan's Home in Rangoon, led by its headmistress, Lillian Bald, who during the trip up from Rangoon had picked up refugee children from at least three other schools. She and her charges had reached Milestone 102 on the road to Fort Hertz and were reaching exhaustion. She appealed to the British army for help, and some of the children and older staff members were taken by truck to the distant outpost. Young and Shaw volunteered to accompany between twenty and fifty children, and Miss Bald, when they were diverted from the Fort Hertz road westward over very difficult trails to Maingkwan and then northwestward through the Hukawng Valley to Shingbwiyang. Young had gone on ahead with a letter from Miss Bald begging for food and transportation to help them get to Shingbwiyang. He had arrived there at the end of June.[10]

Baxter, the Anglo-Indian, made chapattis with flour and served them with jam and tea, and the hungry new arrivals dived into the wonderful food. Fatigue was hitting them with a vengeance, and after a late dinner at General Tu's headquarters, they collapsed on gunny sacks and blankets. Shingbwiyang was a welcome relief after weeks on the trail, but, as Hambleton wrote, it was far from being a comfortable place. It "is almost a swamp from rain—dirt, disease, and death. Flies by hundreds in this place in daytime."

For the time being, there was more food available as long as Hambleton, Lean, and their new friends made it a point to eat breakfast and dinner with General Tu, who lived better than the rest of his men. Enjoying privileges as a commander that were not extended to most of his soldiers, his meals were supplemented by chapattis and marmalade, margarine, and sugar from North's stores. Indian and Chinese supplies were being brought in by airdrops and getting mixed up so that Indian troops and civilians received some of the Chinese foodstuffs and the Chinese were getting the supplies meant for the Indians. Many of the Chinese soldiers were not getting as much food as the Indians and took to looting it at gunpoint. Four or five people were dying daily in the squalor in the town from disease and starvation. Some British officers looted North's stocks, and the assistant district commissioner became extremely wary of all military personnel thereafter. The Fourth of July passed with almost no recognition of it except that General Tu distributed a little brandy with which to celebrate. Hambleton tried to acquire a pair of high boots, as his own shoes were "shot," his feet were always wet, and he could not get his infected foot to heal unless he could keep it dry. "Hope we can get up off floor instead [of] grubbing hands in dirt all time," he noted in his diary. "Beard getting pretty long."[11]

General Tu and his army were settling into a comfortable existence at Shingbwiyang. Part of this had to do with the order Tu had received from Chiang Kai-shek to form a defensive line in the Hukawng Valley instead of moving on to India, but some of it was owing to a growing lackadaisical demeanor brought about by the relatively easy life that the food and clothing drops from American and British aircraft created among the troops. British relief officers working with civilian refugees noticed that they, too, were becoming lethargic and unwilling to travel the remaining ninety miles to Ledo as long as they received provisions. The Chinese asked for 100,000 pounds of supplies to be dropped at Shingbwiyang every day, a request that Colonel Boatner brusquely dismissed as impossible due to shortages of aircraft and undependable weather.[12]

On days when flying weather was good, six or more planes a day could fly in to drop supplies, and food was then plentiful. On 6 July, for example, six American and eight RAF transports made supply drops, and Hambleton and his companions feasted on a veritable banquet of baked beans, tea, beef, jam, figs, and sugar, which they enjoyed in fresh new clothing that was included in the shipment. But, despite the air drops, the supply situation at Shingbwiyang was anything but ample, as many flights were aborted because of bad weather or mechanical problems, and many bags were also lost in the river or jungle. The refugees were selling their personal goods to purchase food, and the soldiers were doing the same. Lieutenant Colonel Coates, a British liaison officer with the Fifth Army, was starting to look "pretty peaked"; Young, Hambleton, Baxter, and Lean were afflicted to varying degrees with malaria, fevers of unknown origin (FUOs) and chills; and Dr. Cheng was administering injections of an unnamed drug (possibly sulfa) to Hambleton for Naga sores. Hambleton was also trying to cure his sores by sponging them each morning in hot water. "Can't seem to gain much strength," he worried. His lack of energy resulting from the steadily inadequate diet and recurring fever caused him to neglect the cleaning of his rifle. He was thinking of ways to signal to American pilots that he was in the camp and met with General Tu to discuss the construction of an airfield for small planes. News circulated that the main "refugee trail" and the Ledo Road past Pangsau Pass were nearly impassable owing to deep mud and landslides, which made the Chinese army and civilian refugees extremely reluctant to cover the last leg of their journey to India, although dumps of food and medications at Hkalak Ga, Hpachet, Ranglum, and Tirap—names that would

10. Hambleton's Story (Continued)   117

become better known to Americans and Chinese in the next two years—were being stocked for the anticipated hordes of people in weeks to come.

General Tu assigned 300 men to build a light plane landing strip (which was never finished and ultimately proved unusable), and Hambleton had the Chinese send a message to Boatner's headquarters saying that it was under way. He fervently hoped that the U.S. Army would see fit to evacuate him by air, a desperate plan at best given the near impossibility of doing so. Boatner sent a message inquiring about the status of the airfield, which Hambleton took to General Liao of the 22nd Division for a response because he had an operable radio. Hambleton also requested a bag of food supplies for himself, and one arrived the next day. It contained twenty pounds of rice, sixty cans of nutritious army rations (meat and beans, hash and beans, meat and vegetable stew), and boxes of C-rations containing biscuits, candy, sugar, atta (a whole wheat flour used in many Indian breads), and coffee. He gave some of the contents to others in his group and picked up additional rice from General Tu, totaling forty pounds, plus apricots, tea, bully beef, and sugar from the Chinese.

At last, on 12 July, General Tu and the Fifth Army headquarters troops, including a bodyguard unit and a battalion of the 65th Regiment, packed up and set out for India, followed by the 22nd Division two days later. They were loaded with supplies airdropped in previous days and would supply themselves from the food dumps up the road to Assam. Hambleton recognized that their departure would greatly ease the supply situation. He made what turned out to be a crucial decision not to risk his fading strength by accompanying them, instead waiting until all hope of air evacuation was gone. "Hard just wasting time though amid these flies, diseased air and dirt, but maybe it has all been a 'Test by Fire,'" he wrote with an almost audible sigh. Besides, he felt that he had to stay behind and nurse Lieutenant Lean, who was suffering from an FUO. By then, Boatner had written off air evacuation, although Hambleton did not know that. If he had, he might have gathered what strength that remained and made a determined attempt to leave Shingbwiyang with the Chinese. "Am too sarcastic and quick tempered," he admitted to his diary. He might also have added stubborn and indecisive. "Lean is too British, selfish, and indifferent for smooth cooperation, but that's another test." In any event, Hambleton was not anxious to be in the company of the Chinese army again, "as am well fed up with Chinese military in general. Broken promises, looting, inefficiency, intrigue, murder, deceit." But they would have at least been a supportive lifeline for his remaining journey to India.[13]

Hambleton and his friends, along with help from Gurkha troops, cleaned up the area around their hut and built a bamboo fence to keep refugees from sleeping—and dying—under it, as well as a drainage ditch around it to carry off mosquito-producing rain water. He spent idle time reading two issues of *Esquire* magazine obtained from North, listening to Captain Young's story of his trek from Myitkyina, and hearing a Gurkha's report of the death of his sergeant major and a padre who was bringing fifty orphan girls from a village back along the trail; some of the girls had perished as well. After the Chinese left, Hambleton began to realize his mistake in not going with them and became increasingly anxious to leave the "pest hole" in which he was living. He was also having daydreams and nightmares arising from the unsanitary and climatically harsh conditions. His twelfth wedding anniversary was on 11 July: "what a place to spend it," he moped in his diary that day.

He sent a radio message to Boatner on 13 July, which had still not been answered five days later, so he wrote another out in longhand and gave it to one of North's native messengers to carry to India. His strength was not improving, and he felt that he was wasting time: "Getting more uneasy and anxious to get out. Always the possibility Japs may bomb this place or catch up to us during lull in weather. Maybe we 'missed boat'—as others must now be in India—but couldn't make it before," Hambleton wrote in his diary on 30 July. General Tu had left for India more than two weeks earlier, and Hambleton thought he must be there by now. "Couldn't have made it then," he wrote. "Lean was sick and couldn't leave him—had no shoes and legs in bad shape. But what a waste of time that could be so much better spent in India." The sores on his hands had healed and his leg was improving, which perhaps accounted for his increasing restlessness, although he still suffered from recurring FUOs. Captain Young was growing steadily worse and delirious from fever and dysentery, and Carroll, his former RMC hut-mate who had moved out a couple of weeks earlier, died along with five others on the same day. Hambleton was fearful of catching some disease from the flies and pestilence around him, although he admitted that he felt good, had a good appetite, and functioned normally, albeit understrength. "Keep trying only [to] look ahead," he reminded himself.[14]

Tu and a contingent of Fifth Army indeed had arrived in India by the end of July, followed in ensuing weeks by the rest of the Fifth Army Headquarters troops and most of the 22nd Division. On 5 August, Colonel Boatner sent a memo to General Sibert in New Delhi concerning Hambleton's situation and that of the Chinese units that had arrived in Assam.

> Capt. Hambleton is reasonably well. He refused to come out with a British liaison officer who came out yesterday, evidently because he did not feel strong enough and also because he had hopes a plane would come in for him—*a definite impossibility* [author's emphasis]. He plans to come out after the monsoons—Sept or Oct. Barring sickness, he should live to get out. However, there are many types of severe sicknesses—diseases—and he might fall victim to them. There has been no radio, communication with Shin[gbwiyang]—for over two weeks. Prior to then I transmitted

10. Hambleton's Story (Continued)   119

[your] orders to march out if possible. I am certain that is the best thing for him to do. In the past 10 days rations came into this area.... I directed that a one months supply be dropped to him. Will check immediately.[15]

It is not known who the British liaison officer was to whom Boatner referred. In the same message, Boatner reported the arrival of the last organized unit of Fifth Army and the 22nd Division.

Lean and Hambleton held "quite a discussion" on 5 August and decided to begin the walk out the following week with a Kachin named LaBing: "Decided it best thing to do and an opportunity to have his escort." North had left the day before on a ten-day trip to help civilian refugees get through to Margherita, and the two men agreed to leave as soon as the political agent returned. The anticipation grew into excitement in Hambleton's mind, and he found it hard to sleep. His thoughts raced ahead to Christmas gifts to give his wife and to formulating home improvement plans for his house back in the United States. He read through the issues of *Esquire*, searching advertisements for gift suggestions "I am going to get my Sunny wife." He also pledged to demonstrate his love for her every day and to give her a small token of that love, "even though its [sic] only a flower from the garden. Tell her I love her and not keep things hidden anymore. At night lying on this hard bed looking out the door for hours on dark wet jungle, battling mosquitoes, and putting a drop of iodine on spot where one got me when I dozed off. Always thinking, thinking, and hoping that the better life is not too far off again."[16]

The supply shipment that Boatner had mentioned in his message to General Sibert on 5 August was dispatched to Hambleton on 10 August. It consisted of five large bundles and one small bundle of K-rations, packed in straw. When it arrived, Hambleton grumbled that he was somewhat disappointed that it contained no tobacco or chocolate. He sorted out the shipment in his corner of his shed and later feasted on clam chowder, beans, canned pears, and coffee. He also received a new pair of rubber boots. He was blessed with ample supplies and started thinking of selling off the surplus items before leaving for India. The air drop also brought letters from his wife, along with some newspapers and a copy of *Time* magazine. "So much to think about and arrange now if we go this week," he wrote in his diary.

North returned the next day and said he planned to keep LaBing at Shingbwiyang for a couple of months. This news caused Hambleton to panic, but he decided to "see what happens" and moped about in gloom and depression. He went on "quite an eating spree" that day, perhaps to partially drown his sorrows in food: "Breakfast—tomato juice, bacon, Army hash, wheat biscuits, coffee and sweet. Lunch—Pork sausages, sauerkraut, biscuits, tea. Dinner—salmon, peas, asparagus, rice pudding." He slept better that night, as the air cooled off and "I calmed down a bit." Then, the following morning, LaBing came in early and said he was leaving for Margherita the next day and was rounding up four coolies for Hambleton and Lean. North had changed his mind once again. "Quite a surprise and what a relief to get underway at last!" But Hambleton's elation was tempered somewhat when he heard that LaBing was going to charge the two men R500/00—"quite a wad," Hambleton wrote in disgust.

The morning of 12 August saw a hard rain that continued until afternoon, so the two men did not start out when they planned. Hambleton killed time eating and preparing to leave the next day. "Had touch of fever come on in late afternoon—made me weak and pretty worried—just at this stage when I'll need all strength. The mist and rains over [the mountains] on our route don't look very inviting. But this is last spurt and then all will be well again. Couldn't take any coffee at night as started fever off again." His diary is blank for 14 August, but on 15 August he wrote that LaBing had arrived with four coolies and they were loaded with supplies, but then word came from North that he was recalling the coolies. Lean dashed off and found one bearer, the men loaded their packs, and they started off for the Tara River crossing. It was an easy walk, and they arrived at about 2:30 in the afternoon. The bridge was washed out, and the men built a "ping," a type of rough shelter of wood and leaves, while waiting for Lean to get coolies from Shingbwiyang to rebuild the bridge. On 16 August they crossed the river on the bridge, and then Hambleton spent "an awful day" going up and down steep grades with a badly cramped leg. His companions were far ahead of him, and by the time he came to the third river (which had no bridge) late in the afternoon, he decided that he had had enough and turned back to Shingbwiyang.

Hambleton sent a boy ahead to give North a note saying that he was returning. It was a slow walk but made easier by being all downhill. He crossed two rivers, fell in one and was soaked, but he found that Lean had left some supplies at the river and there was a ping to rest in. By this time, he was so weak that he could hardly walk. His diary entry on 18 August was frightening: "Rain let up in forenoon and sun out. Laid down all day—got too weak breathing wood smoke. Fever and chill. Took one [of] Lean's [aspirins]. Up to take leak and fainted twice. Scared and nervous. Lean may not have made it. Boy got [a] supply [of] wood and improved roof." The last entry on 19 August was very brief: "Sunshine all day—river going down—three Chinese sitting out in ping on river."

After these last words, Hambleton was silent. He died nine days later in Shingbwiyang. The fever that wracked him on 18 and 19 August worsened and, according to an interrogation of his servant by Father Louis Meyer (a chaplain at 20th General Hospital in Assam), by the time he was brought back to Shingbwiyang, he was vomiting and could not eat. "He all the time want coffee," the servant told Father Meyer. Hambleton died around noon on 28 August and was buried the next day in a bamboo basket with two

10. Hambleton's Story (Continued)

British soldiers. The servant was with him at the end and watched Hambleton being buried. He was clad in old clothes, not a military uniform. The servant and Lean, who had also returned to Shingbwiyang to watch over Hambleton, stayed three or four days and then started out again for India. Lean and the servant split up after two days on the trek and never saw each other again, though they both eventually reached India. Despite efforts by Mrs. Hambleton to locate her husband's grave a couple of years later, it was never found, probably because it was churned up by American bulldozers excavating an airfield over it a year or so later, unaware of its location.[17]

11

The British, Chinese and Civilian Exodus

The scramble to exit Burma was, for the British and Chinese, not nearly so orderly or relatively uneventful as Stilwell had made it for his group. The American general and his staff made plans and preparations in advance for locating a more secure route of retreat and notified the India headquarters of their route, thus ensuring that they had airdrops of food and drinking water (as well as adequate transport) and that additional food stocks were either available or purchasable from native peoples along the way. The British had woefully underplanned for evacuating their troops, and the Chinese had no plans at all. Hambleton's thwarted attempt to reach safety in India was more often the tragic rule than the exception. In the rush to escape the Japanese net, thousands of British and Chinese soldiers and civilian refugees perished of disease and exhaustion in the torrential rains, floods, and mud that poured down on the treacherous mountains and valleys of northern Burma during the nightmarish monsoon months of May, June, July, and August 1942, spawning widespread disease, starvation, and exhaustion among the troops and refugees. The medical problems experienced by the British and Chinese armies during the retreat were monumental and, at least in the case of the British, were chiefly due to the same failure that led to their military defeat: unpreparedness.

For the civilians, there was little or no medical aid available, and, in their frantic rush to flee the country, they had taken few precautions to ensure that they carried food, spare clothing, adequate footwear, or medicines (if they had any). Many of these refugees were single young men who had had no experience with living outside in the heat and rain, let alone walking hundreds of miles through forbidding terrain amid the ever-present threat of being overtaken by the Japanese or attacked by marauding Chinese soldiers and *dacoits* (native bandits who prowled the roads and trails in search of unarmed people to rob and kill). Their physical condition was simply not up

11. The British, Chinese and Civilian Exodus

to the demands that the massive evacuation posed. They had no guidance in obtaining unpolluted drinking water and food or in how to cook it properly; many of these men died in agony from dysentery, cholera, malaria, and typhus. Only a relative few were able to obtain space on the limited number of ships that were available to transport civilians by sea from Rangoon to India. Most had to walk to India or over the mountains on the western side of Burma into the hell of the Arakan to find boats that would take them across the Bay of Bengal.

Women managed much better, on the whole, than the men. They were used to taking care of their families—feeding, clothing, cooking—and at least knew what was required to make a fire, boil water for tea and cooking, and form groups for protection and community welfare. Still, thousands of women and children died as they struggled against the harsh climate, weather and terrain to reach India.

When the front collapsed in Burma, the Allied forces suddenly faced the very real possibility of being trapped by the swift-moving Japanese pincers that were rapidly closing off the routes of escape to the east and west. The eastern sector of the British and Chinese defensive line began to fall apart on 23 April, when the Chinese Temporary-55th Division (a poorly-led and poorly-trained unit) disintegrated into small groups and fled to save themselves from the onrushing Japanese. With its absence, a gaping hole suddenly opened in the defensive line at Loikaw, through which the Japanese raced toward Toungoo. Only the well-trained, tough, and dependable Chinese 200th Division was left to hold the enemy advance at Toungoo before being forced out of the city while fighting a brilliant rearguard action.

In the last weeks of the campaign, the British, Chinese, and Americans were trying to cobble together a plan for a last-ditch stand in northern Burma, one that was in line with the essentials of British strategy and with Stilwell's concept of ultimate defense. General Sir Harold Alexander, commander of British troops in Burma, arrived on 5 March from England, charged with the primary duty of protecting India, while Stilwell's mission was to defend China.[1] Stilwell was under no illusions that Burma could be successfully defended at this late date; early on, he had decided to look beyond the Allied defeat to the future retaking of Burma. With this in mind, he proposed to Chiang Kai-shek that 100,000 Chinese soldiers be airlifted to India to be trained and equipped for the reconquest of Burma. The Generalissimo agreed to the plan "in principle," but fulfillment of the agreement would have to await the end of hostilities.[2]

Alexander issued Operational Instruction 46 on 23 April, coinciding with the collapse of the eastern sector of the Chinese front, in which he planned to "cover the communications between India and China." His task would be to hold the ends of the Allied line of communications (LOC) at its eastern and western extremities. This plan would secure escape routes for the British and Chinese and form the bases for a future overland supply route to China by protecting the Burma Road at Lashio at the eastern end, as well as a jeep track being built by the British from India (at the urging of Chiang Kai-shek) as far as the Burma border at the western end. The Chinese army east of the Mandalay–Pyawbwe railroad line would withdraw to the northeast to defend the eastern link of the Burma Road while those forces to the west of the rail line would regroup to defend Meiktila, and then pull back through Mandalay to Shwebo, which would become the evacuation point to Assam.[3]

Two days later, after conferring with Stilwell, the British commander ordered an immediate withdrawal across the Irrawaddy River, via the Ava Bridge, by Chinese and British troops to escape entrapment by the Japanese. The bridge would then be demolished with explosives, thereby slowing the Japanese advance and allowing the British and Chinese to withdraw to the higher elevations of northern Burma and establish a defensive line to defend India and to which the enemy would be drawn just as the monsoon season broke. In the event of this plan proving to be impossible to implement, Alexander hoped to evacuate as many British and Chinese troops as possible to India. As Stilwell pushed his Chinese toward the bridge—their vital, slender link to safety—he fretted in his diary, "I hope it's still there."[4]

Chiang Kai-shek's growing apprehension at the turn of events in Burma led to a message to General Lo Cho-ying instructing him to continue defending Burma but also to "avoid decisive actions with the enemy's main strength," the desire to hold the LOC clashing with the equally strong need to protect his army from being wasted in expensive (and possibly futile) confrontations with the Japanese. Chiang further directed that the escape route into China was to be defended in the Kengtung-Fuhai area in the eastern Shan States, and that western Yunnan, Myitkyina, Mandalay, and Bhamo would anchor the eastern end of the LOC. General Lo took this message to a conference with Stilwell and Alexander on 29 April, at which a decision was made to attempt to implement Alexander's defensive line along an escarpment in northern Burma, stretching through Kalewa, Katha, Bhamo, and Hsenwi, while preparations were made to move the Chinese to Myitkyina, which Chiang Kai-shek and Stilwell hoped to use as the main defensive base of the LOC. But the Allied leaders were under no illusions that the defense would succeed and agreed that, if the Chinese could not reach Myitkyina and Stilwell failed to maintain effective communication with them, he would head west over the mountains to Imphal, a plan with which the Generalissimo agreed.[5] The Chinese would retreat to either India or China (preferably the latter), and the British would escape to India.

Alexander notified General Wavell, after his conference with Stilwell and General Lo, that he had given "very careful thought to further operations

11. The British, Chinese and Civilian Exodus

and I can see no other alternative which will allow me to carry out my objectives: The defence of INDIA, maintain touch with the Chinese, and keep one or more jumping off places in BURMA."[6] He went on to say that his troops were holding off the Japanese until the track from Ye-U to Kalewa could be improved and stocked with water and provisions for his retreating army. The Chinese 38th Division would be withdrawn to India to be properly re-equipped along with those of the 22nd Division (which Captain Roscoe Hambleton was accompanying). Alexander and his staff planned to join Stilwell at Myitkyina to try to maintain contact with the Chinese and Americans "because I feel sure that the political situation demands that I stay in BURMA as long as I am nominally in command of the allied armies."[7]

The British raced to escape the fast-closing Japanese trap. Withdrawing north and west from Mandalay, they were pursued by the enemy streaming up the Irrawaddy and Chindwin rivers. On 10–11 May, Gurkha units of the 17th Indian Division formed a rearguard to hold off the Japanese until the bulk of the First Burma and 17th Indian Divisions could cross the Chindwin. The British army ultimately escaped from Burma more or less intact, but it suffered the loss of one-third of its men, all of its tanks, and almost all of its motor transport. The British arrived in Imphal at the end of May in deplorable condition: the First Burma Division was dissolved, and the 17th Indian Division had to be rebuilt and re-equipped before it could engage in combat again.

The treatment given to many of the British troops who arrived in India, spent and exhausted, was a bone of contention almost from the beginning. Lieutenant General Noel Irwin (1887–1965) assumed command of IV Corps in northeast India early in April 1942. His intention was to have IV Corps forge the 23rd Indian Division and any remnants of the Burma army that could still fight into a defensive line to hold Assam. However, the wretched condition of British troops streaming in from Burma made their further employment in combat virtually impossible until they had thoroughly rested and been outfitted with fresh uniforms and re-equipped, and Irwin's role instead became one of assuming control of the British units as they arrived in Assam and seeing to their welfare, which he did less than satisfactorily in the eyes of many. To be fair, some of the criticism he bore may have not been his fault: adequate preparations for housing, feeding, and dispensing medical aid generally had not been made, thus putting materials of almost every kind in very short supply. Still, Irwin and the commander of 17th Indian Division, Major General David T. "Punch" Cowan, had a "blazing row" when the latter discovered his men camped out on an exposed rainy hillside with no tents or other cover provided. Cowan was joined in his protest by General William Slim, commander of Burcorps, with whom Irwin had a long-standing grudge.[8] Eventually, the British troops were sheltered in tents and then sent to various camps for rest and rehabilitation.

The story of the 7th Armored Brigade of the 2nd Royal Tank Regiment (2 RTR)—the only armored unit that the British had, having been transferred from North Africa early on in the campaign—provides an example of the difficulties facing military units that were trying to get out of Burma. The brigade formed a rearguard for the retreating army, but as they made their way toward the Chindwin River, their steadfast American-built Stuarts tanks (which the British called "Honeys") began breaking down. Ferrying the tanks across the river was not feasible, and their crews spent the morning of 9 May putting the vehicles out of action, using methods of disabling them without the necessity of burning them lest the smoke give away their position to Japanese aircraft. The personnel of the now dismounted 2 RTR forded the river at night; they were subsequently reorganized as an infantry battalion and began the march toward India. Their outward appearance of stamina masked the men's weakened condition, caused by existing on half rations for weeks and fighting the debilitative effects of malaria and dysentery. They crossed the Indian frontier on 15 May and trucks carried them to Imphal, where they experienced the same treatment as the men of the 17th Indian Division. "There followed a week of boredom and somnolence, on a shelterless hillside devoid of all amenities," wrote the historian Basil Liddell-Hart. "During this time sickness and loss of weight showed what a heavy physical toll had been taken of officers and men during the past weeks. Here the first mail which the unit had seen for nearly four months was received."[9]

The Chinese had had a much tougher time of it. Only a few units escaped intact. One of these was the 38th Division of the Fifth Army, which benefited from strong, capable leadership and came to India in good order from 25 to 30 May. Once they arrived in Assam, however, the troops found that the local tea planters and the British military and civilian authorities resented their presence and treated them like prisoners of war. The Chinese were prohibited from walking along roads for exercise or recreation and from entering towns and obtaining local food supplies because General Irwin considered them to be in short supply and therefore available only to British troops. Irwin deemed the Chinese "mere rabble" and sent a request to Stilwell that they be disarmed upon arrival in Manipur. Stilwell's representative to Wavell, Brigadier General William R. Gruber, replied that this would be an insult and that the Chinese should be assembled at Imphal and Ledo and given care. Nonetheless, they continued to be restricted to the vicinity of their barracks until they were evacuated to Ramgarh on 8 July.[10] After their departure, Irwin declared that no more Chinese troops would be allowed to enter the area.[11]

The remainder of the Fifth Army fared far worse. As Captain Hambleton observed, the headquarters unit was first ordered to Myitkyina to establish the new line of defense. Then contradictory orders from Chungking initially directed the army to evacuate to China, a distance of two hundred miles (much of it through Japanese-held territory), only to later instruct them to turn around and head for the rugged Maingkwan–Fort Hertz–Magalta area in the malarial heart of northern Burma. General Tu dutifully set out for Maingkwan, ninety miles northwest of Myitkyina, on a main road to India and (as illustrated in Hambleton's diary) set up his headquarters in Shingbwiyang, which was also the focal point of the flight of many civilian refugees. Tu, his headquarters troops, and the accompanying 22nd Division were kept supplied by air drops, mostly by U.S. planes and a few RAF transports.

The air drop plan was initially developed by Brigadier Dysart Whitworth of the RAF and the local political commissioner in eastern Assam, Mr. E. T. D. Lambert, in collaboration with Chinese minister Yu Fei-peng (but with no involvement by any American officer). In lieu of any other plan, Colonel Boatner decided to follow the British proposal, according to which (as previously noted) dumps of food, medicines, and other supplies would be stocked by air drops along the Hkalak Ga–Hpachet–Ranglum–Tipang–Margherita track, which ran through the notorious Hukawng Valley. Lambert also set out with a relief column of soldiers and Naga bearers to meet the Fifth Army at Hkalak Ga. To facilitate the air supply of the Chinese army, planes were pulled from the Hump traffic, but no permanent reassignments of aircraft or crews were made. "To reserve planes and pilots exclusively for this use would have been most wasteful and have seriously affected traffic into China," Boatner wrote in a report for Stilwell on 23 August. "Consequently, planes were used only when it seemed certain the weather would be favorable and the reports of locations and needs of the Chinese troops had been carefully evaluated."[12]

The airdrops were especially hazardous because of the mountainous terrain and the often dreadful flying weather. Nonetheless, the pilots persevered in conducting the flights out of a strong sense of obligation to the starving troops and civilians on the ground. The methods used to deliver the supplies were later recalled by one of the pilots:

> We'd fill a smaller burlap bag with rice or salt and sew that into another bag twice the size of the first. When these were dropped from an airplane, the inner bag broke but the rice was saved by the second bag. All we had to do was to fly through the monsoon rains of Burma, dodge the mountains, and find the places to drop the food to the waiting Chinese. Then, dodging the jungle trees, we'd go down as low as we dared and shove the bags out the door. We learned to hit the targets pretty accurately.[13]

Brigadier Whitworth also reported in a similar vein:

> The only available dropping-spaces were very small. The best we had was only about the size of two football grounds, and food dropped 50 yards outside the clearing was generally lost forever in the thick jungle.... [Even] with free dropping, we only expected a pick-up of 60 per cent. Later, when pilots and crew developed the technique and I

hit on the idea of attaching 3-yard-wide cotton streamers to the sacks, the pick-up increased considerably. The white streamers were of great assistance in finding sacks which had fallen in the jungle.[14]

Boatner's report also pointed out that General Tu had consistently exaggerated the number of men in his command and understated the amount of food he received. The Americans and Chinese in India were able to determine, by keeping close track of the food delivered in the air drops, that no shortages should have occurred, either for the Fifth Army Headquarters or for the 22nd Division forces. Tu was known (through information later supplied by General Liao, the commander of the 22nd Division) to have confiscated all the food dropped to both the 22nd Division and the Fifth Army Headquarters unit at Taro and Shingbwiyang. The poor condition of the Chinese army generally was, as Hambleton reported to Boatner from Shingbwiyang on or about 13 July, attributable to "inefficient planning, no discipline, indecision, disregard for troops, trudging all over the country and then getting caught in the rains which multiplied troubles, ruined food ... etc." As a result, he pointed out, 500 out of the 1,700 men in the headquarters unit who had left Indaw died en route to Shingbwiyang.

In conclusion, Boatner wrote, he and his staff were caught between conflicting demands of the Chinese (who insisted that the British should take care of supply and evacuation and receive air drops via U.S. aircraft) and the British (who were only concerned with pressuring the Americans for aircraft and urging them to force the Chinese to leave Burma and Assam as quickly as possible). Boatner ended by making the radical recommendation to Stilwell that the Americans withdraw from participation in military operations in India: "Our presence permits both [the Chinese and the British] staffs to shift responsibility to us and delays action and co-operation [between them]."[15]

The 96th Division, under the command of Major General Yu Shao, was as poorly led as any of the Chinese divisions. It had fought without distinction in several tough engagements around Pyinmana and Mandalay before being sent to a rest area at Myitkyina at the end of April, but by mid–May the division had only gotten as far as Mogaung. On 18 May, orders were received from Chiang Kai-shek to take a defensive position in the Maingkwan–Fort Hertz area as part of his general plan to organize a defense in the inhospitable terrain and climate. Accordingly, the division passed through Shingbwiyang and got as far as Fort Hertz when it radioed for badly needed supplies (27 June). It took some time for the division to be located, even by competent guides aboard search aircraft, and several days of good flying weather were wasted trying to find it.

As the Chinese armies struggled toward safety in India, they indulged in extensive looting of native villages, as the political agent at Shingbwiyang, Clive North, reported on 9 August: "All the villages from [Taro] to Shingbwiyang ... are deserted. The people are living in the forest like animals. Between Shingbwiyang and Hkalak ... there are two villages of whose inhabitants I could find no trace for nearly a month."[16] Some villages in the area of Sumprabum and Fort Hertz were burned; the native Kachins were dying at alarming rates from cholera, dysentery, and starvation, and they sought refuge in the surrounding mountains. They became so resentful of their treatment at the hands of the Chinese that they resorted to using guerrilla warfare tactics against stragglers, especially those of the 96th Division.

On 29 June, General Yu informed the Chinese and Americans that his division was leaving Fort Hertz for Kunming, China. It took some time to locate the division, but, at last, on 16 July, the 96th was found east of Sumprabum, and over the next several days 50,000 pounds of foodstuffs and medicines were dropped in the area by the CNAC under American direction until Stilwell ordered Boatner about 20 July to stop supplying the 96th Division because of aircraft shortages. The division eventually arrived in China with 4,000 soldiers out of its original 6,000-man complement lost to enemy action, disease, starvation, and exhaustion.[17]

The 200th Division was perhaps as well led and as disciplined as the 38th and succeeded in overcoming a tortuous march and surviving the ordeal intact. Though it lost its capable commander, General Tai An-lan, in a skirmish at Hsipaw and encountered fierce Japanese resistance in the Bhamo area, the division battled its way across the Japanese lines of communication on the Yunnan-Burma border and reached China in the summer of 1942.

The Sixth Army was in shreds by the end of the campaign. Its various components were in pieces, and all of them, including the headquarters force, were independently trying to make their way out of Burma and into China. Most of them (mainly the survivors of the 93rd and 49th Divisions) congregated at Kengtung until 18 May, when they were ordered to withdraw further into China. Elements of the shattered Temporary-55th and 28th Divisions (of the 66th Army) continued to dribble into China over the summer. The Temporary-55th was ultimately deactivated, while the 28th was rebuilt and returned to Burma as part of YOKE Force in 1944. Some of the stragglers never returned to China, either perishing or becoming freebooting guerrilla fighters in the rugged border country. They were aided by renegade Burmese in attacking and looting the hill tribes and the Japanese indiscriminately in quest of food and treasure.[18]

* * *

The ordeal of the Chinese and British troops struggling to escape Burma was truly awful, but that of the thousands of the civilian refugees was unquestionably worse. About one and a quarter million Indians lived in Burma, many of them in the large cities of the south. Between five and six hundred thousand fled the country in 1942 by sea, air and land. Hordes of Indian and other refugees who could not pay for tickets on ships and planes walked northward, up the main roads, or westward over the mountains into the Arakan, ahead of the onrushing Japanese. While many eventually arrived safely in India, many more died of disease, primarily dysentery, malaria, and typhus, compounded by starvation and exhaustion in the mountainous jungles of northern Burma. Estimates vary widely, but it is believed that between fifty and one hundred thousand people perished during the exodus.

Put very simply, the government of Burma had neglected to make adequate preparations for evacuating the populace. A combination of official bungling, insufficient planning, and indecision created a chaotic situation that stretched on for several crucial weeks in early 1942. Too late, the government realized that many of the Indian refugees were the very people who provided most of the basic services in the cities, such as transportation, food production and distribution, staffing government offices, and tending the shops and businesses; when they left, these functions completely broke down. Early on in the mass exodus, the authorities tried to persuade the Indians to return with promises of evacuation when the time came, but although many refugees returned to take up their old jobs, they were relegated to refugee camps where they sat for days and days without any work being assigned. At the same time, to ensure that the workers and their families did not try to leave by sea, all adult Indian men were prohibited from purchasing tickets as deck passengers, the cheapest possible passage normally available. Only the wealthy were permitted to buy tickets, and these came at a premium price. Finally, an organization was created for the orderly evacuation of refugees to India by special ships and troop transports, and some 70,000 more privileged citizens departed for Madras and Calcutta. After a month, the lower- and lower-middle-class refugees were allowed to depart, but the delay meant that thousands of people reached the treacherous swamps and hills of the Arakan and the malarial mires and mountains of northern Burma just as the monsoon season set in. Provision of transportation and food was only systematically instituted after the roads and tracks to India were crowded with refugees who were confronting the horrors of negotiating deep mud, drenching rains, flooded rivers, and rampant disease.[19]

British authorities gradually came to realize that if they were to get the refugees out of Burma before the Japanese overtook them, many would have to be evacuated up the Manipur road to Assam. This was a jeep track built and used by the British army that ran from Kalewa on the Chindwin River to Tamu, and then on to Imphal via Palel. The road was usable for all but the stretch from Tamu to Palel, but only in the dry season; when the rains came, the road was nearly impassable. The military officials began working on improvements to the track from Tamu to Palel, which took eight weeks to

11. The British, Chinese and Civilian Exodus

complete. The route was opened near the end of March, and 30,000 refugees traveled over it before the month was out. By that time, however, the monsoon season was in full force, and the refugees had to compete for road space with the British army.

Trails that were dusty but passable in the dry season became mudbaths in the rains. The swamps and glutinous tracks bogged down vehicles, and traversing the soupy mud, sometimes thigh deep, quickly exhausted whatever reserves of strength remained in many of those who had already been walking for weeks. Totally spent, they simply sat down by the side of the road and died. Draft animals collapsed along with their owners, and the filth of humans and animals (together with the increasing numbers of corpses) fouled and polluted the water holes, which resulted in the spread of deadly diseases such as cholera, typhoid, and wasting dysentery. The refugees were also victims of leech bites (which, when left untreated, led to ulcers, called Naga sores, on legs and arms), and malaria was rampant. Theft of personal belongings—sometimes ripped from the travelers by fellow refugees, bandits, and passing troops—added to their misery.

Unlike some British and Chinese army sick and wounded, relatively few refugees were evacuated by air. A Japanese air attack on 6 May had heavily damaged the airfield at Myitkyina (the main air base for evacuating civilians and military casualties) and destroyed all but one plane; this loss forced thousands of men, women and children to walk to Assam through the monsoon season. Their primary escape route, the "refugee road," involved following the main road north to a rest house at the 102nd milestone from Rangoon and then taking a small jungle track northwest to Maingkwan, where a large store of rice had been fortuitously dumped by the Burmese government officials when they saw the magnitude of the refugee problem. The trail went on to Shingbwiyang in the Hukawng Valley and to Tipang, the railhead in Assam, about ninety miles beyond Shingbwiyang. The original path, according to A.R. Tainsh in his excellent postwar book, *And Some Fell by the Wayside*, was about four feet wide and became a "succession of deep mud-holes as thousands of refugees and hundreds of cattle and elephants" slogged over it. Fearing further catastrophic loss of life, the British closed the trail just before they reached Shingbwiyang and kept it closed until near the end of the monsoon season in the fall.[20] Brigadier T.O. Thompson of the British Medical Service recalled several years later that "the main impressions were of dust; endless streams of patients for whom transport had to be found; streams of refugees plodding along, the children happy and well fed, the elders looking desperate."[21] Then, as they reached northern Burma and began the arduous climb over the mountains into India, the refugees were beset by torrential rains; the dust turned to mud, and the jungle teemed with insect-borne diseases and venomous animal life.

The few aircraft available for evacuating refugees and soldiers flew out of Myitkyina dangerously overloaded. Colonel Robert Scott wrote in his memoirs of being unable to open the cockpit windows because they would draw in the fetid air from the people in the cargo hold and the stench was overpowering, forcing the pilots to fly in stifling conditions. C-47s used on these runs had a designed capacity of twenty-four litter cases but often carried twice that number (and occasionally upward of seventy or more ambulatory patients).[22]

Upon reaching India, many people were in such an advanced state of physical deterioration from disease and fatigue that a significant percentage died, mainly from malaria, dysentery, and cholera. Camps overflowed with people in dire need of help, and there was little to go around. The British army was not technically responsible for civilians, but medical personnel struggled valiantly to deal with the seemingly endless stream of refugees who poured into India through the spring and summer of 1942. In particular, a concerted effort was made to prevent infectious diseases (notably cholera) among the refugees from spreading to the wider Indian population as well as the military.[23]

12

Ramgarh
Beginnings

While the retreat in Burma was grimly playing itself out, Captain John Grindlay was kept busy in New Delhi during the rest of May and the first half of June treating the ailing members of Stilwell's staff and trying to cope with the terrific heat and dust in the city.

Six officers (his "old maid colonels," he called them derisively) were constantly complaining about their illnesses—principally jaundice, which was contracted, Grindlay concluded, from yellow fever shots they had received in Chungking before going to Burma. The officers included Lieutenant Colonel Frank Roberts (Stilwell's G-2), Lieutenant Colonel Norman Eckert (Field Artillery), Lieutenant Colonel Harvey Edward (a survivor of the Kunming plane crash that had claimed the lives of General Dennys and Lieutenant Colonel George in China), Colonel Richard Sandusky (Infantry), a Colonel Engelhard, and Colonel George Townsend (Signal Corps). Roberts requested a transfer back to the United States, citing poor health, and Townsend and Engelhard were also ordered home, much to Grindlay's relief. "I am going crazy [with] them," he wrote in his diary on 4 June.[1]

The next day Grindlay met four injured air corps officers, men who had been on Doolittle's Tokyo raid, accompanied by a doctor, Lieutenant Thomas R. White. Their plane had crashed in the sea, one hundred feet off the Chinese coast. The aircraft had split open and hurled them out into the water.

The navigator has bilateral upper arm paralysis & the pilot got a bad leg that had to be amputated—others cut up more or less. Japs looked for them but they found a Chin[ese] guerrilla who spoke English & who led them out to back of Chin[ese] lines. [Lieutenant] White met them in a village 5 days after the crash, found the bad leg of the pilot needed amput[ation] & did so in a former Am. missionary hosp. [with] Chin[ese] doc. & Amer. nurse. Moved the pilot on a cart 24 hours later. Finally arrived Kunming & today (6 weeks after accident) here. The boys told of the bombing—how they approached the [Japanese] coast at 50 ft. & kept only 50 ft. above ground all way—to avoid the new [?] detector, the beam of which doesn't follow earth curve, how the farmers waved at them & anti aircraft burst around them. They couldn't tell anything about take off site but I gather from hints it was from Aleutians.[2]

Seagrave visited on 14 June to say goodbye; he and the rest of the hospital unit were being assigned to Ramgarh, a former British training camp and containment center for prisoners of war, located about 200 miles northwest of Calcutta. In the meantime, while awaiting orders to move, they were installed at the American Baptist Missionary Hospital in Gauhati. Up to three-fourths of the patients were dysentery and typhoid cases, "and all of them starvation," Seagrave wrote to Colonel Williams on 20 June. "[Our] nurses have a most appalling job on their hands. Many of our patients have wide open anal sphincters and stools flow out over the bed with each peristaltic wave, day and night. Some twenty are completely incontinent in just one building." The nurses were also contracting diarrhea, and some had malaria.[3]

Grindlay wrote to his wife, Betty, on 14 June, "I gather that when things get going surgically he [Seagrave] will have one outfit and I'll have another." The unit would be treating the hordes of Chinese troops and refugees who were straggling out of Burma with a host of illnesses and suffering from fatigue and starvation.

On 15 June, Grindlay and his "old maid colonels" were sent to Simla, the British hill station in the Himalayan foothills, for a month's rest and respite from the lowland heat. "They think I need a ... chance to regain weight and other nonsense and am sending me up with the convalescent jaundice cases," he wrote to his wife. Colonel Adrian St. John, Grindlay's colleague from AMMISCA days, preceded the group, which traveled by train. St. John met them at the station late in the morning of 16 June and took them to the Cecil Hotel. Grindlay was assigned to a room with Major Donald O'Hara and another officer named Fullerton. They cleaned up, had a drink, and napped in the cool afternoon air, a great relief from the scorching heat of New Delhi.

The month spent in Simla passed all too quickly, although Grindlay was eager to return to surgery by the end of it. The leisurely social routine was "slow but pleasant," he wrote to Betty on 29 June. At noon almost everyone with nothing to do gathered at the Green Room of the Gayety Theater (a venue for amateur dramatics) to drink tea, coffee, gin or beer and have lunch. People then dispersed for a nap, followed by afternoon tea, after which they went walking or horseback riding, or else they might enjoy a game of tennis. The evening's routine began with a bath and dressing for dinner. "[S]ince most of our officers here lost their uniforms in Burma," Grindlay commented in the same letter, "this amounts in our case to putting on clean khaki shirt and pants. Then to the cocktail lounge and then to dinner. After dinner it is only a little conversation and then bed." Two nights a week a cocktail dance was held at the hotel, which alternated on two other nights with a dinner dance that went on until 2:00 a.m. The town was filled with unattached women whose husbands were away on assignment in other parts of India or abroad or who were widowed, and the Americans and British officers would often escort the local ladies to the dances. Grindlay wrote that he had taken two daughters of the viceroy, Victor Alexander John Hope (1887–1952), and Wavell's daughter, Jean, to the dances. One of the viceroy's daughters was Joan Hope, who was Grindlay's favorite.

One day, Ms. Hope asked Grindlay and St. John to tea and cocktails at her home, a "huge, palatial, baronial mansion and grounds, houses, courts etc." She was enrolled in a volunteer course for nurses and had "very sensible criticisms of it." Grindlay found her "pleasant, democratic, lively and intelligent."

* * *

While Grindlay and his patients were on leave, the other Americans who had escaped from Burma were regrouping and reorganizing in India and China. Planning was beginning at Stilwell's front echelon headquarters in Chungking and his rear echelon headquarters in New Delhi to recapture Burma.[4]

Some members of Stilwell's staff were dispersed after the walkout, but several remained under his command and many were assigned to the New Delhi headquarters, including Grindlay. Some of the AMMISCA veterans stayed behind in Chungking at the China headquarters, while others were ordered to new commands or requested transfers out of the China-Burma-India (CBI) theater for a variety of reasons.

Colonel Robert Williams continued as Stilwell's theater surgeon, a position that placed him in command of all U.S. medical personnel in the CBI theater. Williams set up an office in New Delhi but made his headquarters in Chungking to be near the center, where most long-range planning and decision making were being done, and to interact closely with the Chinese medical organizations because, as he reported, they would only "do business" with him as the highest-ranking medical officer. After arriving in India following the walkout, he found that Colonel John M. Tamraz was in charge of the medical section of the American Services of Supply (S.O.S.) then based in Karachi (later transferred to New Delhi). Tamraz's main task was to establish station and general hospitals under S.O.S.; in the meantime, until more medical assistance could be sent from the United States, the British provided hospital facilities for Americans in India during the first half of 1942.[5]

The U.S. Tenth Air Force set up headquarters in New Delhi in 1942 with personnel transferred from Java and the Philippines after those areas fell to the Japanese. This unit maintained its own medical section and chief surgeon, as did the Air Service Command, which later in the same year was renamed Air

Transport Command and assumed control of all the Hump flights. Colonel Hervey B. Porter was chief surgeon for Tenth Air Force, and he also served as head medical officer for the Air Transport Command throughout 1942. Colonel Thomas C. Gentry was flight surgeon of the American Volunteer Group and was appointed head flight surgeon for Chennault's Fourteenth Air Force after its formation in July 1942.

* * *

Grindlay returned to New Delhi on 15 July and once again roomed with Colonel St. John. He wrote to Betty on 18 July, "[St. John] is an ideal roomate [sic], always cheerful with an amazing wit." He used the excuse of having to watch over St. John's state of health in order to remain roommates with a senior officer three ranks above his own. The heat was still intense and "hard to take after the coolness of Simla." The two men lodged at the Imperial Hotel, where Stilwell's headquarters was located, but they tended to favor socializing at the Gympana Club, with its wide lawns, roofed swimming pool, and cheap drinks. Grindlay did not yet know where he would be permanently stationed, whether with the Seagrave unit at Ramgarh or at a facility in New Delhi. He guessed it would be the former but hoped it would be somewhere in India, for "I'm not keen to go back to China." On 17 July he was notified that he had been awarded the Purple Heart for his services during the Burma campaign, along with Seagrave and O'Hara. St. John also received the award for the demolitions he had carried out in Rangoon in the early days of the campaign, Paul Jones for his efforts in keeping the rail lines operating during the retreat, and Frank Merrill for his liaison activities with the Chinese. "[No] one else got it," Grindlay bragged in his diary, adding that "I think [Brigadier General Benjamin] Ferris is 'browned off'" (Ferris was the chief of staff of Stilwell's New Delhi headquarters).

For several days, beginning on 16 July, Grindlay suffered from a substernal pain that made swallowing painful. When the symptoms persisted, he underwent a fluoroscope test on 20 July, and a cardiospasm was found. Belladonna was prescribed to ease the spasm, and the pain finally subsided two days later. Grindlay had experienced chest pains at times in Burma; it was the start of heart problems that were to plague him for the rest of his life.

Finally, after weeks of inactivity, Grindlay was informed by Colonel Williams on 21 July that "a whole gang of us [including O'Hara and Chesley] are going down to Ramgarh." Accompanying them were another dental officer named Budge, Captains Walter H. Bush (a malariologist) and Gordon Smith (a member of the Public Health Service), Lieutenant Arthur Martin (Quartermaster Corps), and a group of fourteen enlisted men who arrived in mid-July to join Seagrave's unit. The non-commissioned officers were assigned to provide medical technical support for the Chinese troops being sent to Ramgarh for rehabilitation and retraining as part of X Force, which would launch an attack into Burma early in 1943. Major Lamar C. Bevil, assistant theater surgeon under Colonel Williams, was also coming along, as post surgeon in charge of sanitation in and around the buildings at the camp, to supervise the hospital and to arrange for medical supplies to be obtained from the British. Another part of Bevil's job was to assign personnel where needed, Williams explained; Grindlay might be assigned to surgery with Seagrave, "whichever Bevel [sic] wanted." Grindlay immediately fired off a letter to Seagrave requesting that Technical Sergeant Ray Chesley be placed in the laboratory ("Best damn lab man I ever met," Grindlay once said) and that he himself be appointed to head the surgical service ("to circumvent any plans of Bevel's").

The next day Grindlay packed two small trunks with personal belongings to send to his wife back home, while the rest was sent to Ramgarh by train on the morning of 23 July. That evening Grindlay accompanied a group of officers, including General Raymond Wheeler (American commander of the Services of Supply in the CBI theater), to the Viceroyal Palace for a swimming party and buffet supper. There, he met Lady Auckinleck, whom he had previously encountered in Simla:

> She is one I had a long chat [with] while sitting on pool table at Viceroyal Lodge in Simla & she ribbed me for not remembering her. She is Mary Astor–like in appearance & very jolly. Rumor is that she is Viceroy's girl friend. Had delightful swim in the marvelous pool, slide on board etc[.] Gen. Wheeler told me Seagrave had wired asking for me. (The [Seagrave] unit is now under S.O.S. [Services of Supply].) Excellent supper of sausage etc. & lots of Scotch (about the last we'll get).[6]

Grindlay and a small party of officers left New Delhi in a Packard automobile to drive to Agra, arriving in the rain at 5:00 in the afternoon. Their Indian driver killed three dogs and four doves en route, Grindlay noted with some amazement. Grindlay and his companions toured the Taj Mahal that evening and departed the next day for Allahabad, and then on to Ramgarh, arriving at 6:30 in the evening. They stayed in the officers' quarters, where Grindlay was informed that he would be head of surgery with Seagrave, which must have come as a relief to him, although he made no note of it in his diary. The next day, Grindlay rode a borrowed bicycle to the hospital.

Ramgarh was a complex of four camps situated on a plateau about 1,500–2,000 feet in altitude, surrounded by hills (some of them densely jungled). Part of the compound was a former British prisoner-of-war camp in which German and Italians POWs were kept. It was turned over to the Americans to use in rehabilitating and training Chinese soldiers who had walked out of Burma or were flown in from China. Their training took place under the direction of Colonel (later Brigadier General) Frederick McCabe, one of the officers who had accompanied Stilwell on the walkout. Colonel Henry Holcombe (Services of Supply and another walkout veteran) was the post commander. McCabe had served as Stilwell's G-3 at the latter's headquarters in Maymyo and as a liaison officer with the Chinese Fifth Army along with Colonel Harry Aldrich; a white-haired officer with a friendly disposition who wore tortoise shell-rimmed glasses. He was a very good friend of Seagrave, Grindlay, O'Hara, and Chesley.[7] Holcombe had charge of the facilities, including the hospital, which brought the Seagrave unit into closer daily contact with him than it had with McCabe.

The Seagrave unit was housed in the former Italian prison hospital, constructed of brick with a tile roof and concrete floor, surrounded by barbed wire. It held five wards, an operating room, a dental clinic, and an orderly room; living quarters for the doctors and nurses were nearby. The wards had 22 beds each, with verandas on all four sides. Seagrave and his staff were given the task of caring for all the patients sent to Ramgarh until the hospital was full, after which an American station hospital unit would be sent in to help with the overflow. Colonel Williams thought the likelihood that the entire hospital would be filled was remote.[8] Events soon demonstrated that he had greatly underestimated the situation.

When Grindlay bicycled into the hospital compound on 28 July, he was joyously welcomed by everyone: "Tears & shouting," he wrote in his diary. Seagrave assigned some of the nurses to make up living quarters for Grindlay and that evening held a special party for him, where he was reunited with everyone, including all the nurses (now increased to 31, Grindlay noted), Bill Cummings, O'Hara, and Chesley.[9] Grindlay assumed supervision of the five patient wards and the operating room the next day and began seeing "flocks of Chinese"—sick and injured Chinese soldiers from the 38th Division arriving by the trainload. Eighty patients were admitted on 30 July, nearly all of whom had malaria (and half of them seriously ill). A quarter of the men were found to have dysentery and intestinal worms; 80 percent had Naga sores on their legs and feet. Tuberculosis cases were isolated in one ward. Grindlay noted that there were "lots of hernias, appendices & many many fist[ulae] in anus." The soldiers were mainly from peasant or lower-class origins and had "filthy habits, spit & vomit & throw food on floor—even officers."

As he had been in Burma, Grindlay was immediately thrown into surgery, operating first on cases that included removal of a bullet from a buttock, an appendiceal abscess, and an infected gall bladder. His chief surgical nurse was Koi, who had been with him in Burma and on the walkout, and who would remain with him for the rest of his service with the Seagrave Hospital Unit. Koi was also the head nurse at the hospital; a Shan from eastern Burma, she was twenty years old in 1942. Grindlay provided a description of her in a letter to his wife:

She has gained eight pounds, since the battle and trek, but even now, weighs only 5 ½ stone [77 pounds]. Yet, being small and of small bones, she is perfectly turned as a Bali or East Java dancer. In an Oriental way, her face is pretty. Her skin is olive, her hair jet black; she wears Burmese dress (like the other girls), light, long "longyi," and a tiny short, gauze-like, close fitting jacket, over a "chemise." ... Koi's main charm to me is what you could see only if you watched her for a day. She is happy as a lark, skipping about, laughing melodiously, playing little tricks and yet doing the most amazing things. Her capacity for work is infinite. She learns in a flash and then doesn't just follow, but uses true judgment and intellect.... [Her] name is pronounced "Gwai." ... She cared for me on the trek and here. She had no blanket, shoes, etc., having tossed them away in order to carry a few first aid things. She unpacked, first finding my things and packed and fed me and dressed my feet, when I was too tired to move.[10]

In addition to surgery, dental inspection had to be carried out on the floods of Chinese soldiers pouring into Ramgarh. Major O'Hara wrote a report to Colonel Williams late in July in which he mentioned that he had examined 280 patients and extracted teeth from forty-two of them. "We are trying to run through 100 men per day," he wrote, and he was using 250–300 shots of Novocain daily. "So have definite need of more immediately," he urged, as well as more syringes, extra needles, and more and better sterilization equipment. "Chesley has a pretty good lab set up & finally is happy," Williams concluded.[11]

The work of treating patients was never routine, and errors were unavoidable in the rush to deal with such a large patient load. One day, the British pharmacy sent a mislabeled bottle of pure Fowler's Solution (liquid arsenic, usually administered in diluted form as a tonic for stomach disorders and as external treatment for various skin disorders; its use was abandoned in the United States by the 1950s when it was found to cause, among other things, cirrhosis and to contain carcinogens). The arsenic was subsequently dispensed by a nurse to fourteen or fifteen patients in undiluted form. The mistake was almost immediately discovered, and the horrified nurse and medical staff raced to induce vomiting to purge the patients of the poison. They sat up until midnight distilling water for IVs and administering sodium thiosulfate as an antidote. Fortunately, prompt action led to all the patients' recovery.[12]

Major Bevil had written to Colonel Williams on 29 July to report that the hospital was not yet transferred from British to American command, but the operating room and dental clinic had been unofficially taken over. Seagrave and Bevil worked out a plan for operating the hospital, dividing it into administrative and professional sections, with Bevil in charge of the former (records, correspondence, personnel, supplies and equipment) and Seagrave the latter (wards, patients' mess, admission and discharge of patients, X-ray laboratory, medical records, clinical laboratory, surgical operating room, pharmacy, and the dental clinic). There were about 300 Chinese patients in the hospital already, most suffering from malaria and chronic dysentery. Bevil concluded by optimistically assuring Williams that "there will be nothing but the most congenial cooperation between Major Seagrave and myself."[13]

About a month later, Stilwell (accompanied by the commander of the Chinese 38th Division, General Sun Li-jen) arrived to inspect the hospital and award the Purple Heart to Seagrave and Grindlay. "Stilwell winked at me," Grindlay noted in his diary with thinly disguised glee. Seagrave was a bag of nerves before the ceremony and had vomiting and diarrhea. Afterward, Stilwell lectured the staff about how to handle the Chinese: "he said we must never hit [them]." But Grindlay had already beaten ten offenders who had physically abused the nurses and threatened the staff with pistols and knives, and he discovered that it brought respect and cooperation from soldiers and officers alike. Colonel Holcombe mentioned the incident to Stilwell, but the latter said nothing. Order was restored by the beatings, Grindlay remarked, and "we never have trouble now & when I give an order they obey it. The bulk of the soldiers are cooperative, appreciative & jolly. All my surgical cases particularly are very very friendly to me."[14]

On 28 August, the day before Stilwell arrived, Grindlay found time to write his impressions of Seagrave after having served with him for almost five months.

> I've never taken time to give my opinion of Seagrave. He is a chap who is determined to be a martyr, who has unlimited energy, nervous & has a bad hand tremor, is filled with self-sympathy & stresses by action & word that he is a self-sacrificing, very ill martyr bravely carrying on, who loves adoration, news writings ... who is unselfish [with] his own things, but who expects things to be handed out to him. He asks Stilwell on one hand to give the group the hardest nastiest job there is then complains that the nurses & he are working too hard & will soon crack up. He is a missionary & yet he never proselytizes. He smokes & drinks a good deal & swears well. Even with his faults I'd rather be [with] him than anywhere else besides home. He never orders & yet gets excellent cooperation. Well, all this week he has been in his room [with] a little fever & diarrhea— Little Bawk [her name was Maru Bawk, a Kachin] constantly by him (all she is good for these days now that he gives all his days & nights to her, teaching her English etc). He has felt very very sorry for himself but I'm convinced that his troubles are mainly nervous. He is going to Darjeeling tomorrow [on a month's leave ordered by Colonel Williams] & is taking Little Bawk—whose only work here has been to take care of him & spoil & pamper him & who did a hell of a job as ward nurse. Than Shwe [a Burmese nurse] who isn't sick & doesn't need to go but is his second favorite. He is also taking Lulu [Karen], who has T.B. but is leaving behind at least 6 girls [with] active T.B., merely because they aren't favorites.

By the end of August the number of patients at the hospital had risen from three hundred to more than twelve hundred. The staff consisted of thirty-two nurses and four doctors until they were temporarily relieved by the appearance of a British Red Cross unit that arrived on 7 August en route to China headed by Dr. W.S. Flowers (see chapter 13). The British unit left precisely a month later. Grindlay wrote to his wife on 23 August that he was doing the job alone "with damned little to do it with." He was being consulted by "all the big shots" for all kinds of medical problems. "As a result of this present standing I get away with murder as far as regulations are concerned—don't even wear a uniform, just an old pair of pants and white shirt, or no shirt at all. I am somewhat legendary with the British over an incident on account of this—when two General's [sic] came to see me one afternoon and I was seen looking less military than a buck private." In his 9 September letter to Betty, he apologized for sounding conceited but wanted to tell her more of his experiences and widely perceived respect and value as a surgeon:

> I am having a wonderful surgical experience. Sadly enough I don't even have competition. My rank means nothing. It is true that the hospital has momentarily fallen from fifteen hundred patients to twelve hundred fifty, but I am called to see everything surgical, not only in the hospital, but the British and Indians bring their people from coolies and soldiers to Generals to see me. I run the surgical side here (as chief of the surgical service), and spend the whole morning operating and afternoon doing emergencies and consultations and even at night. I am the only American excused from all other duties; I don't have to take Chinese lessons every other night, act as host to Chinese officers, etc. So far I haven't had to stop at anything, orthopedics, open reductions, of fractures, tendon transplants, nerve suturing, chest surgery, rib resections, thoracoplasty, breast surgery and all kinds of abdominal and C-U surgery. You see we not only have all the Chinese, but the Gurkha, Sikh, Pathan, Afridi, Ghoriwalli, etc., Indian troops, British and American troops and local Hindus.

Seagrave returned from a month's leave on 20 September (having been away since late in August, when Williams had ordered him to take a rest) and sat down to write a report to the theater surgeon: "The weather in Darjeeling was awful. Half the time it rained continually, and the other half it rained daily. Only on the last morning we were able to see the main peak of Kinchinjunga and the tip of Everest." However, his energy "went up 500 percent," his dizziness had disappeared, and the trembling in his hands that he had experienced "ever since we reached Assam" had stopped. In addition, Than Shwe and Lulu, who were ailing with tuberculosis, had recovered some of their health and were looking much better; Little Bawk had almost shaken her case of malignant tertiary malaria and was gaining weight. Seagrave's improved health made "it all the harder to wait for the push into Burma."[15]

* * *

As plans for an offensive into Burma progressed in 1942, the need for highly mobile surgical support units became apparent to planners. The large 400-bed surgical hospitals common in the Southwest Pacific Area were too unwieldy and lacked sufficient mobility to operate effectively in the rugged terrain of northern Burma. A replacement facility was designed by Colonel Percey J. Carroll, surgeon for USAFFE, SWPA (United States Army Forces, Far East, Southwest Pacific Area), called the "portable surgical hospital" (PSH) (roughly modeled after the Seagrave Hospital Unit), which could provide highly mobile combat surgical support in forward areas for military units engaged in limited or irregular operations. A model for a PSH was developed, consisting of 25 beds that could be transported from place to place by vehicle, humans, or animals and staffed by four officers (three of whom were surgeons and one an internist-anesthetist) and 33 enlisted personnel. The concept of portable surgical hospitals was also introduced successfully in China, where such units followed the Nationalist armies in their campaigns against the Japanese from 1943 onward. More will be said about this service a bit further on.[16]

In accordance with the stated goal of the United States to "improve the combat efficiency of the Chinese Army," U.S. medical personnel in the CBI were directed to expand the capability of the Chinese medical personnel to assume more responsibility for ministering to and supporting their own troops in combat. This task included training additional Chinese doctors and employing hospitalization and evacuation units arriving from the United States to provide medical support at corps and army levels, while the Chinese would be responsible for unit- and division-level medical aid. The plan called for using PSHs in combat situations. The training of Chinese medical staff took place at Ramgarh in 1942 under a group of U.S. Army Medical Department personnel, plus some English-speaking Chinese physicians and eleven European civilian doctors hired by the Chinese Red Cross. The Chinese medical officers were given basic and refresher courses in anatomy, practical surgery, preventive medicine, and other subjects; members of the Pharmacy Corps received dental training in addition to their functions as pharmacists. All of the men were to be assigned to field units with the Chinese army once it returned to Burma.[17]

Stilwell originally envisioned a six-month campaign that would employ twelve PSHs; however, when the campaign lengthened into 18 months, the number of PSHs requested rose to eighteen. The increase was necessary, first, to handle the anticipated upsurge in battlefield casualties and victims of illness and, second, to meet the expectation that every Chinese division would need at least one PSH. Eventually, each regiment in combat was allocated one PSH drawn from nine that arrived in the theater from the United States in late 1943 and early 1944. Additional PSHs, according to Stilwell's plan, would be raised provisionally from medical personnel and equipment drawn from units already in the theater, including the 13th Mountain Medical Battalion, the 151st Medical Battalion, the 25th Field Hospital, the 73rd Evacuation Hospital, and the Seagrave Hospital.[18]

13

Days and Nights at Ramgarh, 1942–1943

The wards at the Seagrave hospital were already packed by the end of August 1942, belying Colonel Williams' prediction that the hospital would never be full. The first trainloads of sick and wounded Chinese soldiers from the 22nd Division began arriving, and the hospital was filled beyond capacity. Additional medical staff were desperately needed. According to Seagrave:

> We put beds down the aisles of the wards and began to fill the verandas. A British Red Cross unit [under Dr. W.S. Flowers] ... came in to help us.... They had English nurses, supposedly much more efficient than our Burmese girls, and most of their personnel spoke Chinese fluently, having previously been missionaries in China. Our receiving office did its best to assign cases evenly, going so far as to send the worst cases to us. But the Red Cross group griped at the number of their admissions, at their quarters, at their food—at everything else. We were relieved when they finally left for China.[1]

A month earlier, Williams had promised to augment the Seagrave unit if and when its hospital reached capacity. Consequently, the 98th Station Hospital, an S.O.S. unit commanded by Major Clarence B. Warrenburg, arrived on 23 August. Grindlay observed that Warrenburg was "all Texan. He seems to be against me." Seagrave was "chronically ill [with malaria] & sorry for himself but in reality just worried & paying too much attention to [nurse] Maru Bawk ['Little Bawk'] & too little time to [the] rest," Grindlay wrote in his diary. As previously noted, Williams ordered Seagrave to Darjeeling for a month's rest, starting on 29 August; Seagrave took with him three nurses (including Little Bawk) "who were also breaking down," and Warrenburg took over. Relations between the interim director and the staff slowly began to improve, but the nurses and doctors still chafed under the more "by the book" administration: "[Warrenburg is] doing things by 'order' now & wants to make the place 'more military.'" But Grindlay noted with relief that Stilwell's staff was looking out for the welfare of the Seagrave unit and would "not let Warrenburg do us dirt." One day the hospital director and one of his men took all morning to conduct a hernia operation, evoking mild criticism from Grindlay, who nonetheless credited them with doing "a good job—just not smooth & quick" (as he would have performed it). By 19 September, Grindlay's opinion of his chief had softened considerably, and he considered Warrenburg "really a decent chap & tries to do right I have concluded & is a *much* better C.O. than Seagrave."[2]

An intriguing visitor arrived at Ramgarh in the person of Lieutenant Colonel Paul H. Stevenson, a U.S. Public Health Service officer, who stayed overnight on 3 September. Stevenson was one of fifteen officers sent to Burma under the command of Lieutenant Colonel Victor H. Haas to provide advice, assistance, and support in improving sanitation, malaria abatement, and other medical matters to Chinese workers who were building the Yunnan–Burma railroad in early 1942. The railroad had been initiated by the British in 1938 and was well along by late 1941, when the United States became involved and Lend-Lease aid started flowing in. The line was designed to carry supplies from Burma to China, but construction was abandoned when a possible Japanese capture of Burma loomed and Chiang Kai-shek called off the work in favor of attempting to keep the Burma Road open. The public health officers' chief responsibility was to design and implement effective sanitation and drainage systems to control the malarial infestation that was killing workers in great numbers.

The men accompanying Haas had extensive experience in disease control, some in tropical areas. They included Dr. Daniel E. Wright, who had worked in the Panama Canal Zone during canal construction to help eradicate yellow fever and malaria; Dr. Fred P. Manget, a 60-year-old Baptist medical missionary with thirty-two years of experience in China who had assisted in providing medical service for Chennault's AVG; Colonel Henry A. Johnson, a sanitary engineer from Memphis, Tennessee; Major William L. Jellison, a parasitologist and a malaria control officer from the Rocky Mountain Laboratory in Montana; and Dr. Marshall C. Balfour, head of the Rockefeller Foundation in the Far East for 20 years. Also accompanying the group was Captain Nevin Wetzel, the explosives expert who had assisted Colonel St. John in the demolition of Lend-Lease supplies at Rangoon in March 1942.[3]

Grindlay was fascinated to learn that Dr. Stevenson was the first American to travel over the entire length of the proposed rail line, followed by Haas and Wetzel, who had covered the route by jeep, horseback, sedan chair, and on foot. The worst part was the first section, starting from Burma, which crossed the Salween River gorge; the Chinese engineer in charge of the work tearfully told Wetzel that he had begun work with 2,000 men and lost 300 to malaria. When Lashio fell to the Japanese, Johnson and Jellison were ordered to leave the area. They had joined a Chinese pack train heading for Kunming, a walk of 150 miles. An American transport plane flew them back to India, where they met up with the other members of the commission. The men had

13. Days and Nights at Ramgarh, 1942–1943

then been scattered around India and China: Haas was appointed chief medical officer of the Services of Supply Base Advance Section 3, covering much of northeastern India (including Assam), with headquarters in Ledo; he held this post until late in 1943. Jellison and Johnson were posted to Assam and began taking steps to control malaria among the Americans who were piling into the area. Johnson was ordered to build a hospital but could not gather all the supplies he needed, and the project was temporarily abandoned.[4]

Stevenson mesmerized Grindlay with yarns until well into the night. These included stories of his medical school days at Johns Hopkins, his more than two decades spent teaching at the Peking Union Medical College, and trips that he had made into remote areas of western China, Tibet, and Mongolia. On one such trip, Stevenson had accompanied Joseph Rock's expedition to measure Minya Konka, the highest peak in Szechuan Province, in 1929–1930, and he "described the thrilling trip to a point 75 mi northwest of it." Stevenson was a friend of Owen Lattimore, whom Grindlay had met in Chungking the previous year, and they swapped anecdotes about the historian and about Joseph Mendelson, Grindlay's former commander in AMMISCA, and his "facility for being in hot water etc."[5]

The following day Bill Duncombe, an FAU driver, and Dr. Handley Laycock, another FAU member, returned from Assam, where they had spent six weeks north of Margherita treating Chinese troops who had fled Burma, about a fifth of them sick with malaria, while 80 percent had Naga sores. Some of the soldiers had been trying to make their way to a refugee camp between Fort Hertz and Myitkyina, near the China-Burma border, where, Laycock reported, about 1,500 refugees and soldiers were camped and dying at the rate of ten per day. He and Duncombe had arranged drops of food and medicine for the soldiers; many picked up vials of morphine and injected themselves, believing that it cured anything. Laycock told Grindlay of a Chinese colonel who had stopped the train of wounded soldiers "so he could have his 6th I.V. in 2 hrs. for malaria!" These men, possibly part of the 96th Division, were following Chiang Kai-shek's order to retreat along the northern route to China, which, on the map, looked shorter and offered a route for trucks, thus "countermanding Stilwells [sic] order to follow us," Grindlay wrote, "where [the] trail at least was fair & where supplies [were] laid out."[6]

A week later Grindlay reported in his diary that malaria had struck four of the doctors in his unit, leaving only Henry Johnson, Ted Gurney, and himself to cover the wards.

> Medical meeting this P-M. on malaria control.... Impossible to control Chinese. They are very irked at us because Stilwell reorganized the outfit here making it only one big division ... & leaving a few generals out in cold—they have gone off to Calcutta (on S.O.S. truck) in huff—god-damn these Chinese! I am still free from malaria but am about only one here who is.[7]

In connection with the American objective of training Chinese medical personnel to support their troops in Burma, Colonel Boatner met with Grindlay, Warrenburg, and Bevil on 19 September to discuss plans for training the Chinese. "I got out of any active part, thank God," Grindlay wrote with relief.

Seagrave returned the next day from Darjeeling, looking fine and "full of enthusiasm. I'm glad to see him back," Grindlay wrote in his diary. Seagrave announced that he was going to write a book about his hospital at Namkham and the Burma war: the result would be his famous work, *Burma Surgeon*, published in 1943. "Characteristically," Grindlay wrote the same day, "when talking about the project, he dramatized himself by asking me to write an epilogue if he were killed in [the] ensuing campaign [in Burma] & see his wife got the money for the book. He is just made that way. Still I like him & really don't believe he could have organized these girls if he didn't dramatize the thing to himself & weren't convinced he is a martyr." In a letter to Betty on 7 October, Grindlay wrote that Seagrave was now spending all of his time on the book. Left on his own, Grindlay noted with a bit of immodesty that "[Seagrave] tells people that I am a much better surgeon than he is anyway and that he doesn't need to do surgery any more except now and then to keep his hand in. It is very decent of him, though of course most exaggerated."

The same day he also reported in his diary that details were received of the death of Captain Roscoe Hambleton (see chapter 10). "That's 2 of the 12 on the boat [*Hoegh Silverdawn*]," Grindlay sadly noted:

Grindlay with his dog, Tilly, in front of a barracks at Ramgarh in the fall of 1943 (U.S. Army photo, courtesy Grindlay family).

13. Days and Nights at Ramgarh, 1942-1943 147

> H[ambleton] & [Staff Sergeant Francis A.] Astolfi the latter a suicide in Delhi while I was there. I was very close to being left [with] Hambleton at [Kyaukmyaung]—in fact O'Hara says he never expected to see me again & I know that was [the] current impression when I stepped into jeep that day, & I thought so myself.

The details of Hambleton's death reached India from eyewitness accounts and were reported to the Americans, but the exact cause of Astolfi's suicide is a mystery, although it probably was depression. Suicide was not uncommon among U.S. servicemen in the CBI and was usually attributed to homesickness, inability to cope with the rigors of the weather and climate, or difficulties in the men's personal lives.[8]

Grindlay, ever the fussy, detail-oriented surgeon, had developed strong habits that remained his trademarks throughout his professional life. In addition to a fierce dedication to sanitation and strict cleanliness around the OR and the wards, his sense of moral integrity remained high for both Americans and Chinese. In that regard, he was especially critical of Seagrave for his continuing attention to Little Bawk as well as his lackadaisical approach to surgery and his love of publicity, as he wrote on 21, 22, and 27 September:

> Seagrave & Little Bawk still "resting." They give me a pain. Nothing wrong [with] Little Bawk except Doc wants to keep her to wait on him & to pat her & kiss her ... Doc did an appendix on one of the Burmese orderlies today [22 September].... He is really a sloppy surgeon & I don't see how he gets away [with] it—I have a hell of a time getting the nurses out of the bad habits he gets them into ... [Captain Carl] Arnold came around [on 27 September] & showed us pictures. Really the publicity they are giving this thing [the Seagrave Hospital Unit] is shameful. The old man laps it up & loves to pose; yet it "isn't done" in a war, I think.

Chinese discipline and morals were oftentimes a problem at the hospital as well:

> Two of our [patients] were taken out & shot today—they were caught in bed together at night—sodomy. Gen. Sun [Li-jen, commander of the 38th Division] is going to have all drivers who smash trucks shot—they do as much harm as a Jap plane—a sensible gesture & one the Chin[ese] will understand.

Grindlay agreed with the severe punishment that the Chinese officers meted out for relatively minor offenses, partly because of his general lack of respect for the Chinese and the perceived need for strongly disciplining them, as well as from a strong sense of moral obligation, duty, and consideration for the protection of valuable equipment and supplies. His strong sense of duty applied to the Americans, too. He reported on 27 September that two noncommissioned officers had borrowed a truck for half an hour the night before, got drunk, ran out of gas, and spent the night in a native village. As punishment, Grindlay assigned them to dig latrine trenches and pile bricks, despite having "awful hangovers." The next day he talked to them "politely but very firmly: they took it well & worked hard & willingly."

On 29 September Grindlay noted that he was doing "a lot of surgery—what is happening that the SOS group [under Major Warrenburg] (who have over ½ the Chin[ese] wards) are doing only 1–2 cases a week?" But his innate love of his profession led him to add, "Of course I never turn down an op[eration] & look for ops & persuade the cases" to let him do their surgeries. That morning alone, he performed surgery on twelve patients.

On 1 October, a group of journalists arrived at the hospital, and Grindlay recorded a light-hearted moment that occurred during their visit:

> A bunch of about 25 correspondents (Amer, Brit, Russian & Chin.) ... came out & looked over hosp. & heard about it. A fight between Warrenburg & Seagrave to win out in getting the publicity [with] former winning because of his rank & position. I was disgusted & didn't go [with] them [on the hospital tour], but as one of the correspondents (a Brit. named Weatherfield for Reuters) passed through O.R. door I noted a mass on back of neck, touched it & told him I'd take it off. ½ hr. later I had a 2" rigid sebaceous cyst intact off. Took him back to off[icers'] mess & had a drink with him.

Besides deriving his own kind of publicity from this incident, Grindlay once again demonstrated his love for the practice of medicine. As his reputation continued to spread among the Americans and the British, officers from both groups were dropping in constantly for consultation and surgical procedures. He gloated in his diary that a British brigadier "came in [with] a fistula in [anus] & wants me to [operate]. Not only [with] the Amer[icans] but [with] the Brit[ish] am I getting reputation as the surgeon. Warrenburg doesn't like it for the [brigadier] asked for me."[9]

On 4 October Colonel Boatner was appointed by Stilwell as chief of staff of the Chinese Army in India (CAI). The appointment put him in a position to control all the finances and supplies, including rations. Stilwell explicitly told Boatner that he would be chief of staff of *his* headquarters as commander of Chinese troops in India, and no other staff or command had any authority at Ramgarh. This was Stilwell's way of preventing Chinese senior officers from assuming control of supplies and finances. It would take three or four months to root out these men and replace them with officers who had orders from Chungking to "play ball."[10]

A little more than a week later, Boatner sent out a memorandum to Colonels McCabe and Holcombe clarifying the structure and nomenclature of the CAI. First, all Chinese troops at Ramgarh were part of the CAI; its headquarters was known as the Chih Hui Pu. Stilwell was in command of the CAI; the vice commander was Lo Cho-ying. The Chinese Expeditionary Force (CEF) being trained at Ramgarh was the Chung Kuo Yuan Ching Chun, with Lo Cho-ying in command and Major General Y.K. Yang as his chief of staff. Yang was made to understand that he had authority only over the CEF and not the CAI, which was Boatner's responsibility. Boatner's assistant chief of staff was Captain (later Major) Vernon Slater.[11]

13. Days and Nights at Ramgarh, 1942–1943

Major Bevil, the S.O.S. commander at the hospital, departed for a new assignment in Delhi on 6 October and was replaced by Lieutenant Colonel Thomas J. Walsh of Trenton, New Jersey. When Walsh met Grindlay two days later, he asked the surgeon what anesthetics were used. Grindlay told him that they used chloroform and ether. Why not spinals? Because, Walsh was told, there was no procaine; it was all at S.O.S. storehouses in Karachi. Walsh believed that the unit needed "bracing up," Grindlay wrote in his diary on 8 October, without understanding the "fact [that] our lack of equipment is because of poor job in supply he did at Karachi." Walsh had been commander of the 159th Station Hospital and a surgeon at Karachi, Grindlay noted, and it was rumored that he had been "sent here because he fell down on the job there."

Grindlay's comment to Walsh concerning the lack of supplies obviously sank in because Colonel Holcombe wrote a letter to General Wheeler on 15 October reporting that Walsh was worried about surgical equipment shortages, including the antiquated X-ray machine. Seagrave, by contrast, had been all smiles while showing Holcombe and Wheeler through the operating room earlier and had told them "he could not ask for better." Holcombe reported that he was confused: "I don't know where to draw the line between the two points of view," he wrote. "Certainly we have no Mayo clinic [sic] here but we have a pretty good hospital and the Chinese are tickled to death with the whole set-up."[12]

Meanwhile, as the hospital politics were unfolding, Grindlay's loneliness for his wife and young daughter became painfully evident in several of his diary entries from this period, as well as in his letters. He marked the first anniversary of his absence from home on 20 September by drinking champagne with his old comrades Donald O'Hara and Ray Chesley. He was depressed that night, writing in his diary, "I hope I don't celebrate my 2nd anniversary away from home." On 7 October he opened his second (and last) bottle of champagne, purchased at a native liquor store a couple of weeks earlier, to drown his sorrows with Seagrave and Bill Cummings. "Drank to my next anniversary at home [with] Betty, of course," he wrote that night. "By God, I hate to be away from her for the 2nd time in a row. It's hell. Had a letter from her today.... Betty very despondent. I wrote her right back this P.M. [by cable] giving her a pep talk. I need some myself & I wish she'd write me in that vein." He also wrote to Betty about a rumor that men who had served in the theater a year or more after 7 December 1941 would be allowed to go home, but he warned her that Stilwell "hasn't let any of his men go just because they did their bit once." A few had gone back to the United States, but only those who were unfit for their jobs because of illness or incompetence, or, in a few instances, reassignment that Stilwell lacked the authority and influence to successfully override.

On 8 October General Wavell paid a visit to the hospital to confer with several disgruntled Chinese generals who had been ousted from their positions by Stilwell's reconfiguration of the units at Ramgarh. These men had, according to Grindlay, pressured military authorities in China to send 10,000 more troops for training and to beef up the army in hopes of becoming needed once again. The troops were arriving by the plane-load and would soon be at Ramgarh. Grindlay drove into town to have his mail censored and was just in time to see Wavell's caravan drive past in "splendid array"—all riding in Lend-Lease equipment, he noted sarcastically, "the kind of thing they do so well."

The next day, Generals Lo Cho-ying (commander, Chinese Expeditionary Force) and Sun Li-jen (38th Division) arrived for an inspection, which was a "bang-up" job, in Grindlay's opinion. Once again, he chortled over the feud between Warrenburg (who was still in command of the 98th Station Hospital) and Seagrave concerning their publicity efforts:

> *Warrenburg (Walsh hasn't taken over yet) bagged all the honors & Seagrave is mad as hell—he did get the photographers to take picture of our group* [with] *him in lead* [with] *Gen. Lo—don't tell me he isn't publicity wild—of course I think all this recent trouble* [with] *Warrenburg, Walsh, etc., is result of jealousy from success of his publicity efforts.*[13]

Walsh came into the operating room and observed Grindlay's repair of a wounded soldier's ulna, and "it opened everyone's eyes," he wrote later. "I hear Walsh took all the surgery at Karachi & is asking to get me out of saddle here. [But] I still maintain good relationship [with] Warrenburg (despite Doc) & know he is hurt by this latest move. His unit [i.e., 98th Station Hospital] is frozen on the tables of [organization] & he feels badly that he has to remain a major—perhaps that has been done for us also." A Chinese photographer took movies of the Seagrave group for Chiang Kai-shek, "which made Walsh & W[arrenburg] mad."

Once Walsh assumed command, he quickly made himself very unpopular at the hospital by lining up the staff "like a lot of schoolboys—just to impress his authority on us. We've never needed authority before but worked hard & well [with] no orders," Grindlay wrote on 12 October. "Now every day we get a few orders or memoranda—just to handicap us usually & slow things down by having 'all go thru usual channels.'" Two days later, at "the schoolboys meeting this [morning] it came. An O.R. schedule has to be submitted to Walsh by 4 PM daily—this is how he is going to take the surgery—list himself as operator. I am amused not angry." In retaliation for Walsh's reassignment of hospital wards (which left Ted Gurney with only one), Seagrave and Grindlay pulled the nurses from the wards assigned to Walsh, Warrenburg, and Carter (a doctor from S.O.S.). When a soldier complained that afternoon that there had not been a nurse on one of the wards since early

13. Days and Nights at Ramgarh, 1942–1943   151

morning, Grindlay told Walsh and Warrenburg the reason, and they told Seagrave to put the nurses back on and restored Gurney's wards to him.

Matters came to a head on 15 October, when Seagrave, O'Hara, and Grindlay learned that Walsh and Warrenburg had asked Colonel John Tamraz to distribute the nurses to other facilities and merge the Seagrave unit with the 98th Station Hospital. The three men were debating how to handle the situation when Colonel Holcombe, the commander of the Ramgarh training center, appeared with Tamraz. They asked what was going on and

> *Doc skillfully (as we all agreed) made no complaint of other bunch. He advanced arguments for our staying separate & all agreed heartily. Then [Tamraz] lit into Walsh, saying he had failed his job in Karachi & was getting a last chance here, had been turned down for promotion & was a rotter etc. [The plan that Tamraz] proposed was separating our group & 98th hosp. entirely [with] Walsh having no orders over either of them, just titular post surgeon & C.O.... We are all overjoyed for this is just what we want, & celebrated [with] drinks.*

The next day, Grindlay happily wrote in his diary that the situation was resolved:

> *Great relief to feel that Walsh can't spy on me any more, try to discredit me etc. The hell [with] him & Warrenburg (who has turned into a twerp). [Tamraz] got everyone together this Am, told the other group off & gave the new orders.... No more paper work & orders for us.*[14]

Things calmed down somewhat after this episode. The day of 19 September was a relatively quiet one at the hospital. Grindlay learned that one of the hospital's American orderlies had gotten drunk, smashed up a truck, and would be court-martialed. Captain Carl Arnold visited from Stilwell's headquarters to get details of the conflict between the 98th and the Seagrave unit, and he dropped a hint that Seagrave would be promoted to lieutenant colonel. Arnold also said that Stilwell "will bounce Walsh for demanding that Lt. Johnson (Henry Myles Johnson, one of the surgeons) salute him & giving him hell." Grindlay spent that evening reading his diary to Seagrave, who was writing his memoir, *Burma Surgeon*: "I have spent quite a few evenings thus." The next evening he read out loud the section of his diary dealing with Burma and the walkout. "In doing so I have remembered what I never wrote down. I was just too tired to remember it at the time, I guess." Grindlay noted that his diary was the only record of events in Burma and during the walkout kept by a participant, and Seagrave's account would be based on it. Seagrave gave Grindlay the finished manuscript to read on 22 October: "It is really excellent. Really I must cuss & throw my weight around more than I realize," he sheepishly admitted after reading of his conduct in Burma.[15]

Stilwell, Williams, and Arnold (accompanied by Stilwell's aide, Lieutenant Colonel Frank Dorn) arrived on 24 October to inspect the hospital. Stilwell found Grindlay in his surgical ward "& greeted me [with] outstretched hand. Walsh was there; I guess he will never ask to be saluted again," Grindlay noted, gleefully imagining Walsh's reaction to witnessing the informality, warm friendship, and respect that existed between the theater commander and the surgeon. Grindlay had also showed the four officers through the ward and told them of his current cases, including a few skin grafts. "The old man [Stilwell] was much interested. He looked at everything, even the case in the O.R."

When he talked to Seagrave afterward, Grindlay learned that Williams had told him in confidence (to be confided only to Grindlay) that plans called for bringing 23,000 Chinese troops to Ramgarh for training, that the program for retraining and re-equipping was to be accelerated, and that in January or February 1943 the Seagrave unit would go back into Burma in two columns—one led by Seagrave, the other by Grindlay. Warrenburg and his 98th Station Hospital would be sent to an American airfield in Assam. "Warrenburg is in a funk worried about [being bombed]," Grindlay wrote.[16]

> Gen. Stilwell wants our group to do all the frontline work & will have Chinese units behind us ... to be brought down out of [China] for us to evacuate [patients] to.... We will go back over the [mountains] on trails—probably in Assam.... The doc [Seagrave] insists that I lead our half no matter what officer outranks me. The plan is for me to take Cummings, Maj. Budge, Chesley, Walt, Johnson, Koi, Saw Yen & half the other nurses. Doc says Gurney is afraid of me. I'm sorry I'm so damned gruff.[17]

Carl Arnold took Seagrave's book to give to Stilwell to read and approve its publication, in consideration of wartime censorship regulations. Grindlay thought that Seagrave did not praise Stilwell enough "but left the reader with an impression that [Seagrave] (& I also) were gruff & cursing old men." Stilwell took the manuscript with him to read on the flight back to Chungking.[18]

One night in early November, Grindlay and Chesley sat down to figure out how many of the original forty-four AMMISCA officers were still in the Far East. Four were dead: Major James Wilson (whom Grindlay mistakenly called "George Wilson," killed during an enemy bombing attack at Mandalay in 1942), Captain Roscoe Hambleton (died of illness in Burma in August 1942), Staff Sergeant Francis Astolfi (a victim of suicide, having shot himself in Delhi in May 1942), and Captain William M. Clarkson, from the adjutant general's office (date and circumstances of death unknown). Grindlay compiled a partial list of survivors in his diary:

Chungking: Lieutenant Colonel Arcadi Gluckman, Colonel Joseph Heinrich, Major Wyman F. Coudray, Staff Sergeant J.R. Lytle, Staff Sergeant Jacob Moul, Staff Sergeant Hubbard White, Staff Sergeant Melvin Tingly

Kunming: Major George Vaughn, Colonel Thomas Rees

Calcutta: Lieutenant Colonel Edwin M. Sutherland, Master Sergeant J.F. Bradley

13. Days and Nights at Ramgarh, 1942–1943   153

Delhi: Colonel Frank Merrill, Master Sergeant C. T. Bardenhagen
Ramgarh: Lieutenant Colonel George Sliney, Lieutenant Eugene Laybourne, Major Thomas M. Haywood, Lieutenant Ray Chesley, Captain John Grindlay
Dibrugarh: Lieutenant Marcus Ogden[19]

On 7 November, at dinner with Boatner and other officers, Grindlay heard more about the plans that were developing for the attack on Burma. These plans presaged those that were to be further expanded the following year at the QUADRANT and TRIDENT Conferences. An amphibious attack by the British was to be made on Rangoon, while another thrust would come from Imphal. Small parties would invade Burma through Ledo, heading toward Shingbwiyang and down the Hukawng Valley. "We [will] take up advanced positions while a road is made in behind us," Grindlay learned. The artillery would follow after the next rainy season. "Don't like the idea of sitting up in hills next monsoon," Grindlay worried. He also heard that Stilwell and Roosevelt had been informed that the Chinese Nationalists were storing Lend-Lease materials in caves for later use against the Communists, which became the subject of furious debate in later years. "[But we] have to keep up a gesture of aid to China."[20] More Chinese sick and wounded were arriving, stragglers from Burma as well as from surrounding training camps; although the flow was abating somewhat, it was still high. "We have had 3 trainloads of Chinese who escaped from Shwinbyan [sic] lately—not quite as bad as the first for they have been in a Brit. hosp. Enrollment now running 800 daily. Our wards [are] full." The wards operated by the S.O.S. group had fewer cases, because "they kick like hell at every [patient] anyhow so we don't give them many."[21]

On 9 November, Grindlay was shocked and angered to learn that nurse Big Bawk

> is pregnant! by one of our casual [detachment] boys.... I would like to beat him up. Don't really blame Bawk. After all, our codes are imposed on her & she doesn't see the social error. She told Doc some time ago, the time [when] she asked for a shot of strychnine from the pharmacy.... Doc told me tonight. If we have to take the boy [with] us [to Burma] I'll see he is shot.[22]

Grindlay and Seagrave conferred about performing an abortion on Big Bawk. Seagrave was finally convinced, despite his religious concerns, and early in the morning of 9 December the two surgeons carried out an abortion by lantern and flashlight. Big Bawk had told them that she did not want the baby; the procedure was done in secret so no one else would know (and possibly object), including the father, the nurses, and the missionary doctor, Ted Gurney. Afterward, they carried her back to Seagrave's room to let her recover.[23]

In the meantime, medical supplies from the United States were slowly arriving in greater quantities, including IV glucose, saline solutions and medicines. Grindlay asked Boatner for a stock of benzedrine[24] for the soldiers when they went into action in Burma. He returned to the hospital the following day, where he experienced one of those episodes that surgeons learn to mentally and emotionally cope with as part of life and death. One of the Chinese patients with severe Naga sores had his cast removed and was anesthetized with ethyl chloride while Grindlay put on a heavy tourniquet.

> *Then had to switch to* [chloroform]. *Did a Trueta* [tourniquet] *dressing & had* [the] *cast nearly on & told Koi to stop* [anesthesia]. *Soon* [the patient] *started gasping & I recognized that his* [heart] *had stopped—*[with chloroform] *death. The* [patient] *had had typhoid so heart muscle was toxic degen*[erated]. *Koi went to pieces. I then had to get her back to help me sew up a perforated* [duodenal] *ulcer. A hell of a tough day.*[25]

The next day was equally stressful. Big Bawk had to be rushed to an Indian civilian hospital in the area because the abortion had not been fully successful. She registered a fever of 105 degrees with a rapid pulse; clearly infection had set in. Grindlay put Big Bawk into an ambulance and took her to the hospital, where he got her started on sulfathiazole to fight the fever. Seagrave was persuaded to go along with them. "I never saw anyone so thoughtless as he," Grindlay grumbled to his diary. "He can't seem to comprehend she is in a dangerous state & hardly able to take care of herself, nor able to get proper help from the other girls as long as the thing is secret." Grindlay performed another procedure to remove fetal remains that had not been completely cleared. She began improving almost immediately and was much better the next day and fully recovered soon afterward.

The weeks that followed were filled with plans and preparations for the move to Burma, scheduled for February. Seagrave would leave first, with one echelon of the hospital staff, and Grindlay would follow in charge of the second group. His diary is replete with descriptions of days taken up mainly in routine surgeries (hernias, anal fistulas, and a constant stream of fractures and other injuries resulting from Chinese soldiers taking trucks and jeeps on joy rides and wrecking them) and treating malaria and dysentery cases. Chinese troops were arriving by the hundreds daily for inoculations in preparation for the upcoming military campaign. Grindlay also performed gallbladder surgery on the wife of the local British civilian surgeon, and he operated on the wife of Brigadier John McDowell to repair varicose veins. Grindlay himself fell ill for more than a week with an upset stomach, fatigue, and weakness, resulting in intense diarrhea, but he refused to stop working or to take emetrine, as Koi urged him to do. Finally, he sent a stool sample to Chesley, who found that Grindlay had amoebic dysentery. "Hell. If I'd not given up lately on my refusal to eat raw vegetables (tomatoes to be specific)," he wrote angrily, the illness might have been avoided. He turned over some surgical cases to others and finally went on emetrine at Seagrave's request and rapidly recovered.[26]

On 14 March, after much debate and waffling, Seagrave departed for Assam, where the head of the Ledo Road was located, with eight nurses and Lieutenant Kenneth D. Harris, who had arrived on 6 January from Delhi. As a member of the Medical Administrative Corps, Harris was an officer trained to carry out administrative duties in the medical field.[27] Grindlay and others saw the group off on the train to Calcutta. With Seagrave gone, Grindlay was busier than ever, taking many of the former's cases while coping with his own patient load. He was now averaging about fifteen operations per day.

Bill Duncombe (Friends Ambulance Unit). This photograph was taken about 1970 during a reunion of FAU members in London (photograph by Henrietta Thompson, in author's collection).

The third day of April was a red-letter day for Grindlay. As a token of gratitude for taking such good care of his wife during her surgery, Brigadier McDowell brought him a female bull terrier puppy that he had obtained from a friend in Calcutta. This little dog had three champions in her grandparents' lines. Along with the puppy, McDowell brought Grindlay her pedigree, diet lists, and two large tins of dog food. "She is a beautiful specimen, very lively and puppy-like now.... I had already decided to call her Matilda or Tillie." Grindlay had adopted a stray dog in Burma, which he had named Pete, but had to leave him behind when the march out began. He became extremely attached to Tilly (as he later called her), taking her with him when he went into Burma several weeks later and bringing her back home to the United States early in 1944.

14

Winding Down at Ramgarh

As 1943 began, the Seagrave Hospital Unit was entering its final period of service at Ramgarh before packing up and moving to facilities along the Ledo Road, then under construction from Ledo in India to eventually link up with the old Burma Road at Bhamo. Despite the increased amount of medical supplies arriving from the United States, critical shortages continued in the first half of 1943. Grindlay expressed both his frustration with the situation and the state of affairs in his diary on 6 April 1943.

> This business of medical supply is getting bad. They just don't have American medical, surgical or dental supplies. We are supposed to get 60 percent from British (in India) & the Brit. just don't have it—never did have it here—always imported it. That's the trouble [with Lend-Lease]. A Britisher [working] on [Lend-Lease] says "don't send them all those surg. instruments. Send us so many sets of wrenches to No. Africa & let the Americans take our surg. instruments in India." The Amer. [Lend-Lease] head agrees. Neither the Amer. or Brit. knows what can be gotten in India.

That evening, letters arrived from Seagrave and Captain William M. Webb, the latter a surgeon with the hospital unit.[1] Both men were leading parties of nurses and technicians into Burma. While Seagrave was taking one route from Tagap to Hpachet via Pebu, Webb was taking another. Seagrave intended to establish a hospital at Pebu, and Webb's unit had been ordered to provide medical support for a battalion of the Chinese 38th Division assigned to protect the right flank of the division's advance to Hpachet. Seagrave wrote that his group had been walking for six days in the rain and had been sniped at by Japanese troops.

Webb wrote a more dismal letter in which he reported that morale in his group was low because the nurses had not wanted to leave Ramgarh. The situation was aggravated by Little Bawk's peevish behavior, which, in addition to her status as Seagrave's personal nursing assistant, caused her to be disliked by the other nurses. Than Shwe was thrown out of the group for insisting that she be sent to China; Bill Cummings told her that she could either go

14. Winding Down at Ramgarh   157

with him to his outpost beyond Hpachet or return to Ramgarh. Grindlay and Gurney sat down that night and discussed the situation and how morale could be maintained among the nurses remaining at Ramgarh. Grindlay finally decided that he would censor all incoming and outgoing mail for "morale & military" reasons.

Grindlay was also growing disgusted with the lack of action on the Chinese front in Yunnan. Thirty Chinese divisions were supposedly being trained there by the Americans to make up Y ("Yoke") Force for a thrust against the Japanese along the Burma Road. "The surgeon ... operating at Paoshan, has had 9 wounded in last 9 months," Grindlay complained.

> The daily Chin[ese] war communiques are laughable—*not a shot fired for a long long time. I heard story of Clair Luce[']s visit to the Yellow River "front"* [in China].... *The Chin*[ese] *laid the stage there, put a few Chin*[ese] *troops in trenches they dug on one bank & sent a few on other bank to fire a few shots—but no Japs for hundreds of miles—just a show arranged by* [Chinese government publicist Hollington] *Tong*.[2]

Three days later Grindlay heard a report from Captain David McConnell (an old friend from the group that had accompanied Stilwell to China in 1942 and who was serving as legal advisor and provost marshal to the Chinese First Army) that Stilwell was returning to the United States with Ambassador Gauss. "Supposedly due to the madame [sic], who is in the U.S. now being worshipped by the U.S. She is trying to get Stilwell out & Chennault in.... If Stilwell doesn't come back I don't want to stay here," he wrote gloomily. McConnell had served as secretary to Senator James Byrnes of South Carolina before the war.[3] Stilwell wrote in his own diary that he was called to Washington by General Marshall for a meeting late in April at the request of Chiang Kai-shek. The Generalissimo also sent Chennault to present a new approach regarding the conduct of the war in China, but Stilwell considered it the same old "'6-months-to-drive-the-Japs-out-of-China' plan." He and Chennault remained in Washington after the meetings with General Marshall in order to attend the TRIDENT conference of 12–25 May.[4]

Grindlay left with his puppy Tilly on 5 May for a twelve-day R&R leave in Darjeeling and to escape the terrific heat then settling on the Indian plains. He returned to the hospital twelve days later; at this point, his diary entries became brief: "Too hot to write. Sweat pours & I have to keep wiping hands on towel in lap." A lot had occurred in his absence, he discovered. "New surgeon & head nurse [Lieutenant Matilda Dykstra] here & rest of this unit to arrive any day. We may be out in a week." The new unit, the 48th Evacuation Hospital, was from Rhode Island Hospital in Providence and was split between Ramgarh and a site along the Ledo Road. The unit had been activated in August 1942 and was under the command of Colonel Charles L. Leedham, a 40-year-old from Clinton, Iowa, characterized by Grindlay as an antagonistic officer with whom he soon clashed. The issue was, as Grindlay explained in his diary on 19 May, that "I had seen our unit [i.e., the Seagrave Hospital Unit] punched about by everyone who had ever been [in command of] it, & if I was wrong about him O.K. If he behaved I'd apologize." Grindlay and O'Hara met with General McCabe, the commander of the Ramgarh hospital and training camp, and the latter took up the issue with Leedham. Leedham took out his anger at being called on the carpet by McCabe by giving the surgeons grief the next day. That same day a report was received that 85 American soldiers and three officers "have been missing in Assam some time—just disappeared."[5] No other details of this incident emerged afterward; it may have been only a rumor.

Dykstra, the head nurse of the 48th Evacuation Hospital, "is a peach," Grindlay noted on 21 May. But she and the others "have to learn tropical medicine," a conclusion he reached after Dykstra put a sheet over a man with a fever, causing his temperature to soar to an alarming (and potentially fatal) 108 degrees. Grindlay intervened and hurriedly applied wet towels to the patient and the fever dropped, thus saving the man from brain damage and possible death.

The following day, one hundred enlisted men and eleven officers of the 48th Evacuation Hospital arrived: "Good lads. I knew 2 at Harvard & rest have also had good training." Their chief of surgery was Lieutenant Colonel William A. Mahoney, a middle-aged physician from Rhode Island Hospital, whom Grindlay described as "likeable, & the real organizer of the unit."

The next few days were spent trying to organize and orient the newcomers to the routines in the hospital, while at the same time Grindlay and the rest of the Seagrave unit were preparing to join the others in Burma. Grindlay asked General McCabe to request air transport to Ledo. In the meantime, the new doctors from the 48th Evacuation Hospital were confused, disorganized, and (in Grindlay's judgment) "poorly led." "No comprehension of the job, or how long to do it, & little hope for correction of this for a long time." The staff, however, turned out to be fast learners, especially when it came to dealing with and treating large numbers of Chinese patients. Still, everything remained in great confusion because the new commanding officer, Leedham, was regarded by his staff as an outsider—an Iowan among Rhode Islanders—and disparaged as "a complete dope." Grindlay sat down with Mahoney on 25 May to give the latter an orientation talk about the hospital. The latter "shook his head, & said 'what has kept you going?'" On 29 May Grindlay reported that the unpopular Colonel Leedham's "nurse friend arrived on our planes & he & she carried on like 2 college freshmen." He went on to vent his frustration and anger with the situation that Leedham had created in rather strong language: "He is a regular army [surgeon] stooge foisted on them who is a pompous coward [with] a provost brain acting like a Hitler."[6]

15

Back to Burma and Home

On 30 May Grindlay's group flew to Ranchi and traveled in trucks to Margherita on the Ledo Road, where they were met by the commanding officer of the other half of the 48th Evacuation Hospital, Major Eric P. Stone, and shown to their quarters. Tired and dirty, Grindlay took a bath and pulled leeches off his ankles. "Sheets bloody next [morning]," he noted in his diary.

The next day Grindlay and O'Hara went out to find the Northern Combat Area Command (NCAC) headquarters and finally located it fifteen miles farther along the road. Brigadier General Haydon Boatner, the NCAC commander, greeted them heartily and sent a radio message to Seagrave that they were en route. They also encountered the Reverend Brayton Case once again, who was growing a large vegetable garden, usefully employing his extensive agricultural background and experience. In the evening, they hosted the doctors from the part of the 48th Evacuation Hospital stationed near Ledo; alcohol flowed in large quantities, which loosened tongues, and stories were exchanged "roasting Leedham." "Really a fine gang of docs," Grindlay concluded, perhaps because they all shared sympathetic views. He and O'Hara learned that Colonel Warrenburg, their former commander who had been transferred with the 98th Evacuation Hospital to Margherita, had "made a hell of a mess" there, "which is further proof that we were right."

On 2 June Grindlay visited the 20th General Hospital at Margherita, the largest facility in the theater, and went on rounds with Colonel Isador Ravdin, the hospital commander. "Ravdin asked me for my experiences after each case. I am a celebrity here. They probably have only 300 [patients] so are carrying on like a med. School [sic] & dont know what job is about." The rest of that day and the next were spent in dealing with details before setting off for Burma. He had dinner with staff from 20th General, and they "pumped me a lot. Their quarters [are] luxurious for the jungle." More lunches and visits followed two days later (5 June), when Grindlay was shown through the 73rd Evacuation Hospital, which had been raised from the staff of the Los Angeles County Hospital. He met the commanding officer and chiefs of surgery and medicine. He also met with Lieutenant Colonel Vincent Haas of the U.S. Public Health Service ("He & I came [to China] at the same time & are oldest in theater") about getting supplies and equipment for the hospital in Burma and learned that they would start out at noon the next day by truck for Hell Gate (Pansau Pass). That night, the girls sang "as usual & Koi is putting me to bed now while rest of boys are drinking [with] 48th [Evacuation Hospital] gang on veranda."[1]

On 6 June, a Sunday, after lunch, the group climbed into the trucks to ride to Pansau Pass.

> Thru a gap in foothills, thru the densest tangle of jungle of big trees, rattan & bamboo. [Ledo] Road well-engineered Muddy & mud deep in spots. Amer[ican] negro road gangs yelled & cheered at nurses. Finally around Hellgate [sic] in pouring rain. A Major Prescott, a [quartermaster], very nasty in arranging for porters but I insisted on 70+. Camped in jungle & how the trucks ever got in thru mud, deep mud holes, stumps, river etc.... Hard rain. All camped in one basha. Like old days. Girls chipper. [After supper] we had a bunch of negros including quartet in to sing. Excellent singing in real negro fashion. Marvelous spirituals that delighted the girls, who sang too.[2]

The next day they were off again, this time reaching the roadhead in pouring rain and wading through deep mud on the road trace for seven miles to reach a camping point. En route they saw lean-to bashas that contained skeletons of refugees who had perished during the mass exodus the year before. Two of them were arm in arm—a husband and wife, perhaps, who had died together. The following morning the travelers marched eight miles, most of it in the rain. "Skeletons about every 100 yards, usually in groups of old bashas.... Last mile runs along river in deep mud by lots of old refugee huts. Over another bamboo suspension bridge to camp.... Skulls (10) right around basha, [with] lots of other bones.... Bath and clothes wash in rain. Drank some of our bourbon.... This is one of largest refugee camps where lots died or drowned."

On 10 June, the group arrived at Nawlip, on a river of the same name, where they stayed for a day, resting. Everyone was soaked and exhausted. Grindlay picked up a "perfect skull & jaw" and carried them for a while before discarding them because it "[was] too much trouble for I was having all I could do to keep on my feet slipping down the Naga short cuts. Knees gone out & I was wretchedly tired." The leeches were bad, as were the sand flies, whose bites, he wrote, "itch like hell."

From atop a hill on 13 June the travelers glimpsed their destination, Tagap Ga, in the distance. They were close enough that they did not need to carry any food, and Tilly could ride in one of the porters' baskets. The "leech trail," as Grindlay called it, was "really straight down, then straight up. Narrow & the ground & [the] leaves [were] alive [with] many big & tiny leeches." They halted after walking about five miles and picked off leeches. The nurses were "very dejected because of leeches & stiff climb & continual rain." They descended into a deep river gorge, crossed it, and then began a long, sheer ascent on an almost invisible trail through dense jungle. It rained hard the whole time. "Elephants & Chinese horses & other travel made this trail bad, [with] deep mud holes," Grindlay wrote. After a strenuous trek of a dozen miles past numerous bones and skulls, they reached the Seagrave hospital at Tagap Ga. "Lots of shouting," Grindlay wrote happily, as he and his group was greeted by nurses Than Shwei and Ruby. "Bath at the river ... dry clothes, dinner, singing, etc. Lots to talk about—the fighting here, plans etc. To bed late. Leaking roof drenched Koi, Louise & I. Tilly very chipper after her ride today."

The hospital was on the slope of a hill facing north, where Grindlay could see the Himalayas some fifty miles away. A nearby hill to the northeast was covered with Naga villages and blocked a view of the mountains around Fort Hertz. The hills closer to Tagap were thickly covered with jungle, Grindlay noted, in which monkeys and jungle fowl "make a continual din—& are answered by our own roosters."[3]

After resting for a day, Grindlay plunged into surgery. The hospital's patients were mostly Chinese soldiers who were fighting the Japanese to clear the trace for the Ledo Road. The dispensary was very busy with about 100 dressings a day for outpatients; only thirty cases were in the hospital, these suffering mainly from malaria and Naga sores. The nurses were "doing [a] crude job dressing but [patients] too filthy to warrant more," Grindlay wrote wearily. Many of the men also had numerous infected sand fly and flea bites.

After each day's work was finished, Grindlay spent time listening to stories from Bill Cummings (a former missionary and now a member of V Force, a special British detachment that operated mainly behind the Japanese lines) and from Seagrave about his trek to Tagap. The Japanese had counterattacked to within five miles of the hospital when Seagrave had first arrived, and they periodically occupied Shingbwiyang at the northern end of the Hukawng Valley. (It will be remembered that Shingbwiyang was the refugee camp where Captain Roscoe Hambleton and hundreds of other refugees had perished in August 1942, and it would become Stilwell's headquarters later in the year after the area was fully secured.) Seagrave told Grindlay that he was planning to take some nurses and go on to Hkalah in support of the 22nd Chinese Division. Hkalah was some distance beyond the hospital that Captain William Webb had set up along with Tun Shein, Hla Sein, and Lulu. Seagrave was due to leave in a few days and planned to trade places with Grindlay in a month; later, the two of them would each establish small hospitals at intervals along the main trails as well as the Ledo Road trace. Ted Gurney, who was promoted to captain in the U.S. Marine Corps on 18 June, was also destined to depart

Map showing Northern Burma. This is the area where Grindlay was based at Tagap Ga near the Hukawng Valley and spent a week in late 1943 trekking through nearby mountains to the north and west, treating natives in several small Naga villages (Patrick Lathrop).

15. Back to Burma and Home

soon to work among the Nagas and repair some of the damage that the Chinese had inflicted on the native peoples.[4]

> *The Chinese have sadly mistreated the Nagas here* [Grindlay wrote in his diary]— *stolen pigs, chickens & dogs, robbed & beaten them etc.* [This abuse dated back to 1942, when the retreating Chinese armies had pillaged native villages as they tried to make their way out of Burma.] *Now the Nagas fear & loath the Chinks & refuse to do anything for them. They think fairly well of British, but the Brit. have lost face by their retreats etc. (as the V-force that left equip etc. & fled from Hkalah recently, saying 400 Japs had come up, whereas Bills* [Cummings] *Kachin spies said only 40). The Nagas think well of Americans, they haven't fled yet (Bill & Doc have done a lot here to gain their respect) ... Bill laid waste one of the border villages because they had listened to a pro-Jap Kachin. The Nagas respect & fear him & his name* [is] *known all about.*
>
> *Bill almost continually visited by Kachin spies, giving reports of Japs.... Incidently, spies report a lot of Jap bashas* [south] *of here—we bombed & strafed them ... next day; Japs had rafts to float down river to here & take this place—we strafed them & when they were rebuilt & loaded* [with] *food did the same thing* [with] *result Japs had to go back; 2 Kachin villages delegates asked to be strafed because all surrounding villages bad & the Japs would think they were pro-British & punish them; Kachin forced labor asked us not to strafe bridge they were building saying "we will build it poorly & slowly & let you know when it is done, then strafe it & we won't be killed"; etc., etc.*

V Force was a special unit of the British army tasked with collecting intelligence and conducting guerrilla operations behind enemy lines. It was created by Lieutenant Colonel A.A. Donald in April 1942 on the orders of General Wavell (commander in chief, India and Burma), who perceived the threat of a possible Japanese attack into Assam and the Arakan. V Force was not a part of Force 136, the British SOE organization that operated in Burma, but instead reported to IV Corps, which was responsible for the defense of eastern India. V Force was initially drawn from military police battalions made up of Gurkhas led by British officers, and it cooperated closely with both Force 136 and the American OSS, which operated in Burma as Detachment 101. When the anticipated enemy attack did not materialize for almost two years, V Force became chiefly an intelligence-gathering organization, with more native tribesmen—Chins, Kachins, and Nagas—recruited into its ranks because of their knowledge of Assam and northern Burma. The native Assam Rifles continued to be the nucleus of V Force for the next two years. (The first units of the Assam Rifles began operating in Burma in June 1942, serving as guides and porters to help the thousands of refugees reach safety in India.) As time went on, Americans were also assigned to the unit as officers and leaders of native squads and platoons, along with men such as Bill Cummings, who had lived in Burma for years and knew the territory like the natives. Information collected by V Force and its companion, Z Force (both of which operated in the Arakan), was sent to an SOE station (known as GS I(k) until it became Force 136 in March 1944) in India. These special units were responsible for internal security and intelligence gathering up to sixty miles behind Japanese positions. Lieutenant Colonel John Wilson, formerly a tea planter in pre-war India, succeeded Lieutenant Colonel Donald as commander of V Force in 1943.[5]

***

In the meantime, Little Bawk was continuing to cause trouble in the Seagrave unit, and "Doc [is] powerless to stop it," Grindlay fretted in his diary. "When she leaves [with] him [for Hkalah] morale & spirit will pick up again like it did in Ramgarh.... [A] lot of affection & devotion they had for him is lost & has gone to me. I am fair (try to be) & they respect my work, energy, firmness etc. No conceit. Several [nurses] refused to go [with] Doc, then told me they wanted to stay [with] me. (I tried to talk them out of it) ... Bawk has stolen food, caused all sorts of fights etc."[6]

Another concern surfaced on 18 June when Grindlay learned from Seagrave that one of the nurses, Esther Po, was pregnant. The father was rumored to be Lieutenant Kenneth Harris, one of the medical administration officers and a man who claimed to be quite religious. "A hell of a note," Grindlay growled about the situation. He, O'Hara, and Seagrave conferred on how to proceed. "Probably fault of both, but I find it hard to figure Harris. Thought he really understood our 'father & daughter' relations [with] those gals. I can honestly say there has hardly been any temptation even to me, anyhow—too much color etc. difference." (Grindlay seems to have had a distinct dislike for interracial mixing, although he definitely was not a racial bigot and got along with men and women of all races.) The surgeons eventually agreed that an abortion was necessary and decided to administer castor oil as a purgative in hopes of inducing a miscarriage.[7]

An air drop that same day brought a troubling letter from Grindlay's wife, Betty. She had been ill "but was sweet & cheerful anyhow. I felt like hell. How I want to go home.... I hope this thing [i.e., the war] goes fast & I can be spared. But it looks like 6 mo. more at least. I wish I could write of [my] experiences to Betty but a lot of them would worry her." Grindlay recalled that 20 June marked twenty-one months since he had been separated from his wife.

Seagrave and Grindlay had by now served with each other for about a year and a half, and the "Burma Surgeon" had had ample opportunity to observe his brilliant chief of surgery. Their respect for each other was often in evidence, despite sometimes getting on each other's nerves, but perhaps nowhere did Seagrave express his admiration for Grindlay with more undisguised fervor than in his memoir, which he published in 1943 as *Burma Surgeon* (which became a best seller and made him a national hero overnight). This first book was followed three years later by a second, *Burma Surgeon Returns*, in which Seagrave's appreciation for Grindlay continued unabated:

15. Back to Burma and Home

> *Grindlay is a funny cuss. To listen to his claims he is a growling, atheistic, profane hater of all mankind. In practice he is gentle, kind, inordinately interested in humanity, especially in its stranger forms. He sits for hours making the natives talk about themselves, their customs, their strange ideas. By the time he has done he has won them into feeling themselves his equals and they are eager to give him everything they have. Completely antagonistic to the very idea of missionaries, he is the best medical missionary I've ever seen.*[8]

Grindlay busied himself around the hospital compound with clearing brush and generally keeping the hospital sanitary, including destroying contaminated dressings. He built boardwalks to enable people to avoid wading in the mud and burned the brush that he cleared from the area. The case load continued to be heavy, mainly treating many small sores and abscesses on the Chinese soldiers, including old septic Naga sores that had become ulcerous. "I put three [cases into the hospital] today & tonight they left to smoke opium," Grindlay noted resignedly. Two doctors from the 151st Medical Battalion dropped by for a visit on 26 June and toured the facility. "[T]hey saw us all working like beavers at hard labor etc—& tonight had bull session [with] them, over some G.I. gin." Seagrave had built a dam on a small stream and created a swimming pool. "Bulled last night [26 June with] Doc, who got very interested over his appreciation of my help." They discussed Esther's situation again: the castor oil purge had not worked, and other efforts to induce an abortion over the past two days had likewise failed.

The next evening they held another "bull session" that lasted until 1:00 in the morning, again fueled by gin. Grindlay awoke the following morning with a "bit of a hangover." The topic of Little Bawk and her troublemaking arose once more. Seagrave said that she was the only one among the nurses who knew of Esther's condition and the earlier incident involving Big Bawk back at Ramgarh. They realized that she was a threat to all the other girls but came to no conclusions on how to deal with her.

Bill Cummings and Ray Chesley left for Shingbwiyang on the morning of 27 June via the old Refugee Trail ("No white man has gone down this trail to Shing this year [others had gone down the Hkalah trail]," Grindlay noted in his diary) to reconnoiter the town and verify that the Japanese had left and to meet a Kachin patrol coming up the Hukawng Valley from the opposite direction. Chesley went along "for [the] excitement" and to scout likely places to set up another Seagrave hospital. Grindlay received permission from Seagrave to accompany them, but at the last minute Cummings could not find an additional porter and had to deliver the bad news to Grindlay. "I couldn't go far & don't think I could carry even a light bed-roll & Springfield [rifle], & I refused to overreach on the one can of C-ration they had to make do them a week." Instead, he plunged into his work to forget his disappointment, including building "a decent latrine.... Doc's old one beside the stream offends all my medical training" regarding proper sanitation and disease control.

Grindlay also started a hospital library from books scattered around Seagrave's quarters.

Gurney was slated to depart on 2 July for Tarung Ga, a week's march away in Naga country, with FAU member Bill Duncomb, three nurses, and the headman of Tarung. But it was the rainy season, and the party was held up by high water in the streams they would have to cross. The stream next to the hospital "roars like a Niagra," Grindlay wrote. The pervasive dampness made the "V-cigarettes hard to keep dry enough to smoke despite daily heating."[9] Grindlay expressed his deep admiration for the pilots who flew into the rainstorms to drop supplies. "The risks those boys take!" he wrote admiringly on 4 July.

The V Force camp included Lieutenant Colonel Wilson (commander), Bill Cummings (second in command), Captains Vincent Curl and Peter Lutken, and other members of the group at Hkalak Ga and was just up the trail nearby. Wilson had a bottle of Canadian Club whiskey and invited members of the Seagrave Hospital Unit, including Grindlay, to join them. The group sat around and "bulled" for a several hours that night. The V Force members stayed in the area for a month or more, providing Grindlay with some good conversation. Lutken remembered that Grindlay talked about meeting four surviving members of "the Long Walk"—former prisoners who had escaped from a camp in the Russian Gulag in Siberia and trekked across Mongolia and Tibet into northern India in 1942. This story was chronicled by Slavomir Rawicz (who claimed to be one of the walkers) in *The Long Walk*, originally published in the mid-1950s. Debate continues to the present day about whether the story is a fabrication, since Linda Willis, in her book *Looking for Mr. Smith*, offered documentary evidence that seems to prove that Rawicz was elsewhere when the walk supposedly occurred. Grindlay never mentioned meeting any of the former prisoners, which is a curious omission in his diary; he usually was careful to write down all such momentous or interesting events during his service in the China-Burma-India theater.

Gurney finally got off on 6 July, though reluctant to carry opium, his religious foundations clearly showing. "Everyone traveling here takes opium—only opium & silver good as pay, & they [the Nagas] are surfeited [with silver] now," Grindlay wrote.

On 24 July, forty-eight cartons of cigarettes were air dropped along with all the medical supplies that Grindlay had requested, along with a new boiler for the sterilizer, which got badly dented in the drop. This delivery left Grindlay in a good mood: "We have nearly all [the medical] supplies we need, & good stocks of them. Even 12 new lanterns [arrived]." Grindlay was also preparing to leave on 26 July for a weeklong journey into the mountains to Naga villages (similar to that undertaken by Gurney), where he, Koi, nurse Malang Kaw, and Staff Sergeant Chester F. Deaton would extend medical aid.

Gurney had returned on 22 July, but Grindlay's attempt to place him in charge of surgery was met with resistance: "I don't believe he likes the job," he concluded. O'Hara finally agreed to fill in.

Grindlay's group set off at 9:00 in the morning, stopping at the V Force camp to pick up a two-and-a-half-pound box of opium and four cartons of "V" cigarettes as gifts for the Nagas. Bill Cummings said that an American plane had crashed in the mountains near the Gedu Hka (river) and asked Grindlay to try to find the wreckage and look for survivors. He also secretly requested that, if Grindlay did reach the area, where no other white men had previously been, he should try to learn whether the inhabitants were friendly and if a pass existed from the Hukawng Valley into the Gedu Hka Valley, which ran along the northern edge of the Hukawng and was separated from it by a range of steep hills and ridges. The Americans speculated that, if such a pass existed, it might be possible for the Japanese to cross into the Gedu Hka Valley and surprise Allied positions in the Hukawng Valley.

On the first day, the group reached the first Naga village, Tsumpa Ga, situated 3,500 feet above Tagap. The climb to the village was a hot and exhausting one, made more arduous by having to ford the swift-running Tarung River on bamboo rafts and hike up a trail through thick jungle past huge hardwood trees (possibly teak) ten to fifteen feet in diameter and festooned with creepers. Deaton and Malang Kaw were both overweight and became dizzy and nauseated by the heat and exhaustion. The party emerged onto the summit of a grassy knoll and entered the village of about a dozen houses, "2 of them extremely long," Grindlay later wrote. The headman greeted the newcomers, and they were escorted to their guest house, reachable by a ten-foot notched ladder. The group was served tea in black bamboo cups, and then they reclined on mats near the fire to rest. After their nap, Grindlay gave the headman several packages of cigarettes, and the group walked down to a creek and bathed. A meal was prepared for them and more gifts were distributed, including K-ration candy and sugar, "all voraciously accepted."

A lengthy conversation ensued following the meal, with the nurses interpreting (Malang Kaw, a Kachin, translated the Kachin language spoken by the Nagas into Burmese, and Koi translated from Burmese to English). Grindlay learned that the villagers used to be in Tagap but were driven out the year before because of the stench of hundreds of dead refugees around them and by the passing hordes of civilians and soldiers who sacked the village of everything transportable or edible. One family had lost its buffalo because the refugees shot at them and frightened them away. Once the conversation ended, the Naga men settled down to smoke their opium pipes and fall asleep by the fire, while Grindlay's party retreated to the other end of the house for the night, sleeping under mosquito nets.

The next day (27 July) the medical team treated a parade of men, women and children, and Koi brought Grindlay a container of Naga rice beer. The sick were treated for Naga sores, headaches, backaches, and other such relatively minor ailments. One of the young men, the boatman who had navigated the raft on which they had crossed the Tarung River, was diagnosed with a greatly enlarged spleen and anemia, signs of long-term malarial infection; Grindlay gave him a letter for Gurney and told him to go to Tagap for treatment. Every patient was given a few pills or had their sores dressed. Sodium bicarbonate was used for leg pain, aspirin for headaches, and a cathartic pill (purgative) for malingerers. "[M]y most satisfied and enthusiastic patients were those who had received cathartic pills," Grindlay later wrote proudly, but perhaps with tongue in cheek.

The village was situated on the edge of the cliff, and the visitors walked out to take in the view of the country around them from its edge. Grindlay noted the "forbidding valley" at the bottom of a yawning chasm that dropped into a dark jungle through which rushed the Tarung River. Across the chasm to the southeast they saw Tagap, 3,500 feet below them, and Grindlay could pick out his hospital and other buildings. To the south were several ridges and the formidable Hukawng Valley stretching beyond; to the east was some of the most stunning scenery he had seen since he had returned to Burma, with the potentially strategic Gedu Hka Valley visible between two mountain ridges. A few sunlit clouds rose above the mountain peaks, and at lower elevations there were dense gray mists and rain squalls masking a few of the slopes. High white cliffs marked the southern wall of the valley, and Grindlay recalled that it had not been explored. "I realized that I had only one real desire on this trip—to go up the Gedu Hka."

That evening, a 90-year-old man whom the group had met the day before, wearing a tasseled turban and an English public school blazer given him by a refugee in exchange for rice, told them of his life in the old days. He had come to the area about sixty years earlier while on a war expedition and stayed on. He told them of villages in the snowy mountains to the north, reporting

> that no one else has ever been there, that people there are still naked as in old days, that they get their poison for arrows from a small plant that grows near the snow there, that people there probably still use it; of headhunting & dances about heads, that only old people still know these dances, of taking British soldier heads, of their amazement & surprise at arrival of white men.[10]

Grindlay guessed that the plant he mentioned might have been nightshade, from which belladonna was extracted as arrow poison.

Grindlay's stomach was still not quite back to normal, and his evening meal caused him distress exacerbated by the exertion of climbing to the village the day before and the mountaintop chilliness. His dog Tilly was also exhausted and could not hold down her food: "[She] just lies on [a] blanket

15. Back to Burma and Home

under my coat & shivers & sleeps." Grindlay drank Naga beer that night and went to bed early after watching the men get out their opium pipes again. A brother of the headman departed to go to the next village, Tawaw Ga, and introduce the group before they arrived.

On the morning of 28 July, Grindlay and the nurses held sick call for more of the Nagas, and then nine women appeared to act as porters. The group left the village and trekked over steep trails, hugging the streams and crossing another torrential river. Here Grindlay almost lost his dog, whose health was improving as the day progressed. He had carried her through waist-deep water to the opposite bank and returned to assist one of the porters when he was startled to see Tilly being swept past him by the strong current. He dived after her, grabbing her tail and pulling her ashore. The Nagas laughed loudly at Grindlay's performance, and he had to dry out his clothes and wristwatch on a sunny rock.

The group paused for half an hour to rest, bathe, and cool off at the Tarung River, and then they were off again, up a trail that led to the next village. Along the way, Grindlay found himself craving American beer "something awful," even though he had had strong Naga rice beer the day before.[11] Soon after resuming their hike, the guide, Hla Duk, suddenly knelt over and examined the ground closely. He had seen the heel print of a shoe and suggested that, while it might have been made by a Japanese soldier, it was more likely that of a Chinese deserter. These were men who either were wandering through the jungles of northern Burma, trying to find their way back to China, or had become bandits. Most deserters were discovered, Grindlay later wrote, often lying dead along the trails or dying of disease and exhaustion in Naga villages. The Nagas had learned the year before that Chinese soldiers were dangerous because they frequently indulged in looting and rape and were to be avoided unless they were sick and helpless. In those cases, the soldiers would be taken to a Naga village to recover and be watched. A little farther on the travelers saw the footprint again, and this time it was clear enough to be identified as a British army boot, the type issued to Chinese soldiers. Grindlay felt uncomfortable with the idea that a Chinese deserter, who might be trigger-happy and starving, was in their area and could threaten the group, especially the nurses. He, of course, carried a sidearm and was determined to defend them, if necessary.

They reached the top of a hill next to the taller Tawaw Bum and saw the charming village of Tawaw, with a herd of about twenty buffalo grazing and keeping the grass cropped "like a golf course," Grindlay noted. This village had ten houses, with the usual dogs, cats, pigs, chickens, and small children running everywhere and bare-breasted women hanging over porch railings while scolding the youngsters. Again the visitors climbed to the main floor of the headman's house by means of a notched ladder and ate ears of corn roasted in the fire, after which they descended a quarter mile to a spring below the village and bathed, and the women washed their clothes. Grindlay later wrote that

> At bed roll time [we] *found not quite so much room for our* [mosquito] *nets as at Tsumpa. Koi and Kaw wanted me to have everything & I refused & ordered them to take best place & also blanket. They got mad & I had hell of a time consoling Koi telling her I refused to take everything selfishly but finally accepting the blanket.* [Sergeant] *Deaton is certainly a lazy good-for-nothing. I tell him something & he stands (or lies) stubbornly & ignores it. I'll send him elsewhere—he is not good on trail even—too fat & lazy & whining about his supposed ailments.*

Grindlay asked Hla Duk if the Nagas still indulged in headhunting and was told that they had stopped twenty-five or thirty years earlier. He learned that the scattered villages in the area had all spun off from a very large one of roughly 300 houses, surrounded by a wall of sharpened stakes and a moat. The village was now destroyed, the site covered with elephant grass; no one knew where it used to be. Tawaw was about thirty years old and due to be abandoned because the farmland around the village was wearing out.

A village visible on the hill above them was called Gedu Tsu, and another village named Gedu Ga was just beyond it. Hla Duk offered to lead Grindlay to Gedu Tsu if they could go alone, as the climb would be too much for the porters. Grindlay was not only thrilled by the prospect of going up to Gedu Tsu but also flattered that the Naga guide had "respect ... for my ability" to climb the steep trails. "No one had ever been up beyond Gedu Ga until 30 years ago, & no white man has *ever* been beyond Tawaw, & only a few have ever been here," he bragged excitedly in his diary.

On the morning of 29 July, Grindlay treated the headman's feet for Naga sores—"much better already & he is pleased," he wrote later in the day—and then he set off with his guide and a pack containing three D-ration chocolate bars and six cans of C-rations consisting of biscuits and ready-to-eat precooked meals, plus ten pounds of medical supplies. He waved gaily to the rest of the group ("Deaton looks as though he thinks I can't do it"). Just past the village Grindlay and Hla Duk met two Nagas coming toward them. The men carried a message, wrapped in layers of plantain leaf to keep it dry, from a Lieutenant Bramston, an English V Force officer, who had been sent by General Boatner to find the same crashed plane that Cummings had asked Grindlay to help locate before he left Tagap. Bramston had requested a supply drop of Very pistols and flares; although he did not give his location, Grindlay assumed that it was Gedu Ga. He wrote a return note and said that he was heading for Gedu Ga and would give what medical aid he could, assuming there were survivors.

He and Hla Duk continued on a faint trail through dense, dark jungle filled with huge trees, accompanied by the howling of gibbons and sparrow-sized "cicadas going off like sirens, & occasional coo from a huge [green] dove, or chatter of mocking bird." They descended on a steep trail, using roots for footholds, to a tributary of the Tarung River, the Gedu, "a rushing roaring torrent" shadowed in jungle gloom; they crossed the water and immediately started a steep ascent, this time not pausing to bathe in their eagerness to escape the dripping, melancholy forest.

> Wringing wet [with] sweat, & as usual sweat trickling from nose & chin. I thought it hardest, steepest, longest & hottest climb I'd ever made. Wringing wet, panting (despite usual halts) we arrive at a more level trail out of the black jungle, in bamboo thickets & then came to a point where our feeble trail came to a well-traveled one. Here I plopped down & Hla Duk & I drank from my canteen, ate a block of D-ration & smoked a cigarette. At this point was a small totem of forked sticks & an egg & skull on top. I gathered it was a sacrifice (used to put heads there) to [the] bad spirit of [the] trail.... Lying there Hla Duk taught me Kachin (Jinpaw) words for trail (lam), farm (vie).

The village lay only a little farther on and consisted of eight houses with a central buffalo wallow. The villagers cautiously peeked out of the open ends of their houses at the strange white foreigner. Hla Duk comforted them with the explanation that Grindlay was an American, a friend, who had come with medicine to treat them for diseases. To the surgeon's surprise, several men quickly came to him with Naga sores, and others appeared with enlarged spleens and headaches. He was tempted to tell them to go down to Tawaw for treatment, but "I knew the people would think me a fake or impolite so I treated them."

Afterward, he indicated to the Nagas that he wanted to move on, and two men were assigned to Grindlay, wearing dahs (curved knives). One man, the son of the headman, carried his father's smooth-bore muzzleloader rifle. During one of the rest stops, Grindlay demonstrated how his .45 caliber army-issue automatic pistol worked and fired off a couple rounds, to the amazement of the tribesmen. This trail was another laborious climb, steeply upward through dark forested jungle. At the top, Grindlay blacked out and slumped to the ground. He gradually recovered while Hla Duk fanned him, and he ate a piece of a chocolate bar with some fruit that the guide picked from a tall tree and smoked a cigarette. Then they continued on their way, through jungle and bamboo thickets, and arrived in Gedu Tsu after another moderate climb to find a village with the usual "naked children and women, respectively, following and inspecting us." Grindlay noticed that none of the women wore anything above the waist except "wampum beads about [the] neck" and earrings.

The newcomers climbed a ladder to the headman's house and interrupted a council of elders. Exhaustion again caught up with Grindlay:

> I just folded up. The dewar [headman] & his mother took off my leggings & shoes & socks, picking off the leeches & killing [them with] a [fire] brand. I lay on the mat &

dropped into a brief doze. Duk woke me ... & shoved his brass cup to me, filled [with] *delicious cider-like rice beer. I quaffed it & felt swell.... I was soon given a white chicken, & a woman gave me a couple of eggs. The dewar made pot after pot (a tin can pot hung from the frame over the fire) of hpalek* [tea]*; and bamboo tubes were kept going* [filled with tea].... *Soon a pot of rice cooking, & my chicken made into one curry & another curry of spicy jungle vegetables.*

Gifts were exchanged, and Grindlay showed the curious natives his compass, flashlight, and automatic pistol. Two people came to him with Naga sores, which he dressed, and soon "every adult & most children came up [with] aches & pains & moderate spleens [from malaria]." Afterward, he sank down by the fire and drank tea while he smoked and scratched the fleas "torturing my belly, elbows & wrists." He took off his wet pants and rolled up in his raincoat ("it is high there & air very chilly") and slept.

The next morning, after a breakfast of rice and jungle vegetable curry, washed down with tea, Grindlay and Hla Duk, accompanied by the headman, set off for the next village, Gedu Ga. Grindlay learned that Hla Duk had never been in this area, and thus both men were newcomers. On reaching the village, he once again held sick call and treated the usual headaches, Naga sores, enlarged spleens, and other ailments.

On 31 July they started back to Tawaw; once they were close, Grindlay fired his pistol a few times to bring Koi and Kaw "tearing down trail, Koi screaming." Back in his house, he bathed and the girls washed his clothes. In his absence, Tilly had recovered, and Sergeant Deaton looked chipper. While Grindlay ate and drank some tea, the nurses told him about the many Naga sores they had treated during his absence. He learned that some of the natives at Gedu Ga had heard the plane crash but Bramston could not locate it. None of the natives had ever been up in the area where the aircraft went down because the mountains were too steep. "Finally, tired, to bed & a good sleep despite fleas & rats."

Grindlay's group began the return trip to Tagap the following day. He and his dog attracted scores of leeches en route. "One armpit a writhing mass at one time," he wrote in his diary. Naga runners appeared with letters from Lieutenant Colonel Wilson of V Force for Grindlay and Bramston. They walked in the pouring rain and stopped for the night in a village named Rekkau, where they ate roasted ears of corn and drank tea. There were only two bedrolls among the group, and Grindlay insisted that the girls take one and Deaton the other. He slept near the camp fire on a mat and was besieged by fleas.

Rain fell all night, and Grindlay awoke the next day (2 August) with a stiff back and neck from lying on the mat with a log headrest. The usual parade of villagers appeared for medical treatment, and he and the nurses handed out the rest of their pills (purgatives). They set off again and arrived in Tagap early that afternoon to cheers from everyone. "I inhaled a half case [of] pineapple," Grindlay wrote happily. Best of all, there were letters awaiting him from Betty and Seagrave.

Grindlay's strenuous but exciting adventure was over. He learned that the distance from Tawaw to Gedu Ga was thirteen air miles and twenty-six by trail. The plane crash they had searched for turned out to be near Pehai Bum, about where the natives had heard the sound. Wilson suggested that, thereafter, each plane should carry a can of yellow paint for the crew to paint large crosses on the wings so they would be visible from the air, making it easier for supplies and rescue teams to be dropped more accurately to lend medical assistance and evacuate air crews. Tilly was almost recovered from the leeches and the exhaustion of the trip, "but Lord she got thin," Grindlay wrote anxiously of his dog's condition.

By now, the hospital and auxiliary buildings at Tagap had electric lights, thanks to a generator brought in by Martin Davies, one of the FAU men, which he and O'Hara had hooked up. The dentist had also repaired the crushed autoclave boiler. On his first night back, Grindlay, along with Chesley and Major Johnny Wetzel,[12] went down to the V Force camp with Grindlay's bottle of Canadian Club (his monthly officer ration) and spent a wonderful evening drinking and conversing with old comrades and reporting on his trip. Hla Duk came around to bid Grindlay farewell before returning to his village, Tsumpa, and was given a bundle of yellow, black and green cotton yarn and a British blanket as gifts from Lieutenant Colonel Wilson. Grindlay showed the native guide their medical supplies, the electricity plant, operating room, instruments, anesthetics, microscope, and blood serum, with all of his words translated by Seagrave's native medical orderly, Theodore, who spoke Kachin. Hla Duk "was thrilled—said he never knew there were such wonders. Told him we could take care of all villages & do all kinds [of] surgery. Then gave him 2 [tin] foil wrapped cigars & he left." Grindlay never saw his friend and guide again.

On 5 August, with rain falling off and on all day, Grindlay stayed in his basha, suffering from a stomachache, diarrhea and hemorrhoid pains. He removed a cyst from a native's forehead but did little else. More mail arrived from Seagrave: "Doc sent a hell of a lot of stuff, most of it silly—2 letters [with] tales of woe, his 'general order #1' informing nurses they were to rotate as our servants ('aides'), Webbs [sic] tales of woe of [working at] Hpachet— Chinese riots" and other such things. A letter was also received from General Boatner promising that he would personally see that supplies and equipment requested by the unit were dispatched. Theodore and Koi translated Seagrave's order, which was received with smiles, but Grindlay detected an undercurrent of resentment among the nurses at being assigned to work as servants. "The officers then decided to let [the] assignment be made but refuse to let girls do things," he wrote in his diary, a neat way to circumvent the order. Grindlay capped off the day by writing a report for Boatner of his trip to the Naga country, with special notations about Wilson's yellow paint idea, recommending further expeditions in the same area, and suggesting changes that should be made on maps and in methods of rescuing survivors in the extremely rugged area. He gave up writing when the lights went off and bugs swarmed around his lantern.

During a conversation with Wetzel on the evening of 6 August, Grindlay learned that Stilwell had said that Grindlay was the best surgeon he had and that he would not let the Seagrave unit go home until the Burma campaign was over. A "crazy radio" message arrived from Seagrave asserting his desire to go to Shingbwiyang to be closer to the battle lines and the Ledo Road head. "I guess doc really is crazy," Grindlay wrote, "there isn't one good reason he should go there." A report from an officer who had been back in the Ledo area stated that it was rife with malaria and the hospitals were at full capacity.

On 22 August, reports were received that a C-46 transport plane had crashed southeast of Tagap; passengers included John Paton Davies, a political advisor to Stilwell; Eric Sevareid, a war correspondent for CBS radio; and about twenty others. They survived and were in a Naga village not far away; Lieutenant Bramston rose from his hospital bed and flew over the area and said that he saw survivors, but they turned out to be Peter Lutken and his group of V Force Kachins. Davies and the others were further away, southwest of Hkalak in a large Naga village. This group was the first rescued by the newly formed Air-Ground Rescue Unit of the Air Transport Command.[13]

On Thursday, 2 September, Tun Shein (a Karen who had been a kind of Man Friday to Seagrave since Namkham—serving as a truck driver, orderly, cook, and other roles as required) arrived from Hkalak with nurses Ma Koi, Maran Lu, Chit Sein, and Ga Naw. "Much rejoicing," Grindlay wrote. After dinner, Seagrave radioed from Hkalak, ordering Grindlay there for a conference. He decided to go, accompanied by Chesley, Lieutenant Joseph Stohl, and Private First Class Norilla on Saturday.[14] Grindlay spent the evening talking to Tun Shein and later reported to his diary that

> *doc is drunk all the time, that he is trembling & acts crazy. He can't do surgery at all.* [Tun Shein] *says doc has long been fornicating with the girls—mentioning Bawk, Lu Lu & Chit Sein! I am enraged & disgusted. Tun Shein has known it a long time & tells me now because Doc is now openly talking about it lecherously.... He* [Tun Shein] *says he is going to meet Cummings here, talk it over* [with] *him, then go to Ledo & tell Boatner that (1) Doc has to be ordered in on some excuse & me put in charge* [with] *him to help me run the outfit, or (2) the unit will dissolve & he will take the girls to India. I am amazed at a lot of things; I don't know what to do.*

Grindlay and his party set off for Hkalak, which meant crossing through a deep river gorge that exhausted Stohl and Norilla. Chesley and Grindlay were tired and stumbling after "a fair climb" when they arrived at a jungle camp of V Force Kachins. The group resumed their march the next day in drier weather and met Lieutenant Colonel Wilson returning to Tagap from Shagrang, checking up on the Chinese who were supposed to be meeting the Japanese at Nampuk. They had found various excuses not to go into action but were finally prodded into doing so and encountered a group of 75 enemy troops, mostly Burmese; two were killed and one taken prisoner, at a loss of two Chinese killed and one wounded. "He looked tired," Grindlay wrote of Wilson. Wilson told Grindlay that he thought Seagrave was "in a hell of a state, & thanked me for my letter to Boatner" containing a report on his trip to the Naga villages and recommendations.

At about 1:30 p.m. on 6 September the travelers came out of the jungle and saw Hkalak below them. They passed a V Force camp and went on to the hospital. "I shouted & girls [came] out yelling—Hla Sein, Lulu, M.T. Bawk, Naw Shan, Naw Aung, Emily, finally Little Bawk & Doc.... Doc about as I saw him last. Trembling, almost on point of tears (alcoholism)." Seagrave showed Grindlay a radio message from Boatner asking him to come in to headquarters at Ledo, if possible, to discuss his situation. "My trip needless!!" Grindlay stormed. "Doc is going to Ledo thru Tagap." Seagrave had radioed Boatner asking how much authority he would have and whether it should be shared with Grindlay; Boatner had responded by requesting that he come to Ledo to talk it over.

That night, Grindlay met all the nurses and noted the low morale: "Doc & [Little] Bawk still shunned by others, that she is always by him etc.... Watched Doc wreck his new still [with] clumsiness & stupidity." (The still was meant to produce medicinal alcohol for use as an antiseptic.) After lunch the following day, eight Nagas arrived, carrying a wounded Chinese soldier, and Seagrave asked Grindlay to "fix him up." The wounded man had a flesh wound on the left thigh and a deep bullet wound in the right thigh that had fractured the femur. No autoclave was available for sterilization, so the surgical gauze had to be boiled. Grindlay began surgery at 4:30 p.m., first cleaning the wounds (which already had clean dressings and sulfa applied to them) and then putting a pin through the leg above the knee and applying a cast while Lieutenant Wallace of the Quartermaster Corps and three of his men set up the traction.[15]

Over lunch the next day, Grindlay sat down with Wallace and got an earful about Seagrave's drinking and crying jags. He also said that the infamous "Burma Surgeon" had taken over the duty of liaising with the local Chinese contingent and with V Force. Wallace was going to report the liaison interference, and Wilson was going to his superiors with his complaint. Ever a stickler for cleanliness, Grindlay was shocked to discover that Seagrave had acquired two pet monkeys who lived in the hospital kitchen and mess hall and slept on the food shelf at night. "Filthy—Filth & sloppiness & inefficient—the whole place," Grindlay exploded in his diary on 9 September.

The following day, Seagrave left with Lieutenant Harris and Fan Tze, a Chinese orderly, to journey to Ledo to report to General Boatner. Grindlay sent a radio message and a long letter to Boatner "asking him to send Doc on leave for 'nervously sick' & then to keep him in Ledo & get him straight [sober]."

At last, on the morning of 14 September, Grindlay "did the job on Esther"—that is, he stimulated an abortion using a cervical packing of gauze saturated with sulfa crystals. Esther Po was now six months pregnant. The operation was carried out in Esther's basha, with some of the nurses assisting. Overnight she experienced mild labor pains that subsided after midnight. "She didn't have much spunk after that, called me to ask me to take the pack out—because she had too much pain & couldn't sleep. Not much grit!" Grindlay wrote insensitively, but he admitted later that he could not sleep for worrying about complications. At daybreak the nurse Emily called him and said that a baby had been born and the placenta was being expelled. Grindlay checked it over and found that it was intact; nothing had been left behind. At this point, his tender inner nature, normally kept well hidden under a tough, unemotional exterior, came bursting through:

> Couldn't get myself to do more than glance at the tiny 6 [month] old brat. It gasped & cried weakly, living about 20 [minutes]. I couldn't have killed it, I know that. I decided then & there never to do anything like this again no matter what. Sick & disgusted I hunted a shovel & dug a tiny grave. When I had finished the baby was dead. Esther took it very coolly—I think now she is most despicable girl in unit, "weak" & selfish. The other girls surprised me. Hla Sein seemed to feel as I did. Both Bawks & Emily & Naw Aung seemed delighted [with] baby, thought it was cute & sweet, but on other hand had no sense of the tragedy of its helplessness, its cruel treatment by us, & its death. I am used to seeing death, but this was to me a murder.

For the rest of the day, Grindlay "felt rotten & did little," although he did send a brief radio to Seagrave: "Everything finished." Grindlay did not mention the name of the father at this point, but in his diary entry for 18 June, he had stated that he was sure that it was Lieutenant Harris; however, this allegation remained unsubstantiated. Esther was the second nurse to become pregnant; Big Bawk had to have an abortion in December of the previous year (see chapter 13).

Lieutenant Bramston of V Force, now recovered from his malaria, appeared at Tagap on 16 September. "He is a lively, alert likeable chap" was Grindlay's assessment of the young officer. He and Grindlay exchanged stories of their trips to the Gedu Hka villages back in July. On 15 August, Grindlay had heard part of the story of Bramston's search for the wreckage of the downed plane from Lieutenant Colonel Wilson and learned that the V Force officer gave up trying to reach it about a day and a half out of Gedu Ga. Bramston told Grindlay that he had come to within 16 miles of the wreckage of the plane and could see parachutes on a mountain ledge. He could not reach it because of lack of food and the turbulent rivers that had to be crossed. According to what Grindlay wrote in his diary,

> He received a dropping of rations on the mountain and then went on beyond Gedu Ga. [Bramston's] *party was able to go only a few miles in several days. They tried to cross the* [Gedu Hka River] *but got only as far as an island a short distance from shore. Bramston said not even elephants could have gone beyond the island. The men* [two Gurkhas accompanying him], *including Bramston, fell sick with malaria. They ran out of food. They had been told to follow the river so that planes could spot and drop to them. All the food that was dropped and some signal equipment smashed on rocks and went into the river. They were forced to give up and return. After a day's rest at Gedu Ga they returned to Hbawn Ga over the pass on Sanka Bum. I never learned what happened to the survivors, if there were any, of the crash. I learned only that the crash had been spotted on a shelf of cliff of Pehoi Bum.*

Major General Caleb Haynes (the same pilot who had flown many of Stilwell's staff out of Burma in May 1942) took Bramston, who had climbed out of his sickbed, on a surveillance flight over the crash site. No survivors were seen. What Grindlay could not have known at the time was that this was because an earlier supply drop at the site had included a note that mistakenly told the survivors to walk east instead of west. Captain Peter Lutken of V Force told the author of this book many years later that he believed this error cost the survivors their lives, for walking east would have led them to the Japanese, who still occupied the area around Sumprabum. A correction was dropped a couple days later, but by then the survivors were already gone. This is why Bramston never saw them at the crash site. Their ultimate fate was never discovered.[16]

That evening, Lieutenant Wallace and twelve of his African American quartermaster troops came to the hospital for dinner, and Grindlay mixed a cocktail with juice and beer, which "served to mellow [their] voices. Had a hell of a lot of wonderful singing. Bramston & other V-force boys came down later & joined in." In the morning, the hangovers kicked in: "All [quartermasters], including Wallace, feel a bit off today," Grindlay wrote.

A mail drop on 18 September from a passing plane brought nine letters for Grindlay, including one from Betty. The weather was hot and muggy: "I don't feel too well," he wrote on 20 September. "I have a hell of a time sleeping & my stomach feels half nauseated." The insects added to his misery: "Tiny almost invisible sandflies, that are worst at night & get thru mosquito net & sting terribly.... I've never seen [them] as bad as here. [My] hands are covered [with] bloody blisters."

On Thursday, 23 September, Grindlay began the return trip to Tagap. He left in the morning with two nurses (Lulu and Hla Sein), a V Force radio man and nine porters. It rained hard, and they were soon soaked to the skin. As they crossed a 5,000-foot ridge in the Hukawng Valley, they became "cold as hell." In the afternoon the travelers began a steep, hazardous descent down a trail littered with fallen branches, moss, and clumps of orchids. They dried their clothes over a fire and tried to sleep at a camp with some Chinese soldiers. Grindlay and his group started out the next morning and stopped to rest in mid-afternoon. Grindlay pointed out Tagap in the distance and dressed blisters on the nurses' feet. After a 45-minute rest, they set off again. By the time they reached their stopping point atop a steep hill, both nurses had "utterly collapsed" and were vomiting and experiencing pains in their chests and abdomens from fatigue.

Darkness fell, and in pouring rain the leeches "swarmed over us" as Grindlay led the way with his flashlight. Both nurses became hysterical at the ominous blackness (most native peoples did not venture through the jungle at night out of fear of leopards), leeches, blood, and rain. The group became lost for a short time until Grindlay finally got the attention of Chinese soldiers at Tagap by flashing his light and calling to them; "a party came down [and] identified us & led us up" to the camp. "Arrived exhausted at 9 P.M. A nightmare. Got girls dry & to bed." Hla Sein and Lulu were sedated to ease their vomiting. Grindlay remained with Hla Sein, the sicker of the two, until 2:00 the next morning; then he slept soundly in a dry basha with clean clothes and his frantically happy dog, who had welcomed him back. He and O'Hara drank beer, and Grindlay listened to Chesley chastise him for terrifying the girls by pushing them through sinister jungle darkness and pouring rain to complete the return trip in two days.

Grindlay spent the following days resting from the strenuous and stressful trek back from Hkalak. On Sunday, 26 September, he met Colonel John P. Willey, chief of staff of headquarters of the 5303rd (Provisional) Combat Command under General Boatner, who was visiting the Tagap camp. The 5303rd was the service organization that provided support to the Chinese and had the Seagrave Hospital Unit under its command. Grindlay found Willey to be a good man but inexperienced: "[He] left the states a month ago. No matter how good he is he doesn't know the problem of working [with] the [Chinese], let alone out here; I object to [Boatner's] putting him in command." However, Willey was greatly impressed by the cleanliness and neatness of the Seagrave Hospital camp and called it "far & above the best in Tagap," Grindlay wrote proudly in his diary.

Grindlay's work load was increasing and the hospital was filling with sick men. A group of Nepalis turned up to begin building a new hospital; about half of them were ill with malaria or dysentery when they arrived. A radio message was sent to Boatner asking for four American medics to hold sick call for the Nepalis at their camp. Two medics arrived on 2 October from

15. Back to Burma and Home

Namlip, but one of them fell ill with malaria. Eventually, 70 percent of the Nepalis were down with the disease.

On the last day of September, twenty-seven cargo planes appeared overhead and dropped supplies. Unfortunately, much of the contents of the bags were broken. Grindlay moaned, "In fact, so much dropped that many bags broke intact ones on ground. I watched the process—terrific waste." The Chinese tried to grab as much as they could, and two of their soldiers died from injuries suffered when free-falling bags hit them as they ran out into the drop zone. One soldier died within two hours, and another "gasped his last" just as he was brought into the hospital.

Willey visited the Seagrave Hospital again on 1 October and again expressed his pleasure and admiration for the level of cleanliness and neatness of the camp. Grindlay showed Willey a report he had written that included a financial statement and a list of supplies and clothing that the hospital needed. The report "pleased him very much," Grindlay later wrote.

During another "bull session" at the V Force camp on 8 October, Lieutenant Colonel Wilson imparted the confidential news (which only he, Willey, and the man who had decoded the secret order knew) that they would be moving to Shingbwiyang in two weeks. Grindlay had guessed that something big was in the works: suddenly increasing numbers of high-ranking American officers were arriving. "Most are Majors & are liaison," he wrote.

At the same time, many of the American engineers and construction gangs who were arriving to work on the Ledo Road were falling ill with dysentery and malaria, and Grindlay had no place to put them. There were eight new patients by 11 October and no empty beds. After conferring with Willey, Grindlay sent a radio message to Boatner asking for tents to house the American patients. The following day a group of Kachins appeared (led by an American officer), having been assigned to build a new ward at Tagap; it consisted of a bamboo floor on which two pyramidal tents could be erected. An order also arrived for a 350-bed ward for the Gurkha soldiers to be erected at Shingbwiyang, but no plans accompanied the order, so Grindlay and Chesley proceeded to draw up one and give it to an American engineer.

On 20 October word trickled through that Seagrave would soon be returning, leading to increased tension among the staff, especially the nurses. That evening and the next morning a "long powwow" was held with the nurses and Tun Shein. Koi and Ruth wanted to remain with Grindlay, who told them that Seagrave probably had not changed his ways and that "I couldn't promise to 'manage' him." A vote was taken among the nurses, and only one (Kyang Tsui) wished Seagrave to continue as leader; the rest voted for Grindlay. He and Tun Shein met with Willey later that day and discussed the situation and the draft of a radio message that Tun Shein had composed for Boatner. Willey agreed with them that a last attempt should be made to keep Seagrave at Tagap while the bulk of the hospital moved to Shingbwiyang in support of the new American and Chinese push farther into Burma. Willey approved sending the radio message and added a note "that this [situation is] dynamite."

Seagrave suddenly appeared in the camp at tea time on 23 October. Accompanying him were Paul Geren; Lieutenant Carl "Johnny" Antonellis (1915–1986), an army surgeon assigned to Seagrave; and Lieutenant Kenneth Harris. "Doc was very cool," Grindlay noted later. Seagrave went to Kyang Tsui's house and, one by one, called in the nurses for their gifts. He told them that he had spent five thousand rupees on them, but Grindlay thought the gifts were "just junk." Seven of the nurses changed their minds and said they would remain with Seagrave.

After dinner with Colonel Willey, Grindlay met with an angry Seagrave, "who raved at me saying [Boatner] had told him … that [the] unit didn't want him as commander, quoting my letters. In essence he accused me of plotting behind [his] back, of holding meetings behind [his] back etc." It was a "long long session," in which Grindlay was joined by Koi and Ba Saw, who both supported him. Afterward, Koi told Grindlay privately that "she had learned something from me." In her words, "Before [I] was afraid [of] Dr. S. He do wrong thing but me afraid to tell him. Now me learn to tell him & that better. When he get mad he always shout like that. Now I shout back & he get quiet & talk better. The other wards have learned to defy the bully." Seagrave and Grindlay met with Willey the next day, who "read doc the riot act about who [is] in command up here." Seagrave maintained that he was in charge, as the ranking medical officer, but Willey disabused him of that idea. On 27 October a letter arrived from Boatner in which he promised to take official action against Seagrave if necessary. "Very nice letter," Grindlay wrote, perhaps not without a small smile of satisfaction.

That same day, the unit, accompanied by a V Force patrol, packed up and moved to Shingbwiyang. They followed the old refugee trail, which was still littered with the skeletal remains of thousands of people who had died almost a year and a half earlier trying to reach safety in India. The party camped beside a river next to several old refugee bashas and numerous skeletons, their decayed clothing still in evidence. "All kinds [of] rotted shoes & gear on trail," Grindlay noted, along with "whole villages of rotted bones-filled bashas."

The unit decided to build one hospital at Toshung Hka, and Chesley went on with Lieutenant Colonel Wilson to Ningam to build another. But that area still was not entirely cleared of the enemy, which held up construction. A battle was fought on 31 October by the Chinese and V Force Kachins against the occupying Japanese and members of the Burma Independence Army (BIA) before Ningam could be secured, with the loss of several men on each side; a couple of BIA prisoners were also taken. By 2 November wounded Chinese and Kachins were starting to arrive at the hospital for treatment as fierce local firefights occurred south of Ningam. It was the beginning phase of the battle of Yupang, which would last into December, as the Japanese stubbornly tried to hang on to the lower Hukawng Valley. Nepalese laborers built the hospitals according to the plans that Grindlay, Chesley, and others had drawn up. In a moment of rest and reflection, Grindlay idly wondered where Captain Roscoe Hambleton was buried in the area.

The perennial food shortages were starting to affect the health and well-being of the hospital personnel, including Grindlay. On 5 November he noted that there had been no food drops since they arrived in the Shingbwiyang area a week and a half earlier, and they were living on tea, rice, corned beef and beans. "Really I have been starved for 6 [months]," he confessed; "fresh meat (monkey mostly) about 5 times. I feel sick—thin, nervous, [with] diarrhea." Grindlay had written to friends at the Mayo Clinic as far back as 8 August about the shortages, remarking glumly, "our concern is just *food*— something to eat. At last the air force has performed the miracle and can drop us at least quantity [sic]. We are sick of corned beef and dehydrated vegetables and I wish they'd send all the hot dogs back to the White House. At last we have more cigarettes; I had just about decided to join the natives at smoking opium and plantain."[17]

Word came to the camp by messenger from Captain Peter Lutken of V Force that he had been wounded on 31 October during an operation behind enemy lines in the Hukawng Valley. Lutken had been leading a group of Kachins on a reconnaissance mission in cooperation with the 112th Chinese Regiment and was wounded in the buttocks and stomach during a skirmish with the Japanese near a small village named Sharaw. Lutken was hit by machine gun fire while crawling around directing his men, bullets also striking his canteen and his cartridge belt. Lying almost helpless on the ground, he began chewing sulfa tablets to prevent infection. A Chinese medic reached him during the night and foolishly inspected the wounds by flashlight. This action drew the attention of the Japanese, whom Lutken heard moving up reinforcements, and they began to mortar his position. He told the Kachins to carry him into the jungle on a makeshift litter. At the same time, he developed a severe case of dysentery (most likely precipitated from eating contaminated deer meat), which put him in "kind of a coma," he later recalled. His faithful Kachins administered opium that caused temporary paralysis; while he was immobile, he could hear the men discussing his condition in their native language, Jingpaw. They were concerned that "maybe they had given him too much." Lutken awoke several hours later, and he dispatched one of the Kachins to hike back to the Seagrave unit at Tagap with a note about his condition. Lieutenant Myles Johnson, one of Seagrave's surgeons, received Lutken's note and immediately left with a bag of medical supplies and a bottle of plasma along with the Kachin guide and an aide to administer treatment. Lutken lay on the litter for a week, the time it took for the guide to reach Seagrave and for Johnson to return. The surgeon gave him ether and probed for pieces of the bullets, also packing the wounds with antiseptic and Vaseline-soaked gauze to prevent sepsis and at the same time to aerate the wound. During the entire ordeal, Lutken remained with his men and was moved about on a litter to continue scouting Japanese positions. He eventually was able to be carried back to the 20th General Hospital, where Grindlay was then stationed and X-rayed his injuries.[18]

Wilson notified Grindlay that it was now safe to move on to Ningam, closer to the front. Accompanied by twenty-five Naga porters, Grindlay set off and marched to within five miles of their goal by the first night. They camped on the edge of a large river, where the jungle was "very dense," Grindlay wrote that night. "[A] lot of 12 ft. high elephant grass." He carried a thirty-pound pack in debilitating heat and humidity. The group ran across "lots of tracks & beaten down bamboo & high grass from [a] herd [of] wild elephants. Also tracks & tusk marks of wild boar; also very large tiger pug by boar tracks." They arrived at Ningam at 3:00 in the afternoon of the second day as an air drop was in progress.

Grindlay and his party crossed the open field used as the drop zone for the V Force camp. He rested and talked with Wilson over tea before moving on to the hospital where Lieutenant Antonellis was working. Just as he arrived, six patients ("rather minor casualties") were brought in and taken to the operating room that was situated under two parachutes draped under a huge banyan tree on the river bank. "Did the surgery in a short time," Grindlay wrote later. One basha had been constructed for a hospital ward, and the Kachins under Wilson's direction were building two more. There was a continuous sound of mortars and machine guns from the direction of Yupang. "Marvelous moonlight—nearly full," Grindlay wrote. "A greenish silver light—as it comes thru the slight mist that covers us—in jungle & over the high grass clearing of [an] old [native] village."

Grindlay spent the next morning (8 November) organizing the camp and hospital. "Antonellis needs a lot of directing," he noted. Grindlay sent an urgent radio message to General Boatner's headquarters requesting drops of desperately needed tarps, blankets, mosquito nets, surgical dressings and ether—"almost none on hand," he fumed. He told Boatner to stop dropping supplies at Shingbwiyang, where they were not needed, and instead send them to Ningam. He then plunged into surgery: "Slashed away [without] stop until 11 PM—doing 26 major cases.... Very tired. Eyes tired from flashlight work. Several chest cases today—rest [had compound fractures]." As noted previously, fractures were caused by bullets and mortar shell fragments striking and shattering bones.

The next day, Grindlay worked on nineteen patients and finished them by tea time. He was running critically short of supplies, especially ether, of which there was only enough left for about a dozen more patients. Wilson radioed to Boatner, hotly demanding more supplies. Grindlay dined on buffalo and barking deer that night, drank the last of Wilson's Scotch, and fell into bed. The supply situation was slightly alleviated when O'Hara and six nurses arrived on the afternoon of 10 November, bringing an autoclave, enamel pans, and other goods. The ongoing battle for Yupang resulted in more casualties, and Grindlay worked past midnight on three "bad cases" with compound fractures, one head wound, and another with his arm "nearly torn off." In the latter case, he found that the ulnar artery was still good, and "so I patched it up." A message was received that there had been a large drop of supplies at Shingbwiyang despite Grindlay's radio message on 7 November saying that no more should be sent there. "Today [we] got only ether & bandages here. Need blankets badly—to keep [patients] warm—I need 3 blanket layers on top & beneath myself" in the chilly post-monsoon weather.

Grindlay awoke on Thursday, 11 November, "tired as hell" after a night filled with the disruptive cries and moans of wounded men, the sounds of jungle animals, and the shouting and firing of Chinese guards at Yupang. Only three casualties were brought in, one with compound fractures in both legs. "Took a long time on it," Grindlay wrote. There were one hundred Japanese soldiers dug in at Yupang, and persistent Chinese attacks supported by two aerial bombardments had so far failed to dislodge them.

In the meantime, Grindlay received a "nasty" letter from Seagrave at Shingbwiyang, "beginning dear Grindly [sic] & ending yours Gordon S. Seagrave—each sentence beginning 'you will'—& saying briefly he was going to divide us in 3, me to go to Sharaw—(Japs block trail there), he to Ningbywen ... & Gurney (not here yet but holding Hkalak down) to Yuphang [sic]." Grindlay replied bluntly that Seagrave did not know the military situation and that he thought it was dangerous to put the nurses so close to the front lines. He talked the situation over with Lieutenant Colonel Stanley H. Bray (1891–1976) of the Railway Grand Division (and a transportation officer on Stilwell's staff), who visited the unit and agreed to send a message to Seagrave telling him not to make a move without permission from Stilwell's headquarters.[19] Seagrave arrived on Friday, 12 November. "He is still acting the martyr," Grindlay noted, "or maybe his looks at us are that of a master to a worm. Its [sic] evident that his idea is that only we can be wrong. Told [Bray] of some of the recent events in evening & then he went to bed.... O'Hara & I drank a bit of his whiskey. I decided to wait until Doc made overtures before going to him—otherwise he would be sure I thought I was in the wrong."

The next day was Grindlay's thirty-fourth birthday, though he had forgotten about it "until Big Bawk & a galaxy of gals pounced on me.... My 3rd away from home." The day was fairly quiet ("Little work to do"). However, an air drop brought some dangers, for suddenly bags of rice began to fall in the camp, two of them punching through a basha and almost hitting several members of the medical staff, including Grindlay, "& making a mess of things." Some of the requested supplies also arrived, such as dressings, mosquito nets, and blankets, but no sulfonamides.

After supper, Seagrave asked Grindlay to chat with him. Koi had had a long conversation with Seagrave at noon, telling him to split the unit. She later told Grindlay that a little more than half the unit wanted to leave Seagrave. Seagrave had shouted at her, and she shouted back. In the meeting with Grindlay, the "Burma Surgeon" complained that Grindlay had called a meeting behind his back (to discuss Seagrave's inconsistent behavior and drinking), which sounded like rebellion, and said that next time he would put his foot down. The matter of Esther's abortion came up, and Seagrave declared that she had been spreading the rumor that Grindlay had told her that "Doc had bungled the job (he did) for I told her it [was] necessary to finish [the] job since Doc had [probably] messed the baby up," which was patently untrue. At the end of the day a box of crushing clamps and Doyen clamps arrived from Colonel Isador Ravdin at 20th General Hospital. Grindlay rather gleefully showed them to Seagrave and reported how he had obtained them ("he [Seagrave] had failed to get them in all his travels"), and Seagrave asked to have the clamps divided between the two of them.[20]

On 14 November, Grindlay and Chesley—accompanied by two natives, several V Force scouts and porters, and Frank Martin, a reporter for the Associated Press—left with Lieutenant Colonel Wilson for Numbraung to give medical treatment to the Nagas. Along the trail Grindlay saw numerous animal tracks—elephant, tiger, wild buffalo, barking deer, wildcat and boar. The bamboo and plantain beside the trail had been crushed by the passage of the elephants. After tea break in the morning, the group split, and the medics went off to Numbraung, farther down the Hukawng Valley, while Wilson and Martin departed for the village of Jugun.[21]

Later in the day Grindlay's party wended its way back to Ningam, treating sick patients along the way. Back at the base camp, Grindlay was shown two press stories by UPI correspondent Albert Ravenholt that reported extensively on Grindlay (but did not mention Seagrave), as well as some captured Japanese equipment taken during the battle for Nimbwiyang a few days earlier.[22] Supply drops over the next two days finally brought badly needed supplies and mail, including a letter from Betty Grindlay and one from Colonel Vernon W. Petersen, NCAC surgeon, complaining that Grindlay had asked for three times the amount of supplies that the hospital at Sharaw did. Grindlay wrote in his diary, "So what?" Wilson also announced that he was moving the field headquarters of V Force to Numbraung now that the Japanese had been driven from the village. Chesley volunteered to accompany the unit, and Grindlay and others packed supplies for him to take along.

On 17 November Grindlay's longtime friend and colleague Donald O'Hara received a message approving his transfer to Tenth Air Force in India, "& he radioed acceptance," Grindlay wrote mournfully. "I'll be sorry to lose him." The two men had worked together in the Seagrave Hospital Unit for more than a year and a half. Two days later, O'Hara was notified of his promotion to lieutenant colonel.[23]

Grindlay's relations with Seagrave were deteriorating. "Doc very sullen and nasty," he wrote on 17 November. "Seagrave acting very nasty to me—countermanding my medical orders etc.," he wrote five days later. Seagrave's reputation with the rest of the staff was also at a low point. That same evening Grindlay had a conversation with Dr. Ba Saw, a Karen surgeon with the Seagrave Unit: "He definitely doesn't trust Seagrave either. We agreed to continue to try to keep things quiet & smooth." On 24 November he noted that "Doc [was] mean all day. Trying to discredit me but making [an] ass of himself."

Troubles with Colonel Chen, commander of the 112th Chinese Regiment (the unit that Peter Lutken had been serving with when he was wounded), were also worsening. On 21 November, Grindlay reported hearing that lax security precautions had permitted the Japanese to capture a Chinese machine gun post just twenty feet from the gate into the regiment's compound; afterward they had waited quietly to ambush and kill two American members of V Force. This incident had occurred three weeks earlier, when the Japanese had annihilated a company of the 112th on 2 November, mere days after Lutken was shot. (Lutken later remembered that the Chinese had stupidly attacked up a hill three times in succession in the face of withering Japanese machine gun fire, suffering heavy casualties.) Chen, Grindlay wrote, "ignores V-Force [intelligence], leaves supply routes open, steals from Americans & defies them to do anything about it, has his men urinate on Americans as they sleep at night—a royal mess." Bill Cummings reportedly wanted to go to Ledo and tell Boatner in person about the situation. "Wilson bitching too—& discouraged—from nasty letter he got from [Boatner]—telling him [the] language [he used] in his letter was disrespectful etc."[24]

The Japanese had managed to capture Colonel Chen's Chinese headquarters on 3 November and routed the force holding it. In the process, Lieutenant Colonel Douglas Gilbert, chief liaison officer to the regiment, was rumored to have been killed or captured—no one was sure which. At the end of the war, Gilbert was found interned in the infamous Rangoon jail, where he had been held since his capture a year and ten months earlier.[25] Seagrave somewhat grandly announced that he was going to the front to rescue the officer but fortunately was talked out of it. Grindlay was not sure whether Seagrave's motive was heroics or sincere. Eric Inchboard and Bill Brough came in and reported that the Chinese had made only a feeble attempt to rescue Gilbert. The Japanese were reported to be in force on the American/Chinese side of the river, and a blackout was imposed at the hospital camp, making the nurses jittery as the threat of an enemy attack increased. Grindlay asked Seagrave to send Gurney and the nurses back to Shingbwiyang before it was too late, but his request was refused. Ammunition was issued to everyone in expectation of having to fight their way out.

Meanwhile, the Chinese 112th Regiment was surrounded, and attempts to break through for its relief failed. General Sun, commander of the 38th Division, wanted to retreat, but Boatner refused to permit it, saying that only a single Japanese battalion held the area, not the entire 56th Regiment, as Sun claimed. Sun appealed to Major General Thomas Hearn, the chief of staff of U.S. Army Forces in the CBI, to intervene, but Hearn supported Boatner. Finally, the Chinese succeeded in reinforcing the defenders, and the 114th Regiment started arriving by mid-November to break the enemy blockade.[26]

The threat of Japanese counterattack continued to grow, and on 25 November Seagrave finally made up lists of the nurses, after being prodded by Boatner to do so, and divided them into three echelons to be led by O'Hara, Grindlay, and Seagrave himself in the event that they had to flee. A new trail leading to the main track to Shingbwiyang was chopped through the jungle in case evacuation was required. The turkey and trimmings for Thanksgiving dinner that President Roosevelt had promised to everyone serving overseas in 1943 did not materialize; instead, the Seagrave unit dined on corned beef, peas, fried potatoes, rice and tomatoes. A songfest ensued at which Grindlay was requested to sing the army's marching song and "Alouette."

The next day, a message arrived from Boatner ordering all the nurses back to Shingbwiyang and placing them under Lieutenant Colonel Bray. "[Seagrave] raved & ranted," Grindlay wrote, "finally got all girls together & said 'orders are for you all to go to Shing. There you will have to do own cooking, ward & water carrying' etc.... [Who] has courage to stay here [with] me?'" Ten of the nurses chose to stay in Ningam, but the rest were "very happy to get out—as Koi says 'not afraid but don't know how to shoot gun.' Koi very sad at leaving me. I refuse to let her stay. Gurney also goes [with] them but Tun Shein will also join them.... Jap firing—mortars & mach. guns—very close all night."

The nurses packed and were off at 8:30 on the morning of 27 November. Grindlay's dog Tilly was sent with them for safekeeping. "Much crying etc. Koi very, very sad." A dozen American soldiers went along as an escort, and twenty-five natives were hired to carry loads. "Seagrave very nasty & angry [with] departing girls who now openly show their contempt of him. Spectacle of them gathered about me saying goodbye, his striding in & in best sgt. manner ordering 'Fall in,' telling them they were cowards etc." Major Milton

15. Back to Burma and Home

Dushkin, a new doctor who had joined the unit only days earlier, was discovered to be a kind of spy for Boatner, who wanted more information about the condition of the unit, Seagrave's behavior, and the growing animosity between him and Grindlay. Dushkin told Grindlay that sending the nurses to Shingbwiyang might mean that the unit would be disbanded, "in which case I'll sure quit fast…. I'll get out I've decided as soon as all this quiets down & I can quit [without] losing face."[27]

The next several days were very tense. The Japanese were edging closer to Ningam, and the heavy mortar, machine gun and rifle fire could be heard all day. Grindlay continued to work hard on the casualties that were arriving while Seagrave went on "belittling me & discrediting me at every chance." American soldiers were dug in on all sides of the little peninsula that jutted into the river on which the medical facility was located (and on the opposite bank as well). News was received that two men, Lieutenant Rollin C. Brown and Sergeant Daniel Bubrick, had been killed in an ambush while scouting out the location for an airfield in the Sharaw area. Brown's body was later found beheaded, stripped, and mutilated on the trail, and Bubrick was discovered on a river bank shot through the groin; he showed signs of having escaped only to later collapse and die.[28]

On 28 November, Grindlay typed up his letter requesting a transfer and sent it to Boatner the next day. O'Hara had already been reassigned to Tenth Air Force, and Chesley wanted to be transferred. Grindlay did not complain about his situation, only stating that he wished to leave for personal reasons. Wilson carried the letter back to Ledo, accompanied by Ravenholt, the UPI correspondent. On 30 November, a number of patients arrived from Sharaw, where Carl Antonellis and Myles Johnson were now based, and O'Hara received orders to leave for his new assignment at Calcutta. He departed on 2 December and was sorely missed. "Sorry as hell to have him leave. Took picture of him & camp," Grindlay wrote sadly.

The Seagrave Hospital Unit had two diversions that provided a brief respite from the internal rancor that was creating bad feelings among the staff. A mysterious figure passed through the camp on 4 December. He was named Basil Shervashidze, a White Russian and native of Georgia, who claimed to have flown in the Soviet air force in the battle of Nomonhan in Mongolia in 1939. He told a tale of being at the University of Tokyo when the war broke out, leaving him unable to get back to the Soviet Union. Shervashidze had arrived in India in March 1942 and joined the British army. When Grindlay met him, he was acting as a translator for the Americans. He may have been employed by the OSS, but how and when he ended up in Burma is not known, although he apparently spent an undetermined amount of time there, meeting and marrying his wife Tamara, who was born in Burma.[29] That night Shervashidze talked about Nomonhan, a major conflict between Russian and Japanese forces on the border of Manchuria that had resulted in a severe defeat with heavy losses for the Japanese. He also very optimistically said that after Germany was defeated, the Soviets would join the United States in the war against Japan, which proved to be true. Grindlay believed Shervashidze's stories, but, in 1949, when Shervashidze was detained by Indian security police, no evidence of his exploits surfaced.[30]

Another visiting Eastern European was Dr. Viktor Taubenfligel, a newcomer assigned to the Seagrave unit in 1943. He met with Grindlay on the night of 4 December and commented that it was difficult to see how Seagrave could operate with the tremor in his hands. Taubenfligel had a colorful history. A Jew, he had protested against the Nazi presence while studying at a university in Prague by engaging in fistfights with stormtroopers and was expelled. He transferred to the University of Padua and earned an M.D. Immediately after graduation, he had joined the Polish contingent in the International Brigade as a surgeon and served during the Spanish Civil War. In 1939, he left Europe and was employed by the China Medical Aid Committee, a British organization, as one of several foreign surgeons it engaged. The group was turned over to the Medical Relief Corps of the Chinese Red Cross for a year and, in 1942, Stilwell agreed to employ them to provide medical support for the Chinese Army in India. The surgeons were paid $100 a month and doubled their salary when they were transferred to British Lend-Lease funds later on.[31]

* * *

After Grindlay's meeting with Taubenfligel, the FAU men came in and, in the course of a long conversation, reported that they had been talking with Seagrave and that "Doc [was] willing to play ball [with] me!, that I was needed etc etc—I answered I wanted to leave … that it was too late for words now!" Two days later Seagrave was informed that Grindlay indeed wished to leave the unit and "begged me to stay." He wrote to General Boatner to request that Grindlay be given a three-week leave, together with some of the nurses and Tun Shein, and that he be returned to the unit after his leave was over.

On 7 December Boatner sent a radio message authorizing Grindlay to move back to Shingbwiyang with two nurses and wait for permission to go on leave. He left early the next morning with two V Force men (including Lieutenant Bramston) and the two nurses. Grindlay carried only a pistol and a canteen; yet he and the girls were exhausted from their poor diet and lack of exercise for the past month. Their meal at breakfast was only rice—"not even 'willy' [stew]," he wrote. They arrived in mid-afternoon at Shingbwiyang to find a great many surprising changes. It was now a huge camp with a maze of trails that ran off through the jungle and elephant grass to satellite camps, and the 151st Evacuation Hospital was now located there.

15. Back to Burma and Home

The nurses who had been evacuated nearly two weeks earlier *in one mass leapt on me, pulling, fondling, biting & shouting. Tea. Bath in river, Koi gleefully taking care of me again. Told Koi I thought Doc's promises of* [cooperation] *etc., meant change of heart, at any rate he had learned he couldnt abuse girls & get away* [with] *it.... All say I am skinny. No appetite.* [Wilson] *says* [Boatner] *trying to put blame on mishaps, etc., on V-Force.* [Wilson] *says his report to Brit. Army held there in file—not sent on—because they were afraid to have real story of blunders get out.*

Grindlay enjoyed a stiff drink of whiskey and spent the night in an insulated tent of British manufacture, where he slept in warmth for the first time in many days. The next morning he and Bill Brough visited the hospital and noted numerous changes, though it "still look[ed] like [the] old place." After lunch Colonel Vernon Petersen, NCAC surgeon, flew in and told Grindlay that he was to go to the 20th General Hospital and Dr. Norman Freeman would replace him at Shingbwiyang.[32] Boatner had said the assignment was temporary, but Petersen heard a rumor that it would be made permanent. Chesley was also going along. Petersen said that all the medical units at the front, including Seagrave's, were to be sent back to Ledo during the first week of January, but the native nurses might be ordered to Ningam. If they did not want to go, they were free to quit the service.

Grindlay returned to Ningam on 10 December, an easier trip because most of it was downhill and he had had a good rest at Shingbwiyang. Petersen went along but was out of shape and became fatigued. Grindlay operated on several new cases, including one with a bullet wound in the jejunum (small intestine). "Petersen got good idea of difficulties of working [with] torch," he wrote in his diary. A meeting was held that evening with Seagrave, Dushkin, Petersen, and Grindlay. Petersen told them that they would be rotated out for rest, while some new field surgical teams would be brought in during a lull in the combat to get used to the conditions; then the Seagrave Hospital Unit would come back in as a "superclearing" company and mobile surgical unit, stationed in the center of the front, with the new units on the flanks. "O.K. [with] me," Grindlay commented in his diary. Seagrave said that he was going to demand that Grindlay be brought back with the unit and, when the latter left the next day for 20th General, "Doc said he knew he could get [Boatner] to get me back. Petersen said same."

Before leaving, Grindlay met with Freeman at Shingbwiyang and was told that the 20th General Hospital was "thrilled by the work the Seagrave unit [is] doing and the excellent condition of cases they were sending back [to 20th General] and was pleased to be part of the unit." Grindlay replied that he was equally happy to take Freeman's place at 20th General. Grindlay gave the nurses a letter translated into Jingpaw that Seagrave had sent to Boatner. Bill Cummings translated the letter for Grindlay, who was incensed to learn that Seagrave had blamed all the unit's troubles on him (Grindlay) and Tun Shein and asked to have both of them permanently transferred out. "[He] lied to me," Grindlay wrote. "A letter of lies & threats—he hasn't changed. An honest man can't deal [with] him. I said nothing more to [the] girls. Had hot bath at V-Force & Koi & I ate [with] them."

Grindlay met with Colonel Willey the next day and praised Boatner as a strong supporter of the Seagrave Hospital Unit. Willey was angry that Seagrave had gone over his head in certain matters, such as writing to Boatner. Grindlay later met with Tun Shein and told him that the twenty-one nurses at Shingbwiyang would probably quit rather than go to Ningam. They would stay only if Grindlay returned to the unit. Several, including Koi, had cried and begged to accompany Grindlay to the 20th General Hospital. The lone bright spot in that day was the arrival of a letter notifying Grindlay that he had been elected to the American College of Surgeons.

On Monday, 13 December, Grindlay boarded a plane to fly to Ledo, taking Tilly with him. "Tearful goodbye from girls. Splendid view [of the] Hukawng [Valley]." The flight followed the Ledo Road and went up and over Tagap and Gedu. Tagap was now a huge center, Grindlay noted, and Tilly lay in his arms and took a great interest in the view. The plane landed a mile from headquarters, and Grindlay was taken there in a jeep. "I looked like the wild man of [the] jungle, I am sure," he later wrote. "Hordes of new officers." He shared a drink with Colonel (later General) Edward McNally and told

Main entrance of the 20th General Hospital at Margherita, Assam, India, to which Grindlay was transferred in late 1943 (20th General Hospital Records [UPC 15], University Archives, University of Pennsylvania).

15. Back to Burma and Home

him of the situation in the medical bases of the Seagrave Hospital Unit and "advised him that staff men here should go down & visit—he agreed."[33] After a "wonderful dinner ([with] canned fruit & coffee [and] dessert)," Grindlay took a jeep to the 20th General Hospital. There he met Boatner, who was ill with pneumonia and could not receive visitors, but a "nurse let me in." They talked for a while, and Boatner assured Grindlay that he was still his good friend and that he and Stilwell both

> know all the dope. They decided [there was] nothing to do unless we put something in writing officially, that best thing to do is let the lid blow off, that girls will not be sent back to Ningam, that they will come out here & get leave, that if they quit they will be taken care of, that [the] fact that all the old men have asked to leave Doc should be a blow to him, & that [the] fact that Doc once did job for Stilwell makes latter grateful & also that docs [sic] publicity makes them feel he wanted me to rest at Hq. & think things over, go on leave then if I wanted ... then have a month at 20th Gen., then go back [with Seagrave] Unit if I wanted.

Grindlay spent the night in a tent with an actual floor. In the morning he bathed and shaved, including the bushy mustache that had grown during his weeks in the jungle, "& felt better." He later saw Johnny Walker, a British political officer in Assam, who said that he had read Grindlay's report on Gedu. Grindlay found him to be a "sound man [with] vision" and afterward drank "nearly my limit of rum, too. Drove that command car like hell back [to headquarters]."

On 15 December Grindlay visited Boatner again at the 20th General Hospital and shared some of the general's gin and rum. Grindlay was advised to take a few more days to rest and then go on leave. "I broached [the suggestion of] a return home & he said *if* I wanted it he would approve." Boatner ordered Grindlay to rest a couple more days before going to see Colonel Isador Ravdin, executive officer (and later commander) of the 20th General, "but I refused." Grindlay left and visited briefly with Chesley and other friends and "had a few drinks at bar & an excellent dinner there." He tried to see Ravdin, but the latter was not in, so Grindlay returned to headquarters.[34]

The next day Grindlay had his chance to talk with Ravdin. Grindlay told him that he did not know whether he wanted to work at the 20th General Hospital or go on leave; that he had no enthusiasm for starting over again with a new outfit (as good as this one was); that he had been in Asia for two and a quarter years, and the past six and a half months isolated in the jungle; that his wife was under nervous strain; and that he had scarcely seen his child since her birth. Ravdin was sympathetic and asked Grindlay to think some more before coming to a decision.

When he left Ravdin, Grindlay learned that Colonel Williams was in the area and had requested a meeting at the hospital the next morning. Ravdin sat in while Grindlay told Williams the same things he had conveyed to

Ravdin the day before. Williams, disappointed that Grindlay was not going back to the Seagrave unit, asked rather plaintively, "What will they do [without] you & who will take your place?" He requested that, after his leave, Grindlay return to the 20th General Hospital. When the meeting was over, Grindlay went to receive his pay (2,000 rupees), picked up a bottle of whiskey, had a bath and shave, went to dinner, and afterward sat drinking beer and discussing "Hukawng Fever" (only then being recognized as scrub typhus, or *tsutsugamushi*) with Alexander Gilliam (1904–1963) of the U.S. Public Health Service.[35]

On the morning of 17 December, Grindlay took Lieutenant Colonel Wilson, who was suffering from an unidentified malady, to the 20th General Hospital and saw the V Force commander comfortably settled in a room complete with a "marvelous steel bed [with] springs & mattress." He then met with Major John Paul North, the chief of surgery, who suggested that Grindlay choose his job at the hospital. "Decided I'd like to follow up my battle casualties, thus working mainly [with] Henry Royster, a prince. Also

Colonel Isador Ravdin, executive officer and commander of the 20th General Hospital (I.S. Ravdin Papers [UPT 50 R252], University Archives, University of Pennsylvania).

inherited Norman Freemans [sic] job of handling blood bank, taking blood Tues Thurs & Sat. Enjoyed seeing my casualties again." That evening Grindlay took some beer to Boatner, and they sat talking for a long time. The general said he was expecting Stilwell the next day and would broach with him the subject of Grindlay's return to the United States.[36]

A few days later it was Christmas Eve, and Grindlay attended a party in the operating room at 4:00 p.m. Afterward he took a bath, and he also bathed Tilly in front of the stove in his room, where it was "fairly warm." He made his dog look festive by tying a ribbon around her neck, and then he took her out with him to a movie and three parties. At the last gathering ("a sedate party of well-bred people") Grindlay collected several gifts for himself and Tilly, including nuts, candy, and cigarettes.

Christmas morning 1943 dawned with "many hangovers," but Grindlay escaped any ill effects because he had "held back" on his drinking. He received a few blood donors and then attended a cocktail party in mid-afternoon. "Chesley passed out," Grindlay noted. He also had a "date"; he sat beside one of the 20th General Hospital's nurses at dinner and walked her back to her quarters afterward. In the evening, the staff celebrated the holiday with a buffet supper and a dance in the mess hall. Grindlay felt out of place "in my old clothes & g.i. shoes, but [had] a good time nevertheless." He noted that Henry Royster came with "a beautiful nurse to whom he is engaged." The lady was probably Ethel Fisher, whom Royster married in 1946.

By Monday, 27 December, most of the staff had sobered up and were back at work. Grindlay journeyed to NCAC headquarters and found that Stilwell had approved his request to go home, and he immediately asked for air transport. He also had another long talk with Boatner, who had been receiving mail from the Seagrave unit via Colonel Petersen. Petersen was "answering personally Seagrave's mail. He [Petersen] indicates that he is sore at [Seagrave] & said 'I am god-d. fed up [with] this bird.' Evidently his & Stilwells plan is to deal [with Seagrave] by neglect from now on."

On 29 December Lieutenant Colonel Wilson (now out of the hospital), accompanied by Peter Lutken (who had almost entirely recovered from his wounds), arrived with the new head of V Force, a Colonel Scott (though Wilson would remain in charge until V Force was reorganized and could be formally turned over to Scott). Grindlay performed X-rays of Lutken's pelvis, abdomen and chest and could find no bullet pieces remaining from the wounds sustained at Sharaw at the end of October; Myles Johnson had done an excellent job of removing all of them. Lutken stuck around for a couple of days, and he, along with Chesley and Grindlay, celebrated New Year's Eve by quietly drinking in Grindlay's room, with some officers from the sick ward drifting in and out. "Ended by a short visit to the dental crowd's elaborate New Years party. Drank little," Grindlay later wrote before tumbling into bed.

The next day, Grindlay noted (likely with a sense of personal satisfaction), "Felt OK myself (drank little) but others looking green today." Colonel Ravdin threw a New Year's party that started at 5:30 in the afternoon—"A very pleasant time, dancing & drinking moderately." The festivities were made more pleasurable for Grindlay because a new tailored dress uniform (replacing his old tattered clothing) could be worn for the first time.

It was around this time that Grindlay reconnected with one of the former Seagrave nurses, Naomi, an older woman who had first joined the hospital at Namkham in 1932. Naturally, she came to be nicknamed "Grandma" by the younger nurses. She and Grindlay took walks together and went to movies. On one such walk Naomi told him that she had once asked Seagrave for leave and then used the time away to quit the unit and get a new job. She could not get along with Seagrave, she said. Soon after, Grindlay learned that Seagrave had paid a surprise visit to NCAC headquarters on 2 January, and everyone commented on how depressed and worried he looked. Grindlay also heard, via Lutken, that Seagrave had told Boatner that Grindlay was "O.K. & he [Seagrave] would like Chesley, O'Hara & me to return, says he *can* handle unit, that he doesn't want unit to come out on leave, that he hates Tun Shein & Cummings—presented [Boatner] [with] an order that these 2 not [be] allowed 'to interfere' [with] Unit." After his visit, Seagrave sent a man to get Naomi so he could take her back to Shingbwiyang. On 4 January Colonel Petersen returned from Ningam, and Grindlay concluded that it "looks as though Doc [will be] getting his way & Unit will not come out."

On 5 January Grindlay heard that the nurses were quitting and coming up to Ledo from Shingbwiyang. In a snit of pettiness, Seagrave had ordered Lieutenant Harris to take away their clothing and equipment. At 4:30 in the afternoon, Harris phoned Grindlay from the 20th General Hospital gate to say that he, O'Hara and the girls were waiting there in a truck. Grindlay thought the girls seemed very happy when he saw them, and he soon had them settled in a basha in Johnny Walker's compound, which also held Naga and Kachin refugees. Walker arranged for blankets and food, and Grindlay found O'Hara space in the room of an officer who was then ill in the hospital. After dinner and cocktails, Grindlay went to visit the nurses wearing his new uniform. Koi told him "the messy story of how Doc wouldn't listen to requests to quit, how he forced the 4 [nurses] to go back to Ningam, how lots of the girls still [with] him want [to leave] but are afraid to quit." Walker said that he would send the women on leave to Shillong and then help find them hospital jobs on a tea estate at the same pay (if they were willing to work there).

It was time for O'Hara to leave for his assignment with the Tenth Air Force on 6 January, and in his farewell, he told Grindlay that he planned to return to the United States in May. Before departing, O'Hara saw Boatner, "who told him Doc had made a mess but they were going to let him do just

15. Back to Burma and Home

this as it is only thing they can do, & will finish him eventually." On 8 January Grindlay went to NCAC headquarters hoping to see Boatner, but the latter was not there; instead, he conversed with General McNally and discovered that "Mac" was leaving the next day for a new assignment as chief liaison with the 38th Chinese Army. "Mac would like to go home too," Grindlay wrote that night. McNally rightly believed that Seagrave had acted out of spite by taking away the nurses' equipment and that all the nurses "were fed up [with] him." The general gave Grindlay a leather steamer trunk in which to pack some of his belongings for his anticipated return to the United States. Grindlay was informed by Major Vernon Slater that his return was still two to four weeks away, despite a rumor that everyone in the theater with more than two years of service would go home en masse. Such an exodus was unlikely, as manpower was critically short in the CBI.[37]

Mail call brought three letters from Betty on 9 January, informing Grindlay that she would be in Florida on 1 February, the anticipated date of his arrival from India. A bout of diarrhea made him miserable for nearly a week, but he still made the rounds with old friends in the area, visiting them for the last time, sharing cocktails in the officers' club, and administering the blood donation program. At one point, Grindlay visited Chesley, who was in the hospital with a "touch" of bronchopneumonia. He was surprised and delighted to also discover Captain Dick Young, one of Stilwell's aides and an old comrade from the walkout, in the opposite bed suffering from amoebic dysentery. Young told Grindlay that Stilwell was "keeping entirely out of the [Seagrave] Unit mess—that [he] knows all about it." Later that day, Norman Freeman returned from Seagrave's unit and reported that he didn't think Seagrave "knows much about surgery, & that he didn't do any. [Colonel] Petersen did some while he was there. [Seagrave] told Stilwell he could take care of 300 casualties there!"

Meantime, a stool sample that Grindlay had submitted to the lab tested positive for amoebae, and he started a course of chinoform on 13 January.[38] He begged doctors at the 20th General Hospital "not to report me & slap me [into the hospital]—what if orders [to return to the United States] came thru while I'm in." He kept busy with blood donors and happily reported to his diary that his diarrhea was subsiding. He also learned, in a conversation with Sergeant Chester Deaton (who had accompanied him to the Naga villages the previous summer), that the sergeant was being sent back to Seagrave's unit, probably because of something Lieutenant Harris had said to higher-ups. Deaton believed that Harris was out to get him because Deaton had caught the lieutenant and Esther having sex. Grindlay was surprised to find that Harris was now a chaplain, given that he was "singing those dirty songs after Sunday evening services—egged on by [Seagrave]," he wrote on 14 January.

The next day Grindlay's diary was full of news. Koi "hung on me like a leech"; she could not understand why he was not going with them back to the Seagrave Hospital Unit. "Very sad little girl," he wrote. Tun Shein told him that Eric Inchboard, one of the FAU drivers, was going to marry nurse Ruth. Grindlay, who was not in favor of mixed-race marriages, was upset by the news: "I got Eric aside & begged him to wait & think it over—to realize that after the romantic part [was over] he might regret [it] & at least to think of [the] children." Inchboard chose to ignore Grindlay's advice and went on to have a long and happy marriage with Ruth.[39]

During dinner that evening a message was received ordering the nurses, Inchboard, and others to return to Burma. Grindlay was in the middle of a report about his trip to Gedu Hka, but he left the table immediately to say farewell to the "gang." He rode with them in cold weather to the railway station at Tinsukia and saw them onto the train and settled in first-class compartments. "Finally kissed all the girls & promised to see them in Burma again some day. Koi very tearful. Cold foggy ride home. Webb, Robinson & I warmed ... by my fire & talked about Unit. Evidently lots of people now talking of our unit & writing home of events—so [Seagrave's] reputation will soon be tarnished." The next day Grindlay wrote mournfully in his diary, "Very depressed all day. I will miss that little devil Koi. Felt so bad I could do nothing—spent evening [with] Johnny Walker listening to records by fire."

On Thursday, 20 January, "About 11 o'clock I got the big message—a call from Slater saying my orders were in. I had air transp. to Bombay & water thence. Very excited & could hardly do my 3 ops. in P.M."

After receiving his orders, Grindlay went to NCAC headquarters and saw General Boatner for a few minutes; then he met General Benjamin Ferris and had a long talk with him about his son, Benjamin Ferris, Jr., who had graduated from Harvard Medical School and was heading for a career in pediatrics. Grindlay brought up the matter of ship transportation to the United States and discovered that his orders were supposed to specify air transport. Grindlay was told to see Colonel Frank Milani, who would "fix them." Milani, chief of the theater adjutant general's office in Delhi, told Grindlay to fly to Delhi with him and Ferris, and the matter would be straightened out there. Grindlay also had an opportunity for a brief conversation with John Paton Davies, a Foreign Service officer assigned to Stilwell's staff, and visited briefly with Lieutenant Eugene Laybourne and Lieutenant Bramston before taking a bus back to his quarters.[40]

> [January] 21. Fri. Packed in Am. About 10 set off to Hq.... At Hq. Slater called me in & showed me the last 6 mo. officers report Seagrave sent in. I had to see it because under "leadership" it said "unsatisfactory." Lot of the rest he put down as "satisfy" [satisfactory]—about as bad. Also said I was in need of physical & mental rest, & that he had told me this. Slater said [Boatner] was going to kill the thing but that I had to make

15. Back to Burma and Home

reply. I did. Makes me feel low. Returned to 20th in P.M. & wrote some notes answering letters from friends.... Arranged [with] Milaric [sic] to be picked up in [the morning]. Back to 20 & said goodbye to friends. Ravdin told me Rockefeller was going to finance a big surg. project for Chinese after war & asked me to join him.

After a night spent in sleepless tossing, Grindlay was picked up by Davies in a command car at 9:00 and they motored to the airfield, "a cold but lovely ride thru tea estates & towards the cold white Himalayas." At the field he met Ferris and Milani, and they "all [along with Tilly] got on the Lockheed Vega Lodestar—a twin-tailed job that goes over 200 [mph] cruising." They landed at 12:30 at an American airfield and had lunch, after which the flight continued, passing over the "snowy wall" of the Himalayas. They arrived in Delhi at 6:30 and transferred to the Imperial Hotel. Grindlay had a hot bath and then a conversation with Colonel John Tamraz, head of surgical supply in the theater, "who said [General Raymond] Wheeler (CO Services of Supply) showed him my letter, said he [Wheeler] always distrusted Seagrave, & offered me chief of surg. at a new gen. hosp. at home he will get soon."

Grindlay spent the next two days resting in New Delhi due to a relapse of diarrhea and the need to await flight clearance orders. The air corps transportation staff at CBI headquarters made arrangements that would guarantee him through flight from Agra to the States; he received a "4" priority, one of the highest. On 25 January he hopped a ride on a B-25 going to Agra, where the landing was rough: "Pilot said [landing] gear was bad & that was reason he was taking her in for repair—afraid to tell me before." Tilly enjoyed the fifty-five-minute flight, he happily reported. Grindlay checked in with the operations officer, a Captain Carter, and showed him his orders. Carter promised to get him out on the first through plane, either a C-54 or a C-84. The officer took Grindlay into town, where he purchased two bottles of Scotch, took a nap in the afternoon, and read mysteries in the evening. He was in bed by 11:30.

The next morning Grindlay was breakfasting when he heard that a C-46 crew was returning a "worn out plane" to the States and had offered him a ride. He made a trip to the airport but found that the plane was not ready, so he spent another evening at the officers' club. At noon the following day, 27 January, the plane was ready to go, and they were off within the hour. The first leg of the flight was to Karachi, where Grindlay learned that he could get on a more dependable C-54 the next day and deposited his bag at the airport. Grindlay looked in on the staff at the 181st General Hospital and spent the evening "drinking & bulling" with "Kochy" (Captain Thomas Kochenderfer, MC, formerly with the 159th Station Hospital) and Colonel Williams.

On the morning of 29 January he awoke at 5:00 a.m., and he and Tilly took a bus to the airfield, where he briefly saw the crew of the C-46. His own plane left at 6:30, flying over great expanses of desert and landing eight hours later at Aden for lunch. They continued on, crossing over the Red Sea, Eritrea, and the shimmering Nile River to Khartoum, where they landed once more. "Modern airdrome," Grindlay commented. "Almost [got] in trouble over Immig[ration] record. When I said no Yellow fever [vaccination] for over a year [they] were going to hold me here 10 days." He either argued the officials out of the delay or pulled rank, because he was cleared to leave the next day. Two other men were pulled off the plane because they lacked proper medical papers issued by the Air Transport Command; it is not known whether they were detained for the ten-day quarantine period. Grindlay was put up in "very fine quarters—courtyards." He made a trip down to the Nile and commented on the tall stature of the Sudanese people, who had tattooed cheeks and wore "long nightgown clothes."

On 30 January, the flight was off by 6:00, just before sunrise. The travelers covered 1,400 miles nonstop in six hours and landed at Maiduguri, Nigeria, having passed over Sudan and French Equatorial Africa. While eating lunch, Grindlay spotted a sign that listed the distance to Karachi as 5,269 miles and to Washington, D.C., as 5,584. "So I'm half way to Miami," he wrote excitedly, if a trifle inaccurately. Off again, they flew over

> red & gold sandy desert [with] branching net of superficial tree & shrub dotted valleys; then some rocky purple cones & buttes sticking up; then a rocky [mountainous] area [with] colored rock bluffs & gordes [with] more vegetation; then flat [with] more & more vegetation, [with] cactus fences & canals ... then larger oases (really [illegible] gulches), then greenest grass [with] trees, then a few rivers, & we passed over [south] end [of Lake] Chad. Below a herd of elephant. Pilots say lots hippos in rivers here.

Forty-five minutes into the next leg of the flight, one engine started misfiring, forcing the plane to turn back. The engine was repaired, and they took off again for Accra, arriving at 10:00 p.m. Grindlay and the rest of the passengers (mostly men from the Fourteenth Air Force) and the crew spent all the next day at Accra. The number three engine was leaking gasoline and required repairs.

Early in the morning of 31 January the crew and passengers were briefed on the coming trans-Atlantic flight. They were shown how to exit the plane quickly (if they had to ditch in the ocean), how to get the lifeboats inflated, how to work the radio and its generator, and how to use signal flares. They were off at noon—"Tilly very restless"—and flew into the night over the Atlantic. Grindlay woke just as day was breaking over the ocean and soon after saw the black volcanic peaks of Ascension Island off the port side of the plane.

Here Grindlay's war diary ends, in mid-sentence, abruptly and without ceremony, on 1 February 1944. He never took it up again. His overseas service was at an end.

Epilogue

After John H. Grindlay left the China-Burma-India (CBI) theater, the Seagrave Hospital Unit, consisting of many of the original nurses and supplemented by several new surgeons and technicians, became one of the primary medical support units for the Chinese forces who were clearing a path for the Ledo Road. The unit also supported Americans who were injured while working on the road itself and, soon after, those who formed the first U.S. combat force in the theater, called "Merrill's Marauders."

Seagrave wrote more of the unit's experiences in *Burma Surgeon Returns*, published in 1946, which chronicled events from the time the group re-entered Burma in early 1943 until it returned to the hospital at Namkham two years later, almost to the day. His story, unsurprisingly, put a glossy, mainly upbeat face on the unit's work, depicting himself as a modest man plugging along under horrific wartime conditions to bring professional medical aid to people who would otherwise have been denied it. Taken together with his first book, *Burma Surgeon*, the picture that Seagrave drew of his life and work resulted in an international wave of sympathy and adoration among an admiring reading public that came to view Seagrave as not only a hero but also someone living an exotic, intriguing life in a land little known to most Americans. His reputation as a courageous, yet modest, figure remained intact for the rest of his life and long afterward.

Contrary to Stilwell's and Boatner's hopes, Seagrave did not fade into obscurity, nor did his hospital unit collapse in failure, mainly due to the popularity of his two books. Through grit and determination bred from long years fighting the odds of climate, disease, and hostile forces, plus a knack for public relations, the man whom the nurses called "Uncle" and "Daddy" outlasted almost every attempt to shut down his work and his hospital. Every one, that is, except the attempt launched by the government of Burma, which arrested Seagrave on 15 August 1950 on fabricated charges of treason, stemming from an incident involving the rebel Kachin leader Naw Seng. The latter, who had fled to China in 1949, returned to Namkham the following year and demanded surgical supplies at gunpoint; Seagrave had turned them over, which led to the allegations that high treason had been committed. A special tribunal in Rangoon in 1963 sentenced Seagrave to six years in prison at hard labor, but his sentence was commuted to time served under arrest (about six months). After appealing the sentence, Seagrave was exonerated of all charges and freed to return to Namkham, where he practiced until declining health forced him to retire from medical practice. Seagrave died in his home at the hospital in March 1965. His hospital has continued to operate as a clinic (with brief interruptions); at least one of his longtime nurses—Esther Po—still lived nearby in 2004.

Grindlay returned to the United States and served for the remainder of that year and into 1945 as executive officer at McGuire General Hospital in Richmond, Virginia. It was a job he hated; surgery was much more to his liking than paper shuffling. On 29 June, he wrote to his old friend and mentor, Dr. John Bowler of the Hitchcock Clinic at Dartmouth Medical School, that the hospital had only a few patients until it was converted to an amputation and neurosurgery center, after which it filled rapidly. When that happened, Grindlay had asked to be returned to surgical service, performing mainly orthopedic surgery and given the title of assistant chief of surgical service. The administrative duties were dull and onerous, and, because of them, he apologized to Bowler for his lack of communication: "Too much pen pushing spoils a man's zeal for doing the things he wants to do, especially when it involves writing."[1]

In July 1945, Grindlay was transferred to Billings General Hospital at Fort Benjamin Harrison, near Indianapolis, all the while trying to wangle reassignment to Stilwell's command on Okinawa, where the general, now commander of Tenth Army, was busy planning and preparing for the invasion of the home islands of Japan, scheduled for August. Grindlay wrote to Stilwell on 23 June, "My discontent with the jobs I have had in the [Zone of the Interior—that is, the United States], such as executive officer and chief of surgery, might be strange (since I do love my wife and children) if I were only a doctor. I feel I am a soldier, too, however; I want to do and know I can do my real job if I can get back with you.... This won't finish my fight to get back to you and even if you can't ask for me I'll still try to get there. But, if there is any way you can do it, will you send for me?"[2]

Three days later Grindlay wrote in the same vein to Carl Arnold, with whom he had already spoken, now serving at the Army War College in Washington and slated to join Stilwell, enclosing a copy of the letter he had sent to Stilwell. According to Grindlay, "I will have a hell of a time keeping my mind on anything until I get the orders [to join Stilwell]. The sooner I hear the sooner my doubts and worry will be over.... I have to leave my family soon anyhow.... I was transferred to Billings GH and had to report there July

6. Indianapolis is supposed to be very crowded and I am told I needn't expect to find a place for my family for several months.... Even if I can find a place in Indianapolis this summer I'll be afraid to bring a woman, a 4 year old and an 8 month old child, plus 2 dogs out there. Even by your pessimistic guess I'd just get them settled when I'd get my orders."

In mid-August, Grindlay was ordered to Hamilton Field, San Rafael, California. He wrote again to Stilwell saying that he had moved his family to stay with his wife's relatives in Milwaukee, "sold the Mayo Clinic on giving me the job (as soon as I am out of the Army) of research in surgery," and found a house in Rochester, Minnesota. Then he received word that he did not have to be at Hamilton Field until the end of the month. "I don't know whether that will be changed, and I don't know whether you still want me. I'm anxious to get started at the Clinic but if the Army needs me a while longer I hope I can be sent to you."

The war ended abruptly with the dropping of atomic bombs on Hiroshima (6 August) and Nagasaki (9 August) and the Japanese surrender that ensued in less than a week. Grindlay never had the chance to serve with or see Stilwell again. He left the army in 1945 and was appointed a consultant in the Institute of Experimental Surgery at the Mayo Clinic in 1946, where he spent the remainder of his career. But Stilwell and Burma were never far from his thoughts. In 1944, shortly after returning to the United States from the CBI theater, he had published a short article containing his recommendations on the treatment of tropical skin infections.[3]

Grindlay's respect and admiration for Stilwell were expressed in a heartfelt letter of condolence he sent to Mrs. Winifred Stilwell on 16 October 1946 upon hearing of the death of his beloved commander four days earlier. "I am not likely to forget Uncle Joe," he told her. "He was a soldier and the greatest soldier I have ever known. He had strength and toughness, which he never allowed to be sapped by age or the priviledges [sic] of achievement.... [He] was a soldier's soldier.... I am sorry my wife and children, especially my son, will never meet Uncle Joe."

Mrs. Stilwell responded on 20 November:

> The messages have been wonderful, but your letter is one I shall keep. I know how you feel about my darling, and I know how he felt about you. He spoke of you very often, with pride, so the admiration was mutual, which is a good thing.
>
> I saw a great change in Joe on his return from [the atomic bomb test at] Bikini, but no test that he was given showed any trouble except teeth. He never had pain, and until the operation of October third, no one, including doctors, knew of the cancer. He was never given morphine, and all who attended him are forced to believe with me that an unknown power protected him to the end.... His valiant spirit lives on.

Then, in an allusion to her deep-founded belief in the ability of the living to make contact with the dead, she concluded:

He has unfinished work in China, which will take his attention, and I have work to do here. The truth must come out and I know he will help me when the time comes to give that truth to the world.[4]

Mrs. Stilwell's reference to her "work" indicated her intention to gather Stilwell's diaries and other papers for publication as a book, which eventually came to be issued as *The Stilwell Papers* in 1948, edited by journalist Theodore White. Mrs. Stilwell wrote on 2 August 1947 that she had gotten an agent named George T. Bye, "and he has been very helpful," but she worried that her husband's "words are so full of dynamite that many [publishers] were afraid to touch them. Now we have Sloan Associates, who published Teddy White's 'Thunder out of China.' ... The words will not be changed—but there must be some deletions—for I want the truth out but no libel suits."

Grindlay became head of the Section of Surgical Research at the Mayo Clinic in 1952 and held that position until 1961, when he was named a senior consultant. He specialized in aspects of orthopedic problems, neurosurgical techniques, abdominal surgery, and extra-corporeal circulation of the blood. During his career he wrote more than 250 scientific papers and contributed much to the discovery and improvement of new surgical techniques and methods, some of which are still used today. He retired from Mayo in April 1963 and moved to Colorado, where he died on 14 December 1968.

* * *

The war in China, Burma, and India came to an end with Japan's surrender in August 1945. By then the Imperial Japanese Army in Burma was a mere shadow of its former size and power after three years of grueling combat, while the armies of the Allies—Britain, China, and the United States—were overwhelming in their numbers and equipage. British and American air power, in particular, dominated the skies of South and Southeast Asia, as well as China.

Unlike in Southeast Asia, the Japanese armies in China were still relatively intact. A million and a half enemy soldiers occupied a major portion of the country. Nationalist government authority (under the leadership of Chiang Kai-shek) was concentrated in the west and south, while the Communists under Mao Tze-tung held extensive areas in northeastern China. The Russians, who entered the war soon after the atomic bombs were dropped on Japan, swept in and occupied Manchukuo, the Japanese-occupied and -governed former Manchuria, and soon had spread as far south as Peiping (Peking). In 1945, despite efforts by U.S. military and political representatives, China was poised on the brink of civil war, as the Nationalists and Communists vied for control of the country. It would take four more years before the conflict ended with the triumph of the Communists in October 1949.

India, in the meantime, had hardly been touched by actual combat, which was confined to areas in the northeast (Assam and Manipur) and the east (Arakan). But India was wracked by massive uprisings as the independence movement grew and strengthened after Great Britain announced at the war's end that it would give its former possession, the "Jewel in the Crown," its independence in 1947.

The practice of medicine in the CBI theater was constantly hampered by shortages of supplies, equipment, personnel, food, and transportation—in short, almost everything that was needed to provide adequate medical care for military units in the field. Its position at the far end of a lengthy supply line accounted for some of these shortages, but the primary reason was the low priority given to the CBI theater. Europe and the Pacific had the highest priorities, and the CBI became the "forgotten theater." Its veterans know that, and they all resent this status to the present day.

Yet, despite the perennial shortages, the Americans and their Chinese allies were able to accomplish some remarkable objectives. Perhaps the most important one was the goal that had led the United States into Asia in the first place—keeping China in the war, thereby tying down a million and a half Japanese troops from being transferred to the Pacific or possibly capturing India in 1944. In the process, the Americans achieved two remarkable feats: constructing the Ledo Road and the ABC fuel pipeline through some of the world's worst terrain and climate, and creating and operating the Hump, an aerial supply lifeline over forbidding mountains that remained unsurpassed in its magnitude and efficiency until the Berlin Airlift of 1948. These accomplishments are made more impressive by the fact that those involved faced serious shortages—insufficient aircraft and aircrews, pipeline material, and construction equipment and supplies—while combating debilitating (and sometimes deadly) diseases and battle or operational losses, in addition to fighting a tough, determined, fanatical enemy.

In fifteen months, the Ledo Road builders moved thirteen and a half million cubic yards of earth, built 700 bridges, and installed an average of thirteen drainage culverts per mile—all at a cost of $125 million to $150 million and the lives of 1,133 Americans. The ABC Pipeline system used 50,000 tons of pipe and cost 2,000,000 man-hours of labor on the part of Americans, Indians, and Chinese.[5] The Hump, by comparison, utilized up to 725 aircraft and 91,000 personnel, including 3,500 pilots, by 1945. More than 500 planes were lost, along with more than 1,300 crew members, between 1942 and 1945; many of these losses were due to mechanical failures directly attributable to the weather and terrain the planes were forced to fly through and over.[6] Still, the tonnages carried were five times higher by the end of the war than those brought to China over the Ledo Road, which made many critics (including senior commanders and politicians in Washington) wonder whether the expense of the road was worth it. Nevertheless, the accomplishments of the soldiers, engineers, and aircrews stand as perhaps the greatest of the entire war.

The CBI theater came to an end in October 1944 after Stilwell was recalled, at which time it was split into the India-Burma Theater and the China Theater. A year later, thousands of men returned to their home countries—the United States, Great Britain, India, China, and Japan—when the war ended. Unfortunately, thousands more remained behind, the victims of combat, plane crashes, accidental and purposeful death in hundreds of ways, and (more than any other cause) disease.

No enemy that the Allies faced in the CBI was tougher to overcome than disease. None of the nations that fought in this theater had extensive knowledge of or experience with the tropical diseases that would be encountered. The CBI theater, for much of its extent, was a pestilential death trap. Malaria, in its various forms, was the most commonly known and dreaded malady among both the Allies and the Japanese, but, even so, its treatment was limited to quinine and, later, atabrine, distributed in large quantities that were eventually found to be harmful in other respects. *Tsutsugamushi*, or scrub typhus, erupted not long after Allied troops entered Burma, and its introduction was blamed unfairly on the Japanese, perhaps because it had a name derived from Japanese (*tsutsuga* means "illness," *mushi* means "insect"). The carrier is a mite, which lives at the root of elephant grass.[7] As a person brushes past, the mite jumps onto a leg or arm and bites once, causing symptoms to emerge about a week later, of which the worst is a raging fever that can be fatal in many patients. Most of the medical personnel sent to the CBI had never heard of this disease, let alone seen it first-hand.

Treatment of scrub typhus, like many other diseases encountered in the region, had to proceed carefully by trial and error until doctors could be sure whether their measures worked or did more harm than good. A case in point was the introduction of penicillin. When it was first used in the CBI, physicians were amazed at the success of this "wonder drug" in curing previously untreatable fevers in soldiers and civilians. From the outset, they took the attitude of "if a little is good, more would be much better," being unaware of the side effects of excess penicillin, which included serious allergies in some patients. Time and experience soon made penicillin safer for all patients as dosages were adjusted to eliminate (or at least greatly decrease) side effects.

All this experimentation led to what was perhaps the greatest benefit to come out of America's war in Asia: an enormous amount of new knowledge and experience of tropical diseases and their treatment was acquired that would prove invaluable in future wars. The war in the CBI also was a valuable testing ground for innovations such as portable surgical hospitals (PSHs), which were used effectively in Korea and Vietnam in the form of small mobile units designed to work in close proximity to the front lines. There were no front lines in Burma, so the PSHs were positioned to be brought rapidly forward as required. They could also be set up quickly and perform valuable medical services that might last anywhere from a day to several weeks; their proximity to the fighting areas meant that injured men could quickly be triaged, treated, and evacuated by air from nearby landing strips. The PSHs and air evacuation saved the lives of hundreds of men by providing stabilizing treatment until the victims could receive more extensive or specialized care or surgery at larger evacuation, station, and general hospitals in Assam. The Seagrave Hospital Unit's small offshoots were actually PSHs, or MASH units (as such services were called by the time of the Korean War).

Gordon Seagrave and his hospital unit came to symbolize the best in medical missionary activities during World War II, just as the volunteers of the Friends Ambulance Unit and the American Field Service epitomized skilled, unselfish devotion to duty by people who performed under highly dangerous, sometimes life-threatening conditions. Seagrave was a dedicated medical caregiver, despite his foibles and failures, and he and his surgeons and nurses contributed immeasurably to the survival and welfare of countless sick and wounded men, American, British and Chinese alike.

Without question, the Seagrave unit's activities could not be discovered or fully understood and appreciated without the availability of Seagrave's two books, Grindlay's invaluable diary, and the interviews, letters and diaries of medical practitioners who performed these astounding deeds day after day. It is safe to say that no other theater of war presented as many difficulties and obstacles to adequate medical treatment as did the CBI. The steamy jungles, rivers that boomed in torrents through precipitous mountain ravines, flooding rains, muddy quagmires that alternated with choking dust (depending on the time of year), myriads of insects, deadly fauna and flora, and endemic diseases that lurked in the forbidding forests, swamps, and mountains all compounded and complicated the problems of providing careful medical care, which relied so much on cleanliness, sterility, prompt treatment, and ready access to drugs.

Medical personnel adapted to these challenges relatively quickly. Grindlay himself is an exemplary case in point: finding himself in Burma during the drought and overpowering heat of the dry season, he learned to conduct surgery without the sterile conditions that prevailed in the operating theaters he was accustomed to in the United States. Insects, rain and often dust fell into the surgical field; blood was removed from patients and recycled; surgery was conducted by lamplight or flashlights; surgeons smoked as they operated; and the constant rush of cases rarely left sufficient time to give them full attention or complete care. It took Grindlay a long time to conquer his compulsion for strict sterility and learn to accommodate less-than-perfect surgical conditions.

Nurses and doctors at hospitals in and around Ledo in northeastern India found the condition of their facilities abysmal. Inches of water in wards and surgical suites were generally the rule rather than the exception during the monsoon season. Living quarters (often little more than bamboo huts) were riddled with insects, lizards, snakes, and scorpions, and their thatched roofs leaked whenever it rained. Privacy was compromised because of rickety outhouses and primitive bathing facilities. Chinese patients—many of whom were uneducated peasants, and therefore accustomed to living in crude or unsophisticated conditions at home—shocked American and British nurses with their uncouth habits, which included throwing food and spitting on the floors, keeping live chickens tied to their beds, wandering about from ward to ward without concern for spreading contagious diseases, and tearing bandages off to curiously view the wounds underneath. Bloody dressings, removed internal organs, amputated limbs, and other detritus from surgery sometimes lay on operating room floors for hours before they could be collected by staff or Indian dustmen and buried or burned. The unsavory sight of corpses that had been dug up by stray dogs and other foraging animals was a common occurrence. It is remarkable, therefore (if not little short of miraculous), that Western medical personnel adapted so rapidly and so easily to these relatively crude circumstances.

As the volume of equipment and supplies began to increase in 1943, and especially in 1944, the capabilities of surgeons, nurses and technicians grew apace. Perhaps no other single factor was as effective in treating disease and the many types of fevers resulting from both battle wounds and illness as the introduction of penicillin in late 1943. The "miracle drug" was indeed just that: although its uses and application were by no means fully understood or appreciated, and many cases of overdosing with sometimes serious (even life-threatening) consequences resulted, the new drug saved the lives of many men by breaking and eliminating fevers that otherwise would have proved fatal. Good as they were, the sulfa drugs were no match for the curative powers of penicillin.

Until penicillin made its appearance on the world's battlefields, sulfa drugs were the most potent medicines available, especially to Americans. Their widespread use in tablet and powdered form saved hundreds of men from death by infections of many kinds; the drugs were carried by every GI and medic and liberally applied as an antiseptic powder to open wounds. In tablet form, sulfa drugs kept numerous killer diseases at bay, especially fevers, such as scrub typhus and the many FUOs (fevers of unknown origin) that were found in Burma and parts of India and China. Quinine (and later its synthetic counterpart atabrine) were highly effective in fighting the dreaded malaria.

Advances in sanitation were also extremely important in eliminating breeding areas for malaria-bearing mosquitoes by draining the land around camps and hospitals. The use of the Lyster bag, developed in World War I, provided safe drinking and cooking water for troops in the field, and, dangerous as it ultimately was discovered to be, spraying DDT on humans and foliage worked to eradicate the mites, fleas, and insects that carried diseases of many kinds.

In short, medical knowledge and practices made enormous strides during World War II, knowledge that was immensely beneficial and applicable to diseases everywhere. Grindlay returned to the United States with a wealth of experience in treating disease and injuries (often on an experimental basis) that he applied in his post-war research at the Mayo Clinic and promulgated through teaching and publications in the following decades. Horrible and destructive as warfare always is, nevertheless, something good or beneficial usually emerges. Many would argue that the benefit from the CBI theater was, first and foremost, new discoveries in surgical techniques and the treatment and eradication of a number of endemic tropical maladies. Much of that was due to the work of John H. Grindlay.

Chapter Notes

Introduction

1. Letter, Major General Haydon Boatner to Sara, Josh and Lorna (Grindlay), 6 October 1969 (copy made available to author by Dr. Lorna Grindlay Moore, April 1988).
2. "World War II" was so designated by order of President Harry Truman, acting on the suggestion of Secretary of War Henry Stimson and Secretary of the Navy James Forrestal, on 11 September 1945. Concerning the breaking of the Japanese codes, see Rear Admiral Edwin T. Layton, *And I Was There: Pearl Harbor and Midway—Breaking the Secrets* (New York: William Morrow, 1985), and Richard J. Aldrich, *Intelligence and the War Against Japan: Britain, America and the Politics of Secret Service* (Cambridge: Cambridge University Press, 2000), among others.
3. Chong-Sik Lee, *Revolutionary Struggle in Manchuria* (Berkeley: University of California Press, 1983), p. 127. Two excellent treatments of the genesis and conduct of German military assistance to China are Bernd Martin, ed., *Die Deutsche Beraterschaft in China, 1927–1938: Militar-Wirtschaft-Aussenpolitik* (Dusseldorf: Droste Verlag, 1981), and William C. Kirby, *Germany and Republican China* (Stanford: Stanford University Press, 1984).
4. Parks M. Coble, *Facing Japan: Chinese Politics and Japanese Imperialism, 1931–1937* (Cambridge, MA: Council on Far Eastern Studies, Harvard University, 1991), p. 49–50; Christopher Thorne, *The Limits of Foreign Policy* (New York: G.P. Putnam's Sons, 1973), chapter 8; S.C.M. Paine, *The Wars for Asia, 1911–1949* (Cambridge: Cambridge University Press, 2012), pp. 73–74.
5. James William Morley, ed., *The China Quagmire: Japan's Expansion on the Asian Continent, 1933–1941* (New York: Columbia University Press, 1983), pp. 245ff. See also Mark Peattie, Edward Drea, and Hans Van de Ven, eds., *The Battle for China* (Stanford: Stanford University Press, 2011), for discussion of specific activities and operations of the early phases of the Sino-Japanese War.
6. Waldo Heinrichs, "Franklin D. Roosevelt and the Risks of War, 1939–1941," in *American, Chinese, and Japanese Perspectives on Wartime Asia, 1931–1949*, edited by Akira Iriye and Warren Cohen (Wilmington, DE: SR Books, 1990), pp. 147–50, 158.
7. Robert E. Hertzstein, *Henry R. Luce, Time, and the American Crusade in Asia* (Cambridge: Cambridge University Press, 2005), pp. 33–34.
8. For an excellent history of the action at Changkufeng, see Alvin D. Coox, *The Anatomy of a Small War* (Westport, CT: Greenwood Press, 1977).
9. The best account of the causes, action, and results of this bloody but little-known major engagement is found in Alvin D. Coox, *Nomonhan: Japan Against Russia, 1939*, 2 vols. (Stanford: Stanford University Press, 1985).
10. See F.C. Jones, *Japan's New Order in East Asia* (Oxford: Oxford University Press, 1954).

Chapter 1

1. Robert Gillen Smith, "History of the Attempt of the United States Army Medical Department to Improve the Effectiveness of the Chinese Army Medical Service 1941–1945"

(unpublished PhD dissertation, Columbia University, 1950), p. 11.

2. Warren F. Kimball, *The Most Unsordid Act: Lend-Lease, 1939–41* (Baltimore: Johns Hopkins Press, 1969), pp. 9–10; Wayne S. Cole, *Roosevelt & the Isolationists, 1932–1945* (Lincoln: University of Nebraska Press, 1983), pp. 412–22.

3. Maurice Matloff and Edwin M. Snell, *Strategic Planning for Coalition Warfare, 1941–1942* (Washington, DC: Office of the Chief of Military History, Department of the Army, 1953), p. 63.

4. *Ibid.* The Communists, under Mao Tse-tung, had requested military aid from the United States in November 1940, but they were turned down. See Charles Romanus and Riley Sunderland, *Stilwell's Mission to China* (Washington, DC: Office of the Chief of Military History, Department of the Army, 1953), pp. 13–14.

5. Although Hopkins carried the title of Lend-Lease administrator, he had no organization behind him. Nonetheless, he exerted a great amount of influence. Roosevelt created the Division of Defense Aid Reports (DDAR) under Major General James H. Burns to receive foreign requests and to coordinate the activities of various governmental agencies involved in Lend-Lease. Until October 1941, the president personally approved almost every action under Lend-Lease. See Richard M. Leighton and Robert W. Coakley, *Global Logistics and Strategy: 1940–43* (Washington, DC: Center for Military History, United States Army, 1995), p. 78.

6. Romanus and Sunderland, *Stilwell's Mission to China*, p. 28.

7. Leighton and Coakley, *Global Logistics and Strategy*, p. 108.

8. Grace Person Hayes, *The History of the Joint Chiefs of Staff in World War II: The War Against Japan* (Annapolis, MD: Naval Institute Press, 1982), pp. 20–21.

9. Lieutenant General Albert Jesse Bowley (1875–1945) was an aging officer who began his army career in 1897 and held numerous high-level commands at the divisional and corps levels and served a multi-year stint as commander of Fort Bragg in the 1920s. He also served in the Spanish-American War in the Philippines, in China, and in Europe during World War I. He retired in 1939 but must have been considered for recall in 1941.

10. Letter, Brigadier General Sherman Miles to Brigadier General John Magruder, 11 July 1941, AMMISCA File, Library of Congress (Microfilm) (hereafter AMMISCA File).

11. "Proposed Letter of Instructions to General Magruder," n.d. (AMMISCA File).

12. William George Grieve, "Belated Endeavor: The American Military Mission to China (AMMISCA) 1941–1942" (unpublished PhD dissertation, University of Illinois at Urbana–Champaign, 1979), p. 15.

13. Memorandum to Chief of Staff, "Plan of Military Mission to China," by John Magruder, 22 August 1941 (AMMISCA File).

14. *Ibid.*

Chapter 2

1. The information about Major Mendelson is drawn from William Boyd Sinclair, *Confusion Beyond Imagination*, book 5: *Medics and Nurses* (Coeur d'Alene, ID: Joe F. Whitley, 1989), p. 141.

2. Unpublished diary of Colonel Edward MacMorland (Widener University Archives, Chester, Pennsylvania) (hereafter MacMorland diary).

3. MacMorland diary; Philip Ziegler, *Mountbatten: A Biography* (New York: Alfred Knopf, 1985), pp. 149–50. MacMorland may have been "thrilled" by Mountbatten's stories without realizing that the descendent of Queen Victoria had had anything but a successful experience at Crete and that his impetuosity caused him to lose the destroyer *Kelly* to a Luftwaffe air attack. The *Kelly* was a long-suffering ship that Mountbatten had commanded for more than a year and a half: it was almost capsized by an enormous wave off the coast of Norway (which hit the ship while Mountbatten was pushing it along at 28 knots, a far greater speed than he should have been going) and survived a collision with another ship, striking a mine, and being torpedoed twice, much of this misfortune due to Mountbatten's faulty seamanship. In August 1942, Mountbatten would command the disastrous Dieppe raid, which resulted in a significant loss of life (most of those killed were Canadians) and failed because of poor planning, poor intelligence, poor preparation, and a general indifference to casualties for the sake of ego. See Frank McLynn, *The Burma*

Campaign (London: Bodley Head, 2010), p. 184.
4. S.E. Smith, ed., *The United States Marine Corps in World War II* (New York: Random House, 1969), pp. 1–2.
5. Major Lewis A. Hohn, U.S. Marine Corps (1907–1967), served as commander of the Wake Island garrison until mid-October 1941, when he was transferred to Midway. He was in command of the garrison on Midway at the time of the Japanese attack in early June 1942 and taken prisoner.
6. Brigadier General Henry Black Clagett (1884–1952) was born in Fort Wayne, Michigan, in 1884 and graduated from West Point in 1906, in the same class as Jonathan Wainwright. He was a fighter pilot before the war, briefly serving as commander of the 1st Pursuit Group at Selfridge Field, Michigan, in 1938. Clagett was assigned as air commander under General MacArthur in Manila and subsequently was ordered to China in the spring of that year to report on the Chinese air forces and their needs and the potential of the area to support American air operations. He is characterized by Geoffrey Perret in his book, *Old Soldiers Never Die* (New York: Random House, 1996), as a "notorious drunk" who, "when not drying out in a hospital, was out drinking" with his aide, Lewis Maitland (p. 235). Clagett returned to the Philippines and was replaced in November 1941 by Major General Lewis Brereton. Clagett continued to head the 5th Interceptor Command until he was dispatched to Australia to temporarily serve as American air commander until the arrival of Major General George Brett. Afterward, he was given command of the port of Townsville in north Queensland. After residing in Wichita Falls, Texas, for several years, he died in Washington, D.C., in 1952.
7. Major General Christopher Michael Maltby (1891–1980) served in the Indian army, first as an instructor at the Staff College in Quetta in 1938 before being appointed general staff officer in 1939 and then commander of British troops in China in 1941 as part of the British 204 Military Mission. That same year he was ordered to take command of British forces in Hong Kong and was taken prisoner after surrendering to the Japanese in December 1941. Maltby remained a captive until the war's end.

8. A very stark description of the conditions in Chungking at this time can be found in a series of interviews conducted with Chinese women who were trying to eke out a living in the city amid the chaos caused by frequent Japanese bombing attacks starting in 1939. These interviews have been published by Danke Li in *Echoes of Chongqing: Women in Wartime China* (Urbana: University of Illinois Press, 2010).

Chapter 3

1. Unpublished diary of John H. Grindlay, M.C. (courtesy of the Grindlay family, copy in author's personal possession) (hereafter Grindlay diary).
2. S.E. Smith, ed., *The United States Marine Corps in World War II* (New York: Random House, 1969), pp. 34–35; letter, Major General Haydon Boatner to Sara, Josh and Lorna (Grindlay), 6 October 1969 (copy courtesy of Dr. Lorna Grindlay Moore). Grindlay diary, 12 September 1941.
3. Grindlay diary, 12 September 1941. Lauchlin Currie (1902–1993) was an expert in finance and later accused, after disclosure of the Venona decrypts, of being a spy for the Soviet Union. He was never prosecuted for any alleged espionage activities and died in Bogota, Colombia, where he had been a Roosevelt envoy years earlier and developed business ties. Thomas Corcoran (1899–1981) was a Harvard-trained lawyer and at one time called the second-most powerful man in Washington after Roosevelt. He was accused of being involved in a number of shady business dealings throughout his career, several dating back to lucrative wartime shipbuilding contracts that he brokered with, among others, Henry Kaiser, but, like Currie, Corcoran was never formally charged with any illegal activities.
4. The *Silverdawn* was owned by Leif Hoegh & Co. A/S of Oslo. It was built in Copenhagen in early 1940 by Aktieselskabet Burmeister & Wain's Maskin-OG shipyard and registered with Lloyd's as *Hoegh Silverdawn*. The ship weighed 6,900 tons empty and measured 430 feet long and 58 feet wide. It escaped from Denmark in April 1940 ahead of the German occupation forces and sailed to the United States on its maiden voyage. In

May or June 1940, it was equipped with a refrigeration area in which to haul perishable foodstuffs, especially fish (*Lloyd's Register of Shipping*, 26 February 1940 and 24 June 1940). *Hoegh Silverdawn* was torpedoed and sunk by a Japanese submarine in the Indian Ocean west of Australia on 14 July 1943. Twenty-two of its crew members took to sea in a lifeboat certified for 16 persons. Eighteen of the men survived more than 31 days at sea before landing on the coast of India south of Calcutta. Their ordeal, which is reminiscent of the story of Captain Bligh and the survivors of the *Bounty* mutiny more than a century and a half earlier, is chronicled in Leif B. Lillegaard, *Siste Mann fra Borde* (Oslo: J.W. Cappelens Forlag, 1965).

5. Copies of letters from Grindlay to his parents were provided to the author by Ms. Mary Enterline (Grindlay's sister) in November 1988 (hereafter Enterline letters).

6. Men placed on the Detached Enlisted Men's List were those whose duties would not easily assign them to a specific service branch or department.

7. Grindlay learned later that Sergeant Francis Astolfi committed suicide in New Delhi in 1942 or 1943. However, Captain Nevin Wetzel wrote in 1974 that Astolfi died in Kunming in 1942, an apparent suicide, although he did not state this fact directly. The exact details of Astolfi's death are unknown.

8. Captain Dag Arnesen was captain of the *Hoegh Silverdawn* from 18 March 1940 until 20 April 1943. Captain Alf Slaatten took command of the *Hoegh Silverlight* on 5 November 1941. He served in this capacity until 10 March 1942, and then again from 12 August 1944 to 28 February 1945. *Hoegh Silverlight* survived the war and was sold to a Japanese shipping company in 1953. It was scrapped eleven years later. Captains Arnesen and Slaatten survived the war. (Letter, Karin Heum, Hoegh Fleet Services AS, Oslo, to author, 6 March 1996.)

9. Major (later Colonel) Harry S. Aldrich was born Harry Starkey Aldrich in Kalamazoo, Michigan, on 17 May 1895. He graduated from Michigan College of Mining in 1917 and entered the army that same year, serving in the Coast Artillery. He married Keitha Leora Bolles (1894–1985) of West Salem, Wisconsin, in Coronado, California, in 1918. From 1928 to 1932 Aldrich was an army language officer in Peking. He joined AMMISCA in 1941 and became one of two American liaison officers with the Chinese Sixth Army in the first Burma campaign. Afterward, he was appointed commander of the Kunming Area Command under Stilwell. He served a stint in army intelligence before joining the Office of Strategic Services (OSS) in 1944. He was chief of OSS Secret Intelligence in Cairo when General William Donovan, head of OSS, dispatched him to Greece in 1945 to investigate suspicions that the Soviets were behind the unrest in Athens and elsewhere as the Germans withdrew. Aldrich then became head of all OSS operations in the Middle East. In 1945, Aldrich published a Chinese-language dictionary that became one of the standards in the field. He died in Covina, California, in January 1979.

10. Letter, Grindlay to parents, 2 January 1942 (Mayo Clinic Archives, Rochester, Minnesota; courtesy of Dr. Lorna Grindlay Moore) (hereafter Grindlay letters at Mayo). Grindlay was mistaken in his reference to the "Silk Road" of Marco Polo. In the first place, the thirteenth-century Italian traveler came nowhere close to the route of the Burma Road. Second, the Silk Road cannot be attributed to Marco Polo but to generations of traders who journeyed to China via Central Asia more than a millennium before the thirteenth century. Third, while the Silk Road had several routes, most were north of the Tibetan plateau. One side route branched southward to northern India, and there were extensions of that route into southern Tibet and southwestern China. It is possible that Grindlay crossed one of these branches, but only tangentially. Enterline letters.

11. Nicol Smith, *Burma Road* (Garden City, NY: Garden City Publishing, 1942), pp. 273–74.

12. Letter, John Grindlay to Betty Grindlay, 22 December 1941 (Grindlay letters at Mayo). The "69th Mile Bridge" was situated sixty-nine miles northeast of Lashio (see Smith, *Burma Road*).

13. Letter, Grindlay to parents, 2 January 1942 (Grindlay letters at Mayo). Enterline letters.

Chapter 4

1. Danke Li, *Echoes of Chongqing: Women in Wartime China* (Urbana: University of Illinois Press, 2010), p. 17.

2. Charles Romanus and Riley Sunderland, *Stilwell's Mission to China* (Washington, DC: Office of the Chief of Military History, Department of the Army, 1953), p. 37.

3. James Larry Durrence, "Ambassador Clarence E. Gauss and United States Relations with China, 1941–1944" (unpublished PhD dissertation, University of Georgia, Athens, 1971), pp. 14, 30–33, 53.

4. Peter Rand, *China Hands* (New York: Simon & Schuster, 1995), pp. 203–4; Donald Gillies, *Radical Diplomat: The Life of Archibald Clark Kerr, Lord Inverchapel, 1882–1951* (London: I.B. Tauris, 1999), p. 112. After Clark Kerr became Britain's ambassador to Moscow in 1942, he became famous in the British Foreign Office in 1943 and years afterward for writing an amusing memo to his friend, Reginald Herbert (Lord Pembroke), in the Foreign Office, telling him of the arrival of the Turkish envoy with the unbelievable name of Mustafa Kunt, which evoked hilarity in Whitehall, especially when Clark Kerr ended the memo by writing, "We all feel like that, Reggie, now and then" (Matthew Parris and Andrew Bryson, *The Spanish Ambassador's Suitcase: Stories from the Diplomatic Bag* [London: Viking, 2012], p. 46).

5. Robert E. Sherwood, *Roosevelt & Hopkins* (New York: Grosset & Dunlap, 1960), p. 289. For more details on the Arnstein group (formally named the American Commission for the Burma Road), see chapter 20 of Sherwood's book.

6. Major James Wilson later perished in the bombing of Mandalay during the retreat from Burma in April 1942. Major (later Colonel) Barrett headed the first official U.S. military observer delegation to the Chinese Communists in Yenan in 1944, code-named the "Dixie Mission" (Romanus and Sunderland, *Stilwell's Mission to China*, pp. 44, 90–91).

7. "Memorandum of Conference with the Generalissimo, October 27, 1941" (AMMISCA File). Whether the Chinese offer to launch a diversionary attack was genuine remains open to question. One must bear in mind that Chiang Kai-shek had frantically appealed to the British and Americans at the end of October 1941 for help in resisting a Japanese attack on Kunming that Chinese intelligence sources learned was planned for November. Thus it does not seem likely that the Chinese had the military strength in southeast China to attack Indochina. As for the British, they lacked enough aircraft to mount a truly effective defense of Singapore, let alone furnish any to assist the Chinese. The American Volunteer Group, which became a formidable defense force in Burma and China later in the year, was not yet sufficiently trained or equipped to lend much (if any) support to such an attack. (For further discussion of the defense of Singapore and Malaya, see Ong Chit Chung, *Operation Matador: Britain's War Plans Against the Japanese, 1918-1941* [Singapore: Times Academic Press, 1997].)

8. "Memorandum of Conference with the Generalissimo."

9. Romanus and Sunderland, *Stilwell's Mission to China*, pp. 38–40.

10. Colonel (later Brigadier General) Ross G. Hoyt (1893–1983) was ordered to join AMMISCA on 16 October 1941 as an Army Air Corps liaison officer. He was a long-time careerist credited with pioneering developments in in-air refueling a decade or so earlier.

Chapter 5

1. Grace Person Hayes, *The History of the Joint Chiefs of Staff in World War II: The War Against Japan* (Annapolis, MD: Naval Institute Press, 1982), p. 71.

2. Rear Admiral Edwin T. Layton, *And I Was There: Pearl Harbor and Midway—Breaking the Secrets* (New York: William Morrow, 1985), pp. 85–86.

3. The USS *Wake* was a 350-ton river gunboat built for the U.S. Navy in Shanghai in 1926–1927. Originally named *Guam*, the ship was renamed in January 1941 and continued to patrol the Yangtze River from its base in Hankow. It was in Shanghai on 8 December when the Japanese struck Pearl Harbor and several areas in East Asia, including Shanghai. The *Wake* was captured and its crew members were made prisoners of war. The Japanese turned the ship over to the puppet government in Nanking headed by Wang Ching-wei, and it was renamed *Tatara*. In 1945, the ship was recaptured by the United States and given to the Chinese Nationalists; its name was once again changed, this time to *Yuan*. Chinese Communist forces captured it in 1949.

4. "Memorandum of a Conference with the Generalissimo," 8 December 1941 (AM-MISCA File).

5. The Soviet Union had concluded a neutrality pact with the Japanese on 13 April 1941, which would have made it difficult for the Russians to join the United States in declaring war on Japan, although the Soviets were never shy about abrogating treaties if it was in their best interests to do so. Either Chiang did not know this (which seems unlikely) or he chose to ignore it.

6. "Memorandum of Conference with Minister of War," 10 December 1941 (AM-MISCA File).

7. MacMorland diary, 17 December 1941.

8. S.E. Smith, ed., *The United States Marine Corps in World War II* (New York: Random House, 1969), pp. 39–40.

9. Harrison Forman (1904–1978) was a prominent journalist, photographer, and writer who traveled in Afghanistan, the Middle East, Indochina, South America, Tibet and China before and after the Second World War. He was born in Milwaukee, Wisconsin, and graduated from the University of Wisconsin in 1929, where he studied Asian languages. He went to China in the early 1930s to sell American aircraft and train pilots. Forman heard rumors of a mountain in Tibet that was higher than Mount Everest and set off to try to find it. (The rumors proved false.) In July 1937 he successfully eluded the Nationalist blockade of the Communist territories in northwest China and was in Yenan when news was received of the outbreak of fighting between Japanese and Chinese units on 7 July at the Marco Polo Bridge. He covered the Sino-Japanese War for the *New York Times* and NBC Radio and, after the war, continued to travel and photograph in many countries. He died in New York at age 74.

10. Grindlay diary, 22 and 25 December 1941. Lieutenant Colonel St. John was a good friend of one of Grindlay's aunts and served on Stilwell's staff in Burma as supply officer. He collapsed during the arduous "walkout" from Burma to India in May 1942 and had to be carried most of the way on stretchers or mules.

11. The *Tulsa*, as it was commonly referred to, was a freighter launched on 26 July 1919 at the Hog Island shipyard on the Delaware River near Philadelphia. The American International Shipbuilding Corporation built the *Tulsa* for the U.S. Shipping Board (later the U.S. Maritime Commission). The vessel was christened with a bottle of Oklahoma crude oil by Miss Lulu Crosbie, daughter of a prominent Tulsa banker and oil company businessman. It was 400 feet long and 59 feet wide at the beam and was powered by oil-burning engines, one of several ships built at that time which were not fueled by coal. The ultimate fate of the *Tulsa* is unknown, but it was still operating in October 1945; however, it was not called into service during the Korean War, which may indicate that it had been decommissioned and presumably scrapped by then. "Oil Is Used to Christen Tulsa's Ship," *The Oil and Gas Journal* 18 (6 August 1919): 48.

12. General Brett left China for Australia after the conference, where he took command of U.S. Army Forces from December 1941 to April 1942. He then became commander-in-chief of Allied Air Forces in Australia and subsequently held the same position for Allied Air Forces in the Southwest Pacific under General Douglas MacArthur. Brett left the area when he was appointed commander-in-chief of the Caribbean Defense Command in November 1942.

13. Hayes, *The History of the Joint Chiefs of Staff in World War II*, pp. 73–74.

14. "Memorandum of Conference with the Generalissimo," 23 December 1941 (AM-MISCA File).

15. "Memorandum of a Conference with General Wavell on December 23, 1941" (AM-MISCA File).

16. "Memorandum of a Conference with the Generalissimo," 26 December 1941 (AM-MISCA File).

17. Smith, *History of the Attempt of the U.S. Medical Department*, pp. 41–47.

18. Grindlay diary, 31 December 1941.

19. The *Tutuila*, one of six riverboats launched in 1928 in Shanghai, survived a serious collision with a Chinese ferry in 1939, a near-fatal collision with a dock at Chungking in 1940, and a Japanese bombing in 1941 to become the only one among its six sister ships to finish World War II in Allied hands and one of only two ships to escape destruction. The gunboat was handed over to naval attaché Colonel James McHugh, U.S. Marine Corps,

on 19 January 1942; McHugh subsequently turned it over to the Nationalist navy. After being transferred to the Chinese, the ship was renamed *Mei Yuan*. *Tutuila* remained inactive through the rest of the war. From 1945 until 1949 the ship was in service with the Nationalist navy, which scuttled it to prevent its capture. (Kemp Tolley, *Yangtze Patrol: The U.S. Navy in China* [Annapolis, MD: Naval Institute Press, 1971], pp. 178, 180, 286–287.)

20. Grindlay diary, 30 December 1941 and 2 and 3 January 1942.

21. "Weekly Report," No. 13, entry for 5 January 1942 (AMMISCA File).

22. Robert Kho-seng Lim was born in Singapore in 1897. After serving in France in World War I with an Indian army medical unit, he attended Edinburgh University, where he received his medical degree in 1919 and married a charming Scottish woman with whom he had two daughters. Grindlay met one of them, Effie, who, he reported in a letter to his wife after his return to Chungking, planned to attend Smith College in the United States. Lim returned to China in 1924 and taught at Peking Union Medical College before becoming the full-time head of the Chinese Red Cross Medical Relief Commission (CRCMRC) in 1938, which he had founded the year before. Within two years the CRCMRC had 49 medical units in the field, and Lim had started a school to train up to 200 men a month as hospital attendants and stretcher bearers at Kweiyang. In 1941, Lim was appointed inspector general of medical services by Chiang Kai-shek, apparently having forgiven Lim's sin of lending medical assistance to the Communists a few years before.

Dryhurst G. Evans (1905–2000) was born in Wales and came to the United States with his family in 1908 and settled in Wilkes-Barre, Pennsylvania. He graduated from high school there in 1924, going on to attend Oberlin College in Ohio. Evans joined the American Red Cross in 1939 as a field director and during his career was in charge of all operations in India, China, Germany, Korea, Thailand, Austria, and many U.S. cities. He retired in 1970 and returned to Wilkes-Barre as a psychiatric social worker. He moved to Baltimore in 1988 and lived there until his death in 2000.

23. For details on the nature of Lattimore's duties with Chiang Kai-shek, see Robert P. Newman, *Owen Lattimore and the "Loss" of China* (Berkeley: University of California Press, 1992), chapters 5 and 6.

24. Grindlay himself should have been promoted to captain by this time but had not yet gotten notification. It finally arrived on 13 February ("War Diary," entry for 13 February 1942, AMMISCA File).

25. Grindlay diary, 8 January 1942.

26. Grindlay diary, 16 January 1942.

27. Grindlay diary, 18 January 1942. The air drop of plague-infected fleas onto Changteh (Changde), a large city in Hunan Province, was made from a single aircraft on the orders of Colonel Ota Kiyoshi, an aide of Lieutenant General Ishii Shiro, head of Japan's infamous Unit 731, an experimental medicine facility based in Manchuria (Sheldon H. Harris, *Factories of Death* [London: Routledge, 1994], pp. 79, 110). This single "experiment," one of several carried out against the population of Changteh, resulted in upward of 500 deaths. Unit 731 conducted thousands of medical experiments on Chinese civilians and military personnel, in addition to captured Russian soldiers and U.S. air crews. Grindlay's observations were confirmed in 1993 when diaries kept by former high-ranking Japanese officers in the Imperial General Staff Headquarters' strategy section and the chief of the army ministry's medical affairs section were found in the archives of the National Institute for Defense Studies in Japan. The diaries reported that plague-infected fleas were dropped on several cities in Hunan Province in November 1941 ("Diaries Detail Japan's Germ Warfare in China during World War II," UPI Archives (online), 30 December 1993, https://www.upi.com/Archives/1993/12/30/Diaries-detail-Japans-germ-warfare-in-China-during-World-War-II/1516757227600/).

28. Letter, Grindlay to Betty Grindlay, 26 January 1942 (Grindlay letters at Mayo).

29. Grindlay diary, 20 and 23 January 1942.

30. Lanto Kaneti served for two years in Spain; then he went to work with the Communist armies in northwest China about 1939. He later married Zhang Sunfen, and, after the war, the couple moved to Sofia, Bulgaria, where Kaneti practiced medicine and his wife taught Chinese. They were both honored by the Bulgarian and Chinese governments for their activities. Kaneti died in Sofia on 15 June

2004 at age 94. (Guo wu juan xin wen ban gong shi, *1998 Zhong guo da hongshui* [Peking: Wu zhou chuan bo chu ban she, 1998], n.p.)

31. Grindlay diary, 23 January 1942. The story of the dramatic escape of the 2nd MTBS is told by Alexander Kennedy in *Hong Kong: Full Circle, 1939–45* (Privately printed, 1945). In Kunming, the sailors encountered a truck convoy carrying British commandos of the 204 Military Mission. This unit of the British Military Mission was moving from the Jungle Warfare School located at Maymyo, Burma, into China to advise and assist Chinese guerrillas in sabotage operations.

32. Grindlay diary, 25 January and 4 February 1942; "Weekly Report," No. 15, entry for 23 January 1942 (AMMISCA File); MacMorland diary, 23 January 1942. The refugee's full name was Paul Stanley Hawkins. He was born in Peking on 29 January 1915 and graduated from the University of Wisconsin in 1937. He was employed by the National City Bank of New York and sent to Tientsin, China, in mid-1941, shortly after his marriage that July to Helen Roche Julian (b. Oak Park, Illinois, 26 February 1917; d. Van Nuys, California, 24 January 2009), whom he had met in high school in Madison, Wisconsin. Hawkins never got further than Shanghai before war broke out, and he fled the city on horseback. His horses—the one he was riding and a pack animal—disappeared, either taken by the Japanese or having wandered off at some point during his trek, and Hawkins started walking. He eventually met up with a group of Chinese guerrillas who arranged for his safe transit to Chungking. After his return to the United States, he probably remained in banking. He died in Berkeley, California, on 1 August 2000. (*Berkeley* [California] *Daily Gazette*, 18 August 1942: 6.)

Chapter 6

1. Henry L. Stimson and McGeorge Bundy, *On Active Service in Peace and War* (New York: Harper & Brothers, 1948), p. 530.

2. Grace Person Hayes, *The History of the Joint Chiefs of Staff in World War II: The War Against Japan* (Annapolis, MD: Naval Institute Press, 1982), p. 81.

3. William George Grieve, "Belated Endeavor: The American Military Mission to China (AMMISCA) 1941–1942" (unpublished PhD dissertation, University of Illinois at Urbana–Champaign, 1979), pp. 187–90.

4. War Diary, 19 and 26–27 February and 4 March 1942 (AMMISCA File); Theodore H. White, ed., *The Stilwell Papers* (New York: William Sloane Associates, 1948), p. 50.

5. Grindlay diary, 5 March 1942.

6. Nevin Wetzel, "Evacuation of Rangoon," *Ex-CBI Roundup* (November 1974): 13. Captain (later Major) Nevin F. Wetzel (1912–1989) was a mining engineer who had come out to China with AMMISCA as a member of the Corps of Engineers. He was first ordered to work with Major John Ausland on the construction of the Yunnan–Burma railway, and then he went to Lashio to assist in rebuilding the Burma Road. After serving on temporary assignment in Rangoon carrying out demolitions, he returned to his previous assignment at Lashio and was subsequently evacuated to Kunming after the Japanese overran the country. Wetzel was dispatched to Ramgarh in 1942 to train Chinese combat engineers, and the following year he established his headquarters at Tagap to oversee the Chinese who were building the Ledo Road. He moved to Shingbwiyang along with the 12th Combat Engineer Regiment after the town was captured, and in early 1944 he was transferred to China to advise on the demolition of roads ahead of the Japanese advance (Operation I-GO) in southwest China. Wetzel remained in Kunming until the end of May, when General Boatner sent him on a secret mission at Stilwell's request (the latter was then commander of Tenth Army on Okinawa) to reconnoiter the China coast south of Canton in anticipation of future American landings. Wetzel and his party left on 6 June in two jeeps and carried out reconnaissance south of Nanking. Bad road conditions forced them to abandon the jeeps, and for the next ten days they walked from one Chinese guerrilla group to another, gathering information about roads and taking photographs for the final report. The group finished its reconnaissance at Pai Hoi on the coast and was picked up and returned to Nanking, where they remained until war's end. After the war, Wetzel went back to his home state of Utah and established a successful engineering company in Salt Lake City. (See John Allen, "Wetzel's WWII Career Is

History of C.B.I.," *CBIVA Sound-Off* [Spring 1989]: 24–28.)

7. OSS Research & Analysis Report 280, *Evacuation of Rangoon* (as reported by Captain Richard M. Jones), 28 April 1942 (RG 112, National Archives and Records Administration, College Park, Maryland).

8. In actuality, the Japanese took about ten days to regroup before fording the river several miles above the blown bridge. But the damage done to the 17th Indian Division could never be repaired, and its effectiveness as a fighting force was drastically reduced (Wetzel, "Evacuation of Rangoon," 14; Alan K. Lathrop, "The Employment of Chinese Nationalist Troops in the First Burma Campaign," *Journal of Southeast Asian Studies* 12, no. 2 [Summer 1981]: 410; Alan Warren, *Burma 1942* [London and New York: Continuum Books, 2011], pp. 126ff.).

9. Wetzel, "Evacuation of Rangoon," 14–15. William Doyle, a young Royal Marine, was a member of a team of 105 men called Force Viper that landed in Rangoon in the midst of the chaotic evacuation of the city. This group was charged with lending support to the almost nonexistent Burma navy and commandeered three river launches in which to seek out Japanese and do battle. Doyle and his group were present when the docks and oil tanks at the huge Syriam oil refinery near Rangoon, operated by Burmah Oil Company, were detonated to prevent their capture by the enemy, who were bearing down on the city. In a matter of minutes, 150 million gallons of gasoline, aviation fuel, and kerosene went up in an enormous blast set off by British engineers. Force Viper assisted the demolitions personnel in placing charges of gelignite around the oil tanks and loading the company's documents onto barges that were taken upriver for safety. Doyle was given the task of supervising the burning of all the company's payroll and personnel files. The marines also participated in destroying and immobilizing Lend-Lease vehicles left on the docks. After the oil tanks were blown up, they burned fiercely for six weeks. Force Viper escaped on the motor launches. (James Leasor, *The Marine from Mandalay* [London: Leo Cooper, 1988], pp. 27–29.)

10. Gerald Astor, *The Jungle War* (Hoboken, NJ: John Wiley & Sons, 2004), pp. 24, 30–31; Martha Byrd, *Chennault: Giving Wings to the Tiger* (Tuscaloosa: University of Alabama Press, 1987), p. 125.

11. Charles R. Bond, Jr., and Terry H. Anderson, *A Flying Tiger's Diary* (College Station: Texas A&M University Press, 1984), p. 141; Chennault to Colonel Bissell, handwritten draft of radio message, 19 April 1942 (Robert Parton Williams Papers, United States Army Heritage and Education Center, Carlisle, Pennsylvania) (hereafter Williams Papers, USAHEC).

12. Other British personnel killed in the crash were James Percy Russel (a King's Messenger) and Mr. D. Rocson (identity unknown). Philip Fogarty, a former British commissioner in the Shan States, who was on his way to assume the position of representative of the British government of Burma in China, was injured. Coincidentally, the plane crashed on the same day that Sir Archibald Clark Kerr arrived in Moscow as British ambassador.

13. Grindlay diary, 15 March 1942. Grindlay consistently misspelled the names of Colonel Edward and General Dennys throughout his diary. General Brady was Francis M. Brady, who, at the time of the Japanese attack on Clark Field in the Philippines on 8 December 1941, had the rank of colonel and served as chief of staff to General Lewis Brereton. After the latter moved his headquarters first to Darwin, Australia, and then to India, Brady accompanied him in the same capacity. The mission that Grindlay mentioned in his diary entry may have been then Brigadier General Brady's idea in early February 1942 to send heavy bombers (transferred from Java to India) from Akyab via Magwe and Toungoo to Bangkok and Saigon in a retaliatory strike at Japanese installations. Brady later was posted to head the American Air Base Command at Karachi. (See W.F. Craven and J.L. Cate, *The Army Air Forces in World War II*, vol. 1: *Plans and Early Operations* [Chicago: University of Chicago Press, 1948], p. 492, and vol. 4: *The Pacific: Guadalcanal to Saipan* [Chicago: University of Chicago Press, 1950], p. 414.) Colonel Otto George (1904–1942) was a native of Missouri and a member of the Army Air Corps. He also had been sent to Kunming to inspect a C-39 cargo aircraft that had just arrived in the theater, carrying Stilwell and his party. The twin-engine C-39 was

one of several dispatched to India and China for evaluation regarding its suitability for service over the "Hump." It was subsequently found that the aircraft was underpowered and could not fly over 10,000 feet with a full load and was rejected for service in China (War Diary, 9 and 17 March 1942; AMMISCA File). Colonel George's body was removed from China after the war and reinterred at the National Cemetery of the Pacific in Hawaii. General Dennys was reinterred at Sai Won War Cemetery in Hong Kong after the war ended.

14. Grindlay diary, 16 March 1942.

15. Letter, Grindlay to Betty Grindlay, 22 March 1942 (Grindlay letters at Mayo).

16. Joseph Heinrich (ca. 1905–1970) was signal officer with AMMISCA. As a member of the Army Signal Corps he served as advisor to Chinese military and civilian authorities in 1942–1943 and was a member of the Telecommunications Board of India. He was employed by AT&T Long Lines before and after the war. During the Eisenhower and Kennedy administrations, Heinrich traveled with the president overseas to assist in setting up communications with the White House. He became a brigadier general and saw service in the Korean War. Heinrich died in Palm Beach, Florida, in March 1970 at age 65.

17. Grindlay diary, 29 March 1942. Sir Horace Seymour (1885–1978) was the British ambassador to China from 1942 to 1946, replacing Sir Archibald Clark Kerr after the latter moved to Moscow.

Chapter 7

1. The term "Forgotten War" has been used in several book titles—for example, Jon Latimer's *Burma: The Forgotten War* (London: John Murray, 2004) and Christopher Bayly and Tim Harper's *Forgotten Armies* (Cambridge, MA: Belknap Press of Harvard University Press, 2005). Down to the present day, veterans of the China-Burma-India theater, especially members of Merrill's Marauders, still refer to themselves as having fought in the "forgotten war."

2. Letter, J.A. Mendelson to Colonel Williams, Chungking, China, 30 March 1942 (Williams 201 File, Williams Papers, USAHEC).

3. Robert Parton Williams diary, 26 February–19 March 1942 (Williams Papers, USAHEC).

4. Williams diary, 23–26 March 1942 (Williams Papers, USAHEC).

5. Alice-Leone Moats, *Blind Date with Mars* (New York: Doubleday, Doran, 1943), p. 100.

6. *Ibid.*, p. 101.

7. *Ibid.*, p. 111.

8. "The World War II Diaries of General Joseph W. Stilwell (1941–1945)," Hoover Institution Archives, https://digitalcollections.hoover.org/images/Collections/51001/1942_stilwell_diary_rev.pdf.

9. Ian Lyall Grant and Kazuo Tamayama, *Burma 1942: The Japanese Invasion* (Chichester, West Sussex: Zampi Press, 1999), pp. 190–92; F.A.E. Crew, *The Army Medical Services: Campaigns*, vol. 5: *Burma* (London: Her Majesty's Stationery Office, 1966), p. 66.

10. "Burma Retreat, 1942," part I (compiled from letters written by Brigadier T.O. Thompson, D.D.M.S., Burma, to Brigadier H.C.D. Rankin, D.D.M.S., GHQ India), *Journal of the Royal Army Medical Corps* XC (January 1948): 24–25.

11. Grant and Tamayama, *Burma 1942*, pp. 66–67; "Burma Retreat, 1942," p. 25.

12. Crew, *The Army Medical Services*, p. 68.

13. Williams diary, 4 April 1942 (Williams Papers, USAHEC).

14. See Paul Geren's *Burma Diary* (New York: Harper & Brothers, 1943) for his story.

15. The Friends Ambulance Unit was quite separate from the American Field Service (AFS), an entity organized in the United States. The former was made up of British subjects, while the latter comprised Americans. Both groups were active in all theaters of the war. (Letter, Tom Owen, Lashio, to family, 28 February 1942; copy provided to author courtesy of Glyn Owen, United Kingdom.)

16. Bill Brough, *To Reason Why...* (Whickham, UK: Hickory Tree Press, 2001), p. 36.

17. After the war, Dr. Gurney and his family returned to Panglong in 1950. While the date of his death has not been found, Agnes lived until March 2003.

18. Henrietta Thompson, *Walk a Little Faster: Escape from Burma with General Stilwell in 1942* (Privately published, 1980), p. 11.

19. Gordon Seagrave, *Burma Surgeon* (New York: W.W. Norton, 1943), p. 189.

20. Grindlay diary, 3 April 1942. A trephine is an instrument used to drill a round hole in the skull in a procedure known as trepanation. Trepanning is a common means of draining fluid from the brain to relieve pressure and perform brain surgery.

21. A Trueta cast was named after Josep Trueta, a surgeon from Barcelona who had served in the Spanish Civil War. He developed a method of rapidly stabilizing limbs broken by gunshot, shrapnel, or bombs in which the wound would be debrided—that is, the burned and charred edges cut away with scissors—and then wrapped in Vaseline gauze and encased in plaster of Paris. Many patients survived because infection was greatly reduced by this process. Later in World War II, however, it was found that packing a wound with Vaseline gauze actually increased the chances of infection in the excessively damp conditions encountered during monsoon periods or in coastal areas of Burma, such as the Arakan, and the practice was abandoned. (Charles Evans, *A Doctor in XIVth Army: Burma 1944-1945* [London: Leo Cooper, 1998], p. 4; Brough, *To Reason Why*, p. 40.)

22. Williams diary, 12 April 1942 (Williams Papers, USAHEC); Mary Ellen Condon-Rall and Albert F. Cowdrey, *The Medical Department: Medical Service in the War Against Japan*, United States Army in World War II: The Technical Services (Washington, DC: Center of Military History, United States Army, 1998), p. 290.

23. William Harrison Cripps (1850-1923), a British surgeon, was noted for his studies and surgical treatment of rectal and colon cancer.

24. Interview by Henrietta Thompson with Carl Arnold, Oceanside, California, 1 February 1972 (copy of interview provided to author by Ms. Thompson).

25. Williams diary, 29 April 1942 (Williams Papers, USAHEC); "U.S. Forces in China, Burma and India, Headquarters," by R.L. Hambleton, diary, 29 April 1942 (Louis Meyer Papers, University Archives, University of Pennsylvania, Philadelphia) (hereafter Hambleton diary, Meyer Papers, UPA).

Roscoe Lee Hambleton was a native of Orchard Park, New York (born 8 June 1895), and a graduate of Cornell University in 1917, where he received a degree in mechanical engineering. He married Cecile S. Lowder in the American Consulate, Chefoo, China, on 11 July 1930 (she was born in Rockwell, Texas, around 1901). Hambleton was employed by the Sperry Gyroscope Company in Brooklyn, and then by Bodell & Company, both for short periods of time. In 1922 he organized Roscoe L. Hambleton, Inc., a trade organization representing twenty-five American manufacturers of machinery and automotive equipment in the Far East, based in Shanghai and later South America, for a total of fifteen years, beginning in 1924. His company specialized in marine engineering and in 1925 was building the first diesel-powered riverboat for service in the upper Yangtze River. At some point in the late 1930s, he and his wife returned to the United States and had settled in San Diego, California, by early 1939. In November of that same year, Hambleton was employed by General Motors India, Ltd., and moved to Bombay; then he returned to the United States once again after a few months to assume a position in Cincinnati, Ohio, with the Crosley Corporation as export manager. Hambleton left more than a year later to take a commission in the army in June 1941.

Father Louis Meyer, a Roman Catholic priest and chaplain who served the 20th General Hospital in Assam in 1943-1945, held a lengthy conversation with Brigadier General Haydon Boatner (commander of the Northern Area Combat Command under Stilwell) in 1945, and afterward he wrote that Boatner disparaged Hambleton by calling the latter an engineer of "about 3rd rate importance." Boatner went on to say that Hambleton was chosen for the AMMISCA assignment by General Magruder because he had pre-war experience working in China, and the War Department went along with it because Hambleton had well-placed friends in the department. Boatner also told Father Meyer that he was reluctant to have Hambleton on the staff, as "his past dealings with the Chinese had been shady. He was always trying to make something extra out of his job, had gone into bankruptcy in the States, and was tripped up in 'deals' in China." (The exact nature of these "shady deals" is unknown, and perhaps it was merely unsubstantiated hearsay.) Boatner went on to declare that "I did not want him but would let the matter rest since it had been so arranged."

Hambleton may not have had the stamina of a younger man (he was 47 years of age in 1942) to take on the assignment that Stilwell gave him (or for which he may have volunteered), and certainly not to cope with the subsequent difficult chain of events that ended tragically a few months later. But his knowledge of riverboats made him a logical choice, in Stilwell's mind, to handle the transportation of the Chinese 22nd Division across the Irrawaddy River. After arriving in India, Stilwell recommended the Distinguished Service Cross for Hambleton's heroic service in rescuing the 22nd Division at the Irrawaddy River crossing; the DSC was awarded posthumously to Hambleton on 11 March 1943. He was also decorated, again posthumously, by the Chinese for the same action. (Untitled handwritten notes by Father Louis Meyer, 28 January 1945, Ledo, Assam [Meyer Papers, UPA]; Roscoe L. Hambleton File, World War II Servicemen Alumni Files, Department of Rare and Manuscript Collections, Carl A. Kroch Library, Cornell University, Ithaca, New York.)

26. Grindlay diary, 1 May 1942; Williams diary, 1 May 1942 (Williams Papers, USAHEC).

27. Theodore H. White, ed., *The Stilwell Papers* (New York: William Sloane Associates, 1948), pp. 97–98.

28. Hambleton diary, 3–6 May 1942 (Meyer Papers, UPA). Lieutenant (later Major) Denis Guy Lean was born in London on 5 November 1908. He was appointed a temporary captain in the Indian army in January 1943. Nothing more is known of his subsequent military service. After the war, he served for a time as a member of the board of Shell Oil, and he died at age 98 on 4 December 2006 in Perth, Scotland (information provided by Mr. Hans Houterman, Middelburg, The Netherlands, 27 September 2014).

29. Hambleton diary, 10 May 1942 (Meyer Papers, UPA).

30. Hambleton diary, 15–20 May 1942 (Meyer Papers, UPA).

31. Hambleton diary, 21–23 May 1942 (Meyer Papers, UPA).

Chapter 8

1. Arnold interview in Henrietta Thompson, *Walk a Little Faster: Escape from Burma with General Stilwell in 1942* (Privately published, 1980), p. 31; Barbara W. Tuchman, *Stilwell and the American Experience in China* (New York: Book of the Month Club, 1985), p. 291; Williams diary, 1 May 1942 (Williams Papers, USAHEC). A number of first-hand accounts were used in this narrative of the "walkout," some of which will be new to readers, including the diaries of John H. Grindlay and Robert P. Williams. Henrietta Thompson's invaluable privately published book of interviews with walkout survivors, *Walk a Little Faster*, was a godsend in compiling this narrative. Ms. Thompson conducted her interviews at a time when almost all of the participants were still living and their memories of the event had not faded. Several first-hand published accounts (not all of them cited in the notes) were also consulted and will be familiar to students of the China-Burma-India theater and of General Stilwell. These include Jack Belden, *Retreat with Stilwell* (London: Cassell, 1943); Frank Dorn, *Walkout with Stilwell in Burma* (New York: Thomas Y. Crowell, 1971); Fred Eldridge, *Wrath in Burma* (Garden City, NY: Doubleday, 1946); Gordon Seagrave, *Burma Surgeon* (New York: W.W. Norton, 1943); and Theodore H. White, ed., *The Stilwell Papers* (New York: William Sloane Associates, 1948).

2. Colonel Robert L. Scott, *God Is My Co-Pilot* (New York: Ballantine Books, 1962), pp. 78–80. Scott's recollection confirms that Stilwell had his escape route planned by 1 May, probably based on the advice of the Reverend Brayton Case, one of his guides. The itinerary may not have been firm in its details, but Stilwell did know that he would be going by way of Homalin. His radio message of 6 May repeated the Homalin route and asked for a pack train to be sent from Imphal to meet the column. His choice of the exact route depended largely on native guides, Reverend Case, and the driving need to stay ahead of the Chinese and refugees and get safely beyond reach of the Japanese.

3. J.V. Davidson-Houston, *Armed Pilgrimage* (London: Robert Hale, 1949), pp. 254–55.

4. *Ibid.*, p. 259. Brigadier Spear elected to walk out to India. He and a companion, Brigadier Brand, and their party of British troops took a path farther south, one thought to be shorter than the Stilwell route but much

more dangerous, as the Japanese had likely already positioned themselves along it. The party was ambushed in the jungle. Brand later wrote that Spear "had just clambered up a steep slope when a shot rang out and he fell back. I caught him to save a further fall ... I had to take charge. I went up the hill leaving my water bottle for [Spear].... When we made good the hill I came down again to find that [Spear] had already gone. He was courageous, cheerful and a grand companion right up to the end" (letter of Brigadier Brand, 9 November 1942, quoted in Keith Stevens, "A Cautionary Tale for Army Officers Who Study Chinese"; manuscript copy provided by Stevens to the author in May 2005). For Brigadier Spear's background, see Keith Stevens, "'Duncan Force'—the Shanghai Defence Force in 1927, & the Career of Captain Ronald Spear," *Journal of the Royal Asiatic Society, Hong Kong Branch* 48 (2008): 151–72.

5. For a synopsis of Herbert Castens's later wartime experiences with the Chindits, see "Bertie Castens' Secret Track," www.chinditslongcloth1943.com/bertie-castens-secret-track.html. Castens was described by one author as "a big powerful man of over six feet, weighing just short of sixteen stone [224 pounds] and wearing a large black beard" (Lieutenant General Sir Geoffrey Evans, *The Johnnies* [London: Cassell, 1964], p. 21). In 1943 Castens was of great assistance to the Chindits when he led a party of them past Japanese troops on an escarpment on his "secret track."

6. Thompson, *Walk a Little Faster*, p. 59.

7. Letter, Reverend Brayton Case to Clarke Case, Calcutta, India, 31 May 1942 (Reverend Brayton Case Papers, American Baptist Historical Society, Atlanta, Georgia). Case, who has been mistakenly named "Breedom" in several books about the first Burma campaign (including Jack Belden's and Frank Dorn's accounts), was born in Burma to missionary parents, educated in the United States, and returned to the country of his birth as a missionary in 1913. He ran an agricultural extension service and training school in Pyinmana until he was driven out by the approaching Japanese on 13 April 1942. Case (along with a colleague, Professor Dickason, and an Indian cook named Rutnam) fled and linked up with Dr. Gordon Seagrave's medical unit at Tatkon, thirty miles north of Pyinmana. Because of his proficiency in the languages of the Burmese hill tribes and his knowledge of the country, Case came to the attention of Stilwell and accompanied the "walkout" group as a guide. (From all available evidence, Professor Dickason and Case's Indian cook were not part of the walkout.) After reaching India in May 1942, Case went to work at U.S. Army headquarters in New Delhi as an advisor on Burma. At his request, he was flown to Fort Hertz to celebrate Christmas with the Christian Kachins in the area; then he returned to India. He moved to Ledo, Assam, in the summer of 1943 at the request of U.S. Brigadier General Haydon Boatner, who wanted his troops to have fresh vegetables and asked for Case to plant gardens to supply the American and Chinese soldiers with food. Case also helped the native Nagas and Kachins to establish vegetable gardens. He briefly advised OSS Detachment 101 before leaving Ledo in the fall of 1943 to join the forward headquarters of American forces clearing the track for the Ledo Road, who were in need of his knowledge of the country. Case remained in Burma until 14 July 1944, when he drowned after the boat on which he was carrying rice seeds capsized on Indawgyi Lake, near Kamaing, in northern Burma. Unable to swim and wearing heavy military equipment and clothing, Case sank before he could be rescued.

8. See Bill Brough, *To Reason Why...* (Whickham, UK: Hickory Tree Press, 2001).

9. Seagrave, *Burma Surgeon*, pp. 239–40.

10. Gary G. Yerkey, *Still Time to Live: A Biography of Jack Belden* (Washington: GK Press, 2011), p. 84.

11. Thompson, *Walk a Little Faster*, pp. 57–58.

12. Ibid., p. 4.

13. Circular letter by Paul Geren, American Baptist Mission, Gauhati, Assam, India, 27 May 1942 (copy provided to author by Henrietta Thompson).

14. Thompson, *Walk a Little Faster*, p. 24.

15. Letter, Grindlay to Betty Grindlay, Ramgarh, India, 9 September 1942 (Grindlay letters at Mayo).

16. John Nunneley and Kazuo Tamayama, *Tales by Japanese Soldiers* (London: Cassell, 2000), p. 92.

Chapter 9

1. Letter, Robert Williams to Barbara Williams, 4 June 1942 (copy provided to author by Henrietta Thompson).
2. George W. Parsons, recollections, http://www.cotteridge.quaker.eu.org/george_parsons.htm.
3. Grindlay diary, 10 May 1942; letter, Tom Owen (FAU), Calcutta, to family, 27 May 1942 (copy provided to author by Glyn Owen).
4. Grindlay diary, 12 May 1942.
5. Thomas Arthur Sharpe was born on 14 November 1913. He joined the Indian Civil Service on 15 December 1937, the same day that he arrived in India. He was stationed first in Sylhet as assistant commissioner; the following year he transferred to Sadiya in the same capacity and as assistant to the political officer. In February 1939, Sharpe moved to Dibrugarh, again as assistant commissioner, and at the mid-year point he served for two months in Kohima and then relocated to Imphal, where he assumed the position of president of Manipur State Darbar (roughly equivalent to a local governing commission). Sharpe died of wounds received during the battle for Imphal on 11 April 1944. See Office of the Accountant General, Assam, India, *History of the Services of Gazetted and Other Officers Serving under the Government of Assam* (Shillong: Superintendent, Assam Government Press, 1941) (Oriental & India Office Library, London); Williams diary, 14–15 May 1942 (Williams Papers, USAHEC).
6. Naga rice beer, called "zu," is a cloudy yellow beverage that was said to look and smell like homemade cider and was quite tasty (A.R. Tainsh, *And Some Fell by the Wayside* [Calcutta: Orient Longmans, 1948], p. 145). Alastair Tainsh, who assisted hundreds of refugees struggling to walk out of Burma, was deputy assistant director of supplies and transport to the Line of Communications Sub-Area, Ledo. His adventures are also recounted in Felicity Goodall's *Exodus Burma: The British Escape Through the Jungles of Death 1942* (Brimscombe Port Stroud, Gloucestershire: Spellmount, 2011).
7. Williams letter; Williams diary, 19 May 1942 (Williams Papers, USAHEC).
8. Grindlay diary, 19 May 1942; Williams diary, 20 May 1942 (Williams Papers, USAHEC).
9. "The Campaign in Burma," report from Stilwell to War Department, n.d., pp. 91–92 (copy provided to author by Brigadier General Frank Dorn, 1977).
10. Lewis H. Brereton, *The Brereton Diaries* (New York: William Morrow, 1946), p. 124.
11. Williams diary, 23 May 1942 (Williams Papers, USAHEC). Alfred Wagg was a *Chicago Tribune* correspondent in the CBI theater, perhaps best known for his book, *A Million Died!*, which detailed the fate of refugees fleeing from Burma into India in 1942.
12. Williams diary, 21 May 1942 (Williams Papers, USAHEC).
13. Gordon Seagrave, *Burma Surgeon* (New York: W.W. Norton, 1943), p. 285.
14. W.G. Burchett, *Bombs Over Burma* (Melbourne: F.W. Cheshire, 1944), pp. 215–16.
15. Letter, Grindlay to Betty Grindlay, 29 May 1942 (Grindlay letters at Mayo). Contrary to what Grindlay heard, Doolittle's fliers did lose men in the Tokyo raid, both killed and captured by the Japanese after crash landing.
16. *Ibid*.
17. Letter, Tom Owen to Kay (?), 9 June 1942 (copy provided to author by Glyn Owen). Owen wrote that he had discarded or accidentally lost his belongings before and during the trek out of Burma. "This is the most depressing side of the Burma business," he said, "as I landed here [Gauhati] with absolutely nothing apart from the clothes on my back. Pen … and other small articles went into the tributary of the Uyu, passport and all identification documents sailed down the Uyu itself and are probably in the Indian Ocean by now and finally the loss of everything else occurred in the confusion of getting on and off a lorry which brought us from Imphal to Dimapur [where the Seagrave unit boarded the train to Gauhati]. This war business," he concluded, "tends to rid us of any sentimental tenda[n]cies!"
18. Seagrave, *Burma Surgeon*, pp. 293–94.

Chapter 10

1. "Report on Activities in the Dibrugarh-Ledo-Tipang Area from June 20th to August 16th," by H.L. Boatner (New Delhi, 23 August 1942), p. 2, Historical Manuscripts File, Sup-

porting Documents to *U.S. Army in World War II—CBI* (National Archives and Records Administration, College Park, Maryland) (hereafter Supporting Documents to USAWW2); Hambleton diary, 1 June 1942 (Meyer Papers, UPA).

2. Hambleton diary, 3 June 1942 (Meyer Papers, UPA).

3. Hambleton diary, 5 June 1942 (Meyer Papers, UPA).

4. Hambleton diary, 7 June 1942 (Meyer Papers, UPA).

5. Hambleton diary, 9 June 1942 (Meyer Papers, UPA).

6. Radio message, General Tu to USA HQ India, 17 June 1942 (Supporting Documents to USAWW2).

7. Hambleton diary, 21–24 June 1942 (Meyer Papers, UPA).

8. Radio message, General Lin In-Shang (General Liao Yao-shiang), 22 June 1942 (Supporting Documents to USAWW2).

9. Hambleton diary, 2 July 1942 (Meyer Papers, UPA).

10. *Ibid*. Captain Young died at Shingbwiyang on 29 August 1942; Sergeant Shaw had died a short time before in the same camp. Most of the orphans, as well as Lillian Bald, died on the trail before reaching Shingbwiyang.

11. Hambleton diary, 4 July 1942 (Meyer Papers, UPA).

12. Alan K. Lathrop, "The Employment of Chinese Nationalist Troops in the First Burma Campaign," *Journal of Southeast Asian Studies* 12, no. 2 (Summer 1981): 426.

13. Hambleton diary, 14 July 1942 (Meyer Papers, UPA). A young British civilian, Eric Lambert, led a relief expedition from Ledo on 24 June to locate the "lost" Chinese army. He met them on the trail leading out of the Hukawng Valley on 13 July and, with the aid of the Nagas and food supplies from the Americans, he arrived back in Assam three weeks later (Felicity Goodall, *Exodus Burma: The British Escape Through the Jungles of Death 1942* [Brimscombe Port Stroud, Gloucestershire: Spellmount, 2011], pp. 225–29).

14. Hambleton diary, 26 and 31 July 1942 (Meyer Papers, UPA).

15. Draft of message, Boatner to Sibert, 5 August 1942, pp. 1–2 ("Operations—Burma Evacuation," in Supporting Documents to USAWW2).

16. Hambleton diary, 7 August 1942 (Meyer Papers, UPA).

17. Father Louis Meyer, "The Case of Mrs. Roscoe L. Hambleton," 28 January 1945, Typescript draft (Meyer Papers, UPA). This document is based on a conversation that Father Meyer had with Brigadier General Boatner in Assam. Meyer told Boatner that the Chinese servant who was with Hambleton when he died in Shingbwiyang made it out of Burma and was in the 20th General Hospital. Boatner said that Mrs. Hambleton had journeyed to India to find her husband's grave, obtaining work as a nurse in the 73rd Evacuation Hospital, and then fell ill and was placed in the 20th General. Meyer visited her and was loaned a copy of Hambleton's diary, but there is no mention of how the widow obtained the diary in the first place.

Chapter 11

1. Richard Mead, *Churchill's Lions* (Chalford Stroud, Gloucestershire: Spellmount, 2007), p. 42.

2. Charles Romanus and Riley Sunderland, *Stilwell's Mission to China* (Washington, DC: Office of the Chief of Military History, Department of the Army, 1953), p. 136.

3. *Ibid.*

4. Theodore H. White, ed., *The Stilwell Papers* (New York: William Sloane Associates, 1948), p. 92.

5. "General Lo Cho-ying's Report to the Generalissimo on the Operation of the Chinese Expeditionary Force in Burma," 25 June 1942, p. 2 (unpublished manuscript in Joseph W. Stilwell Papers, SNF-21, Hoover Library, Stanford University, Palo Alto, California).

6. Combined Inter-Services Historical Section (India and Pakistan), *The Retreat from Burma, 1941–42* (Calcutta: Official History of the Indian Armed Forces in the Second World War 1939–1945, 1959), p. 467.

7. *Ibid.*, p. 468.

8. The bad relations between Irwin and Slim dated to the British campaign against the Italians in Sudan in 1940, when the 1st Battalion of the 1st Essex Regiment broke and ran during the attack on Gallabat. Slim commanded the 10th Indian Brigade, of which the

1st Battalion of the Essex was a part; after the battle, he sacked the battalion commander, a man who happened to be an old personal friend of Irwin, then serving in the same regiment. Afterward, Irwin harbored a deep resentment and was itching for an opportunity for revenge (Frank McLynn, *The Burma Campaign* [London: Bodley Head, 2010], p. 90). Irwin went on to be appointed by General Wavell to command the First Arakan Campaign in the fall of 1942, an operation that proved a disaster for the British and for Irwin, whom Wavell sacked at the end of it, in May 1943. Irwin was described as a person "whose character did not inspire universal liking" (David Fraser, *Alanbrooke* [New York: Atheneum, 1982], p. 293). He went home to be grilled about his lapses by Field Marshal Sir Alan Brooke, CIGS, and was shunted off to minor commands in Scotland and West Africa for the rest of the war (Mead, *Churchill's Lions*, pp. 221–22).

9. Captain B.H. Liddell Hart, *The Tanks*, vol. 2 (London: Cassell, 1959), pp. 300–301.

10. "Report on Activities in the Dibrugarh-Ledo-Tipang Area from June 20th to August 16th," by H.L. Boatner (New Delhi, 23 August 1942), p. 2 (Supporting Documents to USAWW2).

11. Letter, D.L. Whitworth (Brigadier) to General Yu Fei-peng and General Sun, Dibrugarh, 18 June 1942 (file "Operations—Memos to General Sibert 1942," Supporting Documents to USAWW2).

12. "Report on Activities in the Dibrugarh-Ledo-Tipang Area," pp. 1–2.

13. Colonel Robert L. Scott, *God Is My Co-Pilot* (New York: Ballantine Books, 1962), p. 81.

14. Brigadier Dysart Whitworth, "The Evacuation of Refugees and the Chinese Fifth Army from the Hukawng Valley into Assam, Summer 1942," *Journal of the Royal Central Asian Society* 30, no. 2 (September 1943): 312.

15. "Report on Activities in the Dibrugarh-Ledo-Tipang Area," pp. 3–5.

16. C.W. North, "Starvation in the Hukawng Valley 1942," contained in Military Attaché Report no. 655, 21 September 1942, New Delhi, p. 4 (National Archives and Records Administration College Park, Maryland). Cornelius William ("Neil") North (b. 1917) was a Burma Frontier Service official who had, with great foresight, gathered small stockpiles of whatever food and other supplies he could scrape together for the anticipated onrush of thousands of refugees. He also had huts built at Shingbwiyang to house as many refugees as possible. North was hailed as a hero for his actions, which saved many lives (Felicity Goodall, *Exodus Burma: The British Escape Through the Jungles of Death 1942* [Brimscombe Port Stroud, Gloucestershire: Spellmount, 2011], pp. 183ff.). After the war, he went on to serve in several positions in Africa in the Colonial Service. He retired in 1977 and served as secretary of the Middle East Association until 1981. His date of death is unknown.

17. "The Campaign in Burma," report from Stilwell to War Department, n.d. (copy provided to author by Brigadier General Frank Dorn, 1977).

18. The story (unconfirmed) is that the stragglers left from the recapture of Burma in 1944–1945, plus former native levies who had been released from military service by the British and Americans, were still roaming the countryside after the war was over. American troops garrisoned in Myitkyina in 1945–1946 were forced to build fortifications into which they retreated at night to avoid being killed or injured by these stragglers in their search for food and other provisions (interview with Davis Shryer, former U.S. Army supply officer, Minneapolis, Minnesota, 28 May 2010).

19. Alfred Draper, *Dawns Like Thunder* (London: Leo Cooper, 1987), p. 269.

20. A.R. Tainsh, *And Some Fell by the Wayside* (Calcutta: Orient Longmans, 1948), p. 2. Most refugees used the trail through the Hukawng Valley. Bad as it was, the worst escape route used by a large party of desperate civilians led through the Chaukan Pass further north. This route was steeper, rougher, and (in most places) not previously used, so a path had to be chopped through the jungle. The group that went this way in May 1942 did so in a continuously pouring monsoon rain. Eventually almost everyone reached India (Goodall, *Exodus Burma*, pp. 214–24).

21. "Burma Retreat, 1942," part II (compiled from letters written by Brigadier T.O. Thompson, D.D.M.S., Burma, to Brigadier H.C.D. Rankin, D.D.M.S., GHQ India), *Journal of the Royal Army Medical Corps* XC (January 1948): 58.

22. Scott, *God Is My Co-Pilot*, p. 84.
23. Mark Harrison, *Medicine and Victory: British Military Medicine in the Second World War* (Oxford: Oxford University Press, 2004), pp. 190–93.

Chapter 12

1. Lieutenant Colonel Roberts, who had been an assistant military attaché in China from 1933 to 1938, went on to serve as chief of staff of the U.S. Military Mission to Moscow (1944–1945). Lieutenant Colonel Eckert commanded an artillery regiment in Europe. Colonel Sandusky remained in the CBI, where he became the deputy chief of staff of Y (Yoke) Force under Brigadier General Frank Dorn.
2. Grindlay diary, 5 June 1942. General James Doolittle's planes were launched on their bombing mission of Japan not from the Aleutians, as Grindlay inferred, but from the aircraft carrier *Hornet* more than 600 miles off the coast of Japan on 18 April. The pilot of whom Grindlay spoke probably was Lieutenant Ted Lawson, pilot of plane number 7 (the "Ruptured Duck"), who ditched in the sea off Sanmen, Chekiang Province, and the navigator with the paralyzed arm was Lieutenant C.J. McClure. Four members of Lawson's crew were badly injured and were taken to the Linhai Enze Medical Bureau for treatment. Lieutenant Thomas White, the only doctor on the mission, was flying in plane 15 ("TNT"), which also ditched nearby, though without any injuries to the crew. Upon being informed of the injured men, White rushed to the hospital and amputated Lawson's leg, saving his life (and subsequently receiving the Silver Star for his actions). The American nurse to whom Grindlay referred was most likely a nun from somewhere in the area. The men were later escorted by a Dr. Chen Shenyan to Kweilin, from which point they made their way to Kunming and eventual evacuation to India. The crew members in Lawson's plane were Lieutenant D. Davenport, the co-pilot; Lieutenant C.J. McClure, navigator; Lieutenant R.S. Clever, bombardier; and Sergeant D.J. Thatcher, engineer/gunner. The plane White had occupied was flown by Lieutenant Donald Smith.
3. Letter, Gordon Seagrave to Colonel Williams, Gauhati, Assam, 20 June 1942 (Williams Papers, USAHEC).
4. Colonel John Boyd Coates, Jr., et al., eds., *Surgery in World War II: Activities of Surgical Consultants*, vol. II, Medical Department, United States Army (Washington, DC: Office of the Surgeon General, Department of the Army, 1964), pp. 896–97.
5. Coates et al., *Surgery in World War II*; Blanche B. Armfield, *Organization and Administration in World War II*, Medical Department, United States Army (Washington, DC: Office of the Surgeon General, Department of the Army, 1963), pp. 509–11.
6. Grindlay diary, 21–23 July 1942. Lady Auckinleck's name before her marriage was Jessie Stewart. She and Claude Auckinleck (commander-in-chief of British forces, India) were married in 1921. The viceroy at the time was Lord Linlithgow, though it is not clear whether he and Lady Auckinleck were indeed lovers, as rumor had it. Air Marshal Sir Richard Peirse (1892–1970) was head of Bomber Command for little more than a year (1940–1941), until he was relieved of command for wasting aircraft and air crews and failing to be an effective leader. He was given command of British air forces in India in 1942. His affair with Lady Auckinleck was made known to Lord Mountbatten soon after his arrival in the CBI in October 1943, but Mountbatten kept Peirse on until late November 1944, when the dalliance could no longer be ignored, and Mountbatten refused another extension of his appointment as commander of Allied air forces in SEAC. Peirse and Lady Auckinleck were flown to England on 28 November. Peirse's wife divorced him about a year later, which was followed soon after by the Auckinlecks' divorce. Peirse retired in 1945, and he married Lady Auckinleck in 1946. (See Philip Ziegler, ed., *Personal Diary of Admiral the Lord Louis Mountbatten, Supreme Commander, South-East Asia, 1943–1946* [London: Collins, 1988], pp. 273–74; Michael Dockrill, "British Leadership in Air Operations: Malaya and Burma," in *British and Japanese Military Leadership in the Far Eastern War*, edited by Brian Bond and Kyoichi Tachikawa [Abingdon, Oxon: Frank Cass, 2004], p. 126.)
7. Timothy Fu, *My Experience in CBI, WW II: Memoirs of Stilwell's Ghost Writer* (Bloomington, IN: Authorhouse, 2003), p. 121.
8. Gordon S. Seagrave, *Burma Surgeon Returns* (New York: W.W. Norton, 1946), pp. 36–

37; Major John H. Grindlay, MC, "Report of Medical Department Activities in China Burma India," 29 April 1944 (from interview, Office of Surgeon General, RG 112, National Archives and Records Administration, College Park, Maryland), p. 16.

9. Bill Cummings (1908–1995) was born William Henry Cummings in Burma of missionary parents. He was assistant director of the Pyinmana Agricultural School until Burma fell to the Japanese, when he joined Detachment 101 of the OSS, in which capacity he could use his familiarity with the country and its languages. He died in the United States in October 1995, and his ashes were buried in Kutkai, Burma, at his request.

10. Letter, Grindlay to Betty Grindlay, 9 September 1942 (Grindlay letters at Mayo).

11. Letter, Donald O'Hara to Colonel Williams, 30 (?) July 1942 (Williams 201 File, Williams Papers, USAHEC).

12. Grindlay diary, 30 and 31 August 1942; Seagrave, *Burma Surgeon Returns*, pp. 38–39.

13. Letter, Major Lamar C. Bevil to Colonel Williams, 29 July 1942 (Williams 201 File, Williams Papers, USAHEC).

14. Grindlay diary, 26 and 27 August 1942.

15. Letter, Seagrave to Williams, Ramgarh, 23 September 1942 (Williams 201 File, Williams Papers, USAHEC).

16. S.E. Smith, ed., *The United States Marine Corps in World War II* (New York: Random House, 1969), pp. 72ff.

17. David A. Pattillo, "Portable Surgical Hospitals in the North Burma Campaign: Lessons for Providing Forward Surgical Support to Nonlinear Operations in Airland Operations" (unpublished thesis, Fort Leavenworth, KS: U.S. Army Command and General Staff College, 1993), pp. 39–41.

18. *Ibid.*, p. 41.

Chapter 13

1. Gordon S. Seagrave, *Burma Surgeon Returns* (New York: W.W. Norton, 1946), p. 43.

2. Grindlay diary, 30 August, 2 September, and 19 September 1942 (emphasis in original). The 98th Station Hospital arrived in India on 23 July 1942, and about a month later it reached Ramgarh. The unit assisted in the operation of the hospital until 10 November, when it was ordered to Ledo. It moved there on 1 January 1943, becoming the first hospital to provide medical support for the Ledo Road project. It was reorganized as a 100-bed station hospital in March and, after being relieved by the 20th General Hospital, moved to Chakulia, west of Calcutta, in April and established a station hospital for air force crews. It was enlarged to a 200-bed facility later in the year and, after the Chakulia base closed in 1945, was sent to Shingbwiyang to replace the 73rd Evacuation Hospital. The unit operated there until being relieved by the 25th Field Hospital on 9 September 1945, and then it was transferred to Karachi for shipment back to the United States ("Thumbnail Sketches," Medical Department Units of the India-Burma Theater, p. 33 [RG 493, Box 656, National Archives and Records Administration, College Park, Maryland, ARC Identifier 565623]).

3. For more information about Captain Wetzel, see chapter 6. Victor H. Haas was born in Cincinnati, Ohio, in 1909 and received his M.D. from the University of Cincinnati. He joined the U.S. Public Health Service in 1932 and worked with the National Institute of Health's Plague Laboratory in San Francisco from 1935 to 1939. He went to Burma as chief of the Medical Commission to the Yunnan–Burma railroad and became the commanding officer of Base Section 3 in Ledo. He later was put in charge of the Public Health Service's malaria investigations from 1943 to 1948. He retired as director of the National Institute of Allergy and Infectious Diseases in 1961.

Paul Stevenson (1890–1971) was a native of Monmouth, Illinois, and received his M.D. from Washington University School of Medicine in 1916. The following year he went to China and helped to open the Peking Union Medical College, where he stayed from 1920 to 1937. He was an expert on ethnic groups of southwest China and Tibet. Stevenson returned to the United States that year and received a Ph.D. in public health at the Johns Hopkins University. He was sent back to China to assist with malaria control during the building of the Yunnan–Burma railroad as part of the 15-man group of Public Health Service officers. After the fall of Burma, he and the other officers went to India, where he was placed under the command of Colonel John M. Tamraz, head of the medical section of the theater Services of Supply. The public health officers were sent to sites scattered across India and China to make sanitation and malaria surveys, which was what Stevenson did. He remained in India until 1944, when he was rotated back to the United States. Stevenson subsequently joined the National Institute of Mental Health, where, with one brief break, he stayed until his retirement in 1959.

Daniel Wright (1883–1973?) was born in Winchester, Virginia, and received a B.S. degree in civil engineering from Virginia Polytechnic Institute in 1904. He worked in the Canal Zone for about four years and was awarded the Theodore Roosevelt Medal of Honor in 1921. He came to Burma after being employed by the Rockefeller Foundation in Greece and Turkey; after the war, he joined the United Nations Relief and Rehabilitation Administration until 1949.

William Jellison (1906–1995) was born in Kalispel, Montana, and received his B.S. degree from the University of Montana. He joined the Public Health Service as a parasitologist. He served on the commission sent to work on health conditions on the Yunnan–Burma railroad. He returned to India and served on the U.S. Army Malaria Control Commission and the U.S. Typhus Commission. He returned to the United States after the war and became a world-renowned parasitologist.

Dr. Fred P. Manget (1880–1979), a native of Marietta, Georgia, received his medical degree from the Atlanta College of Physicians and Surgeons in 1906; following internships and postgraduate study, he went to Suzhou and then Huchow, China, to work as a medical missionary. He operated a clinic and hospital in Huchow from 1910 to 1941; then he was asked to serve on the U.S. Public Health Commission. During the war, Manget served in Burma and western China, and then he transferred to Kunming to work with the Flying Tigers. It was Manget who coined the phrase "God is my co-pilot" (which Colonel Robert Scott, Jr., used as the title of his autobiography). He returned to Georgia after the war and opened a clinic in Atlanta, which he ran until 1959, when he moved to Macon. He died in Atlanta in 1979 age 99. See P.A. San, "Malaria Control with the Yunnan–Burma Railway Medical Mission," *Malaria Control in War Areas Field Bulletin* (October 1944): 1–4.

4. James H. Stone, *Crisis Fleeting* (Washington, DC: Office of the Surgeon General, Department of the Army, 1969), p. 14In.; William Boyd Sinclair, "The Battle with Annie," *Ex-CBI Roundup* (March 1990): 6–11; (April 1990): 6–10.

5. Grindlay diary, 3 September 1942. Joseph Rock (1884–1962) was an Austrian American born in Vienna. The first time Rock had attempted to calculate the height of Minya Konka, he miscalculated the altitude; when he reported it to the National Geographic Society, his figure was received with suspicion because it was higher than Mount Everest. Subsequently, Rock recalculated and lowered his estimate of the altitude by 4,650 feet, ranking it about the 41st highest mountain in the world instead of the tallest. Rock established a widespread reputation as an explorer, geographer, linguist, and botanist who lived in Yunnan for many years. He was also well known as something of an eccentric—a man who traveled on his expeditions into China's southwestern mountains in grand style, complete with a small army of retainers and bodyguards, a collapsible rubber bathtub, and his own Austrian chef, and who insisted on having every meal laid out with elegant tableware. For more information about Mendelson, see chapter 3.

6. Grindlay diary, 4 September 1942. Dr. Handley T. Laycock was born in Lanchowfu, Kansu Province, China, on 5 October 1910. He attended St. Paul's School, West Kensington, and went on to St. John's College, Cambridge, and St. Thomas's Hospital, London. He was a resident at St. Thomas's and Addenbrooke's Hospitals. When World War II broke out, Laycock joined the Royal Army Medical Corps and served in China, India, Burma, and Malta. He was a senior surgeon who accompanied the FAU when it moved from China to Burma during the first campaign. He, along with Bill Brough and other FAU members, was ordered to China in August 1942 to assist in setting up a hospital in Waichow in the Hong Kong–Canton area. Laycock appears to have remained in China when part of the FAU group returned to Burma to provide medical support to the Chinese troops and American

engineers building the Burma Road. In 1944–1945 he was in charge of the Surgical Division of the 14th British General Hospital in Bengal and Rangoon. After the war, Laycock joined the Colonial Medical Service and moved to British Somaliland (part of Somalia today) in 1948, where he married Winifred Gladys Worth, a nurse with Queen Alexandra's Imperial Military Nursing Service, in January 1949. A daughter, Patrice, was born in November of the same year. Laycock also served with the CMS in Tanganyika and Nyasaland up to 1964. He became senior surgical consultant to the Natal Provincial Hospitals Service until his retirement. He died on 15 April 1990, location unknown (John P. Blandy and Christina Craig, *Lives of the Fellows of the Royal College of Surgeons of England, 1991–1996* [London: Royal College of Surgeons of England, 2000], p. 205).

7. Grindlay diary, 12 September 1942. Serious U.S. medical efforts to control malaria were just getting under way in mid-1942 as military units began entering areas where the disease was endemic. Such efforts centered mainly on administration of preventative drugs such as quinine, attempts to eradicate potential mosquito breeding areas around camps through the construction of adequate water drainage systems, and instructing personnel to wear clothing that left as few skin surfaces exposed as possible (especially in late afternoon and evening hours, when mosquitos were most likely to be abroad).

Quinine was the chief prophylactic, taken either before or during service in malarial areas. The drug was produced from the bark of the *cinchona* tree, primarily obtained from plantations in Java. An American botanical mission was dispatched to South America in October to search for wild sources of cinchona and establish plantations. In exchange, the U.S. government agreed with officials in Colombia, Ecuador, Venezuela, and Peru to purchase all barks that had the requisite level of alkaloids and to replace harvested trees. Numerous problems developed, including illness among the worker teams, competition with private interests for relatively scarce trees, and the inability of some collectors to recognize the species of cinchona trees whose bark was most desired for quinine. Eventually seed banks and plantations were established in Costa Rica and Guatemala, but the project was cancelled in late 1944 when atabrine, a synthetic product, was developed (Richard A. Howard, "The Role of Botanists during World War II in the Pacific Theatre," *Botanical Review* 60, no. 2 [April–June 1994]: 215–16).

8. Grindlay diary, 20 September 1942. See details of Hambleton's experiences in chapters 7 and 10. Francis A. Astolfi (1918–1942) was a staff sergeant from Plainville, Pennsylvania, and a member of Headquarters, 10th Air Force, assigned as bodyguard and driver to Stilwell; he committed suicide in the air force barracks in Delhi on 25 May 1942, shortly after the "walkout" ("Stilwell's Driver in Burma Kills Self in Delhi," *Brooklyn Daily Eagle*, 26 May 1942: 5). Nevin Wetzel later mentioned the incident but furnished no details other than saying that Astolfi was "a casualty of those dangerous and stressful times in a theatre of war as crazy as a three-ring circus" (Nevin Wetzel, "Evacuation of Rangoon," *Ex-CBI Roundup* (November 1974): 15). Jack Belden went further, describing Astolfi as a "queer case," a "raw-boned, six-foot-two ex-butcher boy." Astolfi had pestered Belden and Darrell Berrigan, a UPI reporter, to write about him. One day he told them that something had been eating at him ever since he arrived in the Far East. "Sometimes I don't feel just right," he had said, wringing his hands. This statement seems to indicate that he was battling inner demons (Jack Belden, *Retreat with Stilwell* [London: Cassell, 1943], p. 150). Astolfi is buried in the National Memorial Cemetery of the Pacific in Honolulu.

9. Grindlay diary, 4 October 1942. The "brigadier" may have been Major John G. McDowell, RAMC. Little is known about him except that he was commissioned into the Territorial Army in 1934 and probably was brevetted as a temporary brigadier (email to author from Keith Stevens, Mersham, Kent, England, 7 June 2010).

10. Stilwell to Boatner, radio message, 4 October 1942 (Williams 201 File, Williams Papers, USAHEC).

11. Memorandum, Boatner to McCabe and Holcombe, 12 October 1942 (Williams 201 File, Williams Papers, USAHEC).

12. Letter, Colonel Henry Holcombe to "Speck" (General Raymond Wheeler), 13 October 1942 (Williams 201 File, Williams Pa-

pers, USAHEC). Lieutenant Colonel Walsh was a former New Jersey National Guard member who was activated in 1941.

13. Grindlay diary, 15 October 1942. Seagrave, by contrast, wrote in his autobiography (with a touch of false modesty) that the correspondents had "pounced upon the Burmese nurses as being unique in the United States armed forces" and nearly broke up the unit because they would concentrate on the pretty girls versus the others. "I came to fear the advent of photographers and correspondents more than I feared the outbreak of an epidemic of bubonic plague, but I had to be courteous and helpful to the press as one of my war duties. I smiled externally but internally I boiled" (Seagrave, *Burma Surgeon Returns*, p. 56).

14. Grindlay diary, 16 October 1942.

15. Grindlay diary, 19, 20, and 22 October 1942. Walsh was relieved of duty and transferred out of Ramgarh by Colonel Tamraz on 27 November. He took over a small 50-bed hospital in Calcutta. In writing that his was the only record of events on the walkout, Grindlay may not have known that Stilwell and Williams also kept diaries in Burma and on the walkout.

Henry Myles Johnson had joined the Seagrave unit in mid-1942, after serving as a medical officer at a rest camp at Ghora Dakka in northwest India. He remained with Seagrave until about the end of August 1944. Johnson was born in Oklahoma City on 25 April 1917. He was educated at the University of Oklahoma and served a residency at Letterman Army Hospital in San Francisco in orthopedic surgery. After the war, Johnson returned to Letterman for three years before moving to Camp Pickett, Virginia, as chief of orthopedics. He resigned his army commission in 1954 and engaged in private practice until his retirement in 1985. During those years, he practiced in Albuquerque, New Mexico, and in Riverside and Sacramento, California. After retirement, he lived in Riverside.

16. The 98th was ordered to Ledo on 10 November and moved on 1 January 1943 (see note 2 above). The unit was replaced by three doctors and 40 staff from the 181st General Hospital on detached service.

17. Grindlay diary, 24 October 1942. Major Budge, as previously noted, was a member of the Dental Corps. He and "Walt" have not been identified. Grindlay certainly did have a "gruff" personality; during the years he spent at the Mayo Clinic after the war, he earned the nickname "Grumpy" among his co-workers.

18. *Ibid.*

19. Grindlay's list in his diary included last names only. Military ranks and first names, where known, have been supplied by the author. This list includes some men who came later to AMMISCA or arrived with Stilwell or, in the case of Wetzel, were part of the Public Health Services team assigned to the Yunnan–Burma railway.

20. The reports of huge warehouses or caves in southern and western China filled with stockpiled American weapons and supplies to be used by the Nationalists in an anticipated conflict with the Communists after World War II ended were the subject of much speculation, but hard evidence confirming their existence has been difficult to obtain. It appears that sources most critical of Chiang Kai-shek and the Nationalists' conduct of the war accepted the rumors, while supporters denied them. Post-war critics such as Graham Peck (*Two Kinds of Time* [Boston: Houghton Mifflin, 1950]) and Fred Eldridge (*Wrath in Burma* [Garden City, NY: Doubleday, 1946]), both proponents of Stilwell, believed that such stockpiles existed. Elliot Roosevelt, writing in his memoir of his father, *As He Saw It* (New York: Duell, Sloan and Pearce, 1946), specifically mentioned that Stilwell had complained to FDR that Chiang Kai-shek was hoarding Lend-Lease supplies for a future conflict with the Communists (p. 207). Chou En-lai visited the U.S. Embassy in Chungking and confirmed Stilwell's claims (S.C.M. Paine, *The Wars for Asia, 1911–1949* [Cambridge: Cambridge University Press, 2012], p. 204). By contrast, Milton Miles, who was commander of the Sino-American Cooperative Organization (familiarly known as "SACO"), firmly stated in his memoir, *A Different Kind of War* (Garden City, NY: Doubleday, 1967), that the Nationalists only began receiving Lend-Lease supplies in 1944; the rest of these supplies were claimed by Stilwell for use in Burma. However, this statement is largely inaccurate: an important part of Stilwell's duties when he was appointed CBI commander was to be in

charge of all Lend-Lease materials sent to the theater; thus he had the authority to appropriate and direct supplies and equipment as he saw fit.

Some official sources also reported on the surreptitious hording of supplies and equipment. In July 1945 the OSS reported that the Communists were complaining that the Nationalists were stockpiling Lend-Lease supplies. Edward E. Rice, an American diplomat in China, told the State Department that U.S. servicemen had seen "many [airplanes] in warehouses near Chengtu" (*Foreign Relations of the United States 1944: China* [Washington, DC: Government Printing Office, 1967], p. 164). Robert Smith, in his valuable doctoral dissertation, "History of the Attempt of the United States Army Medical Department to Improve the Effectiveness of the Chinese Army Medical Service 1941–1945," wrote that there were rumors of caves and temples in Kweiyang and Kunming that were "stuffed to the doors" with medical supplies.

The Chinese were reluctant to permit inspection and inventory of warehouses, further fueling the rumors. Lieutenant Colonel Rolland B. Sigafoos, whom Colonel Williams had sent to Ramgarh to be in charge of the training of Chinese regimental medical detachments, told Grindlay that he found a stash of a half million sulfa tablets somewhere in China, possibly in either Chungking or Kunming. (Sigafoos's identification can be found in Stone, *Crisis Fleeting*, p. 167.) This was after the Chinese had "denied having any," as Grindlay wrote angrily (diary, 5 December 1942). Other Americans, both journalists (including Graham Peck) and members of the military, often observed supplies being sold in China on the black market. Conversely, the Chinese suspected the Americans of siphoning off medical supplies that should have gone to them. Smith noted that there was at least one instance of supplies intended for the Chinese armies being diverted to Yoke Force staff in Kunming (Smith, "History of the Attempt," pp. 106–7, 111–13). Accurate firsthand reports of the Chinese government stockpiling supplies and equipment, however, are difficult to find.

21. Grindlay diary, 10 December 1942.

22. As a "casual detachment" member, the soldier whom Grindlay suspected of being the father was on temporary duty with the Seagrave Hospital Unit, most likely as an orderly or a medical technician.

23. Grindlay diary, 12 December 1942.

24. Benzedrine was a very popular amphetamine (or stimulant) used by soldiers, sailors, and airmen during World War II. During the 1920s and 1930s it was widely used as an inhalant, but it was shipped in large quantities in tablet or capsule form to frontline troops to keep them alert in combat situations. See "What Is Benzedrine?" (http://www.wisegeek.com/what-is-benzedrine.htm). One pilot who flew many Hump flights wrote that "keep awake" or "no sleep" pills were routinely issued to air crews on such missions (Lieutenant Colonel George L. Wenrich, *Silent Valor: World War II in the Himalayas* [Kent Store, VA: Reflective Books, 2005], pp. 67–69).

25. Grindlay diary, 14 December 1942. Chloroform is a very dangerous substance, much more dangerous than ether, and is usually reserved for situations involving euthanasia. In certain patients with hearts weakened by disease and its attendant toxicity, such as the one on whom Grindlay was performing surgery, chloroform can be lethal. He apparently did not know the patient's medical history at the time of the surgery and administered the chloroform in error.

26. Grindlay diary, 8–18 January 1943. For an identification of Brigadier John McDowell, see note 9 in this chapter. Emetrine is made from *Psychotria ipecacuanha* (a plant found in Brazil, Bolivia, and other parts of South America). It has a history dating back to at least the seventeenth century as a cure for amoebic dysentery but was also known to have a toxic effect on the heart, lungs, and intestines and could cause severe secondary illness. It was taken in either powdered or liquid form.

27. Lieutenant Kenneth Harris was reputed to be a fast walker and was frequently assigned to hike between the various medical facilities once the unit was in Burma (Stone, *Crisis Fleeting*, p. 28fn.).

Chapter 14

1. William M. Webb was born in Lawrence, Indiana, on 23 August 1911. He

graduated from Indiana University with a bachelor's degree in science in 1936 and obtained his M.D. from the same institution in 1940. He joined the army after graduation; completed an internship at Fort Sam Houston, Texas; and was assigned to the Seagrave Hospital Unit at Ramgarh in 1942. After the campaign to recapture Myitkyina, Webb was assigned as a medical liaison officer with the Chinese. He returned to the United States in October 1944 and remained in the Medical Corps for 13 years and then the Army Reserve Corps. He retired in 1971 as a colonel and went into private practice. He died on 22 June 2002 in Davis, California.

2. Grindlay diary, 23 April 1943. Hollington Tong (1887–1971) was the propaganda minister for the Chinese government. He was a graduate of the University of Missouri School of Journalism. The staged incident has not been verified and the source of the story is unknown, but it may have been reported from someone at Stilwell's forward echelon headquarters in Chungking to the Northern Combat Area Command in India.

3. *CBI Roundup* (8 October 1942), unpaged.

4. Theodore H. White, ed., *The Stilwell Papers* (New York: William Sloane Associates, 1948), p. 203.

5. Further information on the arrival of the 48th Evacuation Hospital and its commander can be found in *CBI Roundup* (3 June 1943). The circumstances surrounding the loss of the 88 Americans, and their identities, are unknown.

6. Colonel Charles Leedham was transferred to the 112th Station Hospital at Ledo sometime after Grindlay left Ramgarh, and Major Eric P. Stone (who had been with the 48th Evacuation contingent in Ledo) was placed in command. In August, Stone was transferred to the 112th after Leedham requested additional help for his hard-pressed staff ("The Diary of Colonel John M. Tamraz, M.C.: A Record of Trial and Error," in James H. Stone, *Crisis Fleeting* [Washington, DC: Office of the Surgeon General, Department of the Army, 1969], p. 166n.).

Chapter 15

1. Colonel Haas headed a team of Public Health Service officers, including Colonel Paul Stevenson (see chapter 13, note 3), who advised on sanitation and malaria prevention measures for the workers on the Yunnan–Burma railway until work was stopped in early 1942. Grindlay maintained contact with Colonel Ravdin for a few years after the war, visiting the latter at least once during an East Coast trip in 1947 (Grindlay correspondence, I. S. Ravdin Papers, University Archives, University of Pennsylvania, Philadelphia).

2. Many of the laborers on the Ledo Road were African Americans. It is unfortunate that their story has never been fully chronicled, for their contribution to the war effort in the CBI theater was highly significant.

3. The Tagap Ga hospital compound was the principal facility for the Seagrave unit along the Ledo Road.

4. Grindlay diary, 17 June 1943.

5. S. Woodburn Kirby and M.R. Roberts, *The War Against Japan: India's Most Dangerous Hour*, vol. 2: *History of the Second World War* (London: Her Majesty's Stationery Office, 1958), p. 192, and vol. 4: *The Reconquest of Burma* (London: Her Majesty's Stationery Office, 1965), p. 31; Jon Latimer, *Burma: The Forgotten War* (London: John Murray, 2004), p. 139. V Force's initial purpose was to defend the eastern border of India against the expected Japanese attack after the collapse of the Allied defense of Burma. Once it became clear that the Japanese were not going to immediately invade Assam, V Force became an intelligence and special operations organization behind enemy lines. For more information, see Alan Ogden, *Tigers Burning Bright: SOE Heroes in the Far East* (London: Bene Factum, 2013), pp. 447–48.

6. Grindlay diary, 18 June 1943.

7. See chapter 12, note 27, for additional information about Lieutenant Harris.

8. Gordon S. Seagrave, *Burma Surgeon Returns* (New York: W.W. Norton, 1946), pp. 71–72.

9. "V" cigarettes were a British ration that was not popular with American troops because they were made of cheap tobacco that caused sore throats and stained teeth.

10. Grindlay diary, 27 July 1943.

11. Grindlay also noticed that the Nagas felled large trees and left the logs lying in the fields to dry out. Teak, in particular, needs to

be dried, and then soaked in water and dried again, before it can be cut into usable lumber. This information would have been of great benefit to the Chindits the following year, who mistook photos of logs scattered across "Picadilly," one of their strongholds, as a Japanese attempt to block its use. They later concluded that the logs were part of normal Naga logging activity.

12. Identification of Major Johnny Wetzel has been unsuccessful.

13. For a detailed description of the plane crash and ensuing escape from Burma, see Eric Sevareid, *Not So Wild a Dream* (New York: Alfred Knopf, 1946). The training of flight nurses is discussed in Maxine Davis, *Through the Stratosphere: The Human Factor in Aviation* (New York: Macmillan, 1946), p. 210.

14. No identification has yet been made of Lieutenant Joseph Stohl and Private First Class Norilla.

15. Lieutenant Wallace has not been identified.

16. Author's interview with Peter Lutken, Newellton, Louisiana, 24 September 2009 (hereafter Lutken interview).

17. Letter, Grindlay to Mayo Clinic friends, 8 August 1943 (Grindlay letters at Mayo).

18. Lutken interview; Peter Lutken oral history, 28 September 1997, Center for Oral and Public History, California State University, Fullerton.

19. Lieutenant Colonel Stanley Bray served as commander of the Railway Grand Division in the CBI theater until May 1944, when he was replaced by Colonel Paul Yount. He must have been a member of the Corps of Engineers and was up front at the Ledo Road head when Grindlay met him. There were eleven Railway Grand Divisions, each of which operated a section of the worldwide U.S. Military Railway Service.

20. Doyen clamps (or forceps) are used in intestinal surgery or obstetrical procedures and have either curved or straight blades.

21. Frank L. Martin, Jr., was a war correspondent for the Associated Press who reported from North Africa, Burma, and the Pacific theater during World War II. He was born in Missouri and grew up in Columbia, where his father taught in the School of Journalism at the University of Missouri. After the war, Martin was assigned to the Associated Press bureau in San Francisco, but, finding the job unsatisfying, he moved back to his home state and purchased the West Plains Quill Press newspaper in 1946. He ran it until his death in 1995. His son, Frank L. Martin III, edits and publishes the paper today.

22. Albert V. Ravenholt was born in Milltown, Wisconsin, on 9 September 1919. He attended Grand View College in Des Moines, Iowa, briefly, and then he went to New York to work at the World's Fair of 1939. He subsequently traveled on freighters for a year, ending up in Shanghai. In 1941–1942, Ravenholt trucked medical supplies over the Burma Road for the International Red Cross. He served as a correspondent for United Press International and became the UPI bureau chief in China around 1945. He went on after the war to write several books about the Communist movement in China and the activities of Ramon Magsaysay in the Philippines, while also writing for the Chicago *Daily News* and numerous magazines. He married writer and correspondent and wartime OSS member Marjorie Ravenholt in Shanghai in 1946, and the couple continued to cover news from China until they were forced to leave in the late 1940s. They later retired to Seattle, where Marjorie died in 1992; Ravenholt passed away on 25 April 2010.

23. O'Hara commented later that he "didn't particularly want to go back [to Burma in 1943] but I'd rather stay with Stilwell than be assigned to some other theater. I thought it would be easier than it was." After leaving the CBI, O'Hara served at an air base in Amarillo, Texas, and at Eglin Air Force Base, Florida. While at Amarillo in 1945, Stilwell came through and, hearing O'Hara was stationed there, asked to see him. Stilwell requested that O'Hara accompany him to his new command of the Tenth Army on Okinawa to help prepare for the invasion of Japan, but the war ended before the transfer could be effected. After his military career ended, O'Hara eventually retired to Arizona (Henrietta Thompson, *Walk a Little Faster: Escape from Burma with General Stilwell in 1942* [Privately published, 1980], pp. 10, 160).

24. The difficulties with Major Chen were resolved within a few months when his own

men, with whom he had become very unpopular, killed him at Hkalak (Lutken interview).

25. Grindlay learned from a Chinese cook who escaped the battle that Lieutenant Colonel Gilbert was captured and tied to a tree for three days and tortured (Grindlay diary, 27 November 1943).

26. Charles Romanus and Riley Sunderland, *Stilwell's Command Problems*, U.S. Army History of World War II (Washington, DC: Office of the Chief of Military History, Department of the Army, 1956), pp. 47–48.

27. Milton Arnold Dushkin was born in Chicago on 4 January 1911. His father was an immigrant from Lithuania. After graduating from medical school, he set up a practice in Des Moines, Iowa, in 1934. He joined the army reserves before the war and, when activated, was assigned to the CBI theater and subsequently to the Seagrave Hospital Unit. After the war, Dushkin rose to the rank of colonel and served in the Korean conflict. He established a psychiatric practice following his Korean service and became head of the psychiatric department at Cook County Hospital in Chicago toward the end of the 1950s. He died in May 1975 at age 64.

28. Grindlay diary, 28 November 1943; Lutken interview.

29. Tamara Shervaschidze obituary, *Sidney Morning Herald*, 8 December 2012, http://www.legacy.com/obituaries/name/tamara-shervashidze-obituary?pid=1000000161647131&view=guestbook.

30. Grindlay diary, 4 December 1943; Lutken interview. Basil Shervashidze was detained by Indian Security Control Police in 1947 at his home in Kalimpong and brought before the Calcutta High Court in January 1949 on charges that he had not left the country as ordered in 1946. Shervashidze maintained that he had been about to leave when he was arrested and had been in jail ever since, so it was impossible for him to have left India. The court agreed that he should be deported within a month after being released from jail. His ultimate fate is unknown. (See "Calcutta High Court, B.A. Shervashidze vs. Govt. of West Bengal and Anr. on 12 January, 1949," AIR 1951 Cal 474, www.indiankanoon.org/doc/844638/.)

31. Besides Viktor Taubenfligel, the other members of the foreign nationals group and their assignments were as follows: Herbert Baer (German), 50th Chinese Division; Carl Coutelle (German), 38th Chinese Division; Samuel Flato (Polish), China; Walter Freudman (Austrian), 4th Chinese Artillery; David Iancu (Rumanian), 2nd Chinese Tank Battalion; Frederick Kisch (Czech), Ledo; Franz Kreigle (Polish), 1st Chinese Tank Battalion; Erich Mamlok (German), China; and Alexander Volokine (Russian), Ramgarh (Memorandum, "Foreign Contract (Refugee) Doctors with C.A.I.," Colonel Williams (?) to Commanding General, India-Burma Theater (Sultan), 5 January 1945 [Williams 201 File, Williams Papers, USAHEC]). While Grindlay was visiting the hospital at Kweiyang on 20 January 1942, he met some of the International Brigade doctors. He described them disparagingly as "ratty looking wild chaps of Polish, Italian, French, etc., nationality." There was a female physician among them, but her identity is unknown.

32. Dr. Norman E. Freeman was born in 1903 and graduated from Yale University School of Medicine in 1928. He practiced in Boston for a time and later became head of the Department of Surgery, University of California–San Francisco Medical School, specializing in vascular surgery. He died on 9 August 1975.

33. Edward McNally (1900–1968) had been a member of AMMISCA and, after Stilwell arrived in the theater, was appointed assistant chief of staff of the headquarters in Chungking. He was transferred to NCAC in India under General Boatner, and by the time Grindlay met him in late 1943, McNally was in charge of coordinating the assembly and organization of Chinese troops in Assam. He went on to become NCAC's liaison with the Chinese 38th Division.

34. Isador Ravdin (1894–1972) was a native of Evansville, Indiana, who earned his medical degree from the University of Pennsylvania. He was interested in the phenomenon of shock and was engaged in the development of blood substitutes that could be used for casualties when the war broke out. In 1942, Ravdin was asked by the army to research the use of albumin in the treatment of victims of burns and shock. He became the executive officer of the 20th General Hospital when it was formed at the University of Pennsylvania,

later rising to become its commander in 1944. After the war, he rejoined the University of Pennsylvania and shifted his attention to cancer research. He retired in 1956 with the rank of major general in the Army Medical Corps and died in Philadelphia in 1972.

35. Alexander Gilliam (1904–1963) was born in Petersburg, Virginia, and was a graduate of the University of Virginia Medical School. He took a degree in public health at Johns Hopkins University and subsequently became an officer in the U.S. Public Health Service, where he remained for 25 years. After the war, he joined the National Cancer Institute (1948–1960) as an epidemiologist and taught epidemiology at Johns Hopkins from 1960 until his death in 1963.

36. Major John Paul North was a Kirby Fellow in Surgical Physiology at the University of Pennsylvania in the 1930s. After the war, he served in the Veterans Administration for several years. Major Henry Page Royster (1909–1999) was a plastic surgeon on the staff of the 20th General Hospital. He was a graduate of the University of Pennsylvania Medical School (1935) and joined the army in 1942. Royster was assigned to the 20th General Hospital and subsequently earned a Bronze Star and two battle stars. After the war, he returned to the University of Pennsylvania and taught plastic surgery there until his retirement in 1975. Royster died in Raleigh, North Carolina, on 13 June 1999.

37. Major Vernon Slater was an officer attached to the headquarters of the Chinese Army in India, otherwise designated the 5303rd Provisional Combat Troops.

38. Chinoform was an anti-amoebic drug taken orally to control, among other things, amoebic dysentery. It is now universally banned, as it causes a form of neuropathy affecting the spine and eyes, leading to blindness and paralysis.

39. Eric Inchboard (b. 1919) and Ruth (b. 1921) were married in Shillong in 1944. By then, Inchboard had left the FAU and was going to Burma to serve with Seagrave. Later he left the unit and joined the British army as a first lieutenant, assigned to transportation in China because he could speak the language and interact with the Chinese. He and Ruth lived in England for a time after the war ended; then they moved to Burma for several years before returning to England in 1958, most likely to escape the oppressive Burmese military government. Inchboard worked as an architect, designing many hotels worldwide; Ruth retired from nursing, and the couple had one adopted son, Ronald (b. 1953). When he and Ruth were married, Eric was quite ill with rheumatic fever and pneumonia and not expected to live six months (Thompson, *Walk a Little Faster*, p. 186).

40. Brigadier General Benjamin Ferris was deputy chief of staff of U.S. Army Forces in the CBI. He was a native of Pawling, New York, and entered West Point before graduating from high school. He was in the class of 1915 with Dwight Eisenhower and Omar Bradley. Ferris was married in 1917 to a former classmate of Madame Chiang Kai-shek's at Wellesley College. In 1942, he was selected by General Stilwell (who had been Ferris's superior at Fort Benning) to accompany him to China. "I wasn't particularly fond of him but I admired him," Ferris said later. He and other staff members helped Stilwell set up a small headquarters at Maymyo, where he was in charge of supply and morale. Ferris became commander of the rear echelon headquarters in New Delhi after he walked out of Burma with Stilwell.

John Paton Davies, Jr. (1908–1999), was born in China to missionary parents. He graduated from Columbia University in 1931 and, after joining the U.S. Foreign Service, was posted to China in 1933. Davies was assigned as political attaché to General Stilwell in February 1942 and served with him until Stilwell's recall in late 1944. He was a member of the U.S. Observation Group (Dixie Mission) to Yenan in the fall of 1944. He stayed with the State Department until his dismissal in 1954 following political pressure by senators Joseph McCarthy and Pat McCarren. Davies and his wife lived in Peru, Spain, France and the United Kingdom, pursuing various business interests and retirement before returning to the United States.

Epilogue

1. A copy of this letter was made available to the author by Ms. Constance Putnam, Concord, Massachusetts.

2. This letter and the following ones were

made available to the author by Mrs. Betty Grindlay.

3. Major John H. Grindlay, "Treatment of Skin Infections in the Assam-Burma Jungle," *Bulletin of the U.S. Army Medical Department* 74 (March 1944): 74–80.

4. Betty Grindlay told the author in 1969 that she had personal knowledge of Winifred Stilwell conducting séances to contact her husband in the afterlife.

5. Leslie Anders, *The Ledo Road* (Norman: University of Oklahoma Press, 1965), pp. 235–36. At the same time, the ABC Pipeline was being constructed parallel with the road to carry gasoline and oil from Ledo to Yunnan, China. It was a 6-inch pipe as far as Myitkyina, then a 4-inch line to Bhamo and on to China (*ibid.*, 138).

6. Jeff Ethell and Don Downie, *Flying the Hump* (Osceola, WI: Motorbooks International, 1995), p. 7.

7. Richard A. Howard, "The Role of Botanists during World War II in the Pacific Theatre," *Botanical Review* 60, no. 2 (April–June 1994): 210. *Tsutsugamushi* was first identified in Japan in 1930—hence its Japanese name.

Bibliography

U.S. Government Documents

AMMISCA File, Library of Congress (Microfilm).
Foreign Relations of the United States 1944: China (Washington, DC: Government Printing Office, 1967).
Military Attaché Report no. 655, 21 September 1942, New Delhi (National Archives and Records Administration College Park, Maryland).
OSS Research & Analysis Report 280, *Evacuation of Rangoon* (as reported by Captain Richard M. Jones), 28 April 1942 (RG 112, National Archives and Records Administration, College Park, Maryland).
Supporting Documents to *U.S. Army in World War II—CBI* (National Archives and Records Administration, College Park, Maryland).
"Thumbnail Sketches," Medical Department Units of the India-Burma Theater (RG 493, Box 656, National Archives and Records Administration, College Park, Maryland).

Diaries and Personal Papers

Case, Reverend Brayton, Papers. American Baptist Historical Society, Atlanta, Georgia.
Grindlay, John H., diary. In possession of Dr. Lorna Grindlay Moore.
Grindlay, John H., letters. Mayo Clinic Archives, Rochester, Minnesota.
Hambleton, Roscoe L., File, World War II Servicemen Alumni Files, Department of Rare and Manuscript Collections, Carl A. Kroch Library, Cornell University, Ithaca, New York.
MacMorland, Colonel Edward, unpublished diary. Widener University Archives, Chester, Pennsylvania.
Meyer, Louis, Papers. University Archives, University of Pennsylvania, Philadelphia, Pennsylvania.
Ravdin, I. S., Papers. University Archives, University of Pennsylvania, Philadelphia.
Stilwell, Joseph W., Papers. Hoover Library, Stanford University, Palo Alto, California.
Williams, Robert Parton, Papers. United States Army Heritage and Education Center, Carlisle, Pennsylvania.

Unpublished Theses and Dissertations

Durrence, James Larry, "Ambassador Clarence E. Gauss and United States Relations with China, 1941–1944," unpublished PhD dissertation, University of Georgia, Athens, 1971.

Grieve, William George, "Belated Endeavor: The American Military Mission to China (AMMISCA) 1941-1942," unpublished PhD dissertation, University of Illinois at Urbana-Champaign, 1979.
Pattillo, David A., "Portable Surgical Hospitals in the North Burma Campaign: Lessons for Providing Forward Surgical Support to Nonlinear Operations in Airland Operations," unpublished thesis, Fort Leavenworth, KS: U.S. Army Command and General Staff College, 1993.
Smith, Robert Gillen, "History of the Attempt of the United States Army Medical Department to Improve the Effectiveness of the Chinese Army Medical Service 1941-1945," unpublished PhD dissertation, Columbia University, 1950.

Secondary Sources

Aldrich, Richard J., *Intelligence and the War Against Japan: Britain, America and the Politics of Secret Service* (Cambridge: Cambridge University Press, 2000).
Anders, Leslie, *The Ledo Road* (Norman: University of Oklahoma Press, 1965).
Armfield, Blanche B., *Organization and Administration in World War II*, Medical Department, United States Army (Washington, DC: Office of the Surgeon General, Department of the Army, 1963).
Astor, Gerald, *The Jungle War* (Hoboken, NJ: John Wiley & Sons, 2004).
Bayly, Christopher, and Tim Harper, *Forgotten Armies* (Cambridge, MA: Belknap Press of Harvard University Press, 2005).
Belden, Jack, *Retreat with Stilwell* (London: Cassell, 1943).
Blandy, John P., and Christina Craig, *Lives of the Fellows of the Royal College of Surgeons of England, 1991-1996* (London: Royal College of Surgeons of England, 2000).
Bond, Brian, and Kyoichi Tachikawa, *British and Japanese Military Leadership in the Far Eastern War* (Abingdon, Oxon: Frank Cass, 2004).
Bond, Charles R., Jr., and Terry H. Anderson, *A Flying Tiger's Diary* (College Station: Texas A&M University Press, 1984).
Brereton, Lewis H., *The Brereton Diaries* (New York: William Morrow, 1946).
Brough, Bill, *To Reason Why . . .* (Wickham, UK: Hickory Tree, 2001).
Burchett, W.G., *Bombs Over Burma* (Melbourne: F.W. Cheshire, 1944).
Byrd, Martha, *Chennault: Giving Wings to the Tiger* (Tuscaloosa: University of Alabama Press, 1987).
Chung, Ong Chit, *Operation Matador: Britain's War Plans Against the Japanese, 1918-1941* (Singapore: Times Academic, 1997).
Coates, Colonel John Boyd, Jr., et al., eds., *Surgery in World War II: Activities of Surgical Consultants*, vol. II, Medical Department, United States Army (Washington, DC: Office of the Surgeon General, Department of the Army, 1964).
Coble, Parks M., *Facing Japan: Chinese Politics and Japanese Imperialism, 1931-1937* (Cambridge, MA: Council on Far Eastern Studies, Harvard University, 1991).
Cole, Wayne S., *Roosevelt & the Isolationists, 1932-1945* (Lincoln: University of Nebraska Press, 1983).
Combined Inter-Services Historical Section (India and Pakistan), *The Retreat from Burma, 1941-42* (Calcutta: Official History of the Indian Armed Forces in the Second World War 1939-1945, 1959).
Condon-Rall, Mary Ellen, and Albert F. Cowdrey, *The Medical Department: Medical Service in the War Against Japan*, United States Army in World War II: The Technical Services (Washington, DC: Center of Military History, United States Army, 1998).
Coox, Alvin D., *The Anatomy of a Small War* (Westport, CT: Greenwood, 1977).
Coox, Alvin D., *Nomonhan: Japan Against Russia, 1939*, 2 vols. (Stanford: Stanford University Press, 1985).

Craven, W.F., and J.L. Cate, *The Army Air Forces in World War II*, vol. 1: *Plans and Early Operations* (Chicago: University of Chicago Press, 1948).
Craven, W.F., and J.L. Cate, *The Army Air Forces in World War II*, vol. 4: *The Pacific: Guadalcanal to Saipan* (Chicago: University of Chicago Press, 1950).
Crew, F.A.E., *The Army Medical Services: Campaigns*, vol. 5: *Burma* (London: Her Majesty's Stationery Office, 1966).
Davidson-Houston, J.V., *Armed Pilgrimage* (London: Robert Hale, 1949).
Davis, Maxine, *Through the Stratosphere: The Human Factor in Aviation* (New York: Macmillan, 1946).
Dockrill, Michael, "British Leadership in Air Operations: Malaya and Burma," in *British and Japanese Military Leadership in the Far Eastern War*, edited by Brian Bond and Kyoichi Tachikawa (Abingdon, Oxon: Frank Cass, 2004).
Dorn, Frank, *Walkout with Stilwell in Burma* (New York: Thomas Y. Crowell, 1971).
Draper, Alfred, *Dawns Like Thunder* (London: Leo Cooper, 1987).
Eldridge, Fred, *Wrath in Burma* (Garden City, NY: Doubleday, 1946).
Ethell, Jeff, and Don Downie, *Flying the Hump* (Osceola, WI: Motorbooks International, 1995).
Evans, Charles, *A Doctor in XIVth Army: Burma 1944–1945* (London: Leo Cooper, 1998).
Evans, Lieutenant General Sir Geoffrey, *The Johnnies* (London: Cassell, 1964).
Fraser, David, *Alanbrooke* (New York: Atheneum, 1982).
Fu, Timothy, *My Experience in CBI, WW II: Memoirs of Stilwell's Ghost Writer* (Bloomington, IN: Authorhouse, 2003).
Geren, Paul, *Burma Diary* (New York: Harper & Brothers, 1943).
Gillies, Donald, *Radical Diplomat: The Life of Archibald Clark Kerr, Lord Inverchapel, 1882–1951* (London: I.B. Tauris, 1999).
Goodall, Felicity, *Exodus Burma: The British Escape Through the Jungles of Death 1942* (Brimscombe Port Stroud, Gloucestershire: Spellmount, 2011).
Grant, Ian Lyall, and Kazuo Tamayama, *Burma 1942: The Japanese Invasion* (Chichester, West Sussex: Zampi, 1999).
Guo wu juan xin wen ban gong shi, *1998 Zhong guo da hongshui* (Peking: Wu zhou chuan bo chu ban she, 1998).
Harris, Sheldon H., *Factories of Death* (London: Routledge, 1994).
Harrison, Mark, *Medicine and Victory: British Military Medicine in the Second World War* (Oxford: Oxford University Press, 2004).
Hart, Captain B.H. Liddell, *The Tanks*, vol. 2 (London: Cassell, 1959).
Hayes, Grace Person, *The History of the Joint Chiefs of Staff in World War II: The War Against Japan* (Annapolis, MD: Naval Institute Press, 1982).
Heinrichs, Waldo, "Franklin D. Roosevelt and the Risks of War, 1939–1941," in *American, Chinese, and Japanese Perspectives on Wartime Asia, 1931–1949*, edited by Akira Iriye and Warren Cohen (Wilmington, DE: SR Books, 1990).
Hertzstein, Robert E., *Henry R. Luce, Time, and the American Crusade in Asia* (Cambridge: Cambridge University Press, 2005).
Jones, F.C., *Japan's New Order in East Asia* (Oxford: Oxford University Press, 1954).
Kennedy, Alexander, *Hong Kong: Full Circle, 1939–45* (Privately printed, 1945).
Kimball, Warren F., *The Most Unsordid Act: Lend-Lease, 1939–41* (Baltimore: Johns Hopkins Press, 1969).
Kirby, S. Woodburn, and M.R. Roberts, *The War Against Japan: India's Most Dangerous Hour*, vol. 2: *History of the Second World War* (London: Her Majesty's Stationery Office, 1958).
Kirby, S. Woodburn, and M.R. Roberts, *The War Against Japan: India's Most Dangerous Hour*, vol. 4: *The Reconquest of Burma* (London: Her Majesty's Stationery Office, 1965).

Bibliography

Kirby, William C., *Germany and Republican China* (Stanford: Stanford University Press, 1984).
Latimer, Jon, *Burma: The Forgotten War* (London: John Murray, 2004).
Layton, Rear Admiral Edwin T., *And I Was There: Pearl Harbor and Midway—Breaking the Secrets* (New York: William Morrow, 1985).
Leasor, James, *The Marine from Mandalay* (London: Leo Cooper, 1988).
Lee, Chong-Sik, *Revolutionary Struggle in Manchuria* (Berkeley: University of California Press, 1983).
Leighton, Richard M., and Robert W. Coakley, *Global Logistics and Strategy: 1940-43* (Washington, DC: Center for Military History, United States Army, 1995).
Li, Danke, *Echoes of Chongqing: Women in Wartime China* (Urbana: University of Illinois Press, 2010).
Lillegaard, Leif B., *Siste Mann fra Borde* (Oslo: J.W. Cappelens Forlag, 1965).
Lloyd's Register of Shipping (London: Lloyd's Register of Shipping, 1940).
Martin, Bernd, ed., *Die Deutsche Beraterschaft in China, 1927-1938: Militar-Wirtschaft-Aussenpolitik* (Dusseldorf: Droste Verlag, 1981).
Matloff, Maurice, and Edwin M. Snell, *Strategic Planning for Coalition Warfare, 1941-1942* (Washington, DC: Office of the Chief of Military History, Dept. of the Army, 1953).
McLynn, Frank, *The Burma Campaign* (London: Bodley Head, 2010).
Mead, Richard, *Churchill's Lions* (Chalford Stroud, Gloucestershire: Spellmount, 2007).
Miles, Milton, *A Different Kind of War* (Garden City, NY: Doubleday, 1967).
Moats, Alice-Leone, *Blind Date with Mars* (New York: Doubleday, Doran, 1943).
Morley, James William, ed., *The China Quagmire: Japan's Expansion on the Asian Continent, 1933-1941* (New York: Columbia University Press, 1983).
Newman, Robert P., *Owen Lattimore and the "Loss" of China* (Berkeley: University of California Press, 1992).
Nunneley, John, and Kazuo Tamayama, *Tales by Japanese Soldiers* (London: Cassell, 2000).
Office of the Accountant General, Assam, India, *History of the Services of Gazetted and Other Officers Serving under the Government of Assam* (Shillong: Superintendent, Assam Government Press, 1941) (Oriental & India Office Library, London).
Ogden, Alan, *Tigers Burning Bright: SOE Heroes in the Far East* (London: Bene Factum, 2013).
Paine, S.C.M., *The Wars for Asia, 1911-1949* (Cambridge: Cambridge University Press, 2012).
Parris, Matthew, and Andrew Bryson, *The Spanish Ambassador's Suitcase: Stories from the Diplomatic Bag* (London: Viking, 2012).
Peattie, Mark, Edward Drea, and Hans Van de Ven, eds., *The Battle for China* (Stanford: Stanford University Press, 2011).
Peck, Graham, *Two Kinds of Time* (Boston: Houghton Mifflin, 1950).
Perret, Geoffrey, *Old Soldiers Never Die* (New York: Random House, 1996).
Rand, Peter, *China Hands* (New York: Simon & Schuster, 1995).
Romanus, Charles, and Riley Sunderland, *Stilwell's Command Problems*, U.S. Army History of World War II (Washington, DC: Office of the Chief of Military History, Department of the Army, 1956).
Romanus, Charles, and Riley Sunderland, *Stilwell's Mission to China* (Washington, DC: Office of the Chief of Military History, Department of the Army, 1953).
Roosevelt, Elliot, *As He Saw It* (New York: Duell, Sloan and Pearce, 1946).
Scott, Colonel Robert L., *God Is My Co-Pilot* (New York: Ballantine Books, 1962).
Seagrave, Gordon, *Burma Surgeon* (New York: W.W. Norton, 1943).
Seagrave, Gordon S., *Burma Surgeon Returns* (New York: W.W. Norton, 1946).

Sevareid, Eric, *Not So Wild a Dream* (New York: Alfred Knopf, 1946).
Sherwood, Robert E., *Roosevelt & Hopkins* (New York: Grosset & Dunlap, 1960).
Sinclair, William Boyd, *Confusion Beyond Imagination*, book 5: *Medics and Nurses* (Coeur d'Alene, ID: Joe F. Whitley, 1989).
Smith, Nicol, *Burma Road* (Garden City, NY: Garden City Publishing, 1942).
Smith, S.E., ed., *The United States Marine Corps in World War II* (New York: Random House, 1969).
Stimson, Henry L., and McGeorge Bundy, *On Active Service in Peace and War* (New York: Harper & Brothers, 1948).
Stone, James H., *Crisis Fleeting* (Washington, DC: Office of the Surgeon General, Department of the Army, 1969).
Tainsh, A.R., *And Some Fell by the Wayside* (Calcutta: Orient Longmans, 1948).
Thompson, Henrietta, *Walk a Little Faster: Escape from Burma with General Stilwell in 1942* (Privately published, 1980).
Thorne, Christopher, *The Limits of Foreign Policy* (New York: G.P. Putnam's Sons, 1973).
Tolley, Kemp, *Yangtze Patrol: The U.S. Navy in China* (Annapolis, MD: Naval Institute Press, 1971).
Tuchman, Barbara, *Stilwell and the American Experience in China* (New York: Book of the Month Club, 1985).
Wagg, Alfred, *A Million Died!* (London: Nicholson and Watson, 1943).
Warren, Alan, *Burma 1942* (London and New York: Continuum Books, 2011).
Wenrich, Lieutenant Colonel George L., *Silent Valor: World War II in the Himalayas* (Kent Store, VA: Reflective Books, 2005).
White, Theodore H., ed., *The Stilwell Papers* (New York: William Sloane Associates, 1948).
Yerkey, Gary G., *Still Time to Live: A Biography of Jack Belden* (Washington, DC: GK Press, 2011).
Ziegler, Philip, *Mountbatten: A Biography* (New York: Alfred Knopf, 1985).
Ziegler, Philip, ed., *Personal Diary of Admiral the Lord Louis Mountbatten, Supreme Commander, South-East Asia, 1943–1946* (London: Collins, 1988).

Periodical Articles

Arnstein, Daniel, "An Ex-Taxi Driver Checks Up on the Famous Burma Road," *Life*, 6 October 1941.
Allen, John, "Wetzel's WWII Career Is History of C.B.I.," *CBIVA Sound-Off* (Spring 1989): 24–28.
Berkeley (California) *Daily Gazette*, 18 August 1942: 6.
"Burma Retreat, 1942," part I (compiled from letters written by Brigadier T.O. Thompson, D.D.M.S., Burma, to Brigadier H.C.D. Rankin, D.D.M.S., GHQ India), *Journal of the Royal Army Medical Corps* XC (January 1948).
"Burma Retreat, 1942," part II (compiled from letters written by Brigadier T.O. Thompson, D.D.M.S., Burma, to Brigadier H.C.D. Rankin, D.D.M.S., GHQ India), *Journal of the Royal Army Medical Corps* XC (January 1948).
CBI Roundup (8 October 1942); *CBI Roundup* (3 June 1943).
Grindlay, Major John H., "Treatment of Skin Infections in the Assam-Burma Jungle," *Bulletin of the U.S. Army Medical Department* 74 (March 1944): 74–80.
Howard, Richard A., "The Role of Botanists during World War II in the Pacific Theatre," *Botanical Review* 60, no. 2 (April–June 1994): 197–257.
Lathrop, Alan K., "The Employment of Chinese Nationalist Troops in the First Burma Campaign," *Journal of Southeast Asian Studies* 12, no. 2 (Summer 1981): 403–32.
"Oil Is Used to Christen Tulsa's Ship," *Oil and Gas Journal* 18 (6 August 1919).

San, P.A., "Malaria Control with the Yunnan–Burma Railway Medical Mission," *Malaria Control in War Areas Field Bulletin* (October 1944): 1–4.
Sinclair, William Boyd, "The Battle with Annie," *Ex-CBI Roundup* (March 1990): 6–11; (April 1990): 6–10.
Stevens, Keith, "'Duncan Force'—the Shanghai Defence Force in 1927, & the Career of Captain Ronald Spear," *Journal of the Royal Asiatic Society, Hong Kong Branch* 48 (2008): 151–72.
"Stilwell's Driver in Burma Kills Self in Delhi," *Brooklyn Daily Eagle*, 26 May 1942: 5.
Wetzel, Nevin, "Evacuation of Rangoon," *Ex-CBI Roundup* (November 1974).
Whitworth, Brigadier Dysart, "The Evacuation of Refugees and the Chinese Fifth Army from the Hukawng Valley into Assam, Summer 1942," *Journal of the Royal Central Asian Society* 30, no. 2 (September 1943): 311–21.

Online Resources

"Bertie Castens' Secret Track," www.chinditslongcloth1943.com/bertie-castens-secret-track.html.
"Calcutta High Court, B.A. Shervashidze vs. Govt. of West Bengal and Anr. on 12 January, 1949," AIR 1951 Cal 474, www.indiankanoon.org/doc/844638/.
"Diaries Detail Japan's Germ Warfare in China during World War II," UPI Archives (online), 30 December 1993, https://www.upi.com/Archives/1993/12/30/Diaries-detail-Japans-germ-warfare-in-China-during-World-War-II/1516757227600/.
George W. Parsons, recollections, http://www.cotteridge.quaker.eu.org/george_parsons.htm.
Tamara Shervaschidze obituary, *Sidney Morning Herald*, 8 December 2012, http://www.legacy.com/obituaries/name/tamara-shervashidze-obituary?pid=100000016164713 1&view=guestbook.
"What Is Benzedrine?" http://www.wisegeek.com/what-is-benzedrine.htm.
"The World War II Diaries of General Joseph W. Stilwell (1941–1945)," Hoover Institution Archives, https://digitalcollections.hoover.org/images/Collections/51001/1942_stilwell_diary_rev.pdf.

Oral Histories and Interviews

Lutken, Peter, interview by author. Newellton, Louisiana, 24 September 2009.
Lutken, Peter, oral history, 28 September 1997. Center for Oral and Public History, California State University, Fullerton.

Index

Numbers in **_bold italics_** indicate pages with illustrations

ABC Pipeline 203
ABDACOM *see* American-British-Dutch-Australian Command
air evacuation to India 71
air medical evacuation in CBI 205
Air Service Command *see* U.S. Air Transport Command
air supply drops 96, 112-3, 115-7, 119, 127-9, 145, 164, 166, 179, 181; medical supplies mistakenly dropped 182-4; Royal Air Force 84; *see also* Whitworth, Brig. Dysart
Aldrich, Maj. Harry 20, 26-7, 36, 48-9, 138; promotion to Lt. Col. 49
Alexander, Gen. Harold 67, 69, 80, 85; issues Operation Instruction 46, 123-5; proposal to airlift and train Chinese soldiers 123
Allied Line of Communication (LOC)(Burma) *see* LOC
Allies, disagreements 148, 150
American Baptist Missionary compound 79
American-British-Dutch-Australian Command (ABDACOM) 33, 55
American Bureau for Medical Relief to China 49
American College of Surgeons 190
American Export-Import Bank 14
American Field Service 205
American Military Mission to China (AMMISCA) 2-8, 21-2, 27, 29-30, 32-4, 36, 40-1, 44, 47, 49, 56, 57, 60, 64, 152; absorbed into Stilwell's command 63; airplane crash kills members 60; Chinese military preparedness evaluation 34; Chinese resistance to military training 34; convoy to Kunming 28-9; first staff meeting with Stilwell 57; hospital truck 28; living and medical quarters 48; medical group 46; morale 37-39; origins 14-8, 23-4; proposal for U.S. military mission to China 15; Rangoon headquarters files destroyed 58; winding down operations 63
American Volunteer Group (AVG) *see* Flying Tigers)
AMMISCA *see* American Military Mission to China
And Some Fell by the Wayside 131
anesthesia 154; chloroform 149, 154; ether 149; ethyl chloride 154
Antonellis, Lt. Carl "Johnny" 180, 182, 187
Arakan, Burma 123, 130
Arcadia Conference 55
arms shipments to China 14
Arnesen, Capt. Dag Jorgen 26, 27
Arnold, Lt. Carl 78, 84, 151-1, 200
Arnstein, Daniel 34, 68
Asia map **_9_**
Assam province (India) 70, 117, 126, 128, 131, 141, 152, 158; defensive line 125
Astolfi, SSgt Francis 26, 58; suicide 152
Auchinleck, Lady 137
Ausland, Maj. John E. 58
Australian minister 44
Ava Bridge (Mandalay) 78, 124

Ba Saw, Dr. 185
Bald, Lillian 115
Balfour, Dr. Marshall C. 144
Bardenhaugen, MSgt C.T. 153
Barrett, Maj. David 34
Barton, Maj. George Eliot "Beaver" 86, **_94_**
Baxter 116
Belden, Jack 79-80, 88-9, **_94_**, 97, **_103_**, 100
Bevil, Maj. Lamar C. 137, 139, 146, 149
Bhamo, Burma 124, 129
Big Bawk (M.T.) 153, 175-6, 183
Bissell, Col. Clayton 60
Boatner, Brig. Gen. Haydon 5, 112, 116-8, 127-9, 146, 146, 153-4, 159, 170, 173-6, 178-

243

244 Index

80, 183, 185–91, 193–4; promotion to commander of NCAC 159; Seagrave nurses to move to Shingbwiyang 186
Bowler, Dr. John 200
Bradley, MSgt J.F. 152
Brady, Gen. 60
Bramston, Lt. 170, 174, 176–7, 188, 196
Bray, Lt. Col. Stanley H. 183, 186
Brereton, Maj. Gen. Lewis 84–5, 105; radio message of Stilwell's walkout route 103
Brett, Maj. Gen. George 40, 43–4, 46
British army: plans for withdrawal to Mandalay, Burma 70; reaches Imphal 125; retreat from Burma 77, 122, 124
British Casualty Clearing Station unit, Mandalay 71; 1 Casualty Clearing Station, Meiktila 76
British field hospitals (Mingaladon, Moulmein, Rangoon) 70; withdrawal to Mandalay 70
British trade embargo 13
British troops in India: treatment after Burma retreat 125
Brooke-Popham, Sir Robert 21
Brough, Bill 72–3, **87**, 185, 189; abandoned conscientious objector status 87; evacuated to India 87
Brown, Lt. Rollin C. 187
Bruce, Maj. Gen. John G. 61, 85
Budge 136, 152
Bulwer-Lytton, Lord 7
Burchett, Wilfred 106
Burma 10, 18, 20, 34, 42, 122; Chinese assistance to war in 44; Chinese distrust British defense of 44; Chinese offer of troops to British 39; government 27, 130, 131; Japanese military action 57, 67, 69–70; map *162*; plans for recapture 135, 153, 156; Stilwell's responsibilities 54; supply line through 18; war routes of retreat 1942 70
Burma Road 20, 22–3, 26–9, 32–5, 144, 156; Japanese preparations to sever 35–6, 72; Japanese threat to cut 78, 124
Burmah Oil Company 88
Bush, Capt. Walter 136

Calcutta 62; hospital 87
Campbell, Hughie 88
Carroll 118
Carroll, Col. Percy J. 142
Carter, Capt. 197
Case, Rev. Brayton C. 86–7, 93, 159
Castens, Maj. Herbert 86, 93
CBI *see* China-Burma-India Theater
Central Aircraft Manufacturing Company (CAMCO) 59
Chambers, TSgt. Dean 67
Chan Tso-lin 7
Chankufeng, Manchuria 10

Chaunggyi River 82, 94
Chen, Col. 185
Cheng, Gen. Chen 41
Cheng, Dr. Jen-yu 110–1, 116
Cheng Pao-nan 49
Chennault, Capt. Claire 24, 32, 36–7, 59, 82, 157; promoted to brigadier general in USAAF 60
Chesley, TSgt. Ray 26, 96, 104, 107, 136–8, 149, 152–4, 165, 173–4, 178, 180, 185, 187, 189, 191, 193–4; bronchopneumonia 195; ill with bronchopneumonia 195; lab at Ramgarh 139; malaria 106; trip with Grindlay to Nagas 184
Chiang, Madame 35, 45, 52–3, 60, 62, 157
Chiang Kai-shek 13, 15, 25, 30, 34–6, 39–40, 43–6, 49, 52, 54–5, 59, 69–70, 79, 82, 109, 116, 123–4, 128, 144–5, 150, 157, 202; request that U.S. and Britain declare war on Japan with Soviet Union 39
China 6, 8, 10, 14; Air Force 36; China National Airways Corporation (CNAC) 22; Chinese air force 36; Chinese exclusion from Lend-Lease Act 14; CNAC planes destroyed at Hong Kong 39; Communists 43, 49, 153, 202; government relocation 30; lend-lease 13; lend-lease supplies sharing 38, 44; military aid 38; Red River supply route 8; U.S. coordination of war plans 38
China-Burma-India Theater (CBI) 5, 37, 59; ABC pipeline system 203; ceases to exist 204; China Defense Supplies Inc. 17, 24; China Japanese conflict 13, 14; contributions to future medical practice 205–7; creation 65; description 65–6; end of war 202; manpower shortage in 195; Rear Echelon Headquarters 84
Chindwin River 70, 97, 110–1, 113, 125–6
Chinese army in Burma: 5th Army 67, 69, 73, **77**, 81–3, 109, 111–3, 127–9, 138; medical services 46–7; retreat from Burma 122, 124; 6th Army 69, 72–3, 78–9; 22nd Division 79, 82, 111–4, 117–8, 125, 127–8, 143, 161; 28th Division 129; 38th Division 82, 111, 125–6, 129, 138, 156; 49th and 93rd Divisions 129; Temporary 55th Division 123, 129; Advance 65th Regiment 114, 117; 96th Division 113, 128–9; 112th and 114th Regiments 186; 200th Division 70, 110, 123, 129
Chinese army in India 148
Chinese combat in Burma 175; intelligence report 39; looting of Burmese villages 128; National Health Administration 41, 57; Nationalist armies 7, 128, 142; Nationalist medical facilities contrasted with Communists 49; training members of Pharmacy Corps at Ramgarh 142; treatment after retreat to India 126

Index 245

Chinese Communists: medical aid 47–9; Nationalists stockpiling war materials for war with 153
Chinese guerilla fighters in Burma 129
Chit Sein 174
cholera 92, 123, 129, 131–2
Chou En-lai 25
Chungking 22–3, 26, 28–32, 31, 35, 37, 40, 42; air raid warning system 32; allied proposal for secretariat in 44; French Catholic Hospital 47
Churchill, Sir Winston 55
Clagett, Brig. Gen. Henry B. 21
Clark Kerr, Sir Archibald 32, 33, 39, 52–3
Clark Kerr, Tita 33
Clarkson, Capt. William M. 32, 152
Coates, Lt. Col. 116
Collingwood, Lt. C.J. 51
concerns about U.S. aid to China 25
Corcoran, Tommy 24
Coudray, Maj. Wyman F. 61, 152
Cowan, Maj. Gen. David "Punch" 125
Croft, Jack 88
Cummings, Bill 107, 138, 149, 157, 161, 163, 165–7, 174, 185, 189, 194
Curl, Capt. Vincent 166
Currie, Lauchlin 14, 24–5, 31

dacoits 122
Darjeeling (India) 140, 141, 143, 157
Davidson-Houston, Maj. James 85–6, 88, 93
Davies, John Paton 67; plane crash 174, 196
Davies, Martin 72, 173
Davis, Harold 34
DDT: use of 207
Deaton, SSgt Chester 166, 167, 172, 195
Dennys, Maj. Gen. Lancelot 15, 32–4, 33, 39–40, 44, 52; death 60–1
Dennys, Mrs. 62
Donald, Lt. Col. A.A. 163–4
Doolittle raiders 103, 107, 133–4
Dorman-Smith, Sir Reginald 36
Dorn, Lt. Col. Frank 57, 67, 74, 103, 151
Drysdale, Col. 80
Duncombe, Bill 72, 145, 155, 166
Dunnette, William 4
Dushkin, Maj. Milton 186–7
Dutch 8, 10, 13
Dykes, Maj. O.C.T. "Sailor" 85–6
Dykstra, Lt. Matilda 157–8
dysentery 107, 118, 126, 129–32, 134, 138; chronic 140, 178–9

East Asia 6, 10–11
Eckert, Lt. Col. Norman 133
Edward, Lt. Col. Harvey 60–1, 133
Eggleston, Sir Frederick 43
Eldridge, Lt. Fred 90, 91, 107; describes Stilwell on walkout 106

Emily 175–76
Engelhard, Col. 133
Esther Po 164–5, 176, 184, 195, 200
European war 7, 8, 13–4
Evans, Dryhurst 49–50, 62

Fan Tze 176
FAU see Friends Ambulance Unit
Ferris, Col. Benjamin 67, 196; proposes to leave British and Seagrave unit behind on walkout 91
fevers of unknown origin (FUOs) 116, 118, 206
First Burma Division 125
First Washington Conference see Arcadia Conference
Fisher, Ethel 193
Flowers, Dr. W.S. 141, 143
Flying Tigers 8, 24, 32, 44, 60, 66; base 59; dispute with British over supplies 45
food supplies 117, 181, 185
Force 136 163
Fort Hertz 113, 115, 129; soldiers and refugees 145
48th Evacuation Hospital 157–9
Fourteenth Air Force see Flying Tigers
Fowler's Solution 139
Freeman, Dr. Norman 193, 195; replaces Grindlay at Seagrave Hospital Unit 189
French Indochina 8, 10, 13, 35
Friends Ambulance Unit (FAU) 72–76, 87, 95, 96–7, 107, 145, 185, 188–189, 205; ambulances 74; joins Seagrave Hospital Unit 72; members' activities 79, 80, 95, 166, 173, 185, 196, 205; members assigned to Chinese army 72; members assist in surgery 73; salvaging medical supplies and spare vehicle parts at Rangoon 73; saving oil at Yenangyaung 73; walkout 93–4
Fullerton 134

Ga Naw 174
Gardner, TSgt. W.O. 25, 28
Gauhati, India 106–8
Gauss, Ambassador Clarence 31–2, 31, 52, 63, 157
Generalissimo see Chiang Kai-shek
Gentry, Col. Thomas 60, 66, 136
George, Col. Otto "Gus" 32; death 60–1; funeral 62
Geren, Paul 73, 89, 95, 98; circular letter to friends about walkout 106, 180
Gilbert, Lt. Col. Douglas 185
Gilliam, Alexander 192
Gissimo see Chiang Kai-shek
Gluckman, Lt. Col. Arcadi Paul 20, 48, 62, 152
Goddard, Gen. Eric 80
godowns see Rangoon, Burma
Grant, Kenneth 73, 79–80

Great Britain 14
Grindlay, Elizabeth "Betty" 1–2,4, 24, 42, 66, 134, 136, 141, 146, 149, 164, 173, 177, 184, 191, 195
Grindlay, Lt. John Happer 1–2, 5–6, **24**, 33, 35, 40–1, 46–9, 52–3, 57, 71, 73–6, 79, **87**, 88, 91, 93–4, 96, 106, 133–5, 137–8, **146**, 143–55, 157, 161, 164–8, 175–6, 179–80, 183–99, 205; abortion of Esther Po 176; air transport to U.S. 193, 197–8; amoebic dysentery 154; application of experience in tropical medicine 207; argument with Seagrave 180; asked to search for aircraft crash site in Naga area 167; "Battle of Burma" 79; blood bank 193, 195; bull terrier puppy (Tilly) 155; Calcutta 106; with Chesley to Nagas 184; Christmas celebration at 20th General Hospital 193; conference at Hkalak 174; death 202; death of Hambleton 146; death of Sgt. Astolfi 147; death of Stilwell 201; description of trail 99; design of Gurkha hospital ward at Shingbwiyang 179; diaries and letters 23–9, 42, 47–8, 50–4, 56–7, 60–3, 74–5, 77, 80, 93, 95–9, 102–4, 136, 138–9, 141, 146–59, 163–4, 166, 170–98; Doolittle crew members 107; education 23–4; establishes dispensary in Chungking 41; exhaustion 76, 78; heart problems 136; hospital library 166; hospital sanitation and cleanup 165; joins Seagrave Hospital Unit 66; Kweiyang medical training facility 50; leaves 20th General Hospital for U.S. 197–8; leaving U.S. for Rangoon 25–8; to Maymyo 66; Mayo Clinic career 201; mission to Naga villages 166; moves family to Milwaukee 201; to Ningam and organizes hospital 182; nurse Koi 138; opinion of Chinese soldiers' discipline and morals 147; post-CBI military postings 200–1; praise from Seagrave 164–5; promotion to captain 62; Purple Heart 136, 140; Ramgarh 137–8; recovery 107; report to Boatner on Naga medical mission 174; reputation as surgeon grows 148; request for transfer 187; sanitation for Americans along Burma Road 41–2; Seagrave begs Grindlay to stay with Unit 188; Seagrave blames troubles on Grindlay 189–90; Seagrave Hospital at Tagap Ga 160; served Naga rice beer 100; skills as surgeon 78; surgery at Kyaukmyaung 79; term of service 24; 34th birthday 183; tries to join Stilwell's staff of 10th Army on Okinawa 200; 20th General Hospital 189–90; walk-out members' health 104
Grindlay, Dr. Josh 4
Grindlay, Sara 24, 149, 191
Gruber, Brig. Gen. William R. 67, 126
Gurkha troops 117, 125, 141
Gurney, Dr. Theodore 73, 107, 150, 151–3, 157, 161, 166–7, 186

Haas, Lt. Col. Victor H 144, 145, 160
Haigh, Maj. W.D. 86
Hambleton, Capt. Roscoe 25–6, 79–81, 83–4, 109–21, 125, 127–8, 147, 152, 161; death and burial 120–1; ; diary 3, 81–2; dysentery 83, 119; met General Tu and Chinese 5th Army headquarters troops 82; ordered by Stilwell to stay at Kyaukmyaung 80; radio message to Chennault 82; stationed at AMMISCA headquarters Rangoon 57
Hambleton, Mrs. 121
Harper, Dr. Robert 72
Harper Memorial Hospital 72
Harris, Lt. Kenneth D. 155, 164, 176, 180, 194–95
Harrison-Cripps operation 76
Hart, Adm. Thomas C. 22
Hawkins, Paul 52
Hayes, Anna Mae 2
Haymaker, Lt. Kenneth 84
Haynes, Col. Caleb Vance 85, 177
Haywood, Maj. Ted M. 57, 66, 153
Hearn, Maj. Gen. Thomas 186
Heinrich, Col. Joseph 62, 152
Hellman, Marco 34
Heron 81
Hkalak Ga, Burma 116, 129, 161
Hla Duk 169–170–3
Hla Sein 161, 175–7
Ho Ying-chin 31; appointment to allied secretariat 44; offers Chinese troops to Burma 44; war issues of Chinese 39
Hoegh Silverdawn 25–7, 146
Holcombe, Col. Henry 94, 138, 140, 149, 151; malaria 106
Hope, Joan 135
Hope, Victor Alexander John 135
Hopkins, Harry 14, 34
hospital politics 149
Hoyt, Col. Ross 36, 39
Hsipaw, Burma 82, 129
Hsung, General 66
Hukawng Valley, Burma 70, 83, 113, 115, 127, 131, 161, 167; Chinese defensive line 116
Hull, Cordell 36
Hump traffic 127, 136, 203
Hutton, Lt. Gen. Thomas 78

Imphal, India 70, 126
Inchboard, Eric 72, 79–80, 185; marriage to Ruth 196
Indaw, Burma 86, 128
India 10, 202; independence 203
Indian refugees 130
intestinal worms 138
Irrawaddy Flotation Company 80
Irrawaddy River 67, 69, 77, 124–5
Irwin, Lt. Gen. Noel 125–6

Japan: attack on Pearl Harbor 6, 38; bacteriological warfare 51; battles in Burma 69, 77–8, 86, 92, 123, 125, 131, 161, 180, 183, 185, 187; beginning of aggression in East Asia 6–7; concern about U.S. involvement 11; 56th Regiment 186; Greater Far East Asia Co-Prosperity Sphere 10–1; lines of communication 44; Manchuria 7; neutrality pact with Soviet Union 8; preparations to sever Burma Road 35; strategy in Southeast Asia 10, 39; war plan for East Asia 10
Jeep track 124; *see also* Ye-U to Kalewa track
Jellison, Maj. William L. 144
Johnson, Col. Henry A. 144–5
Johnson, Dr. Henry Myles 151–2, 187; Peter Lutken 181–2, 193
Joint Chiefs of Staff (JCS) 15
Joint Planning Committee (JPC) 15
Jones, Bryan 73; with Bill Brough to Myitkyina 87, **87**
Jones, Capt. Paul 67; Purple Heart 136

Kachins 129
Kalewa 124
Kalewa-Tamu-Imphal-Palel road *see* Manipur road
Kaneti, Dr. Lanto 51
Karachi 149
Katha, Burma 81–2, 124
Kengtung-Fuhai defensive line 124, 129
Kirkpatrick, Dr. M.B. 72
Kochenderfer, Capt. Thomas 197
Kohler, Lt. Frederick 60–1
Koi 138, 152, 154, 160–1, 166, 168, 173, 184, 186, 189–90, 194, 196; description 139
Korea 10
Kukis 97, 99
Kume, Burma 77–8
Kung, H.H. 32, 62
"Kungshaven" 49, 56
Kunming 28, 29, 35, 129, 144; Japanese attacks 36
Kuo Chan 28, 37
Kwangtung Army 10
Kyang Tsui 179, 180

LaBing 119–21
Lambert, E.T.D. 127
Lashio 28–9, 39, 78, 124, 144
Lattimore, Owen 45, 49, 145
Laybourne, Lt. Eugene 94, 97, **99**, 153, 196
Laycock, Dr. Handley 145
League of Nations 6, 7
Lean, Lt. Denis Guy 82–3, 109–110, 112–7, 119–20; leaves for Ledo 121
Ledo, India 116, 126, 145, 158–9
Ledo Road 3, 116, 156–7, 159–61, 203; construction crews ill with malaria 179; skeletons of refugees 169

Lee, Lt. Tommy 94
leech bites *see* Naga sore
"Leech trail" 160
leeches 98–9, 131, 159, 160, 178; *see also* Naga sore
Leedham, Col. Charles L. 157–9
Lend-Lease 8, 13–15, 24–5, 32, 34, 36, 38, 42–6, 54, 57–8, 144, 150, 156; medical materials 46; need for a military mission to China 15; planning to share medical materials 46; shipments to China 14–5; tasks for oversight AMMISCA 17
Lend-Lease Act 8
Liao, Yao-hsiang, Gen. 111, 112, 117, 128
lice 76, 110
Liddell-Hart, Basil 126, 158
Life magazine 8, 89
Lim, Dr. Robert 34, 49–50, 66, 76, **77**, 79; Kweiyang medical training facility 50
Little Bawk 80, 143, 147, 156, 164–5, 174–5; infected with tertiary malaria 140–1
Lo Cho-ying, Gen. 81, 86, 150; caused train wreck 124
LOC 123–4
"Long Walk" 166
Louise 161
Lowe, David 60
Lowe, Joyce 60
Luce, Claire 157
Luce, Henry R. 8, 89
Lulu 140, 174–5, 177
Lutken, Capt. Peter 166, 174, 177, 193–4; dispatches Kachin to Tagap Ga for medical aid 181; evacuated to 20th General Hospital 182, 185; wounded 181
Lynch, Dr. Fennimore death 60
Lyster bag 206
Lytle, SSgt. J.R. 26, 152

Ma Koi 174
MacArthur, Gen. Douglas 21, 37, 84
MacMorland, Col. Edward 2, 19–22, **21**, 31–40, 45, 62, 66
Magruder, Brig. Gen. John 15–7, **18**, 27–8, 30–53, 55–7, 61–68; command of Division of General Affairs 57; disagreement with Wavell over Lend-Lease 45; staffing mission 19–23; transfer to U.S. 63
Mahoney, Lt. Col. William A. 158
Maingkwan-Fort Hertz area, Burma 83; defensive line 127–8, 131
mail censorship 157
Malang Kaw 166–7
malaria 76, 96, 100, 104, 106–7, 116, 123, 126, 130–2, 138, 140, 144–5, 161, 174, 178–9, 206; cerebral 87; scabies 76
Malaya 8, 10; Japanese invasion of 39
Maltby, Maj. Gen. Christopher 22
Manchuria 7, 10
Mandalay, Burma 69, 78, 124, 128; city and

248 Index

Fort Dufferin bombed 71, 124, 128; medical depot established 70
Mandalay-Pyawbe rail line 124
Manget, Dr. Fred P. 144
Manipur, India 126; Manipur Road to Assam 130–1
Manning, Capt. E.R. 53
Mao, Pang-tsu, Gen. **33**
Mao, Tse-tung 202
Maran Lu 174
Marco Polo Bridge 7
Marek, TSgt. Frank 25, 28
Margherita, India 119
Marshall, Gen. George C. 15, 54–6, 157; urged to retain AMMISCA 63
Martin, Lt. Arthur 136
Martin, Frank 184
Martin, Brig. John Crawford 80
May, Dr. Wesley 67
Mayer, Lt. Col. William 15
Mayo Clinic 2, 24, 201
McCabe, Col. Frederick **99**; Chinese troops training at Ramgarh 137, 158; Maymyo 138
McConnell, Capt. David 157
McDowell, Brig. John 154; puppy (Tilly) given to Grindlay 155
McHugh, Capt. James 55
McLaughlin, Col. John 84
McNally, Col. Edward 190; Chinese 38th Army 195
medical supply shortage 183
medications: atabrine 204, 206; benzedrine 154; emetrine 154–5; Fowler's solution 139; morphine 145; Novocain 139, penicillin 204; quinine 96, 100, 204, 206; sulfa drugs 106, sulfathiazole 154; yellow fever inoculations 132, 144
Meiktila, Burma 67, 75, 124; bombed 76
Mendelson, Maj. Joseph Aaron 20, 23, 26, 32, 34, 37, 40, 48–50, 66, 145; appointed station surgeon 57; proposed changes in Chinese medical corps and services and withdrawal of Americans 46–7; report on Chinese medical situation and suggestions for improvement 46
Merrill, Maj. Frank 37, 40, 59–63, 67, 71, **100**, 153; AMMISCA headquarters in Rangoon 57; heart attack on walkout 94; Purple Heart 136; swears in Williams as full colonel 100
Merrill's Marauders 37, 199
Meyer, Fr. Louis 3, 120
Mibu, 2nd Lt. Hirano 92
Milani, Col. Frank 196
military aid to China 7
Moats, Alice-Leone 67; convoy to Lashio 68
Mogaung, Burma 128
monsoon 83, 85, 98, 122, 124, 131
Moore, Dr. Lorna Grindlay 2, 4
Moul, SSgt. Jacob 26, 152

Mountbatten, Field Marshal Louis 20
Myitkyina, Burma 69, 124–5, 127–8, 131–2

Naga sores 107, 116, 131, 138, 145, 154, 161, 165
Nagas 97, 127, 163; Grindlay's medical visit to villages 168–173
Naomi 194
Naw Aung 175–6
Naw Seng 199
Naw Shan 175
New Delhi, India 84, 133, 149
98th Station Hospital 143, 151–2
Norem, W.O. Albert 25–6
Norilla, Pfc. 174
North, Clive 114–5, 118–20, 128
North, Maj. John Paul 192
Northern Area Combat Command in Burma and India (NCAC) 19, 159; headquarters 193–4
Nowakowski, Maj. Felix 94, **100**, **102**

Ogden, Maj. Marcus 20, 25, 48, 153
O'Hara, Capt. Donald 73–4, 76, 78–9, 107, 134, 138–9, 147, 149, 151, 159, 164, 167, 173, 178, 183, 186, 194; leaves for Calcutta 187; promotion to major 98, 107, 134; promotion to lieutenant colonel 185; Purple Heart 136; transferred to Tenth Air Force 185
Old China Hands 15, 20, 54
151st Evacuation Hospital 188
151st Medical Battalion 165
159th Station Hospital 149
OSS (Office of Special Services) (Detachment 101), Burma 163
Owen, Tom 72

Panay 48
Pangsau Pass 116
Parsons, George 72, 96
Pawley, William D. 59
Petersen, Col. Vernon 184, 189, 193–5
Philippines 8, 11, 21; Japanese bombing 39; U.S. garrison in 36
Pintha, Burma 80
portable surgical hospitals (PSH) 204–5; Stilwell envisions use 142
Porter, Col. Hervey 136
Prescott, Maj. 160
Putao, Burma 113
Pyawbwe, Burma **77**
Pyinmana, Burma 74, 128

QUADRANT Conference 153

Ramgarh 5, 133–42, 143–55, 156; Boatner in charge of 148; Chinese troops rehabilitating and retraining 137; hospital for Chinese soldiers 108, 126; sanitation and drainage 144; troops treatment at Afridi, Ghorimalli, Gurkha, Pathan, Sikh 141

Index 249

Ranglum, Burma 116
Rangoon, Burma 22-3, 28, 33, 36, 39, 43, 57, 67-9, 123; British casualties moved 71; Brookings Street wharf docks (*godowns*) 35, 58; Raffles Hotel 27
Rankin, Brig. H.C.D. 70
Ravdin, Col. Isador 159, 184, 191, 192, **192**, 194, 197
Ravenholt, Albert 184, 187
Rawicz, Slavomir 166
Red Cross, American 49; British 72, 140-1, 143; Chinese 34, 46-7, 49, 57, 142; International 68
Reese, Col. Thomas 152
"Refugee trail" 116, 165; *see also* air evacuation
refugees 115, 130-1; civilian 129-30; Indian 130; medical situation in India 132
relapsing fever 110
renal colic 75, 78, 107
Retreat with Stilwell (Jack Belden) 89
Reybold, Brig. Gen. Eugene 15
Reynolds, Tony 73
Rhode Island Hospital 157
Roberts, Lt. Col. Frank 56, 84, 133
Robinson 196
Rockefeller Foundation 197
Roosevelt, Franklin D. 7-8, 13-4, 16, 24, 31, 34, 36, 38, 44-5, 54, 153, 186; China military aid 13-4; fear of China military collapse 55; military conference proposal 40; Thanksgiving dinner in Burma fails to materialize 186
Royster, Dr. Henry 192-3
Ruby 161
Russell, Maj. John 57, 62
Ruth 179; marriage to Eric Inchboard 196

Sagaing, Burma 78
St. John, Col. Adrian 42, 88, 91-2, 99-100, 104, 107, 134-5, 144; appearance and health after walkout 106; destruction of all Lend-Lease supplies in Rangoon 58; malaria 106; Purple Heart 136; stationed at AMMISCA headquarters Rangoon 57
Salween River 69, 144
sand flies 160, 177; infected bites 161
Sandusky, Col. Richard 84, 133
Saw Yen 152
Schuler, William death 60
Scott, Colonel 193
Scott, Emil 193
Scott, Col. Robert Lee 85, 132
Seagrave, Dr. Gordon 2, 5, 72-76, 137, 139, 140, 143, 146-54, 159, 161, 174-6, 179, 183, 184, 186-7, 189-90, 194-6, 199, 200, 205; alcoholism 174-5; arrest by government of Burma 199; *Burma Surgeon* 146, 151, 164, 199; *Burma Surgeon Returns* 164; death 200; departs for Assam 155; description of civilian refugees in India 107; deteriorating relations with Grindlay 185; Harper Memorial Hospital 47, 72; knowledge of geography 77; letter to Grindlay about dividing unit 183; malaria 143; ordered to conference at Ledo 175; ordered to rest leave in Darjeeling 140-1; ordered to retreat 77; pet monkeys 175-6; physical condition 175; promotion to major 78; proposal to Boatner to send Grindlay on leave 188; protests possible Grindlay reassignment 78; Purple Heart 136, 140; Ramgarh 134; special tribunal, sentenced and freed 200; unit added to Stilwell command 72; vents anger at Grindlay 180
Seagrave Hospital nurses 74-5, 80-1, 88, **89**, 106-7, 138, 143, 147, 151-2, 156, 160, 164, 175, 180, 183, 186, 189-90, 194-5, 199, 205; accompany Grindlay to Naga villages 166, 172; collect wild food on walkout 96; depart for Burma 155; diarrhea and malaria 134; gifts for 180; Koi head nurse 138; return to Burma 196; roofs for rafts 96; singing on walkout 93; vote on staying with Grindlay or Seagrave 179
Seagrave Hospital Unit 5, 71-2, 77, 80, 87, 93, 96, 99, 106-7, 136, 138, 142, 147, 151-2, 158-9, 164-6, 174, 178-9, 185, 187-93, 195-6, 199, 205; American Baptist Missionary Women's Hospital 106; arrival in India 101; doctors stricken with malaria 145; FAU assigned to unit 72; final period of service at Ramgarh 156; Grindla farewell visit 106; journalists visiting unit 148; move to Shingbwiyang 180; Ningam hospitals 180; ordered to Pyinmana 72; ordered to Shwebo 78; to Ramgarh 108; relied on British medical supplies 77; retreat destination is India 79; rumor unit to be moved to Ledo 189; separated during retreat to Shwebo 78; supported Merrill's Marauders 199; Tagap Ga hospital description 161; trucks to Imphal 104
2nd Motor Torpedo Boat Squadron 51
Sevareid, Eric 174
17th Indian Division 125-6
7th Armored Brigade (British 2nd Royal Tank Regiment) 126
73rd Evacuation Hospital 142, 159
Seymour, Ambassador Sir Horace 66
Shan States, Burma 29, 70, 73, 124, 138
Shanghai Incident 7
Sharpe, Thomas Arthur "Tim" 98-9; Seagrave unit 101
Shaw, Sgt. 115
Shervashidze, Basil 187-8
Shingbwiyang, Burma 113, 115, 127-9, 131; light plane landing strip 117
Shwebo 79; bombing 79, 124
Shwemyo Cliff 75

Sibert, Maj. Gen. Franklin 67, 86, 94, **98**, **101**, 118
Silk Road 29
Singapore 8, 35–6
Singh, Lt. G.B. 86
Sittang River 67, 69, 75
Skau, Olaf 67
Slaatten, Capt. Alf 26–7
Slater, Maj. Vernon 148, 195, 196
Slim, Gen. William 125
Sliney, Lt. Col. George W. 19–20, **100**, **101**, 153
Smith, Capt. Gordon 136
Soderholm, Lt. Col. Walter 34, 37; returned to U.S. 49–50
Soong, TV 14, 17, 19, 25, 30, 49
Soviet Union 10; Long Walk 166; neutrality pact with Japan 8
Spear, Brig. Christopher Ronald 85–6
Stevens, Keith 4
Stevenson, Col. Paul H. 144, 145
Stilwell, Lt. Gen. Joseph W. 1–3, 5, 15, 54–6, 60–1, 69–70, 72–3, 78, 80–1, 84, 86, 88, 89, **90**, **91**, 94, **94**, 97, **103**, 109, 123–9, 138–40, 143, 145, 148–53, 157, 174, 188, 191, 193,195, 196, 200–1, 204; death 201; Fred Eldridge reprimand 90; Grindlay request to return to U.S. 193; headquarters at Maymyo 67; headquarters at Shingbwiyang 161; Magruder's transfer 63; ordered Seagrave retreat 77; physical description after walk-out 106; post-campaign report for War Department 104–5; press conference in Imphal 104; refusal to be flown to India 84; refusal to leave anyone behind on walkout 92; roofs for rafts 96, **97**; split headquarters at Shwebo 79; staff assignments post-walkout 135; staff flown to New Delhi headquarters after walkout 107, 135; walk-out 88–90, **90**, 93; *see also* walkout
Stilwell, Winifred: letters to Grindlay 201–2
Stilwell Papers 202
Stimson, Henry 14, 36, 54–5
Stohl, Lt. Joseph 174
Stone, Maj. Eric P. 159
Stowe, Leland 37
Stuart tanks ("Honeys") 126
Sumprabum, Burma 83, 129
Sun Li-jen, Gen. 140; punishment of troops 147, 150, 186
surgical cases 74–76, 141
Sutherland, Lt. Col. Edwin M. 19, 152
syphilis 76

Tai An-lan, Gen. death 129
Tainsh, A.R. 131
Tamraz, Col. John 135, 151, 197
Tara, Burma 112, 128
Taro River 120
Tatkon, Burma 75

Taubenfligel, Dr. Viktor 188
tea planters 126
Tennant, Peter 72–3, **95**
Tenth of October 31
Than Shwe 140–1, 156, 161
Theodore 173
13th Mountain Medical Battalion 142
Thompson, Henrietta 3
Thompson, Brig. Treffry 67, 70, 71, 131
Tilly (dog) **146**, 155, 157, 160–1, 169, 172–3, 178, 186, 193, 198
Time magazine 8, 89
Tingly, SSgt Melvin E. 26, 152
Tipang, Burma 131
Tirap, Burma 116
Tong, Hollington 32, 45, 157
Toungoo, Burma 59, 70
Townsend, Col. George 133
TRIDENT Conference 153, 157
tropical diseases 204
Tseng, Hsi-kuei Gen. 34, 93
Tu, Li-ming Gen. 80–1, 83, 109–10, 117, 127, 128
tuberculosis 76, 138
Tulsa incident 42–6, **43**
Tun Shein 97, 161, 174, 179, 186, 190, 194, 196
Tutuilla 41; transfer to Chinese under Lend-Lease 48
20th General Hospital 3, 159, **190**, 191–2
25th Field Hospital 142
23rd Fighter Group *see* Flying Tigers
23rd Indian Division 125
Twitty, Lt. Col. Joseph 42, 46
204 Military Mission (British) 32, 85
typhoid 134, 154
typhus 123, 130, 206; scrub ("Hukawng fever") 192, 204

United States: areas of Asia warfare 6–7; distrust of Chinese intentions for Lend-Lease 15; lack of plans for war with Japan 38; Marines in China 38; Neutrality Acts 7, 13–4; plans for oversight of Lend-Lease supplies to China 15; Services of Supply (SOS) 135, Advance Section 3 (northeastern India) 145; 10th Air Force 84, 135; trade restrictions 8, 13; War Department 8, 14, 31, 36, 42, 55, 59
University of Pennsylvania 3

V Force 163, 174–6, 192–3; Assam Rifles in 163; Chins and Nagas in 163; Colonel Scott 193; Gurkhas in 163; Kachins in 163; opium and silver as gifts for Nagas 166–7; relocating to Shingbwiyang 179
Vaughan, Maj. George 25–6, 28, 66, 152; promotion to lieutenant colonel 49

Wake (gunboat) 38
Walk a Little Faster (Henrietta Thompson) 3

Walker, Johnny 191, 194, 196
walkout 3, 84, 93–108, 138, 151; begin mountain climb 98; building rafts for trip on Uyu River to Homalin 95–7; Chin porters *104*; daily routine 95–6; description of participants 93; drop of medical supplies, food and cigarettes 96; end of India motor road 102; end of preparations for 92; final radio message 90; "flea stop" 101; food drops along trail 99; group organization 88–9; last radio message received in India 98; local bearers and mule train 94; met by Stilwell's staff 102–3; nurses and Grindlay weave roofs for rafts 96–7; rafts on Uyu River *96, 97*; received news of Doolittle raid 103; Stilwell's rules for daily food consumption and sanitation 95
Wallace, Lieutenant 175, 177
Walsh, Lt. Col. Thomas 149–52
Wang, Col. "Limey" 76
Warrenburg, Maj. Clarence B. 143, 146, 148, 150–2, 159
Wavell, Gen. Archibald *33*, 43, 45–6, 69, 78, 124, 135, 150, 163
Wavell, Jean 135
Weatherfield 148
Webb, Capt. William M. 156, 161, 173, 196
Wetzel, Johnny 173–4
Wetzel, Capt. Nevin 58–9, 144
Wheeler, Gen. Raymond 137, 149, 197
White, SSgt. Hubbard 26, 28, 1522
White, Lt. Thomas R. 133
Whitworth, Brig. Dysart 127
Willey, Col. John P. 178–80, 190

Williams, Col. Robert P. 2, 66, 71, 76, *77*, 78–80, 89, 99, *105*, 134–35, 137–41, 143, 151–2, 191–2; appointed Theater Surgeon 57; diary 93; offices in New Delhi and Chungking 135; promoted to colonel 100; radio message to wife after walkout 106; walkout 67, 94, 103–5
Willis, Linda 166
Wilson, Maj. James 35, 66, 152
Wilson, Lt. Col. John 164, 166, 173, 175–6, 179–84, 187, 189, 192–3; moving headquarters 184
Wright, Dr. Daniel E. 144
Wyman, Lt. Col. William 67

X Force 136

Yang, Maj. Gen. Y.K 148
Yangtze River 29, 32
yellow fever inoculations 133, 144
Ye-u to Kalewa track 125
Yoke Force 129–157
Young, Capt. 115–6, 118
Young, Lt. Dick 56; amoebic dysentery 195
Yu, Gen. Fei-ping 43, 45, 127
Yu, Shao 128–9
Yu, Maj. Gen. Ta-wei 34
Yunnan-Burma railroad 35, 144
Yunnan Province, China 29, 40
Yupang, Burma 183

Z Force (Arakan) 163
Zigon 79

www.ingramcontent.com/pod-product-compliance
Lightning Source LLC
Chambersburg PA
CBHW051216300426
44116CB00006B/601